A Practical Introduction to HEALTH INFORMATION MANAGEMENT

Aspen Reference Group

Sara Nell Di Lima
Managing Editor

Lisa T. Johns
Editor

Joan Gratto Liebler, RRA, MA, MPA
Consulting Editor
Professor, Department of Health Information Management
Temple University
Philadelphia, Pennsylvania

AN ASPEN PUBLICATION®
Aspen Publishers, Inc.
Gaithersburg, Maryland
1998

All forms, checklists, guidelines, and discussions are presented as examples or generalized information only and should certainly never be used as the bases for a legal document. They are intended as resources that can be selectively used and always adapted—with the advice of the hospital's attorney—to meet state, local, individual hospital, and specific department needs and requirements.

"This publication is designed to provide accurate and authoritative information in regard to the Subject Matter covered. It is sold with the understanding that the publisher is not engaged in rendering legal, accounting, or other professional service. If legal advice or other expert assistance is required, the service of a competent professional person should be sought."

From a Declaration of Principles jointly adopted by a Committee of the American Bar Association and a Committee of Publishers and Associations.

Library of Congress Cataloging-in-Publication Data

A practical introduction to health information management/Sara Nell Di Lima, managing editor; Lisa T. Johns, editor; Joan Gratto Liebler, consulting editor.
p. cm.
Includes index.
ISBN 0-8342-1231-5
1. Medical records—Management. I. Di Lima, Sara N. II. Johns, Lisa T. III. Liebler, Joan Gratto.
RA976.P72 1998
651.5'04261—dc21
98-34764
CIP

Editorial Services: Denise H. Coursey

Orders: (800) 638-8437
Customer Service: (800) 234-1660

Library of Congress Catalog Card Number: 98-34764
ISBN: 0-8342-1231-5

About Aspen Publishers • For more than 35 years, Aspen has been a leading professional publisher in a variety of disciplines. Aspen's vast information resources are available in both print and electronic formats. We are committed to providing the highest quality information available in the most appropriate format for our customers. Visit Aspen's Internet site for more information resources, directories, articles, and a searchable version of Aspen's full catalog, including the most recent publications: **http://www.aspenpublishers.com**

Aspen Publishers, Inc. • The hallmark of quality in publishing
Member of the worldwide Wolters Kluwer group

Printed in the United States of America

1 2 3 4 5

Contents

For a detailed list of chapter contents, please see the first page of each chapter.

Editorial Board

Sharon A. Grass, RN, BSN
Director of Education
Ste. Genevieve County Memorial Hospital
Ste. Genevieve, Missouri

Cindy Holtz, ART
Manager, Health Information Services
Centegra Health System
McHenry, Illinois

Merida L. Johns, PhD
Associate Professor and Director
School of Health-Related Professions
M.S. in Health Informatics Program
The University of Alabama at Birmingham
Birmingham, Alabama

Diane Kearns, MS, RRA
Medical Record Director
Keokuk Area Hospital
Keokuk, Iowa

Ellen MacDonald, MPH, RRA, CCS
Consultant
STAT Records
San Luis Obispo, California

Donna Peters, RN, PhD, FAAN
Senior Product Consultant
Delta Health Systems
Altoona, Pennsylvania

Diane Premeau, RRA, ART
Coordinator, Health Information Technology
Chabot College
Hayward, California

Patricia Rhodes, RRA
Chief, Health Information Management
VA Medical Center
Grand Island, Nebraska

Karen A. Rosendale, RRA
Associate Director of Medical Records
Columbia Presbyterian Medical Center
New York, New York

Patrice L. Spath, ART, BA
Healthcare Quality and Resource Management Consultant
Brown-Spath & Associates
Forest Grove, Oregon

Cheryl S. Thompson, ART
Director of Medical Records and QA
Eastern Oregon Psychiatric Center
Pendleton, Oregon

Victoria D. Wheatley, MS, RRA
Health Information Management Consultant
Plano, Texas

Brenda M. White, ART
Division Director, Record Management
Parkview Memorial Hospital
Fort Wayne, Indiana

Jeannette R. Wood, RN, MA
Director of Patient Care Services
Ste. Genevieve County Memorial Hospital
Ste. Genevieve, Missouri

Introduction

Continuing changes in the health care environment impact the design and implementation of the health information system. The health information manager, therefore, faces the continual challenge of adapting current systems and implementing new systems for gathering and processing critical information relating to the delivery of health care.

These challenges include such issues as the following:

- continued implementation of the computer-based patient record
- development of performance measures appropriate to the organization's patient population
- expanding the clinical information database to include both mandated and recommended data sets, such as the federally mandated OASIS data set or the National Home Care Association recommended minimum data set for home care programs

In an age of mergers and acquisitions, the health care setting is frequently composed of multiple levels of care. The health information system expands accordingly, serving the entire organization, whether in the centralized acute care setting, transitional care units, ambulatory care programs, and even off-site care, such as that provided through telemedicine.

In addition to managing the technical systems aspects of the information system, the health information manager also provides leadership for workers in the department. To be effective, the manager must remain up to date on issues relating to human resource management. This includes knowledge of the actions related to the development of performance measures for each type of job performed in the health information unit. Participation in orientation and training of personnel remains a major responsibility. Thus, the latest interpretations of laws and regulations concerning personnel need to be applied at the department level.

To aid the health information manager in coordinating this multitude of varied responsibilities, we present *A Practical Introduction to Health Information Management*. It contains a blend of sample material as well as articles describing the issues and processes associated with contemporary health information concerns.

To compile the book, our Editorial Board guided us to the most relevant topics and the highest-quality materials. The Board exists as our primary link with current issues pertinent to hospital health information departments nationwide. We collected dozens of forms and sample policies and procedures from leading hospitals to serve as springboards for your own department forms, policies, and procedures development process. From an extensive survey of the literature, we extracted the essentials from narrative text—the concepts, summaries, and guidelines that will be most helpful in putting your objectives into action. The resulting volume showcases the best materials currently used in hospitals across the country. These practical examples of forms, checklists, and guidelines are models that can be tailored to your own particular needs. Management techniques and other information are also provided to supplement daily administrative duties.

To ensure ready access to the subject matter, the first page of each chapter contains a detailed table of contents for the chapter. There is also an alphabetical index at the end of the volume. We encourage a regular use of these tools; a form, guideline, or checklist may be placed in one location but may apply logically in others as well.

Joan Gratto Liebler, RRA, MA, MPA
Consulting Editor

Acknowledgments

In creating a management-oriented reference volume such as *A Practical Introduction to Health Information Management,* tremendous effort is expended during the development period—shaping the focus of the manual, collecting and evaluating items, and ensuring that the format of the book is practical and easy to use. Health information management specialists in various types of settings across the country contributed excellent materials and offered expert suggestions to prepare a manual that satisfies the complex needs of the health information management practitioner. We are most grateful for the contribution of so much quality information.

I especially would like to thank Joan Gratto Liebler, Consulting Editor, whose guidance, expertise, and oversight made this project possible. My sincere appreciation goes to Ms. Liebler for her dedication and assistance in the development of this book.

Our Editorial Board was very responsive in answering queries, providing contacts, and submitting materials. I especially would like to thank Elaine Barnett (Saint Mary's Hospital & Medical Center, Grand Junction, Colorado), James H. Braden (University of Texas Medical Branch at Galveston, Galveston, Texas), Toni Cade (University of Southwestern Louisiana, Lafayette, Louisiana), Nancy Davis (Door County Memorial Hospital, Sturgeon Bay, Wisconsin), Richard Dick (ASCENTechnologies, Inc., Alpine, Utah), Paige Fowler (Eliza Coffee Memorial Hospital, Florence, Alabama), Patricia Rhodes (VA Medical Center, Grand Island, Nebraska), Karen Rosendale (Columbia Presbyterian Medical Center, New York, New York), Patrice L. Spath (Brown-Spath & Associates, Forest Grove, Oregon), Cheryl S. Thompson (Eastern Oregon Psychiatric Center, Pendleton, Oregon), and Victoria Wheatley (Health Information Management Consultant, Plano, Texas).

In addition, I extend thanks to the many people who gave so generously of their materials, including Jennifer Carpenter and Anne Zender (American Health Information Management Association, Chicago, Illinois), Tracey S. Alspach (American Hospital Publishing, Inc., Chicago, Illinois), Luci Hoyt (Briggs Corporation, Des Moines, Iowa), Margret Amatayakul (Computer-based Patient Record Institute, Inc., Schaumburg, Illinois), Raymond Pinder (Crozer-Chester Medical Center, Upland, Pennsylvania), Steven Z. Harris (Information Resource Products, Inc., Woburn, Massachusetts), and Valerie Florance (University of Rochester Medical Center, Rochester, New York).

Finally, this project could have never progressed from a bare-bones idea to a finished product without the support of Rosemarie Cooper, Administrative Assistant; the attention and skill of Greg Balas, Editorial Services; and the guidance and support of Sara Nell Di Lima, Managing Editor, Aspen Reference Group.

1
Introduction to Health Information Systems

Chapter 1

Introduction to Health Information Systems

CLINICAL INFORMATION SYSTEMS OVERVIEW

FUNCTIONS OF CLINICAL DATA SYSTEMS

Clinical data are acquired from and input by patients, physicians, and the institution's providers. The data fall into three general categories. First, there is the historical information that the patient provides; second, there is the information obtained from the physical examination; and third, there are the results of the tests or procedures performed on the patient or the patient's tissues or body fluids. Data gathered by the physician and the institutional provider are the result of observation or examination. These data may be directly entered by any of the three sources (patient, physician, or other health care provider) by a series of different techniques. Input methods include selecting items from a computer screen menu; typing; and using light pens, bar code readers, a mouse, optical scanners, monitors connected to patients, and voice recognition systems as well as traditional handwritten in noncomputerized systems.

Data are stored in the memory of the clinical data systems or on paper, microfiche, computer tape, computer disk, optical laser disk, or smartcards. Primary data are data collected from a source that has not been analyzed. Data analysis allows summarization, linkage to other data elements, and interpretation. Primary data or analyzed data may be transmitted.

Transmission of data may be through hard-wired direct connections, disks, audiotape or videotape broadcast, microwave fiber optic links, or hard copy. Retrieval of data may be by automated prompts, query, search programs, or human memory. The output may be in a typed format, an audio format, or a visual format (e.g., pictures, graphs, and tables), or may consist of X-rays or electrocardiograms.

The input and retrieval functions may be performed by the patient, a member of the family, a physician, or the institutional provider.

The nature of the institutions using the data determines the total scope of the clinical data systems. A vertically and horizontally integrated system of hospitals and other health care facilities requires the most detailed and complex clinical data systems. A single physician's office usually operates with a simple type of data system.

Clinical Information Requirements

The integration of clinical and administrative data systems requires significant philosophical reorientation as well as systems development leading to open access between the data systems. The principal purpose of administrative data systems has been to generate bills and the principal purpose of clinical data systems has been to provide care to individual patients. If clinical data systems are now to support administrative functions as well, access to the data contained in the administrative systems becomes imperative. Furthermore, increasing sophistication in the administrative data systems requires access to individual and aggregate clinical information. For example, imagine that an operating room supervisor wishes to schedule surgical cases for the following day. The age, diagnosis, severity of illness, planned procedure for each patient, and name of each attending surgeon need to be available. Information concerning the average length of time it has taken each surgeon to perform the relevant procedure, as well as clinical information, is also critical in devising an optimum schedule.

Organizational Location

In hospitals, the health records department was traditionally the place where clinical information was collected and stored. With the advent of computerized clinical information systems, the role of the health records department changed, and the data collection, storage, and retrieval functions were transferred to the health information system. Medical literature was contained in the medical library. Both the medical library and the medical records department usually reported to the assistant administrator in charge of ancillary clinical or administrative services. Because of computerization and the increasing sophistication of the clinical data systems, management information system departments were developed to deal (primarily) with administrative data. Developing health information system departments that incorporated certain clinical data systems and the management information systems was the next logical step, and this occurred in the late 1970s and early 1980s.

Management information and health information system departments have generally reported to the chief financial officer. The current interest in information systems as a means of managing larger institutions is leading to the use of a chief information officer (CIO), who serves at the same level as the chief financial officer, the chief operating officer, and the vice president for medical affairs.

Resource Requirements

The requirements for operating clinical data systems include personnel, hardware and software systems, space, maintenance, and updates of system and financing.

Personnel

Two groups of personnel must be properly trained if the clinical data systems are to be effective: the technical experts and the actual users. The first group includes health information management specialists and medical library science experts. Their skills are needed to oversee the medical records and medical literature components of the clinical data systems. Programmers, systems analysts, computer operators, and information system managers are needed to design and keep the systems running.

Each hospital will need at least one certified health information management specialist to advise on the details of diagnosis and procedure coding. Such administrators are similarly expert in the content required for patient care and in regulation and reporting requirements. With the current availability of medical bibliographic material to anyone with a personal computer and modem, a medical librarian is not needed on the staff of many community health institutions.

The second group of personnel requiring training includes all of the care providers in the institution who will be inputting or accessing information. They must have sufficient training to operate the data systems and preserve the security of the systems.

Types of Clinical Data Systems

Clinical data systems may be divided into six types, which are discussed below.

Individual Patient Health Records

The first and most important type of clinical data system is the patient health record system, which contains all of the data concerning individual patients. Ideally, each health record should be a continuous inventory going back to the time of birth and up to the current interaction with the health care delivery system and should be available wherever the patient is seeking care. Most health care managers feel that the problem-oriented medical record approach has significant merit because it orients the information around a problem list and outlines all current and past problems. Each encounter is described and the information is organized into subjective and objective assessment by the physician; the plan is developed for further diagnosis and treatment for each active problem.

Summaries of Clinical and Administrative Data

Some clinical data systems are summaries of clinical data used by providers, third-party payers, managers of the clinical departments, and affiliated institutions for communication purposes. Summaries of administrative data include daily, weekly, monthly, and yearly information, such as the number of admissions by patient classification, by payer classification, and by diagnosis and number of operative procedures.

Disease Registries

Information can be organized into disease registries (e.g., cancer registries) for specific purposes, such as tracking the incidence and prevalence of problems of concern to health planners and policy makers.

Department-Specific Data

Department-specific information is used to manage the individual departments, such as the pharmacy, the laboratory, and the radiology and nursing departments.

Medical Literature and Decision Support Systems

Medical literature information and clinical decision support systems are necessary to assist physicians and other health care providers in keeping abreast of new developments. These systems are helpful for information management, focus the attention of physicians on specific problem areas, and help develop patient-specific recommendations.

Patient-Carried Records

Patient-carried records allow individuals in our mobile society to have medical information about their past and current problems and treatments available wherever they may travel. These records may be in a paper, microfiche, or smartcard format.

Data Elements

The data elements in clinical data systems include the kinds of patient-specific data listed below:

- demographic
- historical
- occupational
- environmental
- social
- physical findings
- results of diagnostic procedures
- treatments (including health education)
- follow-up
- outcomes
- consent

Clinical data systems also contain the following types of institutional data:

- services performed
- individuals who performed the services
- results of the services
- resources utilized

Ideally, a link between the patient and institutional data elements would make it possible to determine for each patient what services were performed and who performed them and also to determine for each kind of service which patients received it.

Source: Edward J. Hinman, "Clinical Data Systems" in *The AUPHA Manual of Health Services Management*, Robert J. Taylor and Susan B. Taylor, eds., Aspen Publishers, Inc., © 1994.

THREE PERSPECTIVES ON INTEGRATED CLINICAL DATABASES

The dramatic transformation of health care organizations from independent local entities into regional and national integrated health care delivery enterprises has forced a reevaluation of the role of information systems. Until recently, nearly all information systems were acquired to support financial and administrative services within single facilities. In hospital settings, patient registration, charge capture, and billing systems are most prevalent; in ambulatory care settings, patient scheduling and claims submission systems are common. Information systems designed specifically to record or to transmit detailed patient specific clinical information for direct use by clinicians are rare, and are mostly limited to the reporting of clinical laboratory and radiology results. In 1990 one study estimated that although clinical data represent 88 percent of all data generated in a typical nonacademic hospital, only 15 percent of those data are stored in any information system.

Even with the development of laboratory and radiology information systems, the methods used for recording, storing, and sharing clinical information have remained mostly unchanged since the inception of formal health recordkeeping nearly 100 years ago. Although many studies have shown serious inadequacies with paper-based, handwritten medical records (especially in multispecialty practices), the convenience of using paper for the individual practitioner has far outweighed any perceived clinical or organizational benefit from using electronic health records. In 1991 the Institute of Medicine (IOM) released a monograph entitled "The Computer-Based Patient Record: An Essential Technology for Health Care," which highlighted the growing inadequacies of isolated paper-based health records and called for a national effort to define and promote electronic health records. The IOM report defined the electronic health record as "An electronic patient record that resides in a system specifically designed to support users by providing accessibility to complete and accurate data, alerts, reminders, clinical decision support systems, links to medical knowledge, and other aids." Although no clinical information systems yet match the IOM's definition, the numbers of vendors and products promoting clinical systems for direct use by physicians have exploded in the past five years, and organizations are rapidly acquiring these systems for use in patient care settings.

The emergence of integrated health care delivery systems (IHSs) and the growing interest and investment in integrated clinical information systems are clearly linked to a desire to make clinically relevant patient-specific information available to all components of health care organizations. The key driver for acquiring these new systems is the need to communicate the clinical record rapidly among relevant practitioners in different locations. The current goal is to move from relying solely on departmental information systems, which focus only on a specific subset of clinical information, to providing comprehensive health records that span inpatient, outpatient, and long-term care over all clinical encounters—the lifelong, longitudinal electronic health record. The current wisdom is that if the goal of a comprehensive electronic health record can be realized, significant improvements in the quality and cost of health care will occur. Initial studies in limited clinical settings support this possibility, although much work remains to be done to prove this hypothesis.

THE CLINICIAN'S PERSPECTIVE

Medical decision making is data-intensive. Not only are the results of current diagnostic and therapeutic interventions important in clinical decisions, but the results of prior tests and therapeutic responses also frequently provide critical information. Thus, from the clinician's perspective, rapid access to the most recent information, along with the ability to place that information into the context of a patient's medical history, is essential to developing optimal patient-specific treatment strategies. In large multispecialty practices, numerous studies have shown that critical clinical information is not available to clinicians who share paper-based records. In one of these studies, the availability of key clinical results in the internal medicine residency clinic at Stanford University was researched by taping all conversations between the house staff and attending physicians. Relevant clinical information could not be located in the paper charts for 81 percent of clinic encounters. Even with an electronic laboratory results system and direct telephone calls to the appropriate ancillary services, desired information could not be located. Using all available avenues to find data, including the patient's family and friends, relevant information still was unavailable in 32 percent of all encounters. When all attempts to locate missing data were exhausted, patients were asked to return at a later date, missing tests were repeated, and clinical decisions were made without the benefit of the unavailable information. In these cases, less than optimal care was delivered because data that were deemed relevant to the patient's care and that were known to exist somewhere were not available at the time of clinical decision making.

Comprehensive integrated clinical information systems promise to eliminate difficulties with locating and accessing patient information. However, there are significant barriers to these systems' delivering on this promise. Unlike the situation in previous decades, today most of the problems associated with clinical data sharing are not technologic ones. Data sharing in a distributed, rapidly changing organizational environment raises a number of highly charged questions for clinicians:

- Who decides which data are sufficiently important to be stored in the clinical information repository? Who decides the criteria for inclusion?
- What relevant data can be excluded? For example, are physician notes—rarely captured in electronic format—entered in the repository? Nurses notes? Medications?
- Who has control over data after they have been entered into the enterprisewide database? For example, who can change

continues

Three Perspectives on Integrated Clinical Databases continued

data after they have been entered? Who can delete data? Should the provider of the data be informed if data are changed?

- Who determines who can access specific data items? Can individuals limit the types of data that are shared and with whom?
- If data can be shared selectively, how does the clinician know when or if she or he has access to the complete health record? If only part of the record is made available to everyone, how does the clinician know when he or she has enough information to safely proceed with a decision?
- Can a clinician trust data generated by others and use these data confidently as a basis of a decision? What is the clinician's liability when he or she bases a decision on information that has been provided by others?
- What data should be stored digitally? How long should these data be stored? A rough back-of-the-envelope estimate suggests that up to 100 terabytes of electronic data could be generated in one year at Barnes Hospital, a 1,000-bed academic hospital in St. Louis. Although this estimate includes radiologic images and physiologic signals and does not factor in digital data compression technologies, it illustrates the point that some decisions regarding what data to collect, retain, and purge have to be made.

Apart from these mostly logistical questions, there are other fundamental questions about how to ensure data validity and integrity. High-quality clinical decision making requires accurate data. No information system, however, can ever achieve 100 percent accuracy. Ensuring that data are valid—that is, that entered information accurately measures the desired property—and that data were entered accurately involves tedious and time-consuming work. As data are gathered from multiple locations, differences in the qualities of different sources' data can markedly diminish confidence in the integrated database. Grossly inaccurate data caused by data entry errors frequently can be recognized or at least questioned because of their physical or logistical implausibility. Vague, ambiguous, or poorly defined data can have a more significant negative impact on clinical decision making because the deficiencies of such data are much less obvious, and they may be the result of subtle differences in how the different data sources defined and categorized information. For example, intravenous fluids used to deliver medications may be recorded in the input-and-output record in one system but in the medication administration record in another system. Failure to recognize these differences and to devise a unified approach to recording and displaying information about these fluids could lead to erroneous clinical conclusions about a patient's fluid status. The designers of clinical data repositories attempt to detect these semantic differences and to remove them by creating enterprisewide definitions that are applied to all data sources. However, clinicians still must understand the limitations and assumptions inherent in the underlying data sources, which may persist in the data repository despite the best efforts of the repository's designers.

Although most of the questions discussed above could also be asked regarding traditional record systems, electronic information systems make patient data available for inspection and use on a scale much larger than what is possible with paper-based records.

THE ADMINISTRATOR'S PERSPECTIVE

An integrated health system is a network of owned, merged, or affiliated facilities organized to act as a single unit to provide comprehensive, coordinated patient care. IHS organizations seek to eliminate the traditional separations between hospital, office, rehabilitation, home, and chronic care facilities. Not only must services be coordinated across previously separate environments but also the integration of strategic planning, management structures, support staff, financial systems, and quality assurance and utilization management programs often must occur for the IHS to achieve an efficient unified approach to medical practice.

For the IHS administrator, the current information systems landscape is a confusing jumble. Faced with the need to provide a comprehensive picture of the cost, quality, and outcomes of IHS services, most IHS administrators must deal with a vast array of differing information systems, both within and among the previously independent organizations that now make up the IHS. With different systems that run on different computer platforms, use different coding systems for similar clinical concepts, and often do not make their data available for external reporting, it is no wonder that the typical administrator of a newly formed IHS cannot create a useful picture of his or her organization's approach to delivering comprehensive clinical care.

An IHS administrator faced with this diversity of information systems has three basic options for responding to the need for integrated information:

1. Allow simultaneous access into multiple systems via windows or sessions, which requires that users know the commands and procedures of each system (integration at the desktop).
2. Determine a small set of corporate standards for information systems in all practice settings and replace systems that do not meet these standards (integration by fiat).
3. Collect data from the existing disparate systems into a single integrated database, called a data repository, from which the unified corporate view of clinical care can be derived (true data integration).

Examples of all three approaches exist today. However, the first option provides only the appearance of data integration; data cannot be combined to provide a comprehensive view of clinical care. The second option usually is not possible in complex and diverse clinical settings. The third option provides the highest degree of data integration, but requires substantial and sustained intellectual and institutional commitment.

By removing barriers separating different practice settings, the IHS administrator has the potential to assess the quality,

continues

Three Perspectives on Integrated Clinical Databases continued

cost, and outcomes of clinical care in a comprehensive manner. For example, in traditional nonintegrated health care systems, obtaining back-to-work or quality-of-life data to assess the impact of new surgical procedures is difficult because data on inpatient risk factors and outpatient outcome measures cannot be readily combined. Further, with the rapid drop in lengths of hospital stays, valid concerns about increased post-hospital morbidity and about the possible negative consequences of shifting significant acute care into ambulatory care practices can be assessed only if the IHS can eliminate the information discontinuity between these settings. From the IHS administrator's perspective, only integrated information systems can provide the required comprehensive clinical view.

To support the analysis of data collected from disparate locations for quality assessment or outcomes studies, the user of an integrated clinical repository must consider a number of questions:

- When are data from different sources comparable? When assessing pneumonia outcomes, for example, are the results of reading a plain chest radiograph similar to or different from the results of reading a digital radiograph for determining initial clinical severity? Using an example from laboratory medicine, are the results of two rheumatologic serology tests comparable if the tests use different techniques and have different "normal" ranges?
- What meaningful clinical studies can be performed on nonrandomized patient data? Sicker patients get more tests performed than do well patients; patients who have chronic diseases see physicians more frequently than do patients with acute illnesses. Patients who have orthopedic problems get bone radiographs more frequently than do patients with seizures. Thus clinical practice data are grossly biased.
- Even if relevant clinical information is stored in the repository, is it in a format that allows analysis? Dictated radiology reports may contain critical information, but if the diagnostic information is not stored in a well-defined coded format, this information cannot be analyzed.
- Even if relevant information is stored in coded form, are different locations using the codes in a uniform manner? If one location uses the same codes differently than another location, differences that appear in an analysis may simply reflect coding differences rather than true practice differences.

Although significant problems exist, most IHSs are proceeding with clinical data repositories on the premise that some integrated data, albeit of limited quantity and of questionable quality, are better than no integrated data. The wisdom of using this heuristic approach remains unknown.

THE PATIENT'S PERSPECTIVE

Of all of the participants in the newly evolving health care system, the patient has the most to gain and the most to lose. From an information systems perspective, making comprehensive clinical information readily available for clinical decision making is an improvement over the current fragmented environment. Patients who undergo the stress, risk, and cost of having tests and procedures performed have the expectation that the information obtained in these ways will be available and used in their care. By eliminating the loss of data that typically occurs when a patient moves from one clinical setting into another—for example, when a patient is released from the hospital into home-based care—more informed treatment and follow-up plans can be devised. Protocols and guidelines, which currently cease to be in effect when a patient moves from one setting to another, can be continued without interruption.

On the other hand, significant privacy and confidentiality issues emerge when data from widely disparate sources are brought together and made available in electronic form. There is an inherent tension between the clinician's need to have relevant data easily available and the patient's legal and ethical right to have control over the dissemination of highly personal clinical information. Although paper-based records may raise similar concerns, the ease and scope with which patient confidentiality can be breached in electronic record systems make them of much greater concern to most patients. Questions patients frequently ask when integrated clinical data repositories are explained to them include:

- What control do patients have over the dissemination of data about them that are stored within an enterprisewide data repository?
- Are sensitive data, such as information about substance abuse or sexual behaviors, given any special protections?
- How much of the information a patient provides to his or her physician actually appears in the data repository?
- Can patients see who has accessed their health records? If so, can a patient also demand to know why these people have requested that access?
- Can patients view their records? Can patients correct errors in their records? Can patients challenge or rebut assertions made in their records?

The IOM addressed many of these concerns in its discussion of patient confidentiality and privacy. The IOM defines information privacy as "the interest of an individual in controlling the dissemination and use of information that relates to himself or herself." The IOM's report on the electronic health record distinguishes three sets of activities that may ensure patient confidentiality.

1. *system security*, or measures taken to keep computer-based information systems safe from unauthorized access and other harm
2. *data security*, or measures taken to protect data from accidental or intentional disclosure to unauthorized persons and from unauthorized alteration
3. *data confidentiality*, or measures taken to keep sensitive information from being disclosed to unauthorized persons.

continues

Three Perspectives on Integrated Clinical Databases continued

Patient confidentiality is an important issue to most information systems' managers. In the 1994 Health Care Information Management Systems Society/Hewlett-Packard survey of hospital chief information officers, 31 percent of respondents used a sign-on password for system access and another 31 percent used both a sign-on password and some form of access logging at the individual data-field level. Available networking and information systems technology can address many patient and institutional privacy concerns, but the inherent conflict between making patient data readily available to clinical decision makers and maintaining patients' privacy remains unresolved.

There is much apprehension about the potential threats to the quality of health care posed by the financial incentives embedded in managed care and capitated services. Major areas of concern are the potential for reduced utilization of effective but costly therapies, higher barriers to timely access to subspecialty care, and loss of long-term patient-physician relationships. Integrated clinical systems, which span all practice settings, may provide the only possible mechanism to detect whether rapidly changing business alignments and incentives do in fact lead to adverse patient outcomes.

Source: Michael G. Kahn, "Three Perspectives on Integrated Clinical Databases," *Academic Medicine*, Vol. 72:4, Association of American Medical Colleges, © 1997.

OPEN COMPUTER SYSTEMS AND HEALTH CARE

The language of health care computer systems has a Top 40 list of phrases that elicit positive nods from decision makers everywhere. As a result of their popularity, these terms become muddled from overuse (and abuse), confusing buyers and making the decision process treacherous.

No term better represents this situation than *open system*. An open system is now almost universally acknowledged to be superior to the *closed* or *proprietary* system. Fortunately, most vendors, if you believe their literature, don't sell closed systems anymore.

Unfortunately, if you're selecting a health care information system, the degree to which it is truly open is critically important. Thus, being able to sift through a stack of vendors who all claim to be selling an open system is a key survival skill.

WHY IS AN OPEN SYSTEM A GOOD THING?

Before I describe how to evaluate a system's "openness," let's explore why an open system is a good thing. The single most important reason is *choice*. Any attribute of a system that expands your choices—as an operator, user, or administrator—is generally desirable.

With the advent of client/server systems, it has become more obvious how many components of hardware and software are required to make a system work. Depending on the system, you will typically be buying some combination of components. Closed or proprietary systems limit the choices of components in some cases to as few as one (no choice). The costs of limited choices are so well understood that vendors go to great lengths to describe their products as open even if they are not.

When only one choice is offered, it is not unusual for vendors to attempt to disguise this fact by bundling. Bundling combines the features of important subsystems with an end-user application so that it appears as if a decision (and a choice) is not required.

Such vendors present a single price for the application with no mention of the proprietary subsystems bundled within it. Note, the client still pays for, and depends on, the subsystems. What's disguised is the fact that a choice is being made implicitly and that there are no options.

The definition of open systems should be extended to include a choice of integration methods. The more methods of integration a system provides (such as those discussed below), the more ways systems can be made to work together.

Here are a number of reasons why open systems have become so popular:

- **Open systems allow clients to select the best hardware and software for their needs.** Every client has requirements that may be best served by a specific combination of components. Open systems make it more likely that you can match the system to your needs. The ability to do this has given rise to another term—*best of breed.*
- **Choices allow customers to select from industry-standard packages provided by established companies.** This can have many benefits, including reliable upgrades, better support, and fewer instances of discontinued products.
- **A choice of integration methods makes it more likely systems can be combined (integrated) to provide more value to the health care enterprise.** The more ways a system can exchange data, coexist on the same screen with other applications, and make features and functions available to other applications, the more open and the more valuable the system.
- **Open systems allow better use of existing resources.** Whenever a system allows customers to use what they are already familiar with or may already own, significant savings can be realized. If the customer has many Windows professionals on staff, the ability to select Windows as the operating system can save considerable sums on training or new hires. Some facilities have site licenses for major brands of software. Such facilities can save money when a system can support the tools they already own.
- **Open systems make it easier to deal with change.** In the computer industry, change is a dominant theme. Product life cycles of two or three years have left many with obsolete and unsupported systems that have had to be replaced at staggering costs. The more open a system, the more likely it will be able to absorb change, whether technical or organizational. As a result, open systems also enable an organization to migrate to new technology as soon as it is available.
- **Open system vendors can focus on what they do best.** As the number and complexity of system components have grown and performance demands have escalated, vendors who focus on one area are able to deliver a higher-quality product. Vertical integration is a thing of the past. Focus has been by far the most successful business strategy. With one exception (the exceptional Microsoft), the best software companies have focused on one or two product areas. Companies that attempt to compete with an application bundled with major subsystems (such as an operating system extension, a database, or an e-mail package) must spend scarce resources on several entirely different areas. The result is a dilution of effort and, usually, a mediocre suite of products.
- **Open systems offer freedom from long-term price gouging.** The history of closed systems has shown a tendency for low up-front pricing followed by gradually increasing long-term pricing. Once customers have invested in a closed system, their choices stay few. Once fully invested in such a system, customers often find the costs of upgrades, maintenance, and support rise rapidly. As there are no options for these services, monopoly pricing becomes the rule. Some software vendors have been able to achieve growing revenues and profits years after all new sales have stopped. They are living on the escalating fees they charge their captive clients.

With open systems, the customer has the choice to find sources for upgrades and support from a much wider number of

continues

Open Computer Systems and Health Care continued

vendors. The open system vendor must maintain competitive pricing or be replaced.

Taken together, these advantages make open systems generally superior to their closed counterparts.

THE DOWNSIDE OF OPEN SYSTEMS

Nevertheless, closed or proprietary systems are sold and new ones continue to appear. There are still some advantages to closed systems.

- **Up-front cost:** Generally an open system costs somewhat more initially than a closed system. A closed system can offer more aggressive pricing by choosing to make less profit on a subsystem. Open systems vendors must earn a profit on their components and so must the vendors of the subsystems. Generally, a closed system vendor who prices aggressively also generates fewer funds for research and development and support. Inevitably this practice leads to poorer products and weaker support.

  Be aware that bargains can be costly down the road. Closed systems usually become far more expensive to upgrade, maintain, and support than open systems in later years as the closed system vendor takes advantage of its monopoly position.
- **Single support source:** Buyers of closed systems generally cite the benefit of buying from a single source that is responsible for several system components and sees that they all work together no matter how often the components are upgraded or modified. One support call for these systems simplifies support and can reduce the overall support bill.

  While this was once a strong advantage for closed systems, open system vendors have risen to the challenge, as have vendors of industry-standard subsystem components. Service and support networks have been formed that tightly integrate, support, and train the open systems vendor. With these networks, vendors can offer single source support at competitive rates. Often these vendors can draw on the support services of their suppliers in a manner transparent to the customer.

  Ensuring that all new releases work together is still a challenge. Increasing use of standards and emphasis on backward compatibility have helped. Open system vendors have to do exhaustive testing of new subsystem releases to ensure ongoing compatibility, and they must continue to make modifications to support the latest releases.

Customers buying open systems should check to see that their vendors have a well-developed procedure for thoroughly evaluating the latest releases of key systems in a timely manner.

Open systems' advantages apparently still outweigh their disadvantages by a substantial margin. The openness of the average health care system has been rapidly increasing in the past several years, and the number of vendors who sell avowedly closed systems has dwindled to near zero.

HOW TO EVALUATE A SYSTEM'S OPENNESS

Since the virtual demise of the totally closed system (defined as a system with all of its components manufactured/developed by a single vendor), almost every system is open to some degree.

Because there is no Bureau of Openness for rating a system and because every vendor seems to want the customer to believe its system is truly open, customers must assess the degree of openness each competing system presents and how much is the right amount for its purposes.

The following has been designed to help the health care buyer evaluate a system's openness.

Networks

Modern health care networks are dominated by two topologies: Ethernet and token ring. While the former is dominant, systems that can support either reflect a greater networking sophistication and can be expected to perform better overall. Be sure to test in advance the performance of systems that require emulators or other adapters to work in your environment.

Hardware

In general, systems that support a wide variety of computers and peripherals are more economical and flexible. The largest dichotomy in the client/server world is represented by the two major operating systems: Windows and UNIX.

Systems that can support Windows and UNIX servers are considerably more flexible and generally can support the full system range from small departmental systems to huge multifacility, enterprisewide systems.

While support for Windows-based PCs is the norm today, some customers have UNIX-based systems such as Sun workstations that only a highly open system will support.

Operating Systems

As noted above, the client/server world has settled into principally Windows and UNIX operating systems. Several varieties of each are now available, and compatibility with one variety does not guarantee compatibility with the other members of the family. Users of Microsoft's Windows 3.1, Win95, and WinNT have already discovered the significant differences among them. Systems that can operate on all three versions have a significant advantage.

The various versions of UNIX come from a variety of vendors and have more significant differences than the forms of Windows. Even the most open of vendors usually support only a small number of the UNIX versions available. Customers should check carefully to see if their preferred version of UNIX is supported.

Software Subsystems

These include all categories of software—operating system extensions (optical platforms and custom device interfaces), databases, word processors, spreadsheets, e-mail, and work flow and other systems that a primary application may rely on.

continues

Open Computer Systems and Health Care continued

In general, the more of the major, industry-standard packages supported by the vendor, the better. Here, bundling with homemade, proprietary versions of industry-leading packages can be especially problematic. Beware of vendors who offer proprietary products and gloss over comparisons with name-brand offerings.

The application you have in mind may not need all the power of one of the industry leaders, but compatibility with them provides options that may prove critical in the future.

Integration and Communication Standards

The health care industry has invested billions of dollars in systems and will invest billions more in the next few years. It will be wholly impractical for hospitals and other care providers to replace major systems in order to gain more features or combine important functions.

As a result, new systems will have to use state-of-the-art techniques to integrate not only with other advanced systems but also with older systems that may have been created with little or no thought to integration.

The most open systems will be able to support

- the latest Microsoft data exchange methods such as object linking and embedding (OLE) and dynamic data exchange (DDE)
- communication and output-based interfaces
- application program interfaces (APIs)
- the ability to interface with Visual Basic (VB) and Visual C (VC) programs
- the ability to interface with terminal emulators for mainframe applications

The latest tools can add one system's functionality to another without significantly changing either system. While both systems are running concurrently, most of the features of both systems are available on the same screen with as little as a mouse click. During this operation, data should be seamlessly exchanged between the systems so, for example, both systems can display a selected patient's data without reentry of basic patient information.

Beware of "integrated" systems that require switching between icons, minimizing one system before working with another, or "toggling," where one system is exited before the other is accessed.

Source: Robert F. Golden, "Open Systems and Healthcare," *Journal of AHIMA*, Vol. 68:3, American Health Information Management Association, © 1997.

INFORMATION SYSTEMS

Computers and information technology have become cornerstones, both in business and private life. Technological capabilities continue to soar, and our youths—the future workforce—rush to get their hands on new technologies. As this trend continues, information technology will become more than a tool; it will become an integral skill equal to reading and writing.

The effects have already been felt in health care. Evidence is all around us—in financing and delivery, planning and control, and clinical and clerical services. In a new book from American Hospital Publishing, *The CEO's Guide to Health Care Information Systems*, Joseph M. DeLuca and Rebecca Enmark Cagan help senior health care leaders make the leap into the world of information technology. In this excerpt, they debunk seven common myths of information technology.

Health care executives have a diversity of continuous clinical, quality, and traditional business issues to resolve; one set of issues relates to health care information technology (IT) implementation and management. Often the IT management process is inhibited by common myths, which are discussed in this chapter.

MYTHS OF INFORMATION SYSTEMS TECHNOLOGY

The complexity of IT management can be intimidating. Many commonly held beliefs regarding technology are overstated, outdated, or simply untrue. In planning, selecting, and implementing IT, managers must overcome these myths to take full advantage of the potential of health care technologies.

We Do Not Need an IT Plan

Many executives believe that IT planning requires only a point-in-time analysis; that is, they will make a plan only when they identify a need or problem. However, effective IT management and planning is a continuous process. As with any other investment, information technology must add constant value and benefit to the organization. In order to do that, IT management must follow a continuous, regenerative systems life cycle, from long-range planning to vendor selection and development to system implementation and update planning. Adherence to a continuous IT management process also develops IT management skills, enabling the organization to gain progressive degrees of expertise and competency for successive planning efforts.

It Is a Peripheral Investment

Information technology is an investment opportunity. Historically, health care providers invested minimally in their information systems (IS): Executives were satisfied if primary business functions such as billing, payroll, and financial reporting were operating smoothly. The lack of industry automation made data on the value of IS technology scarce. Moreover, IT evaluation techniques were costly without sufficient available data to support analyses.

Today, a wealth of data on the potential value of an IT investment is readily available. In addition, numerous methodologies exist for measuring, both objectively and quantifiably, post-implementation results—that is, the return on investment (ROI). This type of analysis is critical because it allows providers to plan for and realize IT benefits often driven by changing market conditions, the need to eliminate unnecessary costs and improve service levels, and other service delivery factors.

Detailed Benefits Analysis Is Prohibitively Expensive

In the past, investigating the benefits of IS technology in detail required a lengthy, expensive effort by provider organizations. Today, unless a technology is so leading edge that no one has ever implemented it successfully, someone knows what the system does and does not do. Executives should seek out that information and examine the "best practices" of people already using the technology, and then adapt those practices to fit their own organization. In this way, providers can learn from the successes and failures of others.

Any Technology Investment Must Be "The Best"

Many executives commonly believe that a new IT system must be leading edge or experimental in order to achieve maximum benefits. Although it is true that to achieve breakthrough benefits (such as a comprehensive electronic health record supporting paperless patient care processes) organizations will have to invest in some form of unproven technology, it is not always necessary to implement the "hottest" technology to achieve the highest levels of benefits and ROI.

There are numerous stable technologies that provide significant economic and strategic benefits. Indeed, existing systems often can provide a source of untapped benefits. Techniques to take advantage of these opportunities include

- **Systems use audits:** These efforts, in which best-practice use of technologies is compared against an organization's use, can increase the use and value of a provider organization's current investments by identifying misused or underutilized areas.
- **Staff retraining programs:** These efforts retrain employees and teach new and updated technology capabilities. This is important because features and functions of major applications are updated as often as once a year by software vendors. Organizational staff can quickly fall behind in maximizing the effectiveness of the technology investment and cannot take advantage of these new features and functions.
- **IT-driven reengineering efforts:** These efforts can be effective when current work processes fail to maximize the technology use. By redesigning procedures and work flow to interact more effectively with existing technologies, organizations can extend the life and effectiveness of their IT investments.

continues

Information Systems continued

Information Technology Equals Data Systems

The term "information technology" is used in today's technological environment to encompass all relevant forms of technology that include information systems, computer system hardware, voice (telephone) systems, and application software, as well as networking (WAN/LAN) and telecommunications technologies. Obviously, current usage of the term encompasses more than data management or data systems. In the field of health care, IT comprises three primary categories of technology:

1. **Data/clinical/information systems:** For example, patient care, patient finance, and managed care
2. **Voice and video systems:** For example, telephone systems, call processors and IVM (interactive voice management), teleconferencing and CATV (cable television)
3. **Networks:** For example, LAN (local area network), WAN (wide area network), CHIN (community health information network), and MAN (metropolitan area network)

It Is Used Primarily for Administrative and Financial Purposes

One of the biggest fears that executives have regarding information technology is that providers and physicians will not use it. However, current experience directly challenges this belief. For example, rapid advances in clinical information technology help save time, make care processes more efficient, and support the diagnostic/therapeutic decision process. This has engendered more support for and use of IT among physicians and other care providers.

In addition, as providers accept more financial risks for treating patients, advanced financial, contract management, and interpretive case management application systems gain clinical converts daily.

We Can Just Extend Our Current Technology for Whatever New Needs We May Have

The belief that current systems can adapt to all new requirements has caused many organizations to waste money on system modifications. Many of the information requirements emerging in today's marketplace are sufficiently new and different that existing systems cannot be modified to meet those needs effectively. For example, integrated delivery systems (IDS), managed care, and capitation all require new capabilities and often new systems to augment and/or replace current systems.

In developing an IS long-range plan, executives should consider the inherent potential or limitations that existing systems offer in meeting new and emerging requirements, and should approach the question of reinvestment, partial reinvestment, or new investment candidly and objectively.

THE IT-BENEFITS CONNECTION

Provider organizations now are focusing on what value IT can provide—the potential benefits and ROI the organization stands to gain (that is, how those functions can translate into direct, quantifiable advantages to the provider). Thus, the ability to maximize IT benefits and the associated ROI is becoming an integral part of the executive management IT skill set.

IDENTIFYING BENEFITS

In many cases, the approach an organization takes to investing in IT will determine the extent of expected returns. In determining potential ROI, provider organizations should consider several environmental and market factors. These include

- **Investment flexibility:** How much capital is available over what period of time
- **Management risk disposition:** Willingness to invest in experimental efforts or vendors
- **Investment motivation:** To reduce cost, position for capitation/managed care, and gain market share

Generally, the potential benefits of IS technology can be categorized into three primary areas:

1. **Quantitative benefits:** These are financial benefits that are clearly measurable and are attributable to the use of a particular technology. For example, the use of electronic data interchange (EDI) technology to submit claims has resulted in widely quantified cost savings for provider and payer organizations.
2. **Qualitative benefits:** These are directly and indirectly attributed to the technology but are more difficult to quantify. For example, implementation of a clinical nursing system may lead to increased ease in recruiting efforts, better nurse retention, more rapid access to clinical nursing data, and decreased charting time. Quantification—and measurement—of benefits usually is difficult because of the task complexity of the nursing function.
3. **Strategic benefits:** These offer substantial benefits to the organization, but at some future date. For example, investments in networking and telecommunications offer significant future strategic benefits, positioning organizations to utilize enterprise-wide patient indexing and electronic medical record (EMR) or distributed case management technologies as they emerge.

MEASURING BENEFITS

In evaluating the potential of a particular technology, health care providers use one of three mechanisms:

1. **Structured, lengthy management engineering analysis:** For example, an organization considering a bedside nursing system may conduct a pre- and post-implementation analysis of nursing time and activities, determining the exact time spent on each patient activity.

continues

Information Systems continued

2. **Eyeball studies of technology potential:** For example, an IDS considering implementation of an enterprise-wide EMR may rely on a logic-based feasibility analysis to project cost and time savings from the system. Suppose the generally accepted IDS estimate states that 10 percent of all tests are reordered due to lack of result accessibility. Logically, an EMR that makes such results available simultaneously to multiple system users would save the costs related to those redundant tests.
3. **Rapid case study and benchmark comparisons:** For example, executives considering installation of a telephone/voice-processing system can look to published literature for any number of case studies on voice technology benefits and extrapolate those findings to their own organization.

No formula can quantify all the critical considerations involved in investing in technology.

COMPUTERIZED PATIENT RECORDS

DESCRIPTION OF THE COMPUTER-BASED PATIENT RECORD (CPR) AND COMPUTER-BASED PATIENT RECORD SYSTEM

Prepared by the CPRI Work Group on CPR Description (WDES). May 1995

BACKGROUND

Computer-Based Patient Record Institute

The Computer-based Patient Record Institute (CPRI) is a non-profit organization of stakeholders in health care committed to facilitating development and implementation of computer-based patient records. Computer-based patient records have the potential for improving health care access, quality, cost, and satisfaction.

CPRI believes a critical element in achieving this objective is a fully articulated, but not prescriptive, description of the computer-based patient record and the computer-based patient record system. The description given in this document is intended to promote a common understanding of the concepts these terms represent.

The descriptions of the computer-based patient record and computer-based patient record system are developed through a series of documents, each increasingly detailed.

This first document defines the scope, characteristics, and general functionality of the computer-based patient record and computer-based patient record system.

Subsequent documents will address

- **Health information framework:** the roles and responsibilities of all stakeholders within and across enterprise boundaries and the agreements that must be developed for the exchange of health information.
- **Computer-based patient record:** the content expected in computer-based patient records to represent the health of individuals across their lifetimes, though not necessarily the content of a given enterprise's computer-based patient record for an individual.
- **Computer-based patient record system:** a description of the requisite functionality to enable implementation of the computer-based patient record.

ACKNOWLEDGMENTS

This document was prepared from the input of several groups within the CPRI. The Concept Model Subgroup of the Work Group on Codes and Structures recognized the importance of description and developed the basic premise. A task force of the Board of Directors focused the work and recommended the series of documents to be developed. Members of CPRI provided input from various perspectives. Finally, numerous individuals contributed text.

COMMENTS REQUESTED

This document is distributed for public comment. Please send comments to

Computer-based Patient Record Institute
1000 E. Woodfield Road, Suite 10
Schaumberg, IL 60173-4742
Telephone: 847-706-6746
Fax: 847-706-6747

INTRODUCTION

Health information is vital. When a person seeks health care, a caregiver needs to know allergies, chronic conditions, current medications, and other pertinent health care information to provide effective treatment. Yet such information is not always easily accessible. There is growing realization that the more widespread use of information technology to increase efficiency and enable changes in health care delivery processes could do much to improve the performance of the health care system, within the bounds of appropriate measures to protect the confidentiality of private health information.

The Institute of Medicine (IOM) conducted a study on improving the patient record in response to increasing functional requirements and technological advances. The result of the study was a report entitled "The Computer-Based Patient Record: An Essential Technology for Health Care." (Published by National Academy Press, 1991, ISBN 0-309-04495-2.) The report defined the computer-based patient record as an "electronic patient record that resides in a system designed to support users through availability of complete and accurate data, practitioner reminders and alerts, clinical decision support systems, links to bodies of medical knowledge, and other aids."

The IOM report also defined the computer-based patient record system as "the set of components that form the mechanism by which patient records are created, used, stored, and retrieved....It includes people, data, rules and procedures, processing and storage devices, and communication and support facilities."

These definitions provide the foundation for further description of the computer-based patient record and the computer-based patient record system.

OVERVIEW OF COMPUTER-BASED PATIENT RECORD

A computer-based patient record is electronically maintained information about an individual's lifetime health status and

continues

Computer-Based Patient Records continued

health care. It is important to clarify that the computer-based patient record replaces the paper health record as the primary record of care, meeting all clinical, legal, and administrative requirements. However, the computer-based patient record is also more than today's health record. Information technology permits much more data to be captured, processed, and integrated, thereby providing meaningful information and contributing to the knowledge of authorized users for legitimate uses.

Content and Structure

The computer-based patient record is a virtual compilation of nonredundant health data about a person across a lifetime, including facts, observations, interpretations, plans, actions, and outcomes. Health data include information on allergies, history of illness and injury, functional status, diagnostic studies, assessments, orders, consultation reports, treatment records, etc. Health data also include wellness data such as immunization history, behavioral data, environmental information, demographics, health insurance, administrative data for care delivery processes, and legal data such as consents. The who, what, when, and where of data capture are also identified. The structure of the data includes text, numbers, sounds, images, and full-motion video. These are thoroughly integrated so that any given view of health data may incorporate one or more structural elements.

Chronology of Health Events

An individual's health data will very likely be distributed over different systems in different locations. Intelligent software agents with appropriate security measures will be used to access data for authorized users with legitimate uses across these distributed systems. Any health data across a person's lifetime must be able to be assembled for a chronology of health information.

Focus on Health Care Recipients

The health care delivery system is dramatically changing to managed care with emphasis on improving outcomes of care and maintaining health. The computer-based patient record, therefore, should not be considered applicable only to patients—that is, individuals with the presence of some pathological condition. Rather, the focus should be on individuals' health, encompassing both well-being and morbidity. The computer-based patient record supports this paradigm shift.

Value-Added Tool for Users

The computer-based patient record is not a record in the traditional sense of the term. Record connotes a repository with limitations of size, content, and location and suggests that the sole purpose of a compilation of health data is to document events. While this is indeed an important purpose, the computer-based patient record additionally permits health information to support both the generation and communication of knowledge.

Benefits

Many organizations are undertaking development of computer-based patient records. These may go by a variety of terms, including electronic health records. Some enterprises are integrating computer-based health record systems across organizational entities. Communities and states are developing networks and alliances to assist in exchange of information across enterprises. Many benefits can be achieved by a single organization implementing computer-based patient records containing information on only its care recipients. However, the more computer-based patient records reflect the full continuum of health data, the more beneficial they become for delivering patient care, maintaining community health, supporting research and education, analyzing health policy initiatives, and meeting the needs of associated stakeholders.

OVERVIEW OF COMPUTER-BASED PATIENT RECORD SYSTEM

A computer-based patient record system includes all the elements that facilitate the capture, storage, processing, communication, security, and presentation of computer-based patient record information. Computer-based patient record systems support health care provision and organizational processes and provide communication linkages to related data and knowledge systems.

Support for Direct Health Care

Computer-based patient record systems support direct health care by supplying tailored views for specific needs, supporting caregiver data entry, offering reminders and alerts, and providing electronic access to health care literature and scientific knowledge.

All caregivers, including physicians, nurses, therapists, diagnosticians, pharmacists, and nonclinical support staff, benefit from improved legibility of and access to health care data, more comprehensive and integrated health care data, and quick retrieval of value-added information. All health care delivery providers, including hospitals, outpatient clinics, physician offices, emergency centers, nursing homes, home health agencies, pharmacies, reference laboratories, and other organizations, utilize computer-based patient record systems.

Support for Health Care Delivery System

Systems that are integrated across all health care stakeholders (including health care recipients, caregivers, providers, researchers, payers, regulators, and retail suppliers) simplify the process and improve the quality of health care delivery, improve the ability of all stakeholders to make choices about health care, facilitate communication and education, streamline and automate the administration of health care, make data available for

continues

Computer-Based Patient Records continued

authorized analysis and research, support policy and public health responsibilities, demonstrate appropriateness and necessity of care based on health outcomes, and manage and contain costs of health care.

Functionality

In order for computer-based patient record systems to accomplish their clinical, legal, and administrative requirements, an information infrastructure must be in place to support the various data capture, storage, processing, communication, security, and presentation functions.

Data Capture Functions

Data capture refers to the collection and entry of data into a computer system. The origin of the data may be local or remote from patient-monitoring devices, from telemedicine applications, directly from the individual recipient of health care, and even from others who have information about the recipient's health or environment such as relatives/friends and public health agencies. Data may be captured by multiple means including key entry, pattern recognition (voice, handwriting, or biological characteristics), and medical device transmission.

All data entered into a computer are not necessarily structured for subsequent processing. Document imaging systems, for example, provide for creation of electronically stored text but currently have limitations on the ability to process that text. Data capture includes consideration of the use of controlled vocabularies and code systems to ensure common meaning for terminology and the ability to process units of information. Structured data entry and text processing provide for that common meaning and processing.

Data capture also encompasses authentication to identify the author of an entry. Authentication may be more broadly interpreted to include the validation of data accuracy. Computer-based patient record system rules and procedures determine how authentication may be interpreted.

Storage Functions

Storage refers to the physical location of data. In computer-based patient record systems, health data are distributed across multiple systems at different sites. Because of this, there needs to be common access protocols, retention schedules, and universal identification.

Access protocols permit availability of data to authorized users for legitimate uses. The systems must have backup and recovery mechanisms in the event of failure. Retention schedules address the maintenance of the data in active and inactive form and the permanence of the storage medium.

A person's identity can be determined by many types of data in addition to common identifiers such as name and number. Universal identifiers or another methodology is required for integrating health data of an individual distributed across multiple systems at different sites.

Information Processing

Application functions provide for effective retrieval and processing of data into useful information. These include decision support tools such as alerts and alarms for drug-drug interactions, lab-drug interactions, allergies, abnormal results, etc. Reminders can be provided for appointments, critical path actions, medication administration, and other activities. The systems may also provide access to consensus- and evidence-driven diagnostic and treatment guidelines and protocols. The caregiver could integrate a standard guideline or protocol into a specific individual's computer-based patient record, modify it to meet unique circumstances, and use it as a basis for managing and documenting care. Outcomes data communicated from various caregivers and health care recipients themselves may also be analyzed and used for continual improvement of the guidelines and protocols.

Information Communication

Information communication refers to the interoperability of systems and linkages for exchange of data across disparate systems. To integrate health data across multiple systems at different sites, identifier systems (unique numbers or another methodology) for health care recipients, caregivers, providers, payers, sites, etc., are essential. Local, regional, and national health information infrastructures that tie all participants together utilizing standard data communication protocols are key to the linkage function. Hundreds of types of transactions or messages must be defined and agreed to by the participating stakeholders. Vocabulary and code systems, previously discussed under data capture, must permit the exchange and processing of data into meaningful information. Computer-based patient record systems must provide access to point-of-care information databases and knowledge sources such as pharmaceutical formularies, referral databases, and reference literature.

Security Functions

Computer-based patient record systems provide better protection of confidential health information than paper-based systems because they support controls that ensure that only authorized users with legitimate uses have access to health information. Security functions address both the confidentiality of private health information and the integrity of the data. Security functions must be designed to ensure compliance with applicable laws, regulations, and standards. Security systems must ensure that access to data is provided only to those who are both authorized and have legitimate purpose for its use. Security functions must also provide a means to audit for inappropriate access.

Information Presentation

The wealth of information available through computer-based patient record systems must be managed to ensure that authorized caregivers and others with legitimate uses have the information they need in their preferred presentation form. Caregivers, for instance, may wish to have tailored views of data by

continues

Computer-Based Patient Records continued

source, caregiver, encounter, problem, dates, or other variables. Data may need to be presented in detail or summary form. Tables, graphs, narrative, and other forms of information presentation must be accommodated. Some users may need only to know of the presence or absence of certain data, not the nature of the data itself. For example, a life insurance company may not need health data content to write premiums for potentially high-risk individuals if computer-based patient records could be probed to determine whether a criteria set has been met. Such limited presentation forms would considerably enhance maintenance of the confidentiality of private health information.

SUMMARY

Computer-based patient records and computer-based patient record systems support health care effectiveness and efficiency with appropriate safeguards for confidentiality. Achieving a health information infrastructure with computer-based patient records supported by fully integrated computer-based patient record systems is obviously a process of incremental steps. However, CPRI believes significant benefits in health care delivery are certain to be realized over the full course of this process.

Source: *Description of the Computer-based Patient Record (CPR) and Computer-based Patient Record System*, Computer-based Patient Record Institute, Schaumberg, Illinois.

COMPUTER-BASED PATIENT RECORDS—HYPE VERSUS REALITY

Few technology assessment issues have been as wide-reaching in today's dynamically evolving health delivery system than those involving health information systems. Variously referred to as hospital information systems (HIS), management information systems (MIS), electronic data systems (EDS), electronic patient records, community health information networks (CHINs), and automated patient record systems, all these permutations of computerized health information have as their stated goal the improvement in the quality of health information gathered, how that data is converted into information for the maintenance of both utilization control, and quality and improvement in health provider productivity.

More often than not, the discriminating feature among these health information variations has been the unique information requirements of the user group that created and implemented the initial information system. In the case of hospital-based medical information systems, the requirement for automated billing and collections of patient services drove the backbone of most organizational information systems. This requirement for a financial or accounting-based system became increasingly important because of the almost infinite variety of cost-discounting provisions, diagnosis-related group billing, and multiple-payer sources that formed the financial infrastructure of America's indemnity health insurance system. Although understandably crucial to the survival of a health delivery system, these electronic financial frameworks often were perceived by nursing management as the automated information legacy on which an ever-increasing health information system was to emerge, the computer-based patient record (CPR).

DEFINING CPR

For the purpose of this current technical analysis, however, a CPR is defined as an electronically based, adaptable clinical tool for the primary input, storage, and recall of patient care–related information. This definition intentionally avoids specification of the technology used for the data input (whether by keyboard, penpad, voice recognition, or automated data collection), the architecture of the data repository (whether mainframe-based, client/server, or freestanding), and the peculiar design of its operating system (whether UNIX, Windows NT, Windows 95, DOS, System 7.5, or OS/2) and the precise relational database management system (RDMS) that houses the patient's health information (whether DB2, Paradox, Access, Lotus 123, or Oracle).

The crucial issue to the technologic analysis of the more than 100 touted CPRs in existence today rests not on electronically erudite issues such as hardware or software availability but on the ability of the primary patient care delivery team to select a patient care record system that satisfies daily clinical care needs in efficient and quality ways, supports the entire health system's organizational infrastructure (from accounting to lab to admissions), and provides a data robustness that allows cross-platform transfer of information both within a community health information network and within the framework of an inevitable national health data repository. Although an admittedly daunting task, these goals can be achieved if the technology assessment committee defines a CPR that meets 12 key features first defined in 1991 in a landmark Institute of Medicine (IOM) study. Despite a computer hardware environment that has rocketed from 80286 to Pentium microprocessor technology and a software environment that has seen DOS 3.2 eclipsed by Windows 95 and OS/2, the IOM's gold-standard criteria continue today due to the evolution of tomorrow's comprehensive CPR.

DEFINING THE PROBLEM LIST

A key supposed benefit of today's evolving managed care delivery system is the ability to comprehensively manage patients across the continuum of care. This mandates that the CPR must have the ability to provide standardized, prioritized, and reliable patient problem lists to all users of patient care information across a time and health system continuum. Of particular concern in creating this problem list is the ability to standardize medical nomenclature among the many internal health system and external users of clinical data. Recall that if the CPR achieves its ultimate structure, it not only supports the ongoing daily clinical care of our patients but also allows the assessment, tracking, trending, and utilization management of particular health outcomes.

To achieve this goal, language must be standardized throughout the health delivery system (which can, for argument's sake, be extended across national boundaries). Colleagues in health records management already acknowledge the tremendous difficulty in obtaining accurate coding of patient primary and secondary diagnoses for purposes such as billing and acuity scaling. These health record experts are essential to helping the technology assessment team select a user-friendly (whatever that means...) clinical interface for translation of patient-observed and suspected signs and symptoms into a set of patient problems that demonstrate high interrater reliability, are reproducible, and meet the frequently very different information needs of the clinical team as compared to those of operations management, billing, quality assurance, and management information systems staff.

The selected problem-recording system must be sufficiently scoped so as to allow all information consumers to understand the problems defined and amply robust to accommodate individual patient nuances of diagnosis. For example, the problem-recording tool might characterize patients with blood pressure of over 160/90 mm Hg as hypertensive but also allow the further definition of this problem as one due to an essential nature, due to a pheochromocytoma, or secondary to a renal artery stenosis. In some cases, the implementation of an expert system to refine diagnoses may allow the real-time education of the information consumer population regarding the classification scheme of the information system itself.

continues

Hype versus Reality continued

MEASURING HEALTH STATUS

Today's CPR must have the ability to record a predetermined set of patient-based functional performance measures that allow the intra- and intercomparison of patient medical status. These recorded data cannot be mere recordings of patient age, height, and weight. A CPR must facilitate the acquisition and tracking of meaningful patient measures that allow independent, accurate assessment of patient outcomes. It is exactly this lack of accepted, tracked, and trended patient outcome data that presently frustrates many managed care delivery systems in accurately making patient care capitation decisions.

Here again, as with the defined problem list, health status reports must be reliable and comparable across the many levels of care through which patients pass—and these measures must be acceptable to a wide information-consumer audience. Too frequently, CPRs are selected based on the particular information needs of a specific operational department or clinical division for either its internal information reporting or to support clinical research projects. Determining a minimal standardized data set should be the goal of the basic clinical patient record. Additional informational requirements should be able to be accommodated by free-text or other specific user-defined data fields, but standardization is essential for the ultimate realization of tomorrow's health information record.

DOCUMENTING CLINICAL REASONING

Particularly in a health delivery environment with increasingly strong quality and utilization review incentives, a method for facilitating the creation and documentation of plans of care is essential. As the technology assessment team grapples with this issue, the clinical staff can offer significant expertise from its already hard-earned experience with critical pathways and/or practice guidelines. Two prime motivations drive this recommendation. First, a prime barrier to the successful adoption of CPR systems in health delivery systems is the impression by the clinical staff that it just creates additional work and takes time away from the primary care delivery process itself. The ability of a CPR to create a framework for the customization of a unique patient plan of care based on a specified health delivery template can save the clinical team time in the creation of patient care plans as well as provide a system for making compliance checking and/or exception analysis of critical pathways easier.

A CPR that facilitates the recording of clinical reasoning can be invaluable to members of the risk-management team. In addition, vital clinical information can be shared by all members of the patient's care team, whether these members be internal hospital clinical consultants, emergency department (ED) personnel, utilization review staff, or pharmacists. In this instance, a well-designed CPR enhances the effectiveness of communication across the care continuum—a factor absolutely essential to sustaining the quality improvement mission of all of health care. As noted by Tierney and associates, "[c]ommunication and information management consume as much as 40% of all inpatient costs, yet errors still occur at an unacceptable rate."

ALLOWING LINKAGE OF DATA

Often variously referred to as data translation or dynamic data exchange issues, the technology assessment members inevitably must confront this management monster. This highly volatile issue usually surrounds the health system existence of a legacy health information system, which is often founded about a financial reporting system, and the attempt to integrate various vendor use-specific packages to support activities as diverse as radiologic image storage, laboratory results reporting, and integration of multigroup provider data systems with those of an emerging integrated clinical delivery system.

It is at this juncture that the technology assessment committee can come to an impasse with health system governance. Demands for improving financial performance of health systems and the constant demands for trimming capital health expenditures may not practically allow the trashing of an existing information system for a new system perceived as better at integrating data exchange functions. Although clinical management often would like to employ a rationale of sunk costs and point to a future of cost-savings with total system integration, more often than not this logic cannot be sustained. In addition, few, if any, vendors of CPR systems provide all the packages necessary to support the incredible information demands of today's health systems.

Even the creation of a health information system around a single RDMS is no assurance of the ability to reliably achieve data linkage. Although the database may itself have the virtue of portability (that is, the ability to operate on multiple platforms), this is no assurance that the data fields stored on these potentially multiple platforms are linked. Frequently, the technology assessment team finds itself in a conundrum—purchasing off-the-shelf information system packages that often require extensive internal system tweaking or bullet-biting and choosing to develop its own unique organizational information system. In the latter case, experience tends to bear out that these unique organizational solutions are more often than not extremely costly, underperform expectations, and literally take years to implement completely, if at all. In many cases, the technology assessment committee finds itself challenged by the requirement to employ a systems integrator to create those data element links or patches necessary to provide an information system that is perceived as seamless or transparent to the user. Some promising standardization of object and data-linking technologies among major system providers shows signs of making this data integration function less overwhelming, but in the near to intermediate future, data linkage remains a major consideration in the selection of a CPR.

CONFIDENTIALITY

As more and more data become available to more and more potential users, how is the security of this often sensitive patient information to be safeguarded? As emphasized by Linda J. Gobis, JD, RN, FNP, because the legal status of computerized medical records still is ill defined, these records are vulnerable to

continues

Hype versus Reality continued

legal challenge, especially regarding their admissibility in court. Who determines what data elements are available to whom? Whose responsibility is it to maintain the security of patient records available if a component of a CHIN? How much medical information is reasonable to share with the health service payer? With a utilization review board? Where will the input of peer review committees be stored—and who can access this information? These security issues grow logarithmically as information technology enters the age of universal telecommunication access. How is information encryption accomplished? By whose standards? And who is responsible for breaks in security?

Intimately intertwined with these information security issues are those of information ownership. Who maintains ownership of a digitized nuclear magnetic resonance (NMR) image? Who is responsible for the cost of moving that image, if necessary? And again, who is responsible for the security of that transferred image? In these discussions, legal counsel well versed in information technology will be invaluable.

MAINTAINING CONTINUOUS DATA ACCESS

Computer health record systems, like all computer hardware, require routine maintenance and are subject to system failure. Technology assessment committees must consider the implications of scheduled system downtime for routinely scheduled maintenance. Although shutting down access to the system from 0200 to 0400 hours may be acceptable in accounting, it would not be for the emergency department (ED) faced with a patient presenting in diabetic ketoacidosis. And where will this data primarily be housed? Although the information systems literature is rife with allusions to data repositories and data warehouses, present hardware configurations support the concept of client/server architecture—that is, information residing on multiple client data storage sites but accessible through established links among the multiple data servers.

In a world espousing national data repositories and a federal government planning for implementation of the Medicare Transaction System (MTS) in the next two or three years, does this storage function need to be centrally based on a supercomputer[s] or portable on an electronically readable patient health record card or maintained on redundant systems? Again, little, if any, national consensus exists on these highly critical issues that inevitably affect the tactical and strategic planning of the technology assessment committee.

SUPPORTING SIMULTANEOUS MULTI-USER VIEWS

Here, again, the requirements for providing acquired data to multiple levels and types of users presents a cogent issue for the technology assessment task force. Will a patient history and physical input screen appear identical for the primary care physician, nurse practitioner, specialist, and ED team? If different, how different can this information appear to maintain the commitment to data comparability across levels of care? And how will all the valuable data the system collects be made available to its customers?

Today, it is not uncommon for queries of patient data to be made on formalized requisition sheets to MIS, which runs a report that may not be available for several hours or days. Certainly, we cannot immediately expect information customers to independently structure real-time queries. Or do we structure a number of predefined information tracking, trending, and reporting templates that attempt to glean the most commonly reported information required by specified information user groups? It is especially important at this juncture that careful, methodical interaction between the technology assessment committee and identified CPR information users occur to maximize the value of queries made as well as to optimize both the presentation style and quantity of information presented to the user.

LINKS TO OTHER CLINICAL RESOURCES

As more and more health care gets driven to a primary care and point-of-service level, the clinician's requirement for clinically relevant, immediate health information resources becomes critical. Facilitating this process are the current rapid advances in telecommunications technologies that allow rapid access to vast medical resources through the National Library of Medicine's MEDLINE system, the availability of multiple drug interaction programs, the availability of expert systems to supplement clinical reasoning, and the great strides made in telemedicine. As with any benefit comes an inevitable cost—both in the acquisition of access rights to the information and the significant investment in the initial and continuing training of staff to optimally utilize the available technology.

ENHANCING CLINICAL PROBLEM SOLVING

As we strive to identify the optimal CPR, what value do we place on the system's ability to enhance clinical problem solving? Can this need be met merely by ensuring telephonic links to a MEDLINE resource? Or should our system of choice contain the health system's internally developed or externally acquired clinical pathways of care? At what point do computer-generated clinical guidance systems become a potential impediment to independent clinical judgment and a potential source of malpractice risk?

Especially in instances where the selected CPR is integrated into an informational architecture provided by several vendors, how is this very important dimension of clinical problem solving created? This value becomes especially compelling as we potentially enter a health environment in which more and more health care is delivered outside of acute and subacute health centers, moving to skilled nursing facilities and into the home. How can valuable information be transferred to a nonacute health delivery environment of which many of us possess little firsthand knowledge? At what point does a clinical decision become an acute care issue or should the selected CPR allow for extending the capabilities of the home care medical staff to yet unimagined heights?

continues

Hype versus Reality continued

FACILITATING DIRECT DATA ENTRY BY STAFF

No clinical research has defined the optimal mechanism for data collection by the CPR. As long as vital signs are scribbled on the dorsum of the hand, as physicians scribble progress notes in office-based records, as microbiology sensitivity data are reported on handwritten pathology forms, as radiological images remain in filed X-ray folders, the ultimate realization of the CPR will continue to evade us. Personal research into the data input issue suggests that the ideal clinical interface will be a combination of keyboard, touch screen, voice recognition, and automated data collection techniques. This ideal user-dependent interface, however, probably is still years from realization.

The important point for members of the technology assessment committee is the realization that no data capture system they review is likely to be ideal. Moreover, significant training, reinforcement, and management support for any chosen data input technology must be anticipated—both in the initial allocation of educational costs of training as well as a potential actual decrease in user productivity in the data charting function in the short run. As long as clinicians and medical support personnel wield a pencil or pen as an essential tool for their job performance, the ultimate CPR will not be realized.

DECISION SUPPORT CAPABILITY

Especially in today's frenetic environment of managed care transition, any selected CPR must contribute to management's requirement for quality, cost, and outcome data that support executive information decisions. In addition, this decision-support capacity must be available to all levels of the information consumer community. Physicians must have the ability to readily access their patient prescription profiles, nursing management must have the ability to examine and consider potential variable staffing ratios, operating room administrators must have procedure and cost data to assist with disposable purchasing decisions, and hospital governing boards must be able to compare their institution's aggregate performance, based on patient acuity and mission, with that of local or regional competitors.

FLEXIBILITY AND EXPANDABILITY

As with home computer systems, flexibility and the intrinsic ability to accommodate new capabilities and growth quickly and inexpensively must be inherent to the technology assessment decision-making process. Few CPR implementations will escape the frustration of being technologically outdated even before the system is fully implemented. In addition, the rapid pace of mergers, consolidations, and strategic partnerships in the health delivery community demand systems that can accommodate new missions with even greater flexibility and efficiency. It is here that the nurse manager must adopt the philosophy of the futurist, supporting the vision of a long-term strategic plan while maintaining the tactical focus necessary to maintain health delivery in the interim.

COST-JUSTIFYING ELECTRONIC MEDICAL RECORDS

Integrated delivery systems increasingly are acquiring electronic medical record (EMR) systems for their owned or affiliated physician practices. As such systems enter the mainstream, computing power grows, hardware prices fall, and EMR software products become more powerful and user friendly. It has been estimated that the market for EMR systems and decision support tools will grow by 60 to 80 percent annually over the next five years.[a]

Given this rapid market expansion, health care financial managers must understand the financial implications of adopting systems that automate patient records and clinical workflow and must be able to assess the potential return on their EMR system investment.

COSTS AND BENEFITS

Estimating the cost of implementing an EMR system is difficult. Windows-based systems, for example, often require that an organization obtain new computer hardware, unless its existing system hardware runs at a minimum of 75 MHz and has 16 MB RAM. In addition, no single standard configuration for hardware exists. Some users equip their examination rooms with PCs; others do not. The two approaches have different cost implications, as does the decision whether to purchase or lease equipment.

Other costs must be considered, too. For example, temporary staff may be needed to enter patient data into a newly installed system. Productivity may drop for several weeks while physicians and staff familiarize themselves with the system. And administration costs for the computer network probably will increase. It is even more difficult to measure a system's qualitative benefits because they may affect diverse parties such as patients, their families, and payers. Financial managers must determine how inclusive their organizations' definition of benefits will be. A purely economic analysis includes the entire value a system offers, such as time freed up for staff to perform other work and any improvements to quality and service achieved. A financial analysis, on the other hand, focuses more narrowly on the effect the investment would have on cash flow.

Independent research and user experience suggest that the use of EMR systems can help organizations save money and can be used as sources of new revenue. Such benefits are listed in the following exhibit, which is organized along a benefits continuum, from the most tangible benefit to the least. Many of the intangible, noneconomic benefits are extremely important, but their economic impact cannot be quantified. Since it is impossible to measure and quantify all benefits, healthcare financial managers should select the benefits that can offer their organizations the greatest financial improvement and incorporate them into a financial model.

a. Robertson, Stephens, & Co., *The Information Imperative*, September 29, 1995, San Francisco, California.

LABOR AND DOLLAR SAVINGS

As the exhibit illustrates, EMR system use can help organizations control costs in the following areas:

Clerical labor costs. By automating the drug prescribing and laboratory reporting processes, organizations can substantially reduce the number of times clerical staffs must pull charts. One health care organization in Arizona, for example, reduced its chart pulling by 60 to 70 percent after implementing an EMR system. The organization reduced its medical record staff from 24 employees to 18 through attrition (saving more than $100,000 annually), even though the organization has added 12 new physicians.

Transcription costs. While EMRs differ in how they handle data entry, virtually all major systems offer templates that allow transcriptionists or physicians to enter notes more efficiently.

Physicians who typically spend $300 to $2,000 per month on transcriptions would reduce costs by $720 to $4,800 if they could realize a 20 percent savings on transcription time. However, for physicians who continue to hand-write their chart notes, there may be an increase in transcription costs, as those physicians will either have to begin dictating or entering notes themselves into the computerized patient record.

Malpractice premium costs. Since EMR systems' improved documentation can lead to better patient care, malpractice insurers are beginning to reduce their premiums for physicians using such systems. Most physicians pay between $5,000 and $20,000 a year for malpractice coverage, and premium reductions, typically about 5 percent, can total thousands of dollars per year per physician.

Storage and supply costs. EMR systems reduce the amount of space needed for paper record storage. If the space is leased, rental costs can be eliminated. If the space is owned by the healthcare organization, it can be put to more profitable use. Memorial Sloan Kettering Cancer Center, New York, New York, estimates that its EMR system has helped realize space savings of 2,000 square feet per year, worth $100,000 annually.[b] A smaller facility, Transylvania Community Hospital, Transylvania, Pennsylvania, estimates that it has realized $3,900 per year in offsite space savings.[c]

Supply savings are less dramatic than space savings, as EMR systems do not completely replace paper records. But providers with EMR systems appear to be reducing the amount of money they spend on chart folders, dividers, and filing cabinets, which are estimated to cost an average of $3 per record, or $9,000 to $15,000 per physician.[d] Memorial Sloan Kettering, for example,

b. Evans, James C., and Albert M. Hayashi, "Implementing On-Line Medical Records," *Document Management*, September/October 1994, pp. 12–17.

c. "Implementing On-Line Medical Records."

d. Nieburgal, Dennis, and Dan Canton, "Cost Benefits of the Computer-Based Patient Record in Doctors' Offices," *Toward an Electronic Patient Record '93: Conference Proceedings of the 9th Annual International Symposium on the Computerization of Medical Records and North American Conference on Patient Care*, Medical Records Institute, pp. 304–308.

continues

Cost-Justifying Electronic Medical Records continued

saved $140,000 annually by reducing their consumption of microfilm, microfiche, and paper and photocopying supplies.[e]

NEW REVENUE

Productivity gains from an EMR system may help medical practices build their revenue bases. Some organizations are adding providers or acquiring smaller practices without having to add support staff. Some users also report being able to see more patients per day, increase per physician revenues by as much as 20 percent, and gain a total return on initial system investment within the first 18 to 36 months after implementation.[f] At Galen Medical Group, Chattanooga, Tennessee, physicians report seeing an average of six additional patients per day since they began using an EMR system in December 1992.

The features of an EMR system encourage more primary care use by automating protocols and other population-wide database queries. Front office staff, for example, may be able to help patients by scheduling them for preventive and primary care, potentially reducing the costs associated with treating severe illnesses, specialty care, and hospitalization.

An additional source of revenue may come from improved charge capture. Industry estimates vary as to how much revenue is lost by inaccurate coding and billings that get lost between the delivery of services and the organization's receipt of third-party payment. One recently published case review found that eight of 18 medical practices were incurring $10,000 to $100,000 per year in lost revenue due to undercoding.[g]

By automating the charge-capture process and linking clinical information to financial systems, lost charges can be reduced substantially. Every one percent improvement in cash flow recovered totals $2,000 to $3,000 per physician per year.

New revenue also may be realized by reducing the length of time accounts receivable are outstanding. Not only do EMR systems move information more quickly from clinician to payer, but such information has greater integrity and thus is more likely to meet payer billing requirements. EMR systems help break the cycle that begins when payers reject poorly documented bills, causing rework and delayed reimbursement. By reducing its accounts receivable by 1.5 days, Memorial Sloan Kettering realizes an annual benefit of $325,000.[h]

Documentation revenue also can increase revenues in the area of home health visit supervision. Primary care physicians who supervise home health visits are finding that through more thorough documentation, they can legitimately justify billing more for management services they provide.

CONCLUSION

EMR systems are becoming an industry standard because they allow providers to deliver better care and service across the continuum of care and over time.

Although financial tools such as return-on-investment analyses can be adequate methods for quantifying an investment in such systems, organizations make system investments for many reasons that are hard to quantify: enhanced efficiency, better patient service, "cleaner" medical records, and improved quality of work life.

Development of EMR systems should not be hindered by an organization's concerns with return-on-investment analyses. If EMR systems set new standards for service and quality of care, organization's return on investment may well be that of its continued survival. In such instances, the organization will not question whether it should invest in a system but, rather, when and in what kind.

e. "Implementing On-Line Medical Records."

f. *Toward an Electronic Patient Record '93.*

g. Damsey, J. Landy, "Limit Loss With Correct Coding," *Family Practice Management*, July 1994, pp. 51–54.

h. "Implementing On-Line Medical Records."

SAMPLE BENEFITS OF ELECTRONIC MEDICAL RECORDS SYSTEMS

	Tangible Financial Benefits	Intangible Financial Benefits	Nonfinancial Benefits
Productivity Enhancements	• Reduction in chart pulls reduces labor cost in medical records department. • Automated interfaces reduce labor costs for personnel involved in coding, billing, manually retrieving lab results, and referral coordination. • Transcription costs. • Malpractice premium lowered. • Less dictation time, faster documentation of encounters. • Improved charge capture, documenting home health management. • Reduced nurse intake time. • Faster billing reduces cash cycle, cuts receivable days. • Document storage space costs reduced.	• Scheduling of resources becomes more efficient. • Easier QA and UR reporting. • Less time spent copying, filing, faxing, and transmitting data. • Lower supply costs. • Fewer lab results lost, repeat tests. • Aggregate patient data improves financial forecasting, risk assumption. • Automation of referral process and more appropriate use of specialists.	
Quality of Care Improvements	• Automated protocols/ guidelines reduce expensive variations in patient treatment. • Less time needed to search through records for relevant patient information. • Decrease in lost lab reports reduces cost of repeat lab tests.	• Reduced medication errors, adverse drug interactions. • Improved primary and preventive care (through automated reminders, protocols, and alerts) reduces disease management costs, specialty and inpatient care. • Availability of chart vastly improved. • Improved data analysis, outcomes measurement, population-based care. • Remote access to patient charts. • Summary screen helps prevent overlooked patient information. • Ease of providing summary information helps specialists with care.	• Improved quality of documentation and legibility. • Improved outcomes reporting. • Less information falls through the cracks in a continuum of care.
Improved Customer Service, Satisfaction		• Less need for repeat lab testing. • Ease of getting medication refills authorized; faster turnaround time on refill requests. • Less paperwork as patients move throughout the health care system.	• Confidence physicians are using the best information technology available. • Improved communication with pre-formatted letters, educational handouts, etc.
Increased Professional Satisfaction	• More time to spend with patients.	• Reduction in paperwork. • Improved communication and less time consumed with routine information exchange.	• Increased satisfaction with availability, documentation of records, efficiency of chart reviews and signing, etc. • Ease of covering for other providers' patients. • Ease of tracking referred patients.

Source: Reproduced, by permission from *Healthcare Financial Management*, October 1996, pp. 63–70. Copyright 1996 by the HEALTHCARE FINANCIAL MANAGEMENT ASSOCIATION.

TIPS ON IMPLEMENTING THE CPR USING REENGINEERING MANAGEMENT TOOLS

Introducing innovative change such as a computer-based patient record (CPR) requires complete reorganization of basic processes within health care institutions. If change fails, conflict and even burnout can result.

Insight into how change messages are processed by employees, however, can make this type of reorganization more efficient and less fear inducing. In the long run, delivering change messages in the appropriate manner will allow the CPR or other new technologies to be accepted more quickly.

Using the example of implementing a CPR, we will describe stages that take place when a process or system is being changed, and suggest how management can respond. To accomplish this, we will draw on the principles of reengineering management. Reengineering involves the fundamental rethinking of both technological advantages and management processes.

PREVIEW: WHAT IS REENGINEERING MANAGEMENT?

When change initiatives are introduced, three basic phases of implementation take place:

1. rethinking
2. redesigning
3. retooling

Rethinking

How did the old system operate, and how can it be improved?

To initiate a CPR adoption process, a health information professional might ask, as a central question, how patient information could be made readily available to health care professionals. Under the existing system, for example, a patient's chart might be needed in both a clinical department and the emergency department at the same time. This stage of reengineering might address how patient information could be in two places at the same time.

Redesigning

Redesign the procedure or system. What procedures need to be redesigned?

The facility introducing a CPR will need to be deliberate in initiating change, rather than allowing change to happen under pressure. This can be done through educating and training staff members who are affected by the automation of health information.

Staff at every level of the organization will need to be trained to access a patient record on the new system, from the file clerks to clinical staff. During this training and education period, jobs may be permanently restructured. For example, the job requirements for a file clerk might be changed substantially to reflect the need for computer literacy.

Retooling

How does this change improve the quality of customer service?

At this stage, those implementing the CPR can fine-tune the job and process changes that have taken place, based on customer responses.

This involves addressing the impact on both internal and external customers, including patients, clinical staff, and facility administrative personnel.

Both problems and improvements will be identified. For example, clinical staff may be surprised by the speed of on-line chart access, but there may be apprehension from some personnel who feel that the system is difficult, complex, or uncomfortably foreign.

SO WHAT DO MANAGERS DO?

So what can managers do, concretely, as the big switch from paper to the CPR is taking place? Simple communication vehicles can make a big impact.

To begin with, the supervisors involved should provide notice about the coming CPR at least three to four months prior to implementation.

This could include a newsletter, circulated throughout the institution, explaining how the CPR will be implemented. In the affected departments, supervisors should place flyers describing the coming changes or posters on the walls, so that awareness of the change becomes part of employees' daily routine.

WHO IS HEARING THIS MESSAGE?

Bear in mind that staff typically react to a major change in routine like a CPR implementation differently, depending on whether there have been other major changes in their institution. In the language of sociology, messages about change can be seen as "transformational" or "processual."

One group of people will see change as transformational. In other words, they will expect the CPR implementation to change their work, personal, and even social roles. To meet the needs of these staffers, those responsible for implementing the CPR will need to point out and illustrate the benefits of the change, such as decreasing the health information professionals' time in finding a record, eliminating lost files, and providing opportunities for upgraded training. Also, employees are more likely to see change as beneficial if they can openly discuss the costs (such as additional computer training or staff discomfort) as they are trained on the system.

Employees who have experienced change such as the adoption of the CPR see change as a natural progression. These employees are processual; they focus on the process instead of the outcome of such a transition.

To support processual employees, managers should explain clearly what education and training will be available in implementing the CPR. For these employees, the staff implementing the CPR should provide a step-by-step schedule, detailing events such as stages of testing, vendor site visits, and the date the system is expected to go on-line.

continues

Tips on Implementing the CPR Using Reengineering Management Tools continued

CONCLUSION

Ultimately, there is no one right way to make innovative changes in health information management. An understanding of how people deal with change, however, can help managers cope with different styles. If a facility makes a point of informing staff about the progress of the CPR and involving them in the process, this technological change can be a more positive process for everyone.

Source: William J. Rudman et al., "Tips on Implementing the CPR Using Reengineering Management Tools," *Clinical Data Management*, Vol. 1, No. 8, Aspen Publishers, Inc., © November 1994.

GUIDELINES FOR ENCOURAGING STAFF ACCEPTANCE OF ELECTRONIC HEALTH RECORDS

LEADERSHIP ATTITUDE

Clearly, if a change to electronic health records is to be made successfully, the organization's leadership must be fully and publicly committed to the change, as well as positive in its approach to the task. Given the impact of change generically and the great degree of necessary change in the specific case of electronic records, a halfhearted commitment or (in the words of one of our interviewees) a "defeatist attitude" could easily spell disaster. The bottom line is that the incredible change involved in implementing a computerized health records system must be constantly presented in such a fashion that its inevitability is clear and any perceived threat is translated into perceived opportunity.

INTERNAL COMMUNICATION AND ACCOMMODATION OF DIFFERING PERSPECTIVES

It should be understood by everyone at the outset that there will be many different perspectives and needs that must—and *will*—be accommodated during the transition to computerized charting. Then, ongoing communication must assure all involved parties that their views will be solicited and their needs will, to the extent possible, be met.

There should be early recognition that the change will likely generate a good deal of fear. This is especially true in the case of providers, many of whom may require periodic reinforcement of the need for (and long-term advantages of) electronic records.

Constant communication must also exist between and among all levels of the organizational hierarchy; that is, every level of constituency must be made a party to decision making at each step of the journey. This will help reinforce the concept that the specific needs of each functional group ultimately affected by the new system will be taken into consideration in the development of the system. Full organizational support will be facilitated if all affected groups feel fully enfranchised in the ongoing decision-making process.

CLARIFICATION OF EXPECTATIONS AND OBJECTIVES

Expectations of, and objectives for, the final electronic records system must be clearly understood by everyone in the user organization. All affected groups and individuals must know what to expect from the system, in terms of both its advantages and its possible problems, and expectations for final results must be both positive and realistic. And, of course, clarification of system possibilities must also be ensured between the user and vendor.

One of the most important expectations must be that staffing will *not* be reduced as part of the change and that total workload may well, in fact, increase. The related systems objective should be understood *not* as a decrease in labor needs, but rather as an *increase* in organizational efficiency and effectiveness resulting from a streamlining of work and an enhanced organizational capacity to respond to opportunities.

An effective way both to clarify expectations and to build excitement for computerized records is to arrange a visit to a site in which the proposed new system has already been fully implemented. This enables people to view the system firsthand and to pose questions to actual users of the system.

COMMUNICATION BETWEEN USER AND VENDOR

Close and constant communication between the organization adopting the electronic records system and the developer and vendor of that system is critical. Anything less may well result in unnecessary hostility between user and vendor, with a resulting degradation of the implementation process.

The user must make all requirements clear at the outset, and all implementation problems must be addressed and followed up with the vendor quickly and routinely. The vendor, in turn, must make the resolution of identified implementation problems a top priority if cordial relations are to be maintained.

ANTICIPATION OF PROBLEMS

All users of the new system must be made to anticipate that problems—many small, some perhaps quite significant—will, in fact, occur before the transition is fully integrated into the organization. While the end product will be distinctly worthwhile, everyone should understand early on that the journey will inevitably be bumpy.

It appears that the most significant provider fear in moving to a computerized records system is that of a computer crash. However, it is a possibility whose effects need not be devastating, and whose correction can be made with a minimum of difficulty.

MAINTENANCE OF ONGOING DICTATION

Good dictation is obviously a key to the success of an electronic records system. Thus, in order to tap the maximum potential of such a system, the organization must continually underscore the importance of accurate, clear, and timely dictation; moreover, accomplishment of such dictation should be routinely monitored and enforced. Poor dictating habits can leach much of the utility from an otherwise good computerized records system.

GRADUAL CHANGING OF CORPORATE CULTURE

A computerized records system cannot be simply inserted wholesale into daily operations. As noted above, the idea of a

continues

Guidelines for Encouraging Staff Acceptance of Electronic Health Records continued

change to electronic records can be a real threat to a number of different stakeholders, for a variety of quite justifiable reasons. Again, the key lies in making clear to each stakeholder (group or individual) that the legitimate needs of everyone will ultimately be met and that the fears of everyone will, to the maximum extent possible, be accommodated.

Once this has been clearly stated, the planning process for making the change must make good on that promise. Then, during actual implementation of the new system, care should be taken not to ram things through too quickly. Fears based in long-standing individual experience or organizational history will not be allayed overnight, and the implementation timetable should accommodate this truth.

FUTURE NEEDS

Finally, while electronic records have obviously come a long way in the past few years, we have not yet reached the end of the development process. Methodologies for better standardization of data, development of improved computer voice recognition, and other important issues need to be continually addressed and the related technologies refined. In addition, the importance of dealing with the issue of patient confidentiality can hardly be understated.

But even with these (and other) questions as yet unresolved, the future is clearly at hand with respect to electronic health records.

Source: Peyton G. Townes, Jr., "Implementation of Electronic Medical Records: The 'People Factor,' " *Journal of Ambulatory Care Management*, Vol. 15, No. 3, Aspen Publishers, Inc., © 1992.

GUIDELINES FOR REDUCING BARRIERS TO PHYSICIAN DATA ENTRY

- **Anticipate change.** Plan for change, and then prepare for unanticipated changes as well. Among these are changes in job definition, status, and professional identity.
- **Involve physicians in the change process.** Physicians should be involved in decision making and in designing changes in their work. Enlist the aid of influential physicians to encourage others to do order entry.
- **Allow time for the change process.** Allow adequate time for changes and adjustments, both in the computerized patient record (CPR) and in the individuals and organizations affected by it. Incremental change, or making change in small steps, is much easier than radical change.
- **Provide benefits.** Take into account what physician users would consider benefits of using a CPR. Ideally, a CPR should benefit everyone, and everyone should know about those benefits. Although physicians have been blamed for resisting computers in medicine, they have *not* been resistant to systems that maintain or enhance their professional status and professional values.
- **Encourage communication.** Involve different specialties, departments, educational levels, and so forth. Encourage communication to share different views of system goals and how to incorporate CPRs into the delivery of care. User groups involved in system implementation generally have been more favorable toward that system.

Source: Adapted from Bonnie Kaplan, "Reducing Barriers to Physician Data Entry for Computer-Based Patient Records," *Topics in Health Information Management*, Vol. 15, No. 1, Aspen Publishers, Inc., © 1994.

DATA REPOSITORIES

ADVANTAGES OF CENTRALIZED DATA REPOSITORIES OVER MINIMAL DATA STORAGE

In an age in which merged health care organizations are scattered throughout large geographical areas, centralized data repositories can provide integrated delivery systems with significant advantages over minimal data storage mechanisms.

MINIMAL DATA STORAGE VERSUS CENTRALIZATION

Many of today's hospitals and health organizations have consolidated their medical data into their own databases, effectively limiting information access to only those individuals affiliated with that particular health care organization. While this minimal data storage approach also enables health care organizations to control the types of patient data that are stored and to ensure that the integrity of the information is not compromised, it can be very limiting for emerging integrated delivery systems. Minimal data storage appeals to many health care groups because they can control their own medical information and who has access to it. This approach is generally inadequate when health care organizations merge.

In fact, the minimal database approach has several distinct disadvantages. In particular, whoever operates the database must purchase the necessary software and hardware—a purchase that can cost millions of dollars. Additionally, the systems must always be on-line to function; network activity is increased, sometimes resulting in slow operations and a lack of standardization control in terms of data integrity, vocabulary, and data interchange.

Centralized data repositories, on the other hand, can provide a wealth of valuable health information without the inconvenience or the expense that comes with operating an independent system.

Advantages of centralized data repositories include the fact that the data are always available; the health care groups with access to the database enforce the rules of privacy, confidentiality, and security; users have guaranteed access to the best available data; data are centralized from among the different health organizations; and users maintain vocabulary and data interchange standards. Databases treated as a population-based system yield valuable comparative information about the patient community and generate a positive return on investment.

CREATING A VALUABLE MASTER PATIENT INDEX

The centralized data repository is only as valuable as the medical data it contains, so it is advisable to include as much detailed information as possible. In particular, the repository should feature the names of all of the health care providers involved in the patient's care, allergies and adverse drug reactions experienced by the patient, a composite problem list, current drug profile, critical health data, immunization information, a record of all health care encounters, and insurance/benefit data. Centralized data provide a very comprehensive look at the patient's total health care picture.

OVERCOMING CONFIDENTIALITY/SECURITY OBSTACLES

While health organizations may shy away from using centralized data repositories because of a perceived lack of security measures, filters can be used to determine who has database access and which types of information they have access to. One approach is to create a master patient index that will use Web-page interfaces to allow individuals to link to the data that they are authorized to view. Another way to protect patient confidentiality within the master patient index is to develop a unique patient identifier more detailed than just the patient's name.

In terms of who will actually control the repository and its valuable contents, a neutral authority rather than a vendor or health institution is recommended.

Source: Kathy Stover, "Centralized Repositories Offer Advantages to Minimal Data Storage," *Report on Healthcare Information Management*, Vol. 5:7, © Aspen Publishers, Inc., 1997.

VENDORS, SOFTWARE, AND HARDWARE

CHOOSING CLINICAL DATA MANAGEMENT SYSTEMS

To effectively compete in today's cutthroat managed care environment, it is vital that any managed care organization be able to manage, monitor, and control its clinical data.

Whether it is in the form of utilization reviews, outcomes studies, HMO or HEDIS reporting requirements, or linkages to other systems, managed care organizations must manage their clinical data as well as their financial data in order to be successful.

But just how do you choose a software program? Where do you start and what do you look for?

With a veritable sea of health care management software, it is important to consider your specific needs and define your goals before choosing one of these programs.

And that is not as easy as it might seem.

Here are some tips and tactics on how to define your focus, evaluate various programs, and contract with a vendor.

DEFINE YOUR FOCUS

The first thing that needs to be asked at the very front end is what are my needs. One issue that needs to be clearly defined at this time is how you define clinical data. Are we talking about the outcomes of clinical activities and looking for utilization review and outcomes studies or are we talking about the electronic medical record?

This is an important step because software packages have very different thrusts depending on different clinical data definitions. It is important to put together a diversified evaluation team consisting of nurses, specialists, physicians, and clinicians.

Always get several physicians' input—not only obtain input as to their needs but also have them work with a few of the programs once you get them narrowed down.

A minimum of three different physicians is suggested, preferably from different specialty perspectives. To obtain dynamic thoughts from physicians who are not in the same discipline, include an oncologist, internist, gastrologist—whoever may be using the system.

However, in evaluating clinical data software for a small- or medium-size hospital, ensure representation from each of the major departments, including both the medical staffs and the nursing staffs.

This is because you need to know if the health records piece is good but the pharmacology piece is terrible. Good representation is vital because all the pieces have to fit together in the hospital.

In light of this, programs should incorporate the straight reporting requirements with the more real-time electronic health record features. However, software programs often do not do this. That they do not is really where the problem is in the industry right now. The current approach measures outcomes such as number of visits, costs and types of visits, hospital days used, and so on; all these elements could be regarded as clinical data.

The other type of clinical data is used to monitor the process of providing care; these data are found mostly in the software packages that develop an electronic health record.

It is also important for potential users to decide if they want a practice-specific program, such as a program specific to obstetrics or cardiology, or whether an enterprisewide, all-encompassing electronic health record would be more practical.

DEFINE SPECIFIC CLINICAL NEEDS

After spending long, hard hours defining the focus of a clinical data management system, potential buyers should go back and refine exactly what elements are necessary for their particular organization—for example, chart tracking and automatic interfaces between the chart and the laboratory. If a sample is sent to the lab, how do the data get back into the medical record?

At this time it is also important to address access and editing issues. Some access and editing elements include the following:

- Who has accessed the record?
- Who has edited it?
- What were the changes in the record?
- Can the original information be retained?

INSIST ON REMOTE ACCESS TO RECORDS

Because the majority of a patient's care is no longer being provided in one location, it is vital that physicians, nurses, and clinicians be able to access records from various locations—specialists' offices, multiple hospital settings, clinics, tertiary centers, ambulatory surgery centers.

EXPLORE DATA ENTRY OPTIONS

Even in our computer-oriented society, there are still people with keyboard phobia. And any system that is going to be effective has to look at other ways of inputting data.

For example, one system that is in pre–beta testing stages uses a touch screen that will move into voice recognition. It also has the ability to input data directly from a faxed form.

continues

Choosing Clinical Data Management Systems continued

RETAIN CONTROL OF PROCESSES

In evaluating these processes and deciding to implement a clinical data management system, it is also necessary to define and ensure a comfortable level of control over your practice and your decisions.

How much control you want the system to have over your practice, the inclusion of built-in formularies, when inappropriate decisions are flagged—these elements should be clearly defined regardless of whether you are evaluating systems for a fee-for-service or a capitated environment.

For example, is a generated prescription checked against a formulary for that patient's HMO? The physician may contract with six different managed care plans, each of which has a different drug formulary. If the user orders a specific prescription, HMOs 1, 2, and 3 may accept the order, but plans 4, 5, and 6 may not. You have to know how you want your system to manage those issues.

The system certainly should develop a standardized health record. This has an economic effect, as insurers may reduce your premiums if you have established the standardized record.

EVALUATE YOUR HARDWARE

After defining and focusing data, access needs and trails, and the specifics of a new system, it is time to evaluate current hardware stock and potential investments in computer systems.

Most of the systems now are working under some form of PC network. If you are operating a Pentium 233 or 266 server with substantial storage space, clinical data management needs will be handled without any enhancement for a two- or three-year period. The cost of hardware has gone down substantially. Small networks can be installed for about $10,000. For the small- to medium-size physician group, hardware costs can range up to $50,000 for a fully equipped server. Clustering software can provide substantial expansion capability.

Small physician offices that wish to tap into hospital-based clinical databases can work with a single PC or small network for under $5,000. Many systems are now using the Intranet concept, which allows modem-based interfaces.

For the small physician group that wants to manage its clinical data, a node or set of terminals tapped into a main database (which, in most cases, resides at the local hospital) can be established. Relatively inexpensive, the node may consist of a single 486 PC and a modem.

SEARCH OUT VENDORS

Once you have defined your needs and evaluated your hardware, the next step is to seek out vendors who are producing the software that you need.

Because it is not widely known where these systems are, start out by reading industry literature and publications. Talking to similar-size groups and organizations that have already implemented systems is also a good way to find the vendors producing the software you may want.

The next step is to contact some of the vendors and get detailed responses about where the systems are in the development process.

EVALUATE SPECIFIC SYSTEMS

The next step is to evaluate the systems and to come up with a list of potential modifications. A lot of these systems are developed in an abstract situation, so try to find out what their strengths and weaknesses are and how they are going to have to adapt themselves. This goes back to narrowing down your needs. The system may look good, but it also may need to add/delete/strip certain elements codes or fields in order to work for you. This customization will add to the cost of the software, but it will also improve the flexibility and life span of the system.

Let the users have a hands-on approach. They must get in there and look at the system, evaluate it, test it, and talk with other physicians who have been working with it.

Along the same lines, small specialty groups should make sure there are good specialty panels and screens in the program that make the specifics of the practice easier.

DECIDE IF THE VENDOR IS RIGHT FOR YOU

After reading the literature, talking to current users, and defining specific system modifications, the next step is to make sure the vendor can provide those modifications.

Through a site visit and visits to current installations and by talking to people who have installed and are actually using the system, evaluators should look at a number of things, such as how well they can work with the vendor, if that vendor is flexible, and if the code can be modified. If the code is so convoluted that it cannot be modified to meet your organization's specific needs, then the system will not work for you.

In addition, it is vital to learn exactly what type of support is going to be available to you. Can you count on ongoing support from two guys who develop what you think is great software in their garage? If your system goes down, will they be around to help?

CONTRACT TIME

After you find a vendor and establish that you can work together, and they are able to modify the program's code to fit your needs, then it is time to develop an agreement with that vendor based on a series of checklists to make sure you are getting what you are paying for.

Another key contract item is to make sure a copy of the source code is kept at an independent location under the contract. If something happens to the system or its primary administrator, others must be able to get to the code so all your files, codes, and data are not lost if the system goes down and the support staff is

continues

Choosing Clinical Data Management Systems continued

no longer around. Get proof that a trusted third party, such as a trust bank, has it in storage that nobody can just gain access to, and that it is there as a backup.

THE CONSULTANT QUESTION

Whether you are a small physician practice or a medium-sized hospital or managed care organization, this decision to purchase and implement a clinical data management software system is going to be a relatively substantial financial investment.

Consider outside help. If you are a large organization and are going to spend a half-million dollars on a system, it is not outrageous to spend $50,000 to $75,000 to have someone outside your organization to make sure you are on the right track.

Likewise, it may be wise for smaller organizations to seek an outside consultant's advice on a smaller scale.

Source: "Navigating the Software Sea: Aspen Special Insert," *Clinical Data Management*, Vol. 2:4, Aspen Publishers, Inc., © 1995.

CHECKLIST FOR DEALING WITH SOFTWARE VENDORS

Prospective purchasers of clinical data information system software should use a structured procurement process when making their selection. This process should include at least the following steps:

1. Conduct a requirements analysis.
   - Define what *you* want the system to do. Don't have vendors tell you what they think you need.
   - Among the variables to consider are the nature of the managed care arrangements in the specific locality, the specialty or specialists involved, and the types of practices (i.e., solo, single-specialty group, or multispecialty group) included in the system.
2. Screen prospective vendors for existing capabilities. Ask what they can do without modifying existing code.
3. Develop a request for proposal and issue it to vendors that appear close to meeting those requirements.
4. Develop objective evaluation criteria and make these available to bidders.
5. Use an evaluation committee with operational representation and an external resource.
6. Conduct vendor demonstrations using live data. Avoid canned presentations.
7. Evaluate proposals. Look particularly for willingness to customize to meet local requirements.
8. Verify references.
9. Narrow choices to the top two or three systems.
10. Visit existing sites without the vendor present.
11. Do a cost-benefit analysis or have it done for you.
12. Select a vendor and develop an implementation plan.
13. Load old data and run them in parallel for at least 12 months to make sure everything works.
14. Train clinical, management, and information systems personnel.

Going through such a process is not foolproof. However, it will eliminate vendors that cannot provide what the organization wants, and it will identify those vendors that have experience in successful problem solving.

CRITERIA FOR CLINICAL DATA SYSTEM SELECTION

A clinical data information system should include capabilities covering the following general areas:

- health record tracking
- automated interfaces between the health record and diagnostic providers
- health record access from remote locations
- advanced user interfaces such as touch screen, fax machine, and voice recognition
- monitoring of treatment protocols
- standardized health record format

There should not be any difference between a provider receiving fee for service or capitation.

Additional criteria to be considered include the following:

- new patient registration—patient history and administrative data
- stratified access criteria based on personnel role and need to know
- ability to check test results over an extended period
- automatic assignment of diagnostic codes
- linkage with purchaser formularies for prescriptions
- health record down- and uploading linkage with referral providers
- transmission of health record data to the hospital when necessary
- summary of next day's patients to prepare staff and automated reminder for patients
- patient outcome data
- ability to interface with existing practice management systems and, if necessary, other clinical data systems
- ability to track all steps in patient care
- justification requirement if proposed procedure steps outside community standard of care

Source: Henry Leavitt and James Kragh, "Navigating the Software Sea," *Clinical Data Management*, Vol. 2, No. 4, Aspen Publishers, Inc., © July 1995.

VENDOR COMPARISON CHART

The selection committee should use the following criteria chart to narrow the number of vendors. The vendors who are selected can be contacted and told they are in the final round. Each should be asked for a customer list and the names, addresses, and telephone numbers of users to contact.

Criteria	**Vendor 1**		**Vendor 2**		**Vendor 3**	
	Yes	No	Yes	No	Yes	No
• Completeness of the proposal	___	___	___	___	___	___
• Responsiveness to the request for proposal (RFP)	___	___	___	___	___	___
• Vendor experience and financial viability	___	___	___	___	___	___
• Ability to satisfy functional requirements specified in the RFP	___	___	___	___	___	___
• Maintenance support and guaranteed level of system availability	___	___	___	___	___	___
• Ease of installation, contract terms, and conditions	___	___	___	___	___	___
• Cost	___	___	___	___	___	___
• Does the system need more hardware than the facility can support or handle?	___	___	___	___	___	___
• Is the vendor support system appropriate for the facility's needs?	___	___	___	___	___	___
• What is the vendor's history, and how stable is it?	___	___	___	___	___	___
• Does the installation just *sound* easy or *is* it easy?	___	___	___	___	___	___
• What is the vendor's update and upgrade history? Are the upgrades significant or merely cosmetic?	___	___	___	___	___	___

Source: Adapted from Patricia M. Haynor and Robin W. Wells, "Taking the Plunge: Selecting a Computerized Staffing and Scheduling System," *Aspen's Advisor for Nurse Executives*, Vol. 4:4, Aspen Publishers, Inc., © January 1989.

GUIDELINES—PROPOSAL EVALUATION

The following guidelines serve as an evaluation methodology for major purchases. Such a methodology would not be practical for minor purchases, although a streamlined version might be appropriate.

EVALUATION METHODOLOGY

- It is important to have a methodology that clearly states exactly how the proposals will be evaluated.
- Generally, scoring of a proposal is a combination of several factors:
  - availability of the feature (installed, not installed, extra cost, etc.)
  - quality of the feature (exceeds requirements, substandard, etc.)
  - priority or criticality of the feature to the client (nice to have versus required)
- Assigning weights to factors is a simple way to consider them when grading a proposal. For example, weight each feature from *1* to *3* depending on its priority (i.e., *3* = required, *2* = important, *1* = nice to have).
- Also, assign availability weights to the evaluation; for example, the feature will get a *3* if it is installed, a *2* if it is not currently installed but will be released within a year at no additional cost, and a *1* if there will be additional cost or if development is not already planned.
- Then assign quality weights to the evaluation; for example, grade a feature *3* if it exceeds expectations, *2* if it is average, *1* if it barely meets the requirement, and *0* if the vendor does not meet the requirement.
- Keep this system as simple as possible.
- For a very small application it may be easier to grade each question "fully meets," "partially meets," and "does not meet," and then tally the scores for each vendor.
- Tailor this area to each specific situation.

EVALUATION CRITERIA

- Once priority weights have been assigned, define the evaluation criteria for each question.
- What constitutes a *3* grade (superior) versus a *2* grade (adequate)?
- Each question needs to be reviewed, and the criteria need to be documented.
- Sometimes it is as simple as saying that a "yes" answer is equal to a score of *2* or a standard programming language (e.g., COBOL) is equal to a *3* and a custom language for that system only is equal to a *1*.
- It is important to do this ahead of time for three reasons. First, objectivity will be lost if scoring has begun. Second, time will be saved by documenting the criteria ahead of time. Finally, consistency will be ensured in the evaluation.
- Some areas require more complex evaluation guidelines. For example, grading the vendors on their client base requires assessment of multiple parameters (sites of comparable size, indication of recent installations, comparable hardware and software). In this instance, points may be given for each area and then totaled.
- The vendors are then compared and ranked.
- The highest ranking would get a *3* and the lowest a *1*.
- There will be other situations in which the value of the answer is relative to the other responses—that is, for which it is difficult to define criteria ahead of time. In those cases, simply indicate that the vendors' responses will be ranked against each other and graded accordingly.

MANAGING THE EVALUATION

Worksheets

- Once criteria and priority weights have been established, it is a good idea to prepare worksheets consisting of a list of each RFP question number, the assigned priority weight, the defined evaluation criteria, and a space to record availability scores and quality scores for use during the evaluation.
- In some instances, the answers will be valuable for information purposes only and will not be scored; this would be indicated on the worksheet.

Organization

- There are several options for organizing the evaluation process once the proposals are received.
- One person can evaluate all the proposals or the user department can evaluate the functional area while information services evaluates the technical/installation area.
- If the RFP is large and complex, functional and technical areas can be divided up among multiple reviewers.
- It is usually best to have more than one person evaluate any given proposal section.
- This can be done jointly or separately, but if done separately, the reviewers must reconcile their differences and develop a single score for each answer.
- Be sure to collate the financial data from all the vendors and distribute them to the appropriate financial officers for their assessment.

Cost Evaluation

- The cost section typically does not lend itself to the described evaluation methodology, and indeed, any attempt to assess the cost aspects of the systems is premature at this point.
- The best way to handle cost is to prepare a single sheet comparing all the cost components for all vendors (hardware, software, installation, etc.).
- Allow the ability to meet functional requirements to drive the selection at this stage; deal with the cost issue later when the field has been narrowed down.

continues

Guidelines—Proposal Evaluation continued

- It is always possible that a vendor will bid a system that is totally out of line with the other bids. In that case, once the evaluation is complete and a vendor appears to be one of the finalists, it is a good idea to talk to the vendor and explain that it has priced itself out of the running.

Calculating the Score

- The simplest way to tally the score is to multiply the priority weight times the availability weight times the quality score.
- These scores can then be summarized by RFP section and by overall vendor for comparison.
- The scores can become very large numbers, and RFP sections may wind up influencing the overall score based on the number of questions in the section (which may or may not have anything to do with its relative importance).
- To solve these problems, use the "% Max" method. The maximum possible score is calculated for each question (priority weight times highest possible quality score times highest possible availability score).
- For each section, the vendor's score is divided by the highest possible score (maximum) to yield a percent maximum score.
- This number is more meaningful for review purposes as well as helpful in eliminating skewing of scores by numbers of questions.

VENDOR CLARIFICATION

- Once all the scoring has been completed, compile any questions for the vendor.
- These should be sent in written form, with a written response required.
- Scores can be adjusted based on the responses to the requests for clarification.
- The response will also become a contractual document, along with the original proposal.

SELECTION OF FINALIST(S)

- Proposal scores for all of the vendors are now calculated. Is now the time to select finalists? Probably not. The scores do not give information about two important areas—how easy the system is to use and how well it supports the operational aspects of the business. How happy are the vendor's clients with the product and the vendor? The answers to these questions may be obtained relatively easily by using client questionnaires and demonstrations.

Client Questionnaires

- To save time, client questionnaires can be prepared during the vendor proposal time, ready to be mailed when the proposal and the associated client base information is received. The purpose of the questionnaire is to evaluate the vendor's level of support as well as the overall satisfaction of the users with the product. This is also a good opportunity to research some of the operational issues of the system, although this area is best evaluated during site visits.
- The goal is to get the needed information while keeping the questionnaire as brief as possible. The following are suggested areas of review:
  - documentation
  - training
  - level of software testing
  - installation planning and support
  - reliability of cost estimates
  - postinstallation support
  - hardware support and reliability
  - software maintenance and enhancements
  - operational ease of use
  - assessment of interfaces
  - response time
  - overall user acceptance and satisfaction
  - realized benefits
- Word the questions so that they are both easy to answer and easy to score and tabulate. Asking the clients to provide a grade on a scale of *1* to *5* seems to work best. Be sure to give clear instructions, to request some operating statistics for comparison, and to state clearly when the response is due. It helps to include a self-addressed, stamped envelope with the questionnaire—it often encourages participation.
- The questionnaire should be scored based on the total number of questions answered, not asked. In some cases, the client is not in a position to answer a question, and the vendor should not be penalized for that. To score, assign a grade to each question based on the *1* to *5* answer and tally all grades. The total is then divided by the maximum possible score, which is the number of questions answered multiplied by the highest possible grade (*5*). The client evaluation scores are then averaged for each vendor.

Demonstration

- The purpose of a demonstration is to evaluate firsthand the ease of use of the system. The demonstration should not be used to perform a detailed functional evaluation (that is the purpose of the proposal, and eventually, the site visits), except in a very general sense.
- Careful preparation for a demonstration is critical and centers on clear communications between the users and the vendors. Prior to scheduling the demonstration, the users need to define the following:
  - the purpose of the demonstration
  - specific areas to be demonstrated, if possible
  - the amount of time to be allocated (enough time should be provided for the vendor to cover the requested issues)
  - the site of the demonstration
  - personnel who will attend

  This information should be clearly communicated to the vendors. In return, they need to provide their requirements, including space, table(s), telephone lines, electrical requirements, and audiovisual aids.

continues

Guidelines—Proposal Evaluation continued

- Once all the demonstrations are planned and scheduled, determine how each will be evaluated. One method is to structure evaluation checklists based on the functional areas to be demonstrated. Include such areas as screen presentation, data highlighting, menu pathways, system standardization, function keys, edits, error recovery, help functions, overall ease of use, and operational aspects. As with the client questionnaires, have the reviewers grade each item on a scale of *1* to *5*. Be sure to base grades on the number of items demonstrated, not the number on the checklist. There are a number of valid reasons some aspects of the system cannot be demonstrated. Overall scoring could be performed as described for the questionnaire.

CLIENT BASE EVALUATION

Once the report is produced, distributed, and approved, the top two vendors will be obvious. The next step is to select the vendor of choice. Do this based on information derived from each vendor's client base. There are three ways to accomplish this, although typically nothing can substitute for the information gathered when actually visiting the clients and observing their system operations firsthand.

Questionnaires

If for some reason site visits cannot be made, client questionnaires as described earlier can be used. Develop new questionnaires that reflect any critical concerns and questions still remaining.

Telephone Interviews

Telephone interviews can be used to follow up site visits or augment client questionnaires. Keep these very brief and specific. If calling clients for the first time, tell them what you want to do and how long it will take, and ask them for a convenient time. Ask them to offer their evaluation in the form of a *1* to *5* rating response. Grading would be done as described earlier.

Site Visits

Site visits are without a doubt the best way to differentiate clearly between products. However, if not carefully organized and managed, the information derived from the visits could be difficult to assess or could be a reflection of how the client manages the product rather than of the product itself. The key is to select the right sites, be well organized, and have clearly defined evaluation criteria.

FINALIST SELECTION

Selection Methodology

- Once site visits are complete, an overall vendor ranking should be prepared to determine the vendor of choice. In addition to the site visit scores, the proposals should once again be considered; in some instances, the demonstration or client questionnaire scores may also be factored in, depending on how much the site visits supersede these evaluations.
- Assign a weight to each area and calculate the final vendor scores. Once this is done, a final document should be produced that includes the following:
  - an executive summary that compares the two finalists' scores in each category and indicates a winner
  - an introduction that recaps the methodology
  - a summary sheet of pertinent vendor background
  - a cost summary of the finalists
  - the vendors' site visit scores by area of evaluation and summarized
  - any comments
- The next step is the approval process.

Source: Patricia Johnson, "System Evaluation and Selection," in *Hospital Software Sourcebook*. Aspen Publishers, Inc., © 1989.

INFORMATION SYSTEM PURCHASE REQUEST

Department: ____________________ Date Requested: ____________ Date Needed: ____________

Software Package: ____

Application: ____

____

____ New System ____ Replaces existing system: ________________________________

Complete information relevant to the system you plan to purchase.

Vendor: ____

Hardware	**Cost**	**Annual Maintenance**
Central Processing Unit	______	____________
Printer	______	____________
Disk Drive	______	____________
Diskette (if needed)	______	____________
Terminals (CRTs)	______	____________
Tape Backup	______	____________
Total Hardware	______	____________

Software	**Name**	**Initial Cost**	**Annual License**	**Annual Maintenance**
Operating System	____________	______	______	____________
Compilers	____________	______	______	____________
Utilities	____________	______	______	____________
Other	____________	______	______	____________
Total System Software		______	______	____________

Application Software	**Package Cost**	**Modification Cost**	**Annual License**	**Onsite/Man-days Budgeted for Training**
____________	______	______	______	______
____________	______	______	______	______
____________	______	______	______	______
____________	______	______	______	______
____________	______	______	______	______
TOTAL APPLICATION SOFTWARE	______	______	______	______

Installation Costs
(Other than software modifications, such as conversion programs, conversion assistance). Please specify.

________________________________ $ ______

________________________________ ______

________________________________ ______

________________________________ ______

TOTAL INSTALLATION COSTS $ ______

continues

Information System Purchase Request continued

Other Costs

Education $__________

Manuals __________

Freight __________

Disk Packs __________

Other supplies (please specify) __________

______________________________ __________

______________________________ __________

______________________________ __________

TOTAL OTHER __________

TOTAL COSTS $__________

Rental Credits

Amount of rental credits applied toward purchase $__________

Period of time involved: ________________

Additional Application Packages Available for Future Phases

Approximate Cost

______________________________ $__________

______________________________ __________

______________________________ __________

______________________________ __________

Are linkages planned to other information systems?

____ No

____ Yes—detail below:

____

____

____

Signature of Person Completing Request: __________________________ Phone: ________________

FOR COMMITTEE USE

Date Reviewed: ________________ Requestor Present: ____ Yes ____ No

Additional Information Needed: ____ No ____ Yes Request date: ________________

Subsequent Review Dates: ____

Approved: ____ No ____ Yes

Action(s):

____ Decision Communicated to Requestor

____ Decision Communicated to CEO/CFO

____ Information Management Plan Updated

____ Other:

Courtesy of Patrice L. Spath, Brown-Spath & Associates, Forest Grove, Oregon.

DEVELOPING TECHNOLOGIES

IMPORTANCE OF STRATEGIC INFORMATION SYSTEMS PLANNING IN A CHANGING HEALTH CARE ENVIRONMENT

Strategic information systems (IS) planning is the process of identifying a portfolio of computer-based applications that will assist an organization in executing its business plans and realizing its business goals. The challenge in strategic IS planning is to demonstrate how IS technology can make the greatest contribution to improving the efficiency and effectiveness of the organization. In particular, it is important that the IS plan be well integrated with the overall strategic plan of the health care organization. In a recent survey of leaders in health care computing, nearly 30 percent indicated that the lack of strategic IS planning within their organization was their greatest IS frustration. Despite the lack of IS planning, more than 60 percent of all health care organizations are in the process of forming an integrated delivery system (IDS), with another 20 percent planning to become part of such a system within the next year. Furthermore, nearly half the respondents predicted that clinicians will be able to share computerized patient information in a nationwide system by the year 2000; another 40 percent predicted that it will happen within the next 10 years.

The reality is that health care organizations are expanding their IS to support an integrated environment with or without a strategic IS plan, running the risk of repeating the same mistakes they made in the past when their acquired ISs could not communicate with each other. To prevent this and other implementation problems, it is essential that IS planning be an integral part of the overall organization's strategic plan. Proper systems planning is of particular importance as many health care organizations strive to build an information infrastructure to support the operations of IDSs.

Source: Karen A. Wager, Shyam Heda, and Charles J. Austin, "Developing a Health Information Network within an Integrated Delivery System: A Case Study," *Topics in Health Information Management*, Vol. 17:3, Aspen Publishers, Inc., © 1997.

POTENTIAL BENEFITS OF ESTABLISHING A HEALTH INFORMATION NETWORK

Just a few years ago, there was a great deal of enthusiasm for and interest in the development of community health information networks (CHINs), in which competing organizations would essentially share clinical and financial information with one another. The sentiment today, however, is quite different. IDSs formed in recent years simply have not been willing to share proprietary information with their competitors. Thus the concept of a true CHIN, in which participants are willing to share information with competitors for the benefit of the broader community, has never come to fruition. Instead, many IDSs are in the process of developing health information networks (HINs) capable of supporting the information needs of their enterprise. From a strategic perspective, HINs can provide health care administrators and providers with the information they need to conduct clinical outcome studies prospectively, evaluate the quality of services provided, and assess financial performance. HINs are also intended to reduce paper shuffling, phone calls, and time delays by providing authorized users access to relevant patient information from multiple sources. Other benefits include rapid transmission of data, elimination of duplicate tests by providing practitioners with access to test results, improved quality of care, and decreased administrative costs.

Source: Karen A. Wager, Shyam Heda, and Charles J. Austin, "Developing a Health Information Network within an Integrated Delivery System: A Case Study," *Topics in Health Information Management*, Vol. 17:3, Aspen Publishers, Inc., © 1997.

CREATING A HIN

Although the potential benefits of HINs are many, organizations must address several key issues in their strategic IS plans to prepare adequately for their implementation. For example, health care organizations cannot afford to build redundant information infrastructures, and appropriate planning for HINs can help avoid such redundancies. Most principal issues can be addressed by including the following activities in the IS planning process:

- understanding business objectives
- defining the type of ownership
- assessing current systems
- identifying participants' IS requirements
- determining the method of financing
- defining legal and security issues

By following this process, organizations can effectively plan for HIN implementation.

Understanding Business Objectives

The decision to participate in or develop a HIN is a business, not a technological, decision. Just as strategic IS plans are developed around key organizational strategic objectives, HIN planning should be based on the ability of the HIN to support the organization's strategic IS initiatives. Consequently, it is important to identify and understand each participating organization's individual and common business objectives and evaluate their critical success factors. HIN projects that are moving forward among large IDSs have relied on extensive discussions among participants to build trust and gain consensus on business objectives. To succeed, many agree that a HIN needs strong leadership that can move the process beyond mere discussion to actual implementation.

Experts in health IS and technology suggest that true leaders think broadly when evaluating business objectives. The overall problem is that of making the transition from an enormous cottage industry to a true national health care system. This transition will not require just the implementation of a broad range of technologies—networks, new applications, and so forth—but, more important, will require a fundamental change in the role of the management information services department.

It is suggested that leaders move from having a single-institution perspective to having an IDS perspective. This implies a willingness on the part of executives to subordinate their individual organizational priorities to those of the broader delivery system. The single greatest challenge facing health care IS professionals will be defining the boundaries of their organizations.

Source: Karen A. Wager, Shyam Heda, and Charles J. Austin, "Developing a Health Information Network within an Integrated Delivery System: A Case System," *Topics in Health Information Management*, Vol. 17:3, Aspen Publishers, Inc., © 1997.

DEFINING TYPE OF OWNERSHIP

In planning to develop a HIN, it is also important to consider the various ownership models and how the HIN will be financed. Some HIN models require that all information be stored in one mainframe computer at a single site, called a central data repository. Other models use a distributed database, which allows organizations to keep information in their own systems and create a virtual network by allowing others to call up specific information as needed. Some argue that no one has been able to make a fully distributed system work and that solving the problem will take time. Furthermore, the lack of a central repository raises the question of who is responsible for the information in a HIN. One suggestion is that the issue of ownership models is both a political and a practical one. Selecting the appropriate HIN ownership model depends on the IDS and its needs. Historically, most HIN ownership models included the vendor-owned model, the community coalition model, and the accountable health plan–owned (AHP) model.

In the vendor-owned model, the vendor generally funds and operates the HIN as a for-profit enterprise. The mission of this type of HIN is to generate significant revenues and profit for the vendor through usage, transaction, operation, and maintenance fees. These HINs generally focus on transmitting claims information more efficiently, with the long-range goal of creating community databases containing patient care, cost, quality, and outcomes performance information. They usually do not contain a central data repository but rather use existing data available through payer and provider IS. Furthermore, most vendor-owned HINs maintain control of the network by securing at least 51 percent ownership. This model offers the health care organization the benefit of having the vendor bear the costs of implementing the HIN hardware, software, network, and technical support staff. From a strategic planning perspective, however, the vendor-owned model may offer less flexibility in system design.

The second type of ownership model is the community coalition HIN. In contrast to the vendor-owned model, the community coalition model is generally formed by a coalition of employers, providers, payers, and government agencies to address the needs of the community at large. This model is designed to improve quality of care and reduce costs within the community by establishing a not-for-profit entity that contracts with a vendor for development and operation of the HIN. The community coalition HIN is owned and funded by the coalition participants, possibly with some assistance from vendors. Within this model, the coalition can set up its own HIN and incur the associated costs or select one or more vendors to build and operate the HIN. The coalition determines its own charges for users and pays vendors the necessary transaction or operating fees for their services. Health care organizations that choose to adopt the community coalition model should be prepared to address issues related to sharing clinical and financial information with their competitors.

A third model is the AHP HIN, which is similar to the coalition model but is generally sponsored and funded by a smaller group of providers. The mission of an AHP is to create a shared, open infrastructure to increase efficiency and lower the cost of communicating patient information throughout the community. Simply stated, the AHP's goal is to develop a network of ISs that aid in providing care to a defined population of patients. Frequently this model is used in specific integrated community networks or by managed care organizations that have contractual relationships with a group of providers. The AHP is owned, funded, and managed by the AHP providers and payers and can therefore control database development and access. This model offers the health care organization and provider greater flexibility than the coalition model in that it tailors the HIN to meet the unique goals and needs of the IDS.

In addition to these three primary models, several hybrids of HIN ownership models are emerging. Some state governments are playing an increasing role in health care reform and may allocate state funds to implement a statewide network. Alternatively, in areas where a particular payer dominates the state, it may be possible to implement a HIN that evolves into the de facto community CHIN. Regardless of the model chosen, it is important to take into account cost, control, functionality, and other strategic considerations. Conducting an economic analysis in the planning stages to estimate costs and cost savings is recommended. The four components of the economic analysis are start-up costs, estimated cost savings, cost to develop and operate the network, and the profit and loss statement of the HIN entity. Although these estimates are unlikely to be precise, given the early stage of HIN development, the analysis is useful for planning purposes.

Assessing Current Systems

In addition to understanding the common business objectives of the organizations involved in establishing a HIN and defining the type of ownership, it is important to inventory and assess the current systems used both within the individual organization and among the various participants. Most organizations begin by conducting an inventory of systems. This inventory should include assessment of the hardware, communication systems, software, and manual and automated interfaces. Generally, one of the first systems assessed is the registration system, primarily because a community master patient index is needed to organize information around patients regardless of where they are seen and where information is captured. Most of the facilities participating in the HIN will have different methods for identifying patient records, and each will maintain its own master patient index. Accessing information stored in multiple systems requires an application that identifies and links patient records. Many health care organizations are struggling to find ways to link records contained in disparate systems. Providers and administrators, however, must be able to track a patient across multiple facilities and through multiple episodes of care to control costs and manage care effectively.

Identifying IS Requirements

Many different types of individuals and organizations may be interested in developing a HIN within an IDS. Each organization will have either paper-based or computerized administrative, clinical, and financial systems. Therefore, it is important to identify IS requirements. One approach is to determine the IS requirements based on the relative volume of transactions exchanged with any given participant. For example, if hospital A submits 5,000 claims a month to payer 1 but only 200 per month to payer 2, hospital A should be more interested in participating in a HIN with payer 1 than with payer 2. This does not mean that payer 2 should not participate, but including payer 1 would provide greater potential benefits to hospital A than including payer 2.

Throughout the planning process, it is important to identify not only the IS requirements but also the infrastructure needed to support the system requirements. Some organizations designate managers with authority and accountability to manage processes that cut across traditional boundaries. These managers are charged by senior management to develop and manage processes, such as patient registration, on an ongoing basis.

Building a strong infrastructure to support the HIN needs also requires defining a telecommunications network, establishing data and language standards, and planning for systems integration. Creating a telecommunications network requires answering a number of questions: What are the numbers and geographical locations of the various sites? How much information is communicated, and in what form (text, forms, or images) must it be communicated? How much imaging data must be stored and sent to the various providers? Is telemedicine to be part of the network? Currently, no single organization can supply all the components necessary to build an enterprisewide HIN. Consequently, it is important to build strategic alliances with vendors and other constituents.

An organization developing a HIN should also establish data and language standards. Data standards are useful in ensuring accurate flow of information among various organizations. Typically, a standard process for building interfaces between individual computer applications (referred to as a *universal interface engine*) is needed to ensure the smooth transfer of data. Similarly, members of the HIN should establish language standards. Often, the definition of a single test or procedure may have one meaning in a hospital and another meaning in a physician practice. Participants must decide whether communication is best accomplished by developing a universal dictionary that ensures that the parameters for all tests and procedures are defined the same way. If organizations choose to maintain individual standards and definitions, it is important to plan a system that will accommodate and respond to these customized meanings. Finally, in building an infrastructure to support the HIN, an organization should plan for systems integration. The goals of systems integration are to provide access to the information in a format that is easy to use and to deliver the information in a manner consistent with the standards defined by the organization.

Determining Method of Financing

How the HIN will be financed should also be addressed in the organization's strategic IS plan. Actual expenditures may vary depending on the type of HIN and an organization's scope of involvement. It is important to identify the major categories of expenditures, however, such as the cost of staffing, feasibility studies, legal services, request for information development, vendor selection, contract negotiations, and business plan development. In addition to identifying major expenditures, it is important to consider potential funding sources such as subscriber fees, private grants, government funding, and vendor-supplied capital.

Defining Legal and Security Issues

As with ownership and financing issues, legal and security issues should also be considered in the planning stages of a HIN. Unfortunately, no definitive guidelines address all the legal and security issues associated with HINs. A number of issues should be addressed, including formalizing the legal structure to reduce the risks of conflict during the operation and termination of the network, selecting the right vendor and the right technology and taking all precautions to ensure the continued availability of the technology, establishing procedures and security mechanisms to protect patients' right to privacy and to the confidentiality of their records, and managing the risks associated with the technology (e.g., reliability of electronic health records, evidence/admissibility of computer-based records, threats to security, backup disaster recovery, and compliance with licensure). Until laws and policies are better adapted to the technical and business realities, those involved in HINs should be cautious.

Source: Karen A. Wager, Shyam Heda, and Charles J. Austin, "Developing a Health Information Network within an Integrated Delivery System: A Case Study," *Topics in Health Information Management*, Vol. 17:3, Aspen Publishers, Inc., © 1997.

EVALUATING A TELEMEDICINE DELIVERY SYSTEM

To develop an effective evaluation plan for a telemedicine delivery system, it is useful to review both the problems and the promise of previous models used in telemedicine. Historical review reveals that experiments with electronic transmission of images to physicians date back as far as the early 1900s. In the United States, two of the earliest telemedicine delivery systems were developed in the late 1950s, at the University of Nebraska and at the Papago Indian Reservation in Arizona, in a joint program developed by Lockheed, the National Aeronautics and Space Administration (NASA), and the U.S. Public Health Service. In the 1960s and 1970s, Massachusetts General Hospital and Dartmouth Medical School also had telemedicine projects in place. During the 1980s, although there was less activity in the United States, Canada saw an increase in telemedicine that was largely attributed to the establishment of socialized medicine and to the vast expanse of that country. Also in the 1980s, Norway successfully implemented a video conferencing medical network that has progressed from the experimental stage to regular medical practice.

The 1990s have seen an increase in telemedicine projects, with advances in communications technology that merge the capabilities of telecommunications with computer technology. Currently, at least 20 states in the United States have telemedicine projects in place. Three projects in Texas include the MedNet system at Texas Tech University in West Texas, the Texas Telemedicine Project serving central Texas, and the MEDTEL system, which is a global system based at Texas Medical Center in Houston. Other systems in the United States have been described, including the Rural Options for Development and Educational Opportunities Network (RODEO NET) in eastern Oregon and military applications abroad, including disaster response in 1988 after the earthquake in Soviet Armenia and linkage between Walter Reed Hospital in the United States and physicians based in Somalia during Operation Hope. NASA has gone beyond the boundaries of the globe with its telemedicine linkage to astronauts during space flights.

The telemedicine systems developed during this decade use technologies that provide the capability to offer four similar types of services. Clinical consultations can be offered via interactive (two-way) digital video and audio with signals transmitted via T1 links, which require a smaller bandwidth than regular television broadcast and thus involve lower costs. Static video imaging systems using existing telephone lines for transmission allow high-resolution X-ray images, color pathology images, and other still images to be delivered to the consulting physician for diagnosis. Medical information can be transmitted via facsimile machines, including reports such as continuous fetal monitoring strips. Finally, the telemedicine set-up can provide remote areas with continuing medical education, which is critical in the rapidly changing health care environment. With currently available technology, remote diagnosis has been found to be successful in a number of medical specialties, including pathology, dermatology, otorhinolaryngology, cardiology, ophthalmology, psychiatry, speech therapy, rehabilitation, and radiology.

EVALUATING GOALS

Medicine today is an information-intensive practice, and telemedicine allows health care providers to move information rather than people. Technology infrastructure is the key to developing telecommunications in the rural areas to be served by telemedicine. Elements that can help in the development of a successful telemedicine system include using the least complicated and least costly technology necessary to meet a need, keeping the system flexible to adapt to rapid changes in technology, involving the users in the development phase to ensure a user-friendly system, and providing adequate training to the users at each site. Comprehensive planning and coordination can result in the immediate, interactive, personal, and lifesaving capabilities offered by a telemedicine system.

An evaluation plan for any new project should be ongoing, particularly during the initial implementation phase of such a complex undertaking. Evaluation should focus on three major areas. In order of priority, the goals of such a plan should be to provide quality patient care, to address legal issues such as ensuring confidentiality of patient information, and to provide cost-effective medical services.

Quality of Patient Care

Quality-of-care issues include the reliability and replicability of telemedical diagnoses, patient response to treatment, determination of the types of consultations that can be carried out safely and effectively via telemedicine, identification of risks of telemedical consultations versus no consultation or a delayed consultation after the transport of a patient, and identification of other mortality and morbidity risks related to patient recovery (such as impact on a patient who must be transported away from family and home). Also involved in the quality-of-care issue is the reliability of the transmission technology. Minimal standards should be developed to ensure that equipment is dependable and accurately depicts the patient's condition. Effective use of the equipment would also be affected by user satisfaction, with users including the patient, referring physician, and consulting physician.

Legal Issues

The main legal issue in telemedicine involves the protection of the confidentiality of patient information. As accessibility to medical information and administrative convenience increase, assurance of patient privacy decreases. Although videotaped clinical sessions would become part of the patient's existing health record and would be protected by the same legal confidentiality guidelines that are currently in place, the issue becomes more troublesome as clinical information is computerized, networked, and sent to distant locations. Slow progress in the development of the computer-based patient record (CPR) has been due to a number of issues such as nonstandardization of hospital information systems and patient data, poorly integrated computer and networking systems, lack of expertise for choos-

continues

Evaluating a Telemedicine Delivery System continued

ing appropriate hospital systems, lack of input of users (especially the health information manager), costs of hardware and software, poor data quality, and lack of consensus about electronic data interchange. One major concern involving the CPR has been the issue of security and confidentiality.

Other legal issues in telemedicine involve ownership of data, medical malpractice, and, where distance delivery crosses state lines, the potential problems of physician licensing. Hospital privileges and ordering of prescription drugs also have to be addressed.

Cost Effectiveness

The final major goal of an evaluation plan involves the cost effectiveness of health care delivery via the telemedicine system. Cost comparisons of each approach of delivery should be studied to determine the cost feasibility of such a system. Costs include expenses for the technology versus the cost of the provider's time and travel, the cost of patient transport, and the potential cost of delay in diagnosis and treatment. Another cost factor, which is one of the reasons why some providers have been hesitant to become involved in telemedicine, is the fact that reimbursement for telemedical consultations between patients and physicians is usually denied by Medicare, Medicaid, and other third-party payers. It is clear that major health care policy changes will be required to ensure a smooth transition to new ways of delivery of medical services.

INFORMATION REQUIRED TO ASSESS GOALS OF EVALUATION PLAN

In most cases, the information that would ensure that these goals are reached is already being collected. Whenever a patient is seen by a health care provider, whether as an inpatient, an outpatient, or a patient visiting a physician's office, a lot of patient data is routinely collected. The amount of information contained in an average patient health record has greatly increased over the past 20 years as a result of increased requirements for reimbursement, legal protection, and documentation of an increased number of complex procedures performed. Although the format of information that is collected is not standardized, all health records are required to include certain information such as demographic data, medical history and physical examination data, diagnostic and therapeutic information, patient progress and course of treatment, disposition, and follow-up treatment plans. These requirements are guided by the standards of accrediting and licensing agencies as well as by federal and state reporting requirements. Although standards for ambulatory patient health records have historically lagged behind inpatient record requirements, outpatient facilities now keep documentation that is equivalent in quality to the inpatient health record. Even though uniform types of information are being documented, the format and quality of the data have been inconsistent. Therefore, for the purposes of an evaluation plan, information that is already being documented and collected may have to be rearranged and monitored for quality to serve a telemedicine project.

In addition to existing information at the sites, each of these facilities should also have in place some type of quality-of-care review program that routinely monitors and evaluates the quality of services being provided. The same mechanisms used in these established programs can be used to evaluate the telemedical delivery system, with the appropriate specialty areas determining the most important aspects of care, the measures to be used, and the appropriate thresholds for evaluation.

New information that is needed but is not currently being gathered on a routine basis is cost information (physician salary ranges, projected travel expenses, etc.) that will be used to justify the cost of the telemedicine system. Also, additional information will be needed to determine user satisfaction (patient, referring physician, and consulting physician) during each interactive telemedical conference.

The statistics to be kept during the monitoring of a project would be determined by the specific clinical specialty area that establishes the measures and thresholds in each type of case. The types of statistics used in quality review studies involve percentages of cases meeting or not meeting the established criteria of quality care. For example, if the specialty area decides to review 50 cases, it may compare the diagnoses made via direct consult versus video consult to determine the accuracy of diagnosis and response to treatment. This comparison could determine whether there were any significant differences in quality of care. Again, each type of clinical case requires the input of the specialists in that clinical area to determine which medical indicators are most appropriate to be reviewed, what type of statistics are reported, and how often the review and reporting takes place.

Source: Janis L. Huston and Timothy A. Smith, "Evaluating a Telemedicine Delivery System," *Topics in Health Information Management*, Vol. 16:3, Aspen Publishers, Inc., © 1996.

SAMPLE HEALTH INFORMATION SYSTEMS

THE UNIVERSITY OF ROCHESTER MEDICAL CENTER (URMC) INFORMATION ENVIRONMENT FOR THE 21ST CENTURY

VISION

The URMC integrated information environment is a collaboration of people and technology that delivers information needed for caring, learning, teaching and discovery.

CORE CHARACTERISTICS OF THE INTEGRATED INFORMATION ENVIRONMENT

Ubiquitous Information is available where and when it is needed, in a suitable format.

Robust The technology infrastructure and information resources are designed to accommodate present and future needs at the best balance of cost and benefit.

Managed There is high level, coordinated leadership for design, operations, planning, standards and policies that govern the information environment.

Comprehensive There is a single point of access to institutional information resources for all authorized users. Core services and training enhance connectivity among community members.

BENEFITS OF THE INTEGRATED INFORMATION ENVIRONMENT

- Desirable uses of information for caring, learning, teaching and discovery are independent of circumstances of time, space, organization or technology.
- The quality and quantity of information that informs decision-making and discovery are improved.
- The efficiency of information management is improved throughout the enterprise by eliminating unnecessary duplication of expenditures, recordkeeping and human effort.
- URMC's ability to recruit and retain the best students, faculty and staff is enhanced.
- The timing, nature and extent of investments in information technology and resources are optimized and integrated with institutional priorities.

RISKS IN BUILDING AN INTEGRATED INFORMATION ENVIRONMENT

- A sizable, ongoing financial investment is required.
- Changing costs & features of information technology are difficult to predict, impossible to control.
- Lack of local expertise, clear goals and commitment may lead to inadequate results.
- Organizational and financing models are ill-defined.
- Integrated Advanced Information Management Systems (IAIMS) development can take a decade.

RISKS OF NOT BUILDING AN INTEGRATED INFORMATION ENVIRONMENT

- URMC is unable to compete successfully in the health care marketplace.
- URMC is unable to function effectively as an integrated delivery system.
- URMC is locked out of emerging research domains (e.g., visualization, techniques, biotechnology, digital imaging, computational biology, informatics).
- URMC is unable to recruit and retain best quality students, faculty, and staff.

Courtesy of the University of Rochester Medical Center, Rochester, New York. http://www.urmc.rochester.edu/iaims/mp.html

THE URMC INTEGRATED ADVANCED INFORMATION MANAGEMENT SYSTEMS (IAIMS) MASTER PLAN

IAIMS INSTITUTIONAL CULTURE	The integrated information environment at URMC is a joint product of committed, high-level leaders and a broad-based, capable community of users. To achieve this we will
Central, High-level Leadership	• Create a high level Medical Center management function that provides leadership for the development and management of a robust, well-executed integrated information environment. • Provide encouragement for the development, careful management and effective use of network-based information resources through appropriate institutional recognition and incentives for participation. • Promulgate information policies that define principles of ownership, access, standardization and authority to assure the quality, confidentiality and security of institutional information.
User Participation	• Develop mechanisms that foster active participation in information systems planning by all types of stakeholders and end users, employing, where appropriate, proportionate representation from major constituencies.
Information Literacy	• Determine the basic information competencies required for work and study in the integrated information environment and provide formal and self-guided instruction opportunities that support achievement of those competencies.
IAIMS INFORMATION INFRASTRUCTURE	URMC's integrated information environment is a well-managed, shared system of human, technological and information resources. To achieve this we will
Network Infrastructure & Core Services	• Provide access to information resources needed for work and study regardless of the location of the requestor, the type of computer platform, the location of the database or the time of day. • Design and build to a uniform standard a new infrastructure that can support simultaneous voice, data and video traffic for in-house and off-campus sites. • Equip all appropriate education and training facilities for multimedia development and utilization. • Implement a set of core network services, including management of firewall systems to prevent intrusion, domain name servers to support Internet protocols, network monitoring systems, network logical and physical documentation systems, teleconferencing connectivity facilities and network user authentication systems.
Support Services	• Provide a coordinated set of consulting, troubleshooting and technological support services to assist Medical Center faculty, staff and students in their use of information technology. • Provide a central point of support for instructional computing for the Medical Center, staffed by trained personnel who can work with instructors to develop interactive computer-based modules. • Provide a centralized network infrastructure management group to assure a robust, proactively monitored, quickly repaired and well documented network infrastructure. • Provide support for resource booking, room set-up and testing for multimedia presentations, regardless of time of need, including evenings and weekends as appropriate.
Knowledge Resources	• Expand and enhance access to the published knowledge bases that support education, practice and research in the health sciences. • Provide remotely-accessible, platform independent educational resources that support formal curricula and independent learning. • Provide access to appropriate knowledge resources and multimedia, interactive software, tailored to the health care consumer. • Provide online, up-to-date access to the full range of University and Medical Center official documents, publications and announcements.
IAIMS TOOL BOX	URMC's diverse population of staff, faculty, students and clients requires an array of general and specialized tools for creating and working with information. To make appropriate tools available we will

continues

The URMC IAIMS Master Plan continued

Standards	• Establish a mechanism for the development and regular review of essential and/or useful institutional standards for both hardware and software for standard applications, including basic user services and database access, and site license negotiations. • Establish standards for hardware and operating systems that maximize interoperability and the secure exchange of information across technology platforms. • Develop criteria for determining which databases should be considered "institutional data", and to develop a central administrative function for registering users and managing user access privileges to these institutional databases.
General Tools	• Develop a common interface, with both a set of standard functions and the capacity for user customization, that allows an authorized user access to all appropriate information resources through a single menu. • Provide and promote the use of a "universal," remotely accessible email system that includes a directory capability, the ability to attach and read documents, and the use of a graphical user interface. • Develop appropriate data dictionaries for both administrative and clinical databases, and encourage their use by providing convenient access to their content. • Acquire or develop software tools that support (1) intra- and inter-institutional activities, (2) management of business operations, (3) central calendaring and scheduling of meetings, equipment and facilities.
Specialized Tools	• Acquire or develop software tools for special purposes including (1) grant proposal preparation and submission, (2) patient education and decision making, (3) the management of information about students and courses. • Acquire or develop decision support tools that are integrated and interactive with the communication, documentation and information handling functions of the CIS. • Build an integrated clinical research environment that will allow access, retrieval and manipulation of clinical and project information for research purposes.

Courtesy of the University of Rochester Medical Center, Rochester, New York. http://www.urmc.rochester.edu/iaims/mp.html

2
Information Management Standards/Requirements

Chapter **2**

Information Management Standards/Requirements

THIRD-PARTY PAYERS

ADMINISTRATION OF THE MEDICARE PROGRAM

Introduction

The Health Insurance for the Aged and Disabled Act (Title XVIII of the Social Security Act), known as Medicare, has made available to nearly every American 65 years of age and older a broad program of health insurance designed to assist the nation's elderly to meet hospital, medical, and other health costs. Health insurance coverage has also been extended to persons under age 65 qualifying as disabled and those having end-stage renal disease (ESRD). The program includes two related health insurance programs—hospital insurance (HI) (Part A) and supplementary medical insurance (SMI) (Part B).

The conduct of the program has been delegated by the Secretary of the Department of Health and Human Services (DHHS) to the Administrator of the Health Care Financing Administration (HCFA). Congress has also provided substantial administrative roles for the states and for voluntary insurance organizations in recognition of their experience in the health care and insurance fields.

The law does not permit the federal government to exercise supervision or control over the practice of medicine, the manner in which medical services are provided, and the administration or operation of medical facilities. The patient is free to choose any qualified institution, agency, or person offering services. The responsibility for treatment and the control of care remains with the individual's physician and the hospital or other facility or agency furnishing services. Individuals may keep or obtain any other health insurance they desire.

Financing the Program

Part A is financed through separate payroll contributions paid by employees, employers, and self-employed persons. The proceeds are deposited to the account of the Federal Hospital Insurance Trust Fund, which is used only for hospital insurance benefits and administrative expenses. The cost of providing Part A benefits to persons who are not Social Security or railroad retirement beneficiaries is met by appropriations to the Federal Hospital Insurance Trust Fund from general revenues or through premium payments.

Part B is financed by monthly premiums of those who voluntarily enroll in the program and by the federal government, which makes contributions from general revenues. All premiums and government contributions are deposited in a separate account known as the Federal Supplementary Medical Trust Fund. Money from this fund is used only to pay for Part B benefits and administrative expenses.

Discrimination Prohibited

Participating providers of services under the hospital insurance program—for example, hospitals, skilled nursing facilities (SNFs), home health agencies (HHAs), hospices, outpatient physical therapists (OPT), comprehensive outpatient rehabilitation facilities (CORFs), occupational therapy and speech pathology providers, and ESRD facilities—must comply with the requirements of Title VI of the Civil Rights Act of 1964. Under the provisions of that Act, a participating provider is prohibited from making a distinction on the ground of race, color, or national origin in the treatment of patients, the use of equipment, other facilities, and the assignment of personnel to provide services. DHHS is responsible for investigating complaints of noncompliance.

FRAUD AND ABUSE—GENERAL

Providers and suppliers have an obligation, under law, to conform to the requirements of the Medicare program. Fraud and abuse committed against the program may be prosecuted under various provisions of the United States Code and could result in the imposition of restitution, fines, and, in some instances, imprisonment. In addition, a range of administrative sanctions (such as exclusion from participation in the program) and civil monetary penalties may be imposed when facts and circumstances warrant such action.

Following are definitions and examples of fraud and abuse. These definitions and examples give a better understanding of the types of practices that are forbidden, under law, in the Medicare program.

Definition and Examples of Fraud—Fraud is defined as making false statements or representations of material facts in order to obtain some benefit or payment for which no entitlement would otherwise exist. These acts may be committed either for the person's own benefit or for the benefit of some other party. In order to prove that fraud has been committed against the government, it is necessary to prove that fraudulent acts were performed knowingly, willfully, and intentionally.

Examples of fraud include, but are not limited to, the following:

- Billing for services that were not furnished and/or supplies not provided. This includes billing Medicare for appointments that the patient failed to keep.
- Altering claims forms and/or receipts in order to receive a higher payment amount.
- Duplicating billings that includes billing both the Medicare program and the beneficiary, Medicaid, or some other insurer in an effort to receive payment greater than allowed.
- Offering, paying, soliciting, or receiving bribes, kickbacks, or rebates, directly or indirectly, in cash or in kind, in order to induce referrals of patients or the purchase of goods or services that may be paid for by the Medicare program.
- Falsely representing the nature of the services furnished. This encompasses describing a noncovered service in a misleading way that makes it appear as if a covered service was actually furnished.
- Billing a person who has Medicare coverage for services provided to another person not eligible for Medicare coverage.
- Repeatedly violating the participation agreement, assignment agreement, and the Maximum Allowable Actual Charge (MAAC) limits or limitation amount.
- Completing certificates of medical necessity (CMN) for patients not personally and professionally known by the provider.
- Completing a prohibited CMN by suppliers.
- Using another person's Medicare card to obtain medical care.
- Giving false information about provider ownership in a clinical laboratory.
- Conspiring to submit or manipulate bills by a provider and a beneficiary, two or more providers and suppliers, or a provider and a carrier employee that results in higher costs or charges to the program.
- Billing procedures over a period of days when all treatment occurred during onc visit (e.g., split billing schemes).
- Using the adjustment payment process to generate fraudulent payments.
- Billing for gang visits—a physician visits a nursing home, walks through the facility, and bills for 20 nursing home visits without rendering any specific service to the individual patients.

Definition and Examples of Abuse—Abuse describes practices that, either directly or indirectly, result in unnecessary costs to the Medicare program. Many times abuse appears quite similar to fraud except that it is not possible to establish that abusive acts were committed knowingly, willfully, and intentionally.

Following are three standards that HCFA uses when judging whether abusive acts in billing were committed against the Medicare program:

1. medically necessary
2. conform to professionally recognized standards
3. provided at a fair price

Examples of abuse include, but are not limited to, the following:

- Charging in excess for services or supplies.
- Providing medically unnecessary services or services that do not meet professionally recognized standards.
- Billing Medicare based on a higher fee schedule than for non-Medicare patients.

- Submitting bills to Medicare that are the responsibility of other insurers under the Medicare secondary payer (MSP) regulation.
- Violating the participating physician/supplier agreement.
- Breaches in the assignment agreement.
- Violating the MAAC or limitation amount.

Although these types of practices may initially be categorized as abusive in nature, under certain circumstances they may develop into fraud if there is evidence that the subject was knowingly and willfully conducting an abusive practice.

Responsibility for Combating Fraud, Waste, and Abuse—The Office of the Inspector General (OIG), in DHHS, is responsible for investigating instances of fraud, waste, and abuse in the Medicare and Medicaid programs. OIG concentrates its efforts in the following areas:

- Conducting investigations of specific providers suspected of fraud, waste, or abuse for purposes of determining whether criminal, civil, or administrative remedies are warranted.
- Conducting audits, special analyses, and reviews for purposes of discovering and documenting Medicare and Medicaid policy and procedural weaknesses contributing to fraud, waste, or abuse, and making recommendations for corrections.
- Conducting reviews and special projects to determine the level of effort and performance in health provider fraud and abuse control.
- Participating in a program of external communications to inform the health care community, the Congress, other interested organizations, and the public of OIG's concerns and activities related to health care financing integrity.
- Collecting and analyzing Medicare contractor and state Medicaid agency-produced information on resources and results.
- Participating with other government agencies and private health insurers in special programs to share techniques and knowledge on preventing health care provider fraud and abuse.

FEDERAL GOVERNMENT ADMINISTRATION OF THE HEALTH INSURANCE PROGRAM

DHHS has overall responsibility for administering the hospital insurance and voluntary SMI programs. Two major agencies—HCFA and the Public Health Service—are involved in specified administrative functions.

HCFA is responsible for policy formulation. The central and regional offices are responsible for the general management and operation of the program. In brief, HCFA's responsibilities include the following:

- Determining an individual's entitlement to benefits in consultation with the Social Security Administration (SSA).
- Determining the nature and duration of services for which a beneficiary's benefits may be paid.
- Establishing, maintaining, and administrating agreements with state agencies, providers of services, and intermediaries.
- Formulating major policies regarding conditions of participation for providers (except SNFs) in consultation with the Public Health Service.
- Developing and maintaining statistical research and actuarial programs.
- Managing general finances of the program.
- Determining reasonable costs and amounts to be paid to providers who have elected to deal directly with the government.

The Public Health Service is responsible for administering the professional health aspects of the program. In brief, its responsibilities include the following:

- Consulting and recommending to HCFA matters concerning the development of health and safety standards and other guidelines needed for determining whether or not providers of services meet the conditions of participation under the program.
- Consulting and advising state agencies concerning the application of standards for providers.
- Coordinating programs and activities necessary in studying the utilization of services under the program.

STATE AGENCIES

The states, by agreement with the secretary, are assigned significant administrative functions to the extent that each is willing and capable of discharging such responsibilities.

Certification—Facilities desiring to participate in either the Medicare or Medicaid programs must meet participation conditions for certification. State agencies certify to the DHHS whether or not providers satisfy, and continue to satisfy, their respective conditions of participation in the Medicare and Medicaid programs. The secretary, DHHS, certifies facilities requesting participation in the Medicare and Medicaid programs. States certify those facilities that request participation in the Medicaid program only. The state function of making certifications is intended to be a natural adjunct to ongoing state activities (such as the licensing of health care facilities and the setting of standards).

Consultation—A state consults with providers of services that need and request participation condition assistance. For Medicare participation, the secretary, DHHS, must approve the consultation service rendered by the state certifying agency.

Coordination—A state coordinates activities with other state programs that involve payment for health care, quality of care, and location of health facilities. Coordinating these activities is essential in ensuring effective and economical use of existing state facilities and trained personnel and to prevent duplication of effort.

State Agency as a Medical Insurance Intermediary—Where a state enters into an agreement with the government to pay the medical insurance premium on behalf of its aged welfare recipients, the agreement may provide for a designated state agency to serve as an intermediary on behalf of its welfare recipients.

ROLE OF PART A INTERMEDIARIES

The Part A intermediary is a public or private agency or organization that has entered into an agreement with HCFA to process Medicare claims under both Part A and Part B for providers of services (e.g., hospitals, SNFs, HHAs, hospices, CORFs, OPT, occupational therapy, and speech pathology providers, and ESRD facilities).

Intermediaries make payments to providers. The amount of payment to a provider is restricted to the lesser of (a) the reasonable cost of covered services and items, and (b) the customary charges with respect to such services. Hospitals are paid based on a prospective payment system (PPS). Under this system, Medicare payment is made at a predetermined, specific rate for each hospital discharge. In addition, intermediaries assist in applying safeguards against unnecessary use of covered services, furnish consultative services to serve as a center for communicating with providers, conduct audits of provider records, assist in the beneficiary appeals process, and provide information and advice to institutions and organizations that wish to qualify as providers of services.

ROLE OF PART B CARRIERS

The law requires the secretary to enter into contracts with carriers to serve as intermediaries in the operation and administration of the nonprovider Part B program. A principal function of these carriers is to determine whether or not physician and supplier charges (including facility-based physicians) for covered Part B services constitute reasonable charges within the meaning of the law, and, also, to make payment. Other major functions include, for example, controlling overutilization and communicating with the health community.

Source: *Medicare Hospital Manual*, U.S. Department of Health and Human Services, Health Care Financing Administration, HCFA-Pub 10 Thru T703, Rev. 7/97.

MEDICARE PROSPECTIVE PAYMENT SYSTEM

BACKGROUND OF THE PROSPECTIVE PAYMENT SYSTEM (PPS)

When Medicare was introduced in July 1965, federal expenditures for health care began a period of rapid growth. Medicare represents nearly one third of hospital admissions in this country; the program did not contain incentives for providers to control costs.

The Medicare Prospective Payment System (PPS) was introduced by the federal government in October 1983 as a way to change hospital behavior through financial incentives that encourage more cost-efficient management of medical care. Under PPS, hospitals are paid a predetermined rate for each Medicare admission. Each patient is classified into a diagnosis-related group (DRG) on the basis of clinical information. Except for certain patients with exceptionally high costs (called outliers), the hospital is paid a flat rate for the DRG, regardless of the actual services provided. The incentives are that cost-efficient hospitals can keep any surplus in DRG payment over costs, while less efficient hospitals must absorb the loss.

Under PPS, the rate of growth in hospital costs has declined. Payments to hospitals, however, have not kept pace with increases in costs, causing PPS operating margins to decline during the first eight years. As hospitals have become increasingly proficient in managing costs, margins have improved.

A peer review organization (PRO) is designated for each state to ensure that hospitals are in compliance with regulations and to ensure that the quality of care is not compromised as the result of financial incentives to limit services. PROs routinely review Medicare discharges and can deny payment for admissions deemed medically unnecessary.

Though simple in concept, the system involves many technical complexities regarding the adequacy of DRGs as a patient classification scheme, the setting of DRG payment rates, the process for PRO review, and the equity among different kinds of hospitals in different settings.

HOW PPS WORKS

Each Medicare patient is classified into a DRG according to information from the health record that appears on the bill

- principal diagnosis (why the patient was admitted)
- complications and comorbidities (secondary diagnoses)
- surgical procedures
- age
- gender
- discharge disposition (routine, transferred, or expired)

Diagnoses and procedures must be documented by the attending physician in the patient's health record. They are then coded by hospital personnel using ICD-9-CM nomenclature. This is a numerical coding scheme of over 13,000 diagnoses and 5,000 procedures.

The coding process is extremely important because it essentially determines what DRG will be assigned for a patient. Coding an incorrect principal diagnosis or failing to code a significant secondary diagnosis can cause thousands of dollars in lost reimbursement for a single patient.

Over 490 DRG categories are defined by the Health Care Financing Administration (HCFA). Each category is designed to be clinically coherent. In other words, all patients assigned to a DRG are deemed to have a similar clinical condition. The Prospective Payment System is based on the average cost of treating patients in the same DRG.

Each year HCFA makes technical adjustments to the DRG classification system that incorporate new technologies (e.g. laparoscopic procedures) and refine its use as a payment methodology. HCFA also initiates changes to the ICD-9-CM coding scheme. The DRG assignment process is computerized in a program called the *grouper* that is used by hospitals and fiscal intermediaries.

Each year HCFA also assigns a relative weight to each DRG. These weights indicate the relative costs for treating patients during the prior year. The national average charge for each DRG is compared to the overall average. This ratio is published annually in the *Federal Register* for each DRG. A DRG with a weight of 2.0000 means that charges were historically twice the average; a DRG with a weight of 0.5000 was half the average.

The 10 highest volume Medicare DRGs represent about 30 percent of total Medicare patients. Each of these higher volume DRGs represent from about 2 to 6 percent of total Medicare volume.

Top 10 DRGs for Medicare

DRG	DRG Description	% Total	Rel Wt
1. 127	Heart Failure and Shock	5.99	1.0234
2. 089	Simple Pneumonia and Pleurisy Age > 17 with Comorbidity and Complication (CC)	3.85	1.1447
3. 014	Specific Cerebrovascular Disorders except Transient Ischemic Attack (TIA)	3.18	1.2056
4. 430	Psychoses	3.18	0.9153
5. 088	Chronic Obstructive Pulmonary Disease	3.11	1.0067
6. 209	Major Joint and Limb Reattachment Procedures, Lower Extremity	2.78	2.3491
7. 140	Angina Pectoris	2.33	0.6241
8. 182	Esophagitis, Gastroenteritis, and Miscellaneous Digestive Disorders Age > 17 with CC	2.09	0.7617
9. 174	Gastrointestinal Hemorrhage with CC	2.07	0.9657
10. 296	Nutritional and Miscellaneous Metabolic Disorders Age > 17 with CC	1.93	0.9313

Source: Health Care Financing Administration, 1994.

The DRG payment for a Medicare patient is determined by multiplying the relative weight for the DRG by the hospital's blended rate:

DRG PAYMENT = WEIGHT × RATE

continues

Medicare Prospective Payment System continued

The hospital's blended rate is defined by federal regulations and is updated annually to reflect inflation, technical adjustments, and budgetary constraints. There are separate rate calculations for large urban hospitals and other hospitals. There are also technical adjustments for local wage variations, teaching hospitals, and hospitals with a disproportionate share of financially indigent patients.

The average DRG weight for all of a hospital's Medicare volume is called the case mix index (CMI). This index is very useful in analysis as it indicates the relative severity of a patient population and is directly proportional to DRG payments.

The DRG classification system is a useful tool for managing inpatient quality measurements and operating costs. It groups patients by diagnostic category for analysis and provides several key measurements of resource utilization (e.g., average length of stay versus published national averages).

The Medicare Prospective Payment System was first introduced to reimburse hospitals for inpatient operating expense only. Reimbursement for capital costs, however, is also being phased into DRG payments. Outpatient business is currently paid under a variety of reimbursement mechanisms, but will eventually be covered under some form of prospective payment system.

IMPACT OF PPS ON HOSPITALS

It is extremely important for hospitals to understand the rather complex regulations related to PPS and ensure that DRG assignments support full and accurate reimbursement.

Source: © QuadraMed, Compliance and Education Division, 561 Main Street, Bethlehem, PA, 18018. Phone 800-373-5620. QuadraMed offers compliance consulting, auditing, educational services, and software products to hospitals across the couuntry.

BALANCED BUDGET ACT OF 1997

Change presents different challenges and opportunities. Among the changes that will affect the health care industry are these ramifications of the Balanced Budget Act of 1997.

PROSPECTIVE PAYMENT SYSTEMS

- freezes hospital prospective payment update for fiscal year 1998
- phases in a prospective payment system (PPS) for skilled nursing facilities (SNFs) on July 1, 1998
- implements prospective payment system for home health services by October 1, 1999
- implements prospective payment system for rehabilitation hospitals by October 1, 2000

FRAUD AND ABUSE

New anti-fraud provisions include the following:

- permanent exclusion for those convicted of three health-care-related crimes on or after date of enactment
- authority for the Secretary of Health and Human Services (HHS) to refuse to enter into Medicare agreements with a physician or supplier convicted of a single felony that the secretary determines is detrimental to the best interests of the program
- exclusion of an entity controlled by a family member of a sanctioned individual
- civil money penalties for individuals who contract with an excluded individual or entity and civil money penalties for kickbacks up to three times the remuneration offered
- a new toll-free number for beneficiaries to report fraud and billing irregularities directly to the HHS Inspector General
- surety bond requirement of no less than $50,000 for suppliers of durable medical equipment
- requirement for Medicare providers to supply employer identification and social security numbers, including the numbers of individuals with ownership interests
- binding advisory opinions on a physician self-referral to designated health services (other than clinical laboratory services) or parties requesting the opinion
- requirement for diagnostic information when ordering certain items or services
- replacement of reasonable charge
- methodology by fee schedules for items and services including home dialysis supplies and parenteral nutrients
- applying inherent reasonableness to all Part B services other than physicians' services
- competitive bidding demonstration projects

AMBULATORY PAYMENT CLASSIFICATION

- requires the secretary of HHS to establish a prospective payment system for covered OPD services furnished beginning January 1, 1999
- the secretary would be required to develop a classification system for covered OPD services, such that services classified within each group would be comparable clinically and with respect to the use of resources

MEDICARE REIMBURSEMENT FOR TELEHEALTH SERVICES

- the secretary would be required to make Part B payments for telehealth services effective January 1, 1999

Source: Kathleen A. Frawley, "Balanced Budget Act of 1997 Presents New Challenges for HIM Professionals," *Journal of AHIMA*, Vol. 68:10, American Health Information Management Association, © 1997.

OVERVIEW OF AMBULATORY PATIENT GROUPS

Ambulatory patient groups (APGs) constitute a patient classification system designed to explain the amount and types of resources used in ambulatory visits. Patients in each APG have similar clinical characteristics and similar resource use and cost. Similar resource use means that the resources used are relatively constant across the patients within each APG. However, some variation in resource use remains among the patients in each APG. In other words, the definition of the APG is not so specific that every patient is identical, but the level of variation in resource use is known and predictable. Thus, while the precise resource use of a particular patient cannot be predicted by knowing the APG of the patient, the average pattern of resource use of a group of patients in an APG can be accurately predicted.

Patients in each APG also have similar clinical characteristics. This means that the patient characteristics included in the definition of the APG should relate to a common organ system or etiology and that a specific medical specialty should typically provide care to the patient in the APG. In addition, all available patient characteristics that medically would be expected to consistently affect resource use should be included in the definition of the APG. For example, patients with a chronic stomach ulcer may or may not be hemorrhaging. Although these patients are the same from organ system, etiology, and medical specialist perspectives, the APGs assign these patients to different patient classes, as the presence of hemorrhage is expected to consistently increase the resource use of chronic stomach ulcer patients. On the other hand, sets of unrelated surgical procedures are not used to define an APG as there is no medical rationale to substantiate that resource use is expected to be similar.

The definition of similar clinical characteristics is, of course, dependent on the goal of the classification system. For APGs, the definition of clinical similarity relates to the medical rationale for differences in resource use. If, on the other hand, the classification goal were related to patient prognosis, then the definition of patient characteristics that are clinically similar might be different. The requirement that APGs be clinically homogeneous caused more patient classes to be formed than would be necessary for explaining resource use alone. For example, patients with a D&C or a simple hemorrhoid procedure are quite similar in terms of most measures of resource use. However, different organ systems and different medical specialties are involved. Thus, the requirement that APGs have similar clinical characteristics precludes the possibility of these types of patients being in the same APG.

APGs were developed to encompass the full range of ambulatory settings including same-day surgery units, hospital emergency rooms, and outpatient clinics. APGs, however, do not address phone contacts, home visits, nursing home services, or inpatient services. While the anticipated initial application of APGs focuses on Medicare patients, APGs were developed to represent ambulatory patients across the entire patient population. For example, APGs relating to pregnancy were developed even though pregnancy is not usually encountered in the Medicare population.

APGs were developed to differentiate facility costs and not professional costs. However, professional costs relate primarily to professional time and, therefore, directly relate to facility time. Professional time can serve as a proxy for the amount of time a patient used the resources of the facility. During the development of APGs, facility costs such as supplies and equipment as well as professional time were taken into consideration.

The data elements used to define APGs were limited to the information routinely collected on the Medicare claim form and consist of the diagnoses coded in ICD-9-CM and procedures coded in CPT. The patient characteristics used in the definition of the APGs were restricted to those readily available in order to ensure that the APGs could be readily implemented.

Source: *Ambulatory Patient Groups Definitions Manual*
Courtesy of: Information Resource Products, Inc. (IRP)
One Presidential Way, Suite 109
Woburn, MA 01801-1071
Voice: 800-634-0496
Fax: 781-938-6543
E-mail: sales@irp.com
Website: www.irp.com
IRP produces a complete line of DRG, APG, severity DRG, reimbursement, and Expert Coding products for health care and insurance industries on PC, AS/400, Unix, and mainframes.

APGs: SELECTION OF THE INITIAL CLASSIFICATION VARIABLE

The first step in developing a patient classification system is to choose the initial classification variable. In the DRGs, the principal diagnosis is used to classify patients into a set of mutually exclusive major diagnostic categories (MDCs). Within each MDC, procedure, age, and complications and comorbidities are used to complete the DRG classification system. APGs use procedure instead of diagnosis as the initial classification variable. The decision to use procedure as the initial classification variable was based on the following considerations:

- When a significant procedure is performed in an ambulatory setting, it is normally the reason for the visit. The procedure is normally scheduled in advance and consumes the vast majority of resources associated with the visit.
- With procedure as the initial classification variable, each procedure is assigned to only one APG. With principal diagnosis as the initial classification variable, the same procedure could be assigned to many different APGs, depending on the MDC of the principal diagnosis. Having each procedure in only one APG reduces the number of APGs and simplifies the establishment of prospective prices.
- Several relative value unit (RVU) scales are available for CPT procedures. With procedure as the primary classification variable, the RVU scales can be used directly in the formation of the initial procedure classes.

Once the decision to use procedure as the initial classification variable was made, it was then necessary to partition all procedures into a set of mutually exclusive and exhaustive procedure groups. The first step in the process was to identify all procedures that can be done only on an inpatient basis. An inpatient procedure was defined as a procedure that requires at least 24 hours of postoperative recovery time or monitoring before a patient can be safely discharged. Some procedures, such as craniotomies, are clearly inpatient procedures. However, other procedures, such as the treatment of an open fracture, are normally done on an inpatient basis but can sometimes be done on an ambulatory basis. Further, patients with the same CPT procedure code can have a great deal of variation in the complexity of the procedure performed. For example, the treatment of an open humeral fracture can vary considerably in complexity.

Only the simplest cases of procedures normally done on an inpatient basis are done on an ambulatory basis. Thus, an open humeral fracture treated on an ambulatory basis will have minimal bone displacement and tissue damage. Such procedures are included in the APG procedure classification. When grouping procedures together to form homogeneous procedure subclasses, it is important to recognize the variation within a CPT code and that only the simplest cases of complex procedures are treated on an ambulatory basis.

The procedures that can be performed on an ambulatory basis were then assigned to one of the following three classes:

1. **Significant Procedures and Therapies**—A significant procedure or therapy is a procedure that is normally scheduled, constitutes the reason for the visit, and dominates the time and resources expended during the visit. An example of a significant procedure is the excision of a skin lesion. Also included in significant procedures are significant therapies such as physical therapy and significant tests such as a stress test.
2. **Ancillary Tests and Procedures**—An ancillary test is one that is ordered by the primary physician to assist in patient diagnosis or treatment. Radiology, laboratory, and pathology services constitute ancillary tests. An ancillary procedure is one that increases the time and resources expended during a visit but does not dominate the time and resources expended during the visit. Examples of ancillary procedures are immunizations and the insertion of an IUD. The term *ancillary services* is used to refer to both ancillary tests and ancillary procedures.
3. **Incidental Procedure**—An incidental procedure is an integral part of a medical visit and is usually associated with professional services.

Only patients with a significant procedure are assigned to significant procedure APGs. All medical services provided to the patient are assumed to be an integral part of the procedure. Patients with no significant ambulatory procedures but with incidental and ancillary procedures are assigned to medical APGs. For example, if a patient has a skin lesion and a skin excision is performed, the patient is assigned to a significant procedure APG based on the CPT code that describes the precise procedure. Conversely, if a patient has a skin lesion but a procedure is not performed, then the patient is assigned to a medical APG based on the ICD-9-CM diagnosis code.

Source: *Ambulatory Patient Groups Definitions Manual*
Courtesy of: Information Resource Products, Inc. (IRP)
One Presidential Way, Suite 109
Woburn, MA 01801-1071
Voice: 800-634-0496
Fax: 781-938-6543
E-mail: sales@irp.com
Website: www.irp.com
IRP produces a complete line of DRG, APG, severity DRG, reimbursement, and Expert Coding products for health care and insurance industries on PC, AS/400, Unix, and mainframes.

OVERVIEW OF THE APG PAYMENT SYSTEM

In the APG system a patient is described by a list of APGs that correspond to each service provided to the patient. The assignment of multiple APGs to a patient is in contrast to the DRGs, which always assigns a patient to a single DRG. If a patient has multiple procedures, then the DRGs use a procedure hierarchy to select the most appropriate DRG. The DRG payment includes the cost of all ancillary services provided to the patient. In the outpatient setting, the diversity of sites of service (for example, same day surgery units, ERs, and outpatient clinics), the wide variation in the reasons patients require outpatient care (well care to critical trauma care), and the high percentage of cost associated with ancillary services (the cost of ancillary services can often exceed the cost of the base visit) necessitates a patient classification scheme that can precisely reflect the services rendered to the patient. The APGs address the diversity among outpatient settings by assigning patients to multiple APGs. For example, if a patient had two procedures performed plus a chest X-ray and a blood test, then four APGs would be assigned to the patient (one APG for each procedure plus the APGs for the chest X-ray and the blood test). In a prospective payment system, each APG would have a standard payment rate, and the payment for a patient would be computed by summing the payment rates across all the APGs assigned to the patient. However, in order to provide incentives for cost control and to minimize opportunities for upcoding of APGs, not all the APGs assigned to a patient are used in the computation of the payment. In the APG system, different services provided during the same visit may be grouped into a single payment unit or discounted.

Ancillary Packaging

A patient with a significant procedure or a medical visit may have ancillary services performed as part of the visit. Ancillary packaging refers to the inclusion of certain ancillary services into the APG payment rate for a significant procedure or medical visit. For example, a chest X-ray would be packaged into the payment for a pneumonia visit.

MULTIPLE SIGNIFICANT PROCEDURE AND ANCILLARY DISCOUNTING

When multiple unrelated significant procedures are performed or when the same ancillary service is performed multiple times, a discounting of the APG payment rates is applied. Discounting refers to a reduction in the standard payment rate for an APG. Discounting recognizes that the marginal cost of providing a second procedure to a patient during a single visit is less than the cost of providing the procedure by itself.

In general, a per-visit prospective payment system has three components: (1) the patient classification scheme, (2) an ancillary packaging process, and (3) a payment computation.

As part of the APG payment model, ancillary packaging routines and discounting strategies were developed.

Source: *Ambulatory Patient Groups Definitions Manual*
Courtesy of: Information Resource Products, Inc. (IRP)
One Presidential Way, Suite 109
Woburn, MA 01801-1071
Voice: 800-634-0496
Fax: 781-938-6543
E-mail: sales@irp.com
Website: www.irp.com
IRP produces a complete line of DRG, APG, severity DRG, reimbursement, and Expert Coding products for health care and insurance industries on PC, AS/400, Unix, and mainframes.

ANCILLARY PACKAGING

In the context of a per-visit payment system, *packaging* refers to the inclusion of certain ancillary services in the payment for the visit. The significant procedure or medical visit combined with the packaged ancillary services is considered a single unit for purposes of payment. In the case of ambulatory surgery, for example, a packaged visit combines the significant procedure with the related ancillary services into a single payment amount. Packaging gives providers the incentive to use the packaged ancillary services efficiently.

Under Medicare's DRG-based prospective payment system for hospital inpatient care, all ancillary services provided to a patient are packaged into the payment for the DRG to which the patient is assigned. Due to the nature of outpatient care, it is not clear that all services provided or ordered during a visit can be packaged into one payment rate. Medicare's current payment system for ambulatory care involves separate payments for ancillary services provided in conjunction with a visit. Payments for laboratory services are based on a fee schedule, while radiology services are reimbursed based on a blend of a hospital's reasonable costs and a radiology fee schedule. This payment method is designed to contain the cost per unit of service; however, it provides no incentive for providers to control the volume of services. Packaging ancillary services into the payment rate for a visit provides that incentive.

Ancillary packaging allows the Medicare program to make a single payment for a well defined package of ambulatory services, thereby creating a consistent definition of services across providers. Further, packaging facilitates comparison across providers and may encourage continuity of care by making providers financially responsible for ancillary services. Consequently, the providers may be more likely to incorporate the findings of tests into patient treatment plans. Finally, packaging gives providers the incentive to improve their efficiency by avoiding unnecessary ancillaries and by substituting less expensive but equally effective ancillary services for more costly options.

There are also some potential difficulties in the packaging of ancillaries. Packaging places providers at financial risk. If expensive ancillaries that are not usually performed for a particular type of visit are included in the packaged payment, then the financial risk may be excessive. As initially only hospital outpatient departments will be paid on a prospective basis, ancillary packaging may encourage hospitals to set up freestanding clinic centers that would not be covered under the PPS. This is more likely to occur if the payment rates attached to the APGs do not adequately account for the cost of the packaged services. In addition, although Medicare's payment per visit is controlled by the packaging, there is no control over the number of visits. Thus, there may be an incentive to increase the number of visits and spread the costs of packaged ancillary services across the visits. However, this incentive is not different than incentives under the current unpackaged payment system. Though a similar incentive was provided by the DRG system, hospital admissions fell after the DRGs were enacted.

Despite potential difficulties with the packaging of ancillaries, it is clear that in a visit-based payment system, some degree of ancillary packaging must occur in order to introduce the incentive to use ancillary services efficiently. If there were no packaging of ancillary services, then the system would be similar to Medicare's current payment method for outpatient care in that it involves additional payments for each ancillary service. This approach is risk free for providers, encourages ancillary utilization, and discourages comparisons of cost across providers.

There are basically two alternative approaches to packaging: partial packaging and all-inclusive packaging. Under partial packaging, ancillary services that are inexpensive or frequently provided are packaged into the payment for the significant procedure or medical visit. However, other ancillary services, particularly those that are expensive or infrequently performed, are paid as separate ancillary APGs. Partial packaging limits the providers' risk. Under all-inclusive packaging, all services (including expensive ancillaries) that are provided during a visit are packaged into the visit payment. Thus, under an all-inclusive approach, if a $500 test occurs on average once in 100 visits, then the packaged payment for each visit would include $5 for this test. The partial packaging option was selected as the most appropriate option because it is feasible and would not impose a high level of risk for hospitals.

Given that partial packaging was selected for use in the APG payment system, it was necessary to select the ancillary services to package into a procedure or medical visit. There are two alternative approaches to selecting the ancillaries to be packaged: clinical and uniform.

A clinical packaging approach selects the ancillaries to be packaged on an APG-specific basis. The ancillaries to be packaged are selected primarily on clinical grounds. Thus, only ancillaries that are clinically expected to be a routine part of the specific procedure or medical visit are packaged. The clinical approach has the benefit that the resulting package visit is clinically meaningful. Further, as only routine ancillaries are packaged into each APG, the distribution of ancillary costs within the APG is relatively homogeneous.

The alternative to clinical packaging is to develop a uniform list of ancillaries to package into every procedure or medical visit. There are several advantages associated with a uniform packaging of ancillaries. The approach is administratively simple. Once the uniform list of ancillaries is developed, both the Medicare fiscal intermediaries and hospitals know with certainty that every ancillary of a particular type is always packaged. Thus, the tracking of the exact ancillaries that are packaged is straightforward. Further, a uniform list of packaged ancillaries is simple for hospitals to explain to their medical staff and thus the incentive to efficiently utilize the packaged ancillaries can be effectively communicated.

A uniform list of ancillaries is less prone to manipulation by hospitals. With a clinical packaging of ancillaries, procedure or medical visits have different levels of ancillaries packaged across the different APGs. Thus, the incentive is to code the patient into the procedure or medical APG with the fewest packaged ancillaries. This presents a particular problem for medical visits in which multiple diagnoses are present. For medical visits with multiple diagnoses, the ancillary tests may be performed for the secondary diagnoses. The uniform packaging of ancillaries also removes the incentive to perform nonroutine tests. Under a clinical packaging approach, low-cost nonroutine tests are not packaged into the visit payment. This provides a financial incentive for providers to perform such nonroutine tests. A uniform packaging approach includes in the packaging for each APG a wider army of ancillaries, thus reducing opportunity for additional payments from nonroutine ancillaries.

The uniform packaging of ancillaries was selected for use in the APG payment model. An attempt to develop a clinical packaging of ancillaries proved difficult. Relatively few ancillaries are truly routine for particular APGs. Thus, the scope of the clinical packaging would have been fairly limited. The administrative simplicity, the relative freedom from manipulation, and the wider scope of uniform packaging of ancillaries led to its adoption.

The APGs included in the uniform packaging are primarily simple laboratory tests (e.g., basic chemistry), simple pathology, anesthesia, simple radiology (e.g., plain films), other minor tests (e.g., EKGs), and minor procedures and therapies (e.g., simple pulmonary function tests). In general, the ancillaries in the uniform packaging include ancillaries performed for a wide range of visit types and are relatively low cost compared to the average cost of the procedure and medical APGs. Only relatively low-cost ancillaries are included in the uniform packaging because if high-cost ancillaries were packaged into the visit payment, the patients who required such ancillaries would cause a substantial financial loss for the hospital. Hospitals would have a financial incentive to avoid treating those patients, causing a potential access problem for Medicare beneficiaries. In addition to the ancillary APGs, the cost of any incidental procedure APGs is always included in the payment for a significant procedure or medical visit. The cost of medical surgical supplies, drugs, and all other facility-related costs are included in the payment for a significant procedure or medical visit. The only exception is the cost of chemotherapy medication.

Source: *Ambulatory Patient Groups Definitions Manual*
Courtesy of: Information Resource Products, Inc. (IRP)
One Presidential Way, Suite 109
Woburn, MA 01801-1071
Voice: 800-634-0496
Fax: 781-938-6543
E-mail: sales@irp.com
Website: www.irp.com
IRP produces a complete line of DRG, APG, severity DRG, reimbursement, and Expert Coding products for health care and insurance industries on PC, AS/400, Unix, and mainframes.

DISCOUNTING

In addition to ancillary packaging, the visit payment computation may also include discounting. *Discounting* refers to a reduction in the standard payment rate for an APG. The need for discounting occurs when multiple procedures or ancillaries are performed. For example, discounting could compensate for the reduced cost per procedure of doing multiple significant procedures at the same time. When multiple significant procedures are performed, in general, the patient preparation, use of the operating room, and recovery time is shared among them. Thus, the cost of doing two procedures at the same time is less than the cost of doing the two procedures at two different times. Discounting can also be used to provide a financial incentive not to repeat the same ancillary service multiple times. Each nonpackaged ancillary in the same APG results in an additional payment. However, in order to provide some financial incentive not to repeat ancillary tests, multiple ancillaries in the same APG could be discounted. The level of any discounting is a policy decision and would be determined during system implementation.

Source: *Ambulatory Patient Groups Definitions Manual*
Courtesy of: Information Resource Products, Inc. (IRP)
One Presidential Way, Suite 109
Woburn, MA 01801-1071

Voice: 800-634-0496
Fax: 781-938-6543
E-mail: sales@irp.com
Website: www.irp.com
IRP produces a complete line of DRG, APG, severity DRG, reimbursement, and Expert Coding products for health care and insurance industries on PC, AS/400, Unix, and mainframes.

ANCILLARY APGs INCLUDED IN UNIFORM PACKAGING

- 310—Plain Film
- 321—Anesthesia
- 332—Simple Pathology
- 343—Simple Immunology Tests
- 345—Simple Microbiology Tests
- 347—Simple Endocrinology Tests
- 349—Simple Chemistry Tests
- 350—Basic Chemistry Tests
- 351—Multichannel Chemistry Tests
- 356—Simple Clotting Tests
- 358—Simple Hematology Tests
- 359—Urinalysis
- 360—Blood and Urine Dipstick Tests
- 371—Simple Pulmonary Function Tests
- 373—Cardiogram
- 383—Introduction of Needle and Catheter
- 384—Dressing and Other Minor Procedures
- 385—Other Miscellaneous Ancillary Procedures
- 386—Biofeedback and Other Training
- 411—Psychotropic Medication Management

OVERVIEW OF THE MEDICAID PROGRAM

Title XIX of the Social Security Act is a program that provides medical assistance for certain individuals and families with low incomes and resources. The program, known as Medicaid, became law in 1965 as a jointly funded cooperative venture between the federal and state governments to assist states in the provision of adequate medical care to eligible needy persons. Medicaid is the largest program providing medical and health-related services to America's poorest people. Within broad national guidelines, which the federal government provides, each of the states

- establishes its own eligibility standards
- determines the type, amount, duration, and scope of services
- sets the rate of payment for services
- administers its own program

Thus, the Medicaid program varies considerably from state to state as well as within each state over time.

Source: Health Care Financing Administration.

MEDICAID ELIGIBILITY

The following describes information about Medicaid eligibility.

NOTE: The Medicaid eligibility requirements listed below are accurate at present. However, they are expected to change somewhat in the near future as states implement the new welfare reform bill, which was signed into law on August 22, 1996.

States have some discretion in determining which groups their Medicaid programs will cover and the financial criteria for Medicaid eligibility. To be eligible for federal funds, states are required to provide Medicaid coverage for most individuals who receive federally assisted income maintenance payments, as well as for related groups not receiving cash payments. Some examples of the mandatory Medicaid eligibility groups are

- recipients of Aid to Families with Dependent Children (AFDC)
- Supplemental Security Income (SSI) recipients (or, in states using more restrictive criteria, aged, blind, and disabled individuals who meet criteria that are more restrictive than those of the SSI program and that were in place in the state's approved Medicaid plan as of January 1, 1972)
- infants born to Medicaid-eligible pregnant women. Medicaid eligibility must continue throughout the first year of life as long as the infant remains in the mother's household and she remains eligible, or would be eligible if she were still pregnant
- children under age 6 and pregnant women who meet the state's AFDC financial requirements or whose family income is at or below 133 percent of the federal poverty level. (The minimum mandatory income level for pregnant women and infants in certain states may be higher than 133 percent, if as of certain dates the state had established a higher percentage for covering those groups.) States are required to extend Medicaid eligibility until age 19 to all children born after September 30, 1983, in families with incomes at or below the federal poverty level. This phases in coverage, so that by the year 2002, all poor children under age 19 will be covered. Once eligibility is established, pregnant women remain eligible for Medicaid through the end of the calendar month ending 60 days after the end of the pregnancy regardless of change in family income. States are not required to have a resource test for these poverty level–related groups. However, any resource test imposed can be no more restrictive than that of the AFDC program for infants and children and the SSI program for pregnant women.

- recipients of adoption assistance and foster care under Title IV–E of the Social Security Act
- certain Medicare beneficiaries (described later)
- special protected groups who lose cash assistance because of the cash programs' rules, but who may keep Medicaid for a period of time. Examples are persons who lose AFDC or SSI payments due to earnings from work or increased Social Security benefits, and two-parent, unemployed families whose AFDC cash assistance time is limited by the state and who are provided a full 12 months of Medicaid coverage following termination of cash assistance.

States also have the *option* to provide Medicaid coverage for other "categorically needy" groups. These optional groups share characteristics of the mandatory groups, but the eligibility criteria are somewhat more liberally defined. Examples of the optional groups that states may cover as categorically needy (and for which they will receive federal matching funds) under the Medicaid program are

- infants up to age one and pregnant women not covered under the mandatory rules whose family income is below 185 percent of the federal poverty level (the percentage to be set by each state)
- certain aged, blind, or disabled adults who have incomes above those requiring mandatory coverage, but below the federal poverty level
- children under age 21 who meet income and resources requirements for AFDC, but who otherwise are not eligible for AFDC
- institutionalized individuals with income and resources below specified limits
- persons who would be eligible if institutionalized but are receiving care under home and community-based services waivers
- recipients of state supplementary payments
- tuberculosis (TB)-infected persons who would be financially eligible for Medicaid at the SSI level (only for TB-related ambulatory services and TB drugs).

Medically Needy Eligibility Groups

The option to have a medically needy program allows states to extend Medicaid eligibility to additional qualified persons who may have too much income to qualify under the mandatory or optional categorically needy groups. This option allows them to spend down to Medicaid eligibility by incurring medical and/or remedial care expenses to offset their excess income, thereby reducing it to a level below the maximum allowed by that state's Medicaid plan. States may also allow families to establish eligibility as medically needy by paying monthly premiums to the state in an amount equal to the difference between family income (reduced by unpaid expenses, if any, incurred for medical care in previous months) and the income eligibility standard.

Eligibility for the medically needy program does not have to be as extensive as the categorically needy program. However, states that elect to include the medically needy under their plans are required to include certain children under age 18 and pregnant women who except for income and resources would be eligible as categorically needy. They may choose to provide coverage to other medically needy persons: aged, blind, and/or disabled persons; certain relatives of children deprived of parental support and care; and certain other financially eligible children up to age 21. In 1995, 40 medically needy programs provided at least some services to recipients.

Amplification on Medicaid Eligibility

Coverage may start retroactive to any or all of the three months prior to application if the individual would have been eligible during the retroactive period. Coverage generally stops at the end of the month in which a person's circumstances change. Most states have additional state-only programs to provide medical assistance for specified poor persons who do not qualify for the Medicaid program. No federal funds are provided for state-only programs.

Medicaid does not provide medical assistance for all poor persons. Even under the broadest provisions of the federal statute (except for emergency services for certain persons), the Medicaid program does not provide health care services, even for very poor persons, unless they are in one of the groups designated above. Low income is only one test for Medicaid eligibility; assets and resources are also tested against established thresholds. As noted earlier, categorically needy persons who are eligible for Medicaid may or may not also receive cash assistance from the AFDC program or from the SSI program. Medically needy persons who would be categorically eligible except for income or assets may become eligible for Medicaid solely because of excessive medical expenses.

States may use more liberal income and resources methodologies to determine Medicaid eligibility for certain AFDC-related and aged, blind, and disabled individuals under section 1902(r)(2) of the Social Security Act. The more liberal income methodologies cannot result in the individual's income exceeding the limits prescribed for federal matching (for those groups that are subject to these limits).

Significant changes were made in the Medicare Catastrophic Coverage Act (MCCA) of 1988, which affected Medicaid. Although much of the MCCA was repealed, the portions affecting Medicaid remain in effect. The law also accelerated Medicaid eligibility for some nursing home patients by protecting assets for the institutionalized person's spouse at home at the time of the initial eligibility determination after institutionalization. Before an institutionalized person's monthly income is used to pay for the cost of institutional care, a minimum monthly maintenance needs allowance is deducted from the institutionalized spouse's income to bring the income of the community spouse up to a moderate level.

Medicaid-Medicare Relationship

The Medicare program (Title XVIII of the Social Security Act) provides hospital insurance (HI), also known as Part A coverage, and supplementary medical insurance (SMI), which is known as Part B coverage. For persons aged 65 and older (and for certain disabled persons) who have insured status under Social Security or Railroad Retirement, coverage for HI is automatic. Coverage for SMI, however, requires payment of a monthly premium. Some aged and/or disabled persons are covered under both the Medicaid and Medicare programs.

For Medicare beneficiaries who are also fully eligible for Medicaid, Medicare coverage is supplemented by health care services that are available under the state's Medicaid program. If a person is a Medicare beneficiary, payments for any services covered by Medicare are made by the Medicare program before any payments are made by the Medicaid program. Medicaid is always payer of last resort. As each state elects, services such as eyeglasses, hearing aids, and nursing facility care not covered by Medicare may be provided by the Medicaid program.

Limited Medicaid benefits are available for certain qualified disabled working individuals (QDWIs) who have earnings sufficiently high to preclude entitlement to Medicare coverage except if the individual purchases coverage, and whose earnings are less than 200 percent of the federal poverty level (FPL). State Medicaid programs must pay the HI premium for QDWIs with income less than 150 percent of the FPL, and may pay some or all of the HI premium for QDWIs with earnings between 150 and 200 percent of the FPL. Medicaid does not pay SMI premiums for these individuals.

For certain poor Medicare recipients known as Qualified Medicare Beneficiaries (QMBs) (those beneficiaries with incomes below the federal poverty level and with resources at or below twice the standard allowed under the SSI program), the Medicaid program pays the Medicare premiums and cost-sharing expenses for Medicare HI and SMI. For Specified Low-Income Medicare Beneficiaries (SLMBs) (those like QMBs, but with slightly higher incomes), the Medicaid program pays only the SMI premiums.

Source: Health Care Financing Administration.

MEDICAID SERVICES

Title XIX of the Social Security Act requires that in order to receive federal matching funds, certain basic services must be offered to the categorically needy population in any state program

- inpatient hospital services
- outpatient hospital services
- physician services
- medical and surgical dental services
- nursing facility (NF) services for individuals aged 21 or older
- home health care for persons eligible for nursing facility services
- family planning services and supplies
- rural health clinic services and any other ambulatory services offered by a rural health clinic that are otherwise covered under the state plan
- laboratory and X-ray services
- pediatric and family nurse practitioner services
- federally qualified health center services and any other ambulatory services offered by a federally qualified health center that are otherwise covered under the state plan
- nurse-midwife services (to the extent authorized under state law)
- early and periodic screening, diagnosis, and treatment (EPSDT) services for individuals under age 21

If a state chooses to include the medically needy population, the state plan must provide, as a minimum, the following services:

- prenatal care and delivery services for pregnant women
- ambulatory services to individuals under age 18 and individuals entitled to institutional services
- home health services to individuals entitled to nursing facility services
- if the state plan includes services either in institutions for mental diseases or in intermediate care facilities for the mentally retarded (ICF/MRs), it must offer either of the following to each of the medically needy groups:
  - the services contained in 42 CFR sections 440.10 through 440.50 and 440.165 (to the extent that nurse-midwives are authorized to practice under state law or regulations)
  - the services contained in any seven of the sections in 42 CFR 440.10 through 440.165

States may also receive federal funding if they elect to provide other optional services. The most commonly covered optional services under the Medicaid program are:

- clinic services
- nursing facility services for the under age 21
- intermediate care facility/mentally retarded services
- optometrist services and eyeglasses
- prescribed drugs
- TB-related services for TB-infected persons
- prosthetic devices
- dental services

States may provide home- and community-based care waiver services to certain individuals who are eligible for Medicaid. The services to be provided to these persons may include case management, personal care services, respite care services, adult day health services, homemaker/home health aide, habilitation, and other services requested by the state and approved by HCFA.

Amount and Duration of Medicaid Services

Within broad federal guidelines, states determine the amount and duration of services offered under their Medicaid programs. The amount, duration, and scope of each service must be sufficient to reasonably achieve its purpose. States may place appropriate limits on a Medicaid service based on such criteria as medical necessity and utilization control. For example, states may place a reasonable limit on the number of covered physician visits or may require prior authorization to be obtained prior to service delivery.

Health care services identified under the EPSDT program as being medically necessary for eligible children must be provided by Medicaid, even if those services are not included as part of the covered services in that state's plan.

With certain exceptions, a state's Medicaid plan must allow recipients freedom of choice among health care providers participating in Medicaid. States may provide and pay for Medicaid services through various prepayment arrangements, such as health maintenance organizations (HMOs). In general, states are required to provide comparable services to all categorically needy eligible persons.

There is an important exception related to home- and community-based services: waivers under which states offer an alternative health care package for persons who would otherwise be institutionalized under Medicaid. States are not limited in the scope of services they can provide under such waivers so long as they are cost-effective (except that, other than as a part of respite care, they may not provide room and board for such recipients).

Payment for Medicaid Services

Medicaid operates as a vendor payment program, with payments made directly to the providers. Providers participating in Medicaid must accept the Medicaid reimbursement level as payment in full. Each state has relatively broad discretion in determining (within federally imposed upper limits and specific restrictions) the reimbursement methodology and resulting rate for services, with three exceptions: (1) for institutional services, payment may not exceed amounts that would be paid under Medicare payment rates, (2) for disproportionate share hospitals (DSHs), different limits apply, and (3) for hospice care services, rates cannot be lower than Medicare rates.

States may impose nominal deductibles, coinsurance, or copayments on some Medicaid recipients for certain services. Emergency services and family planning services must be exempt from such copayments. Certain Medicaid recipients must be excluded from this cost sharing: pregnant women, children under age 18, hospital or nursing home patients who are expected to contribute most of their income to institutional care, and categorically needy HMO enrollees.

The amount of total federal outlays for Medicaid has no set limit (cap); rather, the federal government must match whatever the individual state decides to provide, within the law, for its eligible recipients. However, reimbursement rates must be sufficient to enlist enough providers so that Medicaid care and services are available under the plan at least to the extent that such care and services are available to the general population in that geographic area.

States must augment payment to qualified hospitals that provide inpatient services to a disproportionate number of Medicaid recipients and/or other low-income persons under what is known as the DSH program. Legislation passed in 1991 has curtailed some states' DSH payments.

The portion of the Medicaid program that is paid by the federal government, known as the Federal Medical Assistance Percentage (FMAP), is determined annually for each state by a formula that compares the state's average per capita income level with the national average. By law, the FMAP cannot be lower than 50 percent nor greater than 83 percent. The wealthier states have a smaller share of their costs reimbursed. The federal government also shares in the state's expenditures for administration of the Medicaid program. Most administrative costs are matched at 50 percent for all states. However, higher matching rates (75, 90, and 100 percent) are authorized by law for certain functions and activities.

Medicaid Trends

Initially, Medicaid was a medical care extension of federally funded income maintenance programs for the poor, with an emphasis on the aged, the disabled, and dependent children and their mothers. Over time, however, Medicaid has been diverging from a firm tie to eligibility for cash programs. Recent legislation ensures Medicaid coverage to an expanded number of low-income pregnant women, poor children, and some Medicare beneficiaries who are not eligible for any cash assistance program and who would not have been eligible for Medicaid under earlier Medicaid rules. Legislative changes focus on enhanced outreach toward specific groups of pregnant women and children, increased access to care, and improved quality of care. Legislation also continued specific benefits beyond the normal run of Medicaid eligibility and placed some restrictions on states' ability to limit some services.

In addition to the increase in numbers of beneficiaries from new legislation, the most pronounced Medicaid service-related trends in recent years have been the continued sharp increase in expenditures for intensive acute care and for home health and nursing facility services for the aged and disabled.

The most significant trend in service delivery is the rapid growth in managed care enrollment within Medicaid. In 1995, almost a quarter of all Medicaid recipients were enrolled in managed care plans. One vehicle for the expansion of managed care, and of new eligibility groups, is the 1915(b) waiver process, which allows states increased flexibility to research health care delivery alternatives while controlling program costs. Another vehicle is the section 1115(b) waiver authority, which permits states to implement managed care delivery systems within prescribed parameters.

Source: Health Care Financing Administration.

MAKING THE CASE FOR STANDARDIZED DATA COLLECTION

As more states begin to mandate managed care for many of their Medicaid populations, the case for standardized clinical data reporting sets surfaces in yet another venue. While health information management experts and clinical researchers have long touted the importance of collecting data in a uniform, standardized format to enable data comparisons and linkages among different populations, diseases, and plans, managed care is now forcing the Medicaid world to open its eyes to the issue.

Without standardized data collection, state- and plan-level Medicaid administrators run the risk of basing million-dollar decisions and quality of care initiatives on skewed data analysis results. But a specific data set developed by the Health Care Financing Administration's (HCFA's) Medicare-Medicaid Common Data Initiative (McData) combined with a Medicaid- and Medicare-specific data analysis system is allowing states, and in the near future individual Medicaid managed care organizations, to adjust for severity of illness and demographic factors and to compare quality, cost, and access on a level playing field.

HCFA requires McData for Medicaid managed care organizations and HMOs operating under 1115 waivers.

While states often use the reported data to ferret out fraud and abuse, access to care, and utilization patterns, many of the plans run the risk of flying blind, evaluating only their own internal data with no external benchmarks with which to compare their performance.

One advantage of participating in McData reporting is that plans can perform comparisons of how they are doing relative to plans of similar size. They can develop a yardstick that may help them measure their strengths and weaknesses.

A Closer Look at a Medicaid Management Information System (MMIS)

Huge repositories of data are useless unless the numbers can be analyzed, compared, and applied to the major functions of a state's Medicaid program.

MMIS is the generic name for the monitoring systems that oversee providers, recipients, and health plans and produce analyzed data for the state. MMIS system development firms include Consultec, EDS, Unisys, First Health, and Arthur Anderson, among others.

Although transmission rates, data linkages, and transfer methods are not often specifically defined for participating Medicaid MCOs, it is the responsibility of the contracting provider to make sure the complete data set is collected and reported to the state.

While the HL7 and ANSI X.12 interface have been suggested as official data interchange interfaces, neither HCFA nor the states may mandate such a requirement for Medicaid providers.

However, the recently passed Kennedy-Kassebaum Act requires the Secretary of the Department of Health and Human Services to set that interface standard by February 1998.

But even 100 percent reporting compliance does not do a state any good if the numbers cannot be crunched and interpreted. All MMIS systems consist of at least six subsystems that allow state administrators to evaluate and track data on their Medicaid programs. Once they are designed and implemented, HCFA performs site visits to ensure that they are working properly and that the state is eligible for the federal tax dollars available to help pay for these systems.

The system uses a recipient subsystem, much like a membership tracking system, that monitors all Medicaid recipients and their children and assigns unique identification numbers. This module tracks member eligibility on a monthly basis, thus helping to eliminate services paid for and provided to patients who no longer qualify for Medicaid benefits.

The provider subsystem keeps track of all providers and health systems rendering care to Medicaid recipients in a specific state. It also tracks which doctors are approved primary care physicians, pharmaceutical specifications, referrals, etc.

The claims and processing module adjudicates claims, confirms valid diagnosis and procedure codes, determines the reimbursable amount, and generates the capitation payment to the MCOs or primary care physicians in a gatekeeper system.

Through the management and administration subsystem, MMIS keeps tabs on budgetary items and predicts trends in cost and care. Fraud and abuse detection and utilization review are performed through the surveillance and utilization review subsystems.

Not only do the standardized and severity-adjusted data help state and federal Medicaid administrators keep track of Medicaid managed care contract compliance, they also play a role in many other aspects of Medicaid managed care.

Quality of Care

Because many managed care organizations contract with specialists and hospitals on a fee-for-service basis (utilization assumptions about which are built into an MCO's capitation rate), one of the most common fears about managed care comes from the MCOs' financial incentive to withhold medically necessary health care.

Detailed encounter data are needed to monitor the quality of care within these MCOs so that significant changes in utilization patterns can be explained by legitimate factors. For example, reducing hospital days per 1,000 covered lives from 1,200 to 800 is reasonable, but dropping it below 300 would probably signal withholding necessary care. The same would be true if the number of primary care visits or number of prescriptions per 1,000 covered lives dropped precipitously.

Expanding MMIS Functions

MMIS systems are undergoing developmental changes. The largest of these is the development of decision support systems and executive information systems that lay on top of the MMIS. These systems provide decision makers with information, rather than just data, about the quality of care being delivered, its cost-effectiveness, and its appropriateness.

The firms involved in this work, in addition to MMIS development companies, include Medstat, Codman Research Group (CRG), VIPS, and Adminastar.

Source: "Making the Case for Standardized Data Collection: Medicaid Management Information Systems Rely on Uniform Data Reporting Set," *Clinical Data Management*, Vol. 4:1, Aspen Publishers, Inc., © 1997.

HEALTH CARE FRAUD AND ABUSE: AN HIM PERSPECTIVE

HEALTH CARE FRAUD AND ABUSE

Fraud and abuse in the American health care system account for as much as 10 percent ($100 billion) of the $1 trillion spent annually for health-related services, according to the U.S. General Accounting Office. As a result, the federal government has raised the priority of investigating and pursuing reparation to the number-two law enforcement priority, preceded only by the prosecution of violent crime.

Providers are being held accountable even in the absence of conscious knowledge of wrongdoing on the part of their employees. Proof of specific intent to commit fraud and abuse is not required. The law assumes that the provider should know or be aware of the practices and standards followed by its employees and should have programs in place to ensure that all employees understand and comply with regulations.

Investigations are being conducted by the Office of the Inspector General (OIG), the FBI, the U.S. Attorney General's Office, state Medicaid Fraud Control Units, and HCFA as aggressive methods of recovering program overpayments and assessing penalties and fines associated with improper practices. Permanent or temporary exclusion from the Medicare or Medicaid program may result when a health care provider is proven to have committed fraud or abuse. In addition, criminal prosecution and imprisonment are very real possibilities for offenders.

Health care fraud and abuse, combined with the ever-escalating cost of health care and the limited number of Medicare/Medicaid dollars available, has necessitated the enactment of legislation and the implementation of state and federal programs to curtail the drain on the Medicare and Medicaid systems.

Operation Restore Trust (ORT)

This program was piloted by the Department of Health and Human Services (HHS) in 1995 as a two-year project in Illinois, New York, Florida, Texas, and California. These five states account for one third of all Medicare and Medicaid beneficiaries and, therefore, represent significant national and state health care expenditures. Multidisciplinary teams consisting of federal, state, and private-sector representatives were utilized to target areas of abuse and misuse in nursing homes (including hospice care), home health agencies, and durable medical equipment suppliers. After one year into the pilot, 35 criminals were convicted, 272 cases were under investigation, 93 providers were excluded, and $38.6 million were returned to the Medicare Trust Fund (over $9 returned to the fund for every $1 spent).

Physicians at Teaching Hospitals (PATH)

The PATH program was implemented to identify fraud and abuse issues associated with the billing practices of physicians supervising residents at teaching clinics and hospitals. The areas of greatest concern are: (1) supervision of residents while providing services to patients, (2) documentation supporting the presence of the teaching physician during the service, and (3) appropriate assignment of evaluation and management (E/M) codes for the level of service provided. In the December 8, 1995, *Federal Register*, HCFA outlined new standards for teaching physician billing, which were further clarified in the July 1, 1996, revisions to the Medicare Carrier Manual.

The clinical practice at the University of Pennsylvania was audited with findings extrapolated to $10 million in false claims. The university ultimately settled with the government for $30 million in damages (treble damages) and a government-mandated compliance program.

Voluntary Disclosure Program (VDP)

This program was implemented by the Department of Justice and the OIG for those corporate entities who have billed for nonexistent or unbundled services, provided medically unnecessary services, or have not followed HCFA's new documentation guidelines for teaching physicians. Voluntary disclosure was implemented to allow providers to disclose potential problems that they discovered within their organizations. This could lead to negotiable settlements, reduced fines and penalties, reduced (or no) criminal prosecution, and continued participation in the Medicare or Medicaid programs.

The Jefferson Faculty Foundation of Thomas Jefferson University voluntarily disclosed to the government their discovery of improper billing, which was extrapolated to $12 million in false claims to Medicare. Their settlement consisted of $12 million in damages and development of an internal corporate compliance program.

Health Insurance Portability and Accountability Act (HIPAA) (PL 104-191)

In addition to ensuring the portability of health insurance for Americans, HIPAA also made health care fraud and abuse a federal offense. PL 104-191 addresses intent as it relates to health care fraud and abuse when associated with claims coding (Title II, Subtitle D, Sec. 231.d). It also identifies the establishment of a fraud and abuse control program, a Medicare integrity program, and beneficiary incentive programs. Additionally, revisions were made regarding exclusions to the Medicare and Medicaid programs, monetary fines, and criminal prosecution and imprisonment. All revisions result in stiffer penalties associated with health care fraud and abuse.

Office of the Inspector General's (OIG) 1997 Work Plan

For fiscal year 1997, the OIG identified 16 areas for review in the hospital setting. These include violations to the 72-hour payment window and the targeting of DRG miscoding.

The OIG is looking at improper hospital outpatient billings and nonphysician outpatient billings associated with violations of the 72-hour payment window rule. The rule states that outpatient services provided by the hospital or a nonphysician outpatient entity owned or operated by the hospital within 72 hours of inpatient admission should not be billed separately but should be included in the DRG payment for the inpatient admission. Based on a nationwide computer search performed by the OIG, over

continues

Health Care Fraud and Abuse continued

$200 million in potentially improper billings (for outpatient services) were made in 1992 and 1993. The OIG and the Department of Justice have entered into a joint project to recover overpayments and assess penalties and interest.

The OIG is also looking at improper coding associated with DRG assignment for inpatient hospitalization. This is a joint project of the OIG and HCFA and focuses on identification of facilities for audit of potentially inappropriate code assignments leading to inappropriate DRG classification for Medicare reimbursement.

In response to the increase in legislation and investigations being initiated by state and federal programs, hospitals across the country are beginning to implement compliance programs to detect and correct potentially improper practices. If a facility is targeted for investigation and improper practices are identified, a government compliance program may be mandated in the absence of a facility-developed program.

HOSPITAL COMPLIANCE PROGRAMS

A hospitalwide compliance program helps to identify and prevent fraudulent activities within the organization. Such a program helps ensure the accuracy of billing practices and provides a mechanism for handling any wrongdoing that may be discovered.

Usually a corporatewide compliance program ensures that all aspects of business are in compliance with the 1991 U.S. Sentencing Commission Guidelines for Organizations. The program should include, at a minimum

- **Established standards**—Expectations must be set so that all employees know the organization's parameters regarding legal and ethical conduct. These should be written in a manner that precludes misinterpretation by any member of the organization.
- **Designated compliance officer**—This person should be a high-level individual chosen to oversee the organization's compliance program. In a corporate setting, this may be the head of the internal audit function or chief legal counsel. In a smaller facility, the head of risk management may be appropriate. A decision should be made as to the extent of involvement by legal counsel. In the presence of improper practices, legal counsel's involvement at a high level could ensure attorney-client privilege for the facility and protection from later discovery.
- **Established annual education and training of all personnel on corporate commitment to compliance and company standards**—A structured program should be conducted on an annual basis to ensure that all personnel understand the importance of compliance, their role in maintaining compliance through application of the standards, and their obligation to report any breach according to the hospital compliance program protocol. Education should be provided on the mechanisms employees have available to them for reporting potential violations. Additionally, the organization's disciplinary measures for violations should be covered during the training.
- **Established monitoring and auditing procedures to ensure compliance**—Whether performed as an internal function or outsourced, monitoring and auditing are key elements in ensuring that the appropriate standards are being followed. Monitors should be established to identify those instances where there are variations to the defined standards.
- **Established mechanisms for communicating potential violations**—Mechanisms must be in place to facilitate employee communication of potential violations according to the hospital compliance program. This should include a mechanism for providing anonymous information related to potentially improper practices within the organization.
- **Established disciplinary measures**—Information on disciplinary measures should be disseminated to all employees during the education program. Consistent application of these measures is necessary for employees at all levels within the organization. Any noncompliant behavior should result in disciplinary action.
- **Established response to proven violations**—The internal identification of improper practices should require the activation of several steps within the organization to ensure an appropriate response to the situation. This should include appropriate steps to prevent recurrence of the improper practice in the future.

A corporate compliance program should ensure appropriate documentation, coding, and billing practices within the health care facility. This includes cost reporting, UB-92 billing of inpatient services, and appropriately assigned chargemaster items. Additionally, practices related to Stark rules, Clinical Laboratory Improvement Amendments (CLIA), and confidentiality (to name a few) should be reviewed and standards included as a part of the program.

Although most compliance-related investigations to date have been specific to physician services or outpatient services, the hospital health information management department should become proactive in deterring risk related to inpatient coding and billing.

ROLE OF THE HEALTH INFORMATION MANAGEMENT DEPARTMENT

The health information management (HIM) specialist should become involved on the front end in sharing the responsibility of hospitalwide compliance. The status of the facility in implementing a corporatewide compliance program should be determined to ensure that the work being performed by the HIM department is monitoring for more than just DRG miscoding; monitoring other processes may be included as part of an expanded role within the organization.

The health information management department is a crucial part of any hospitalwide compliance program. Because the de-

continues

Health Care Fraud and Abuse continued

partment manages clinical documentation for patients, it may be appropriate to assume responsibilities that are in addition to traditional roles. For example, the department might be accountable for verifying the accuracy of certain billing considerations such as

- compliance with the 72-hour rule for outpatient services preceding an admission
- accurate discharge dispositions for patients transferred to other acute care facilities
- whether Medicare is a secondary payer

The HIM department may share responsibility with the medical staff, the business office, and other areas of the hospital in making certain that clinical documentation is appropriate, coding is accurate, and services are correctly billed.

The HIM department should also make certain that its traditional responsibilities are in compliance. This may involve

- **Periodic audits**—Periodic audits need to be conducted in order to ensure the accuracy of clinical documentation, coding, and DRG assignment. Audits should be scientifically designed to provide a reliable assessment of current practices and should encompass both inpatient and outpatient services.
- **Data monitors**—Data monitors should be implemented to track key indicators of patient mix and coding practices. Such indicators may include case mix index, complication rates, and reporting of potentially problematic diagnoses and procedures. Identification of abnormalities or variations should trigger the need for a comprehensive audit.
- **Process controls**—Process controls should be instituted to establish responsibilities and accountability among departments. There should be quality controls and feedback mechanisms to help identify any wrongdoing so that it can be corrected.
- **Departmental compliance plan**—A departmental compliance plan should be developed and documented in concert with the hospitalwide plan. The departmental plan should include written standards for documentation and coding.
- **Educational programs**—Educational programs should be conducted on a regular basis to make certain that employees understand the regulatory requirements associated with the documentation and billing of services. This training should be continually reinforced to keep up with regulatory changes, newly identified issues, and turnover among personnel.
- **Internal response mechanism**—An internal response mechanism must be in place that allows an employee to report any concerns without fear of reprisal. For example, a coder should be able to report pressure that may be applied to upcode patient accounts in order to improve reimbursement. Such reports must be dealt with quickly and decisively.

The need for corporate compliance programs is becoming increasingly important, and HIM departments need to be prepared to be an effective partner in a hospitalwide program. As with any new initiative, there will be a period of experimentation and learning as hospitals respond to requirements. It is critical, however, that hospitals take a proactive stance. Implementation of a compliance program helps to prevent problems and demonstrates the organization's intentions to detect and prevent fraudulent activities.

Source: © QuadraMed, Compliance and Education Division, 561 Main Street, Bethlehem, PA, 18018. Phone 800-373-5620. QuadraMed offers compliance consulting, auditing, educational services, and software products to hospitals across the couuntry.

AMERICAN SOCIETY FOR TESTING AND MATERIALS (ASTM)

7. THE OVERALL STRUCTURE OF THE COMPUTER-BASED PATIENT RECORD (CPR)

7.1 The discussion of the structure of the CPR must relate the major entities (objects) of the record to the identified record segments. The clinical heart of the CPR is the core of the entities: patient, provider, problem, encounters, orders, services, and observations. The record segments that relate to these entities are shown in the Patient Record Object Model figure. The focus of these relationships is the RADT object model. The Patient Record Content Structure Data Categories, Segments, and Entity Relationships table shows how the segments currently accommodate the entities.

7.1.1 Notice that most of the entities listed in the Patient Record Object Model figure have their own attributes. For example, the patient has the attributes of sex, race, birth date, etc. Each order includes attributes that identify the item(s) ordered, the date of the order, the ordering provider, the urgency of the order (stat, now, routine, etc.), the ordering instructions and can be further broken down into amount, frequency, duration, special conditions for many orders.

7.1.2 With some of these entities, the industry has enough experience that the overall structure is well understood and easy to describe. In some information areas, especially those that are represented by free text in the traditional record, much is yet to be learned.

7.2 *Perspective*—Representing the overall structure of the record is difficult because it is complex and has a number of dimensions. It also can be viewed from many perspectives. Four of these are chronological, by encounter/episode, by problem, and by topic. Each of these views looks at the same stored data in a different way. There can be many perspectives and even more ways of displaying the same data.

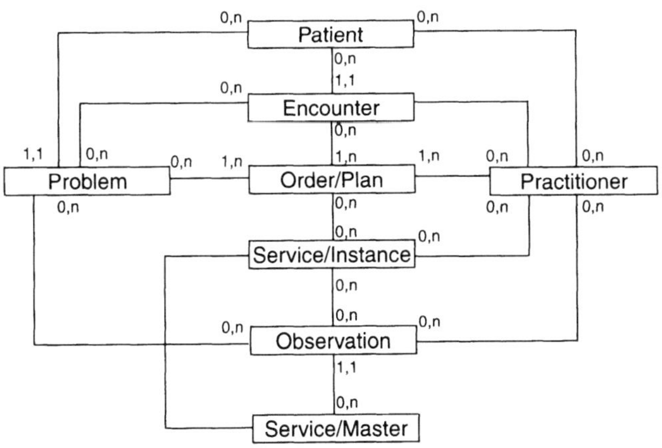

Figure 4. Patient Record Object Model

Another difficult task is that of representing the data needs of different settings in a manner that captures the diversity and complexity of the observations as they relate to service instances and requests. These aspects will be further expanded in the discussion of the appropriate segments.

7.3 *Segment Categories:*

7.3.1 In order to provide a comprehensive structure for the CPR, it must be organized into major segments that are clearly identified and to which information can be consistently added from one setting and episode to another over time. The segments were identified through analysis of the content of the existing data sets, and each segment describes and represents a category or type of information that can be seen in all patient care records.

7.3.2 As noted in the Patient Record Content Structure Data Categories, Segments, and Entity Relationships table, these segments have been regrouped for a more universal understanding of administrative and clinical aspects. The following discussion deals with the essential data elements in each segment. These elements may be utilized in different constellations in different settings, but each element's meaning remains the same wherever it is used.

7.3.3 Segments 1 to 13 (see Patient Record Content Structure Data Categories, Segments, and Entity Relationships table) contain elements that are widely used in all settings and apply to both patient record and the longitudinal precis regardless of setting. They are not specific to any one episode or encounter, though they may be initiated or updated during an encounter. The way they reflect the relation-

Table 4
Patient Record Content Structure Data Categories, Segments, and Entity Relationships

Data	Category and Segments	Entity
Administrative Data		
I	Demographics	Patient
II	Legal agreements	Patient
III	Financial information	Patient
IV	Provider/practitioner	Provider
Clinical Data: Problem/Diagnoses		
V	Problem list	Problem
Clinical Data: History		
VI	Immunization	Service instance
VII	Hazardous stressor exposure	Observation
VIII	Health history	Observation
Clinical Data: Assessments/Exams		
IX	Assessments	Observations
*	Patient-reported data	Observation
Clinical Data: Care/Treatment Plans		
X	Clinical orders	Orders
Clinical Data: Services		
XI	Diagnostic tests	Observations
XII	Medications	Service instance
XIII	Scheduled appointment/events	Encounter
Administrative Data: Encounters		
XIV a	Administrative data	Patient
f	Encounter disposition*	Encounter
Clinical Data: Encounters		
b	Chief complaint/diagnoses	Observation
c	Clinical course	Observation
d	Therapy/procedures	Service instance

*These are new concepts or reordered data, or both. Note that the clinical heart of the CHR is the core of the entities (Objects). The record segments that relate to these are shown.

TYPE	VALUE
EARLY	Early tray
LATE	Late tray
GUEST	Guest tray
NO	No tray
MSG	Tray message

Figure 5. Values for Type

ships shown in the figure and the table will be discussed in the following sections.

7.4 *Occurrence and Utilization of Record Segments in Different Settings*—The Sites of Care table outlines the classes of settings that maintain a patient record of care, which contains the identified segments to some degree.

7.5 *Segment One, Demographics*—These are personal data elements, sufficient to identify the patient, collected from the patient or patient representative and not related to health status or services provided. Some of these elements may require updating at each encounter or episode and must satisfy various national standards and regulations such as Joint Commission standards, conditions of participation for Medicare, and uniform hospital discharge, ambulatory, and long-term care data sets.

7.6 *Segment Two, Legal Agreements*—This includes data elements indicating legally binding directions or restraints on patient health care, release of information, and disposal of body or body parts, or both, after death.

7.7 *Segment Three, Financial*—This segment contains the references to the financial bodies that will cover the cost of care. This segment may be referred to from within the record, as during encounters/episodes. Such reference would obviate the need for a redundant collection of such data during the visit.

7.8 *Segment Four, Provider/Practitioners:*

7.8.1 This segment contains in one place the descriptive data about each provider/practitioner and may then be referenced when recording data about the events of health care. This includes the provider-identifying data on the primary organization, or establishment responsible for the availability of health care services for a specific episode or encounter.

7.8.2 Practitioner-identifying data elements are those associated with the individuals licensed or certified to deliver care to patients, who had face-to-face contact with the patient, and provided care based on independent judgment.

7.9 *Segment Five, Problem List:*

7.9.1 This includes specified clinical problems, a diagnosis summary and stressor exposure, an ongoing list of clinically significant health status events and factors, resolved and unresolved, in a patient's life. This list should contain all past and existing diagnoses, pathophysiological states, potentially significant abnormal physical signs and laboratory findings, disabilities, and unusual conditions. Other factors such as social problems, psychiatric problems, risk factors, allergies, reactions to drugs or foods, behavioral problems, or other health alerts may be included. The problem list is to be amended as more precise definitions of the problems become available. Controlled vocabulary for problem lists may be contained in a problem list directory master table.

7.9.2 This segment contains a master list of all of a patient's problems or diagnoses. It may be referenced, in presenting the diagnostic summary beginning each encounter/episode. All problems or diagnoses initially recorded in a specific encounter/episode will also be entered in this master list.

7.9.3 Whenever possible, identification of risk factors (health alerts) that should be known prior to implementing any health service should be included in this section. They can be considered to be instances of a special type of patient problem and include allergies, contagious conditions, and adverse reaction to specified treatments.

7.10 *Segment Six, Immunizations*—Considered a component of patient health history, this segment contains, chronologically, all immunizations administered to the patient and their current status. This synopsis may also be copied to an emergency record to accompany medical alert data. Acquired (active or passive) or induced immunity or resistance to particular pathogens produced by deliberate exposure to antigens is included.

7.11 *Segment Seven, Exposure to Hazardous Substances:*

Table 5
Sites of Care

Ambulance/aid-car	Hospital, government
Ambulatory surgery facility, free-standing	Hospital, outpatient department
Ambulatory surgery facility, hospital-based	Hospital, psychiatric
Birthing center, free-standing	Hospital, rehabilitation
Birthing center, hospital-based	Hospital, trauma center LVL 1
Clinic/health center, comp outpatient rehabilitation	Imaging services facility, free-standing
Clinic/health center, dental	Independent laboratory
Clinic/health center, free-standing	Industrial health/occupational health center
Clinic/health center, health maintenance organization	Intermediate care facility
Clinic/health center, outpatient mental health	Intermediate care facility, mentally retarded
Clinic/health center, pain	Mental health multiservice organization
Clinic/health center, rural	Mental health partial care organization
Clinic/health center, urgent care center, walk-in, free-standing	Private office, group, fee-for-service
	Private office, group, prepaid
Clinic/health center, vision	Private office, solo practice
Custodial care facility	Residential treatment center, emotionally disturbed children
Day care center	
End-stage renal disease treatment facility	Residential school
Home health	Retirement center
Hospice, free-standing	School clinic/infirmary
Hospital, acute care	Sheltered employment workshop
Hospital, acute care with psychiatric services	Skilled nursing facility/nursing home
Hospital, burn center	Special education program
Hospital, cancer	Substance abuse treatment facility, resident nursing center
Hospital, children's	
Hospital, emergency room	Vocational rehabilitation unit

7.11.1 The what, where, when, and how data on actual or potential exposure to all biological, physical, or chemical agents that might be associated with adverse health effects are listed in this segment. This segment should provide data for epidemiological studies to determine correlation of disease with exposure to environmental stressors.

7.11.2 Because of the potentially long latency period in exposure to hazardous substances before the appearance of effects, the chronological record of exposure—both in the workplace and out, where appropriate—to hazardous chemical, physical, biological, or radiologic stressors to the body is contained in this segment. It has particular importance when accessed as part of the synoptic record because its completeness acts as a prompt to providers/practitioners long removed in time or space, or both, from the original entry that the signs and symptoms of health conditions may be due to previous exposure. Absence of such data does not rule out such exposure but presence provides direct clues needed to identify the possible cause of an observed condition.

7.12 *Segment Eight, Family/Prenatal/Cumulative Health/Medical/Dental Nursing History*—The long-term relevant natural family and patient history and signs that would aid practitioners in predicting or diagnosing illness, or actual or potential alterations in health, or predicting outcome of the patient's care are all the focus of this segment. The historic record of previous signs and symptoms complements the problem list in itemizing, in an integral way, the manifestations of prior disease, illness, or health status not yet documented in the problem. It characterizes those already present in that list and it takes the form of a categorized list of questions of the form: "Have you ever _____? If so, when?" During each encounter/episode this list may be updated by the preface: "Since the last visit have you ever _____? If so, when?" so that the most recent observations can be added to the growing list. This integral process then collects the most reliable observations from the patient (historically categorized in patient records) review of systems, and nursing history or other method, and adds them to the historic body of (at the time) freshly collected data. Ideally, this process begins during gestation and the initial observations are transferred from the mother's record to that of the newborn at birth. Fresh observations are added throughout the patient's lifetime. If continuity can be maintained, the practitioner need not have to reconstitute the early record, at least not often, at each encounter. Recommended and optional attributes of patient history are included in a master table.

7.13 *Segment Nine, Assessments/Exams:*

7.13.1 Assessments/exams characterize the patient's health status in tandem with the history. Depending on the setting, this segment may include a general or specialty medical or dental exam or assessments by nursing, dietary, social service, therapy, or dental hygiene specialists, or all of these. The assessments may be all-inclusive or may relate only to hands-on care of very special problems (that is, particular body systems, psychosocial assessment, dental vision communication, etc.). All data pertinent to pre- and perinatal care including monitoring during delivery are also included in a postdelivery exam assessment. Details of the actual delivery for the newborn are to be entered in the specific section containing health factors of the neonate. Recommended attributes of assessments/exams are identified in master tables.

7.13.2 This segment records the observations of the practitioner during structured and systematic examinations of the patient's body during encounters/episodes. It contains objective observations and measurements that quantify attributes of each body system. These are the same body systems about which patient questions are asked during the history. Such common categories allow characterization of expressed problems with observational evidence in explicit common terms and measures that, over time, allow practitioners to follow the course of illness and recovery. This focuses on the physical assessment of the patient and is combined with appropriate psychosocial assessment to compose overall patient assessment status. These observations complement the diagnostic terms described in 7.15. They also relate to the effects of therapeutic interventions, such as medications, as described in 7.16.

7.14 *Segment Ten, Care/Treatment Plans and Orders:*

7.14.1 Data entries that direct a patient's treatment include detail data on deliverance of orders and compliance with any diagnostic or therapeutic treatment plans, whether written, oral, or standing.

7.14.2 A care treatment plan may be a broad perspective program that identifies planned clinical encounters, education, and scheduled events related to specific diagnosis or set of problems (for example, diabetes). It may also be a short-term tool applied, for instance, in acute care or other setting that arranges interdisciplinary roles to carry out therapies, nursing services, and other activities. While not always explicitly defined, care plans are typically based on protocols and guidelines. In some cases, they are developed via consensus.

7.14.3 A clinical order is an action-oriented message describing an intervention in the health of a specific patient originated by, or under the supervision of, a practitioner. A clinical order has legal implications regarding responsibilities for the ordered intervention as well as quality-of-care implications that may be assessed by supervisory bodies or clinical researchers, or both. It is therefore necessary to specify the logical structure of this message and to define the representations to be used for each constituent data element. The clinical order acts also as a communication and coordination mechanism for all of the practitioner and ancillary professionals who may participate in the actions set in motion by the order. The clinical order structure is complex and may be thought of as a network structure because of the complexity of relationships between specific data elements within the clinical order and other data elements located elsewhere in the care record. Because this complex structure is difficult, and perhaps practically impossible, to represent by means of two-dimensional paper forms, there is no explicit manual-mode model for this kind of data structure. Paper records have relied on plain-text representations in recording the order. In practice, these relationships among the data elements have been implicit in the inculcated practices of professional training. This guide attempts to explicitly define this structure.

7.14.4 Because a clinical order is a message, it has a heading and a body. The heading specifies the originator, the object patient, the routing, and the addressee(s). The body contains a structure that is greatly dependent on the action addressee but does have a large degree of commonality across all types of orders. As the message objective is a specific patient, a copy of all orders for that patient are filed in the patient's health record. This follows current accountability practice regarding the manual record and its legal status as the record of care received by a patient. Other copies may be stored for use by the action or information addressees, as appropriate. A given clinical order may be more appropriately created by means of preexisting templates, or sets of templates, that contain preassigned data.

7.14.5 The data elements in each order are in the following functional groups:

7.14.5.1 Those that identify the patient,

7.14.5.2 Those that identify the action or ancillary service,

7.14.5.3 Those that identify the orderer(s),

7.14.5.4 Those that control the timing or delivery of services, or both,

7.14.5.5 Those that describe the requested service and conditions of delivery,

7.14.5.6 Those that document the delivery of results, and

7.14.5.7 Those that are used for quality assurance.

7.14.6 The logical structure lists these data elements showing their structural relationships within the message and the data elements to which they may be related in other segments of the clinical record.

7.14.7 *Orderer Group of Data Elements*—The elements in this group provide a means of tracking the initiation and responsibilities for each order. This group also helps ensure that various subordinate practitioners do not exceed the bounds of their training by ordering, unaided, procedures they have not yet been qualified to use. At the same time, these steps must, many times, be started in the absence of a practitioner having adequate authority to fully initiate the procedure or service ordered. In hospitals, the actions of the nursing staff and health practitioner students or those in training may require review and validation by cosigning for services having major health or cost implications from the aspect of accountability. Institutional policy must provide the criteria for expeditious action in identifying services needing higher permission levels from the responsible staff; this two-tier approach allows actions to be initiated in a timely fashion but yet rescinded, if appropriate. Therefore, the data elements in this group identify the needed information applying to a wide variety of situations. Nevertheless, not all elements may apply in a given situation.

7.14.8 *Action/Ancillary Service Data Elements*—The elements in this group identify the action performers and the type and priority of the order.

7.14.9 *Order Content Data Elements*—This group of data elements conveys the explicit service/actions desired for the patient. It may include patient data extracted from other segments of the record as required to conduct the services or to carry out the action. Each ancillary service or treatment site must be able to define the data that will be required in this group in order to be able to carry out the ordered actions. Such data requirements will be found in appropriate subordinate files and will control, by prompting, the construction of the text of the order to meet these requirements. Modifications to the order shall be appended to the original text, while other data elements shall document the course of each modification.

7.14.10 *Result Group*—This group of data elements documents the delivery of the result data from the service or action, as appropriate, while the results themselves are stored separately in the appropriate segments of the record.

7.14.11 *Quality Assurance Group of Data Elements*—This group of data elements documents the circumstances of actions that are exceptions to the routine process for each ordered action or service. They assume that a process is evaluating the specific criteria for each clinical order in order to establish the regular bounds. Because health care must deal with the unexpected and the unusual, recording of events that are unusual because they are outside the bounds of routine experience in no way implies that they are not required for treatment. Rather, these data elements flag such events so that they can be easily recognized for review. That they were reviewed is also documented in order to ensure that significant findings are not overlooked.

7.15 *Segment Eleven, Diagnostic Tests*—Significant details of tests performed aid the practitioner in the diagnosis, management, and treatment of the patient. Documentation of the results from the clinical laboratory, radiology, nuclear medicine, pulmonary function, and any other diagnostic examinations would be included. This segment contains the chronological list of all diagnostic tests ordered and conducted on the patient. The attribute data about each such test reference the order, problem list, appropriate physical exam or medication segments, or all of these, that may relate to the monitoring of therapeutic interventions to either measure therapeutic effects or detect adverse affects. It should be remembered that the problem list, encounters, and physical exam segments may, likewise, contain references to specific dates and types of tests that are associated with those problems, encounters, or examinations and that help document the full implications of the meaning of such tests.

7.16 *Segment Twelve, Medications:*

7.16.1 A list of all long-term medications and significant details on all medications prescribed or administered, or both, in the course of, or as a consequence of, an encounter or episode.

7.16.2 This segment contains data about the therapeutic chemical substances and treatments that have been prescribed as interventions in the disease process. All of the attributes of the order described in 7.14 are linked to this record by reference to the orders segment. Additional attributes provided by the pharmacist are also added to the record, including adverse effects reported in the history or the physical exam segments, or both. The problem list that identifies the problem being treated may also be referenced.

7.17 *Segment Thirteen, Scheduled Appointments/Events*—This segment includes the list of planned or scheduled appointments that implement a treatment plan. It includes attributes that characterize the planned services, location, and practitioners that constitute the plan.

7.18 *Segment Fourteen—Encounters/Episodes:*

7.18.1 The concept of an encounter is usually defined to be a face-to-face session of the patient with a practitioner during which information about the patient's health status is exchanged. The encounter record should capture the facts related to the events that took place—whether they occur in an inpatient setting or an ambulatory care environment. Certain information that characterizes the time, place, and circumstances of the initiation of the encounter are first required. Then the information characterizing the patient's condition and reason for seeking care must be recorded. Next, the identification and characterization of the patient's problem(s), including referencing the encounter to the problem list, must be included. Finally, the interventions ordered, the response to the actions performed, the departure condition, and the required follow-up actions must be recorded including a record of the services rendered. Because the circumstances leading to an encounter may be as direct as inpatient rounds by the attending physician to emergency room care (for example, traumatically injured patients), the data collected in the encounter may vary from brief to extensive. The collected data may not include all data elements identified, if these elements are not applicable to a given encounter.

7.18.1.1 A discussion of this segment must first explain that the pointer arrows leading from the identified data elements to a logical file mnemonic are intended to portray that that element is represented in a lexicon. The lexicon has associated attributes that are not dependent on the context of the term in the encounter record, and the recorded element is the index into this lexicon. This notation enables discussion of the complexity of interrelationships among data elements of the record that occur across and within segment boundaries. In order to reflect how the structure of the record parallels the practitioner's thought processes, these logical interrelations must be depicted using a generic convention and the data that are global to the individual encounter must be so identified in order to foster data independence wherever possible. This means avoidance of recording redundant data when these data are independent of the context. It also means using a key identifier or term to represent the invariant data stored in a logical list that can be referenced from within the context. This procedure avoids a common error in forms design in which specific instances, or data values, of a given data element are identified as separate data elements. A specific instance of a class name, for example, might be a specific drug or a unique lab test name. Use the above notation to convey membership in a lexicon name class.

7.18.2 *Segment Fourteen A, Administrative/Diagnostic Summary:*

7.18.2.1 These are the data elements clarifying time/date, location, type, and source of encounter or episode as they differ from information already contained in the related major 7.5 through 7.17. These should include the problems and the list of admitting and all other diagnoses that are factors in the patient's care during the specific episode or encounter and that should be added to the patient's problem list in 7.9.

7.18.2.2 This subsegment contains all of the data that characterizes the origin of the episode and the manner of arrival at the provider's facility, including the condition of the patient. It also summarizes the administrative conditions concerning the termination of treatment, excepting the disposition that is contained in 7.18.6.

7.18.3 *Segment Fourteen B—Chief Complaint Present Illness/Trauma Care*—This contains health/medical/nursing/dental history reference to Section 8 and history of chief complaint and reasons why the patient came in for care. This will include a review of systems as appropriate to the individual case and reference Section 9 as described in 7.13. It also includes reported prehospital care of emergency patients and assessment of the nature of traumatic injury and the results of stabilizing interventions.

7.18.4 *Segment Fourteen C—Progress Notes/Clinical Course:*

7.18.4.1 This includes the components that form an ongoing chronological picture and analysis of the clinical course of the patient during an episode or encounter. This segment is applicable in any health care setting. These elements serve as a means of communication and interaction between members of the health care team. They may also occur as narrative or flow sheets. They constitute the record of patient response to therapies, procedures, and other events.

7.18.4.2 This subsection contains all those data elements that characterize the clinical course of care and the condition of the patient. They will link to tests, therapies, and procedures and will be represented by test or flow sheets.

7.18.5 *Segment Fourteen D—Therapies:*

7.18.5.1 This includes significant details on all preventive or therapeutic, or both, services performed at the time of the episode or encounter or scheduled to be performed before the next episode or encounter. This subsection would not include any surgery performed in an operating room or that could be documented under either Section 12 or 17.8.6. Transfusions, physical, occupational, nursing, respiratory, rehabilitative, and mental health therapies would be included.

7.18.5.2 These elements are recorded to characterize all of the conditions of nonmedication therapy, and they represent interdisciplinary therapy programs and results.

7.18.6 *Subsegment Fourteen E—Procedures:*

7.18.6.1 This includes significant details on all procedures performed in an operating room for diagnostic, exploratory, or definitive treatment purposes.

7.18.6.2 This subsection contains data that characterize those procedural events that accompany treatment of the patient, exclusive of laboratory phases of diagnostic procedures, which are recorded in segment 11.

7.18.7 *Segment Fourteen F—Disposition:*

7.18.7.1 This subsection identifies the circumstances under which the patient terminated the encounter or episode and includes data about the length of stay, condition of patient on disposition, recommended treatment, and other information necessary for follow-up care.

7.18.7.2 This subsection contains data that characterize the conditions under which the encounter or episode was completed and the arrangements for appropriate follow-up either by the current or by other providers. It contains information needed to maintain continuity of care over several episodes or multiple encounters.

STANDARDS FOR CONFIDENTIALITY, PRIVACY, ACCESS, AND DATA SECURITY

"Accredited by the Joint Commission on Accreditation of Healthcare Organizations" means that a health care facility has met certain standards set by the Joint Commission. "Meets ASTM standard xxxx" means that the product or policy/procedure of the organization has incorporated a standard developed by the American Society for Testing and Materials (ASTM). Today, a careful reading of product information may reveal a statement regarding health care information standards, much like the Underwriters Laboratories tag that appears on products. This statement may be in a series of product specifications, or an individual can note that ASTM standards were used in the development of a health information system, a policy, or a procedure.

ASTM

ASTM is an accredited standards development organization that has been producing standards for more than 90 years. Much of its early work was specifically directed at developing standards for testing and setting standards for materials. Standards in the areas of computerization and quality improvement preceded the development of standards in health care informatics in ASTM. The computerization and quality improvement standards are widely used in the business community. Health care informatics is a more recent area of development in ASTM.

Even so, ASTM's Healthcare Informatics Committee (E31) has several standards of interest to health information professionals. For example, standards are available for the following topics: universal identifiers, electronic signatures, content and format of a computer-based health record, and exchange of clinical messages. As needs for standards emerge, ASTM and its member committees address those needs. Many standards for health care informatics are currently in development stages.

STANDARDS DEVELOPMENT PROCESS

The process of standards development proceeds via the following steps:

1. identification of a needed standard
2. research in the topic area
3. development of a proposed standard or set of standards by a group of volunteers with a variety of backgrounds (industry representatives, end-users, academics, and others)
4. gaining formal consensus at several levels
5. publication of the standard
6. review and revision of the standard after publication and use
7. modifications as appropriate
8. formal consensus on changes
9. publication of the revised standard

Consensus of the initial development group as well as of the parent committee is required for approval of a standard. This process, although taking time and effort, is designed to produce a high-quality, usable standard. Standards are reviewed and updated on a regular schedule. The term *standard* does not imply that, once determined, the standard never changes.

Although the standards development work in the United States is a volunteer effort, Europe has decided to fund the standards development process and is spending a considerable amount of money to develop health information or health care informatics standards for the European community. Because we live in a global society and computer products and systems have international potential, the standards community recognizes the need to work in this larger context. A number of joint meetings have been held in the last two years, and work is shared in draft form among working committees.

BENEFIT OF STANDARDS

Standards frequently make life easier. For example, certain specifications were agreed on by manufacturers to allow us to go into the video store, rent tapes, and bring them home to play on our home VCR. In much the same way, we need standards that will allow us to develop and use health information systems more efficiently and more effectively. ASTM and other standards organizations are actively working at many levels to develop useful standards.

Standards can take several forms. For example, a standard can be a specification regarding an information system, or it can be a guideline as to how something should be done. A standard can be technical, or it can be a guide to use when a process is being developed.

ASTM CONFIDENTIALITY, PRIVACY, ACCESS, AND DATA SECURITY STANDARD

ASTM, through its Subcommittee on Confidentiality, Privacy, Access, and Data Security (E31.17) recently balloted a standard on the principles of confidentiality, privacy, access, and data security of health information, including computer-based health records. The areas of confidentiality, privacy, and access to health information have received substantial attention in the last four years.

There is widespread recognition that computerization of health information and the ability easily to accumulate, access, and transfer data electronically add new dimensions to protecting the privacy and confidentiality of health information. The health care community works diligently to respect an individual's privacy and to maintain the confidentiality of an individual's information. There is general agreement that the individual should exercise reasonable control over the health information if it leaves the purview of the caregiver and that the individual has a right of access to his or her own health information. The potential uses of and the demands for health information, however, frequently push the information out of its traditional boundaries. Everyone who has contact with the infor-

continues

Standards for Confidentiality, Privacy, Access, and Data Security continued

mation must recognize the individual's right to privacy and need for confidentiality.

The standards document developed by ASTM Subcommittee E31.17 is a statement of principles to be used in the move to the computerized environment. It is also anticipated that standards will not be sufficient and that laws will continue to evolve to address key issues embodied in the statement of principles.

In some arenas the full development of a computer-based or electronic health record is slowed or limited by confidentiality issues that have not been resolved. For example, large systems that put all patient data on line and then make the entire system available to all clinical staff and employees to facilitate easy access are not addressing privacy and confidentiality on behalf of their patients, clients, residents, or enrollees. Systems can be designed to incorporate safeguards, organizations can develop and enforce sanctions, and staff can be educated regarding their responsibilities and the changes required in a computerized environment.

ASTM Subcommittee E31.17 found it necessary to agree on a set of principles to move to the next level of more specific standards development within E31.17. Therefore, the document currently available contains a statement of principles with a discussion of each principle. This document will be used for future development of ASTM standards. It covers the topics of

- privacy
- confidentiality
- collection, use, and maintenance
- ownership
- access
- disclosure/transfer of data
- data security/integrity
- penalties/sanctions
- education of users

EXAMPLES FROM THE ASTM STANDARD

To provide more than a description of the standard, a few examples from the standard are included in the following sections.

Privacy

Principle: Individuals have a right to know that identifiable, personal information is available in a health record, health information system, or other information system and a right to know to whom the information is available and the use(s) of the information.

Individuals recognize the need to maintain records regarding health care. There are, however, many uses of patient information beyond direct care. Those who collect data and maintain record systems should notify individuals of the types of information collected, generally how the information will be used, and, if known, specific uses and locations of health information databases that will contain a patient's information, especially those that go beyond the boundaries of the health care organization. Examples are regional registries for cancer, trauma, and implants; the Medical Information Bureau; third-party payers; health data organizations; state and regional data systems; and research databases.

Confidentiality

Principle: Health information that has not been disidentified shall be considered confidential.

Individuals share confidential information to receive care. Individuals must be able to trust that the confidentiality of the information will be maintained. Disidentification refers to the processes or mechanisms used to obscure the identity of the person related to a set of data. At a minimum, this involves removing obvious identifying information (name, date of birth, Social Security number, etc.) from the data set. Care must also be taken to ensure that the person associated with the data cannot be deduced via inference.

Access

Principle: Providers, including practitioners and other organizations, must adopt systems that address the use, availability, clarity, and integrity of health information.

Providers must have systems in place to produce accurate information about an individual's health. The information should be legible and reasonably easy to decipher. It is understood that some holders of information will have summary information and that others may hold detailed information. Accessibility over a lifetime could be provided by a longitudinal health record kept by the patient, maintained in components by providers, or maintained in a clinical data center.

The computer-based health record system and other health information databases should allow users and managers of health information systems to classify data for access purposes. The data classification process may address data by related data groups or by individual data elements. The system/database use should be supported by policies and procedures that identify users/roles authorized to read, enter, modify, amend, or download data.

The computer-based health record system and other health information systems should be designed to verify the identity of the user and to record each access to the record/database and the action taken (e.g., read, copy, update, print, download, or transfer). In addition to documenting the access by time and individual, it is also recommended that the purpose of the access be documented. Many authorizations contain a purpose statement that could be related to the reason for access. Internal organizational users should provide a purpose by category (e.g., patient treatment, patient billing, or utilization management).

The organization should periodically review the assignment of access privileges based on job duties, roles, and requirements. Inappropriate browsing of the system by authorized users and others who attempt to access the system should be prohibited by policy, and the system should be reviewed to identify and prevent this activity. Finally, the system should record and audit any apparently inappropriate access, breach of level, or unauthorized access by a user.

continues

Standards for Confidentiality, Privacy, Access, and Data Security continued

Disclosure/Transfer of Data

Principle: The sharing and transfer of data shall be in a manner that ensures the integrity, quality, and security of the information.

Systems should ensure that the quality and integrity of the data are not lost in the data transfer process. Controls should be used to limit the transmission of data to other sites only as authorized. Sites may be internal or external. Encryption should be used when the transmission between systems is not secure.

Fax machines and other devices used to transmit or receive identifiable information and/or to copy identifiable patient information should be in secure areas. Copies, printout, or faxes containing patient information should be destroyed after use or retained in a secure location. Faxed and other transmitted material should be accompanied by a statement of confidentiality and responsibility.

HOW TO USE THE ASTM STANDARD

Health information management specialists are familiar with the use of voluntary standards for accreditation, such as those of the Joint Commission, and for professional practice, such as the professional practice standards of the American Health Information Management Association. Standards provide a guide to action. Although standards do not have the force of law, they are frequently used by organizations and the courts to determine reasonable and prudent behavior.

The ASTM standard guide to the principles of confidentiality, privacy, access, and data security for health information, including the computer-based health record, provides a guide to action in an important area of computerization of health information. It will serve as the basis for future development with the E31.17 Subcommittee and is used by other ASTM subcommittees in their work.

For those with an interest, the standards process is open to all who wish to participate. The goal of standards work is to provide a useful standard. Suggestions to improve the standards based on practical experience with the standards are especially helpful. A copy of this standard and other ASTM standards as well as information about how to participate in the standards process can be obtained from Terri Luthy, ASTM, 100 Barr Harbor Drive, West Conshohocken, Pennsylvania 19428-2959 (voice: 610-832-9500; fax: 610-832-9555).

Source: Mary Alice Hanken, "Standards for Confidentiality, Privacy, Access, and Data Security," *Topics in Health Information Management*, Vol. 16:4, Aspen Publishers, Inc., © 1996.

GUIDE FOR WRITING SPECIFICATIONS FOR HARDWARE PROCUREMENT

X7.1 Purchase of equipment, particularly of elaborate units or complete systems, requires specifications that are complete, detailed, clear, and well-organized. The following outline is a guide to composing comprehensive specifications. Specifications are sent to suppliers with requests for quotations. The purchaser should reserve the right to change the specifications before purchase orders are issued. (The purchaser is the system users' organization or the system users' purchasing agent.)

X7.2 *General Description:*

X7.2.1 Purpose or use of equipment.

X7.2.2 Type or nature of equipment

X7.2.3 Functions (of whole or subsystems).

X7.2.4 List of major units (list should indicate the function of each unit). Include a block diagram when helpful.

X7.3 *Operating Characteristics and Performance:*

X7.3.1 List operating characteristics of the whole or the subsystem. State particularly: modes of operation, modes of control and control ranges, and sequence of operation. (Include, with each of the above, the performance and accuracy desired, that is, range limits, resolution of controls, sensitivity, stability, etc.)

X7.3.2 *Monitoring*—List indicators, meters, etc. (for whole system). Include performance and accuracy desired.

X7.4 *Functions, Operating Characteristics, and Performance (of Each Major Unit):*

X7.4.1 List functions to be performed and operating characteristics of each major unit. Tabulate separately for each unit. State particularly modes of operation, modes of control and control ranges, sequence of operation, signal data. (Include with each of the above the performance and accuracy desired, that is, range limits, resolution of controls, sensitivity, stability, etc.)

X7.4.2 *Monitoring*—List indicators, meters, etc. Include performance and accuracy desired. Repeat this list for each major unit.

X7.5 *Electrical Supply, Safety, and Environment:*

X7.5.1 *Electrical Power*—Input voltage (include range), phases, frequency, maximum power consumption desired, etc.

X7.5.2 *Electrical Safety*—High-voltage protection. State or other code requirements.

X7.5.3 *Operation or Storage Environment, or Both*—Ambient temperature range, humidity range, altitude. Vibration, shock, radiation resistance. Submersion, explosion protection.

X7.5.4 Protection from hostile operators.

X7.6 *Construction:*

X7.6.1 System layouts and installation requirements.

X7.6.2 Size and weight limitations.

X7.6.3 Portability.

X7.6.4 Cabinet, chassis, and panel details; layout, color, panel notching, accessibility for servicing; and marking of controls, plugs, and components.

X7.7 *Quality and Reliability:*

X7.7.1 *Quality of Construction Requirements:*

X7.7.1.1 Conservative design.

X7.7.1.2 Reliable and conservatively rated components.

X7.7.1.3 Use of high-quality construction materials (for example, XXXP boards are not acceptable).

X7.7.2 *Reliability Requirements:*

X7.7.2.1 Mean-time-to-failure analysis.

X7.7.2.2 Worst-case analysis of system operation.

X7.7.2.3 Mean-time-to-repair analysis.

X7.8 *Acceptance Requirements:*

X7.8.1 *Criteria for Acceptance:*

X7.8.1.1 Use of industry-accepted standard test procedures.

X7.8.1.2 Special tests required.

X7.8.1.3 Individuals authorized to accept the system.

X7.8.2 *Inspection or Test at Vendor's Plant:*

X7.8.2.1 Right of purchaser's representatives to witness tests.

X7.8.2.2 Notification in time to send representative to witness tests.

X7.8.2.3 Submission of written test data to purchaser.

X7.8.2.4 Provision of test equipment to vendor by purchaser.

X7.8.3 *Inspection or Test at Purchaser's Facility:*

X7.8.3.1 Test or inspection to be made at purchaser's site (included where necessary to ensure that equipment is not damaged during shipment).

X7.8.3.2 Tests to be made on installation and extent of participation by vendor in such tests.

X7.8.3.3 Purchaser's review and approval of arrangements for any tests to be performed at installed site.

X7.9 *Supplementary Requirements:*

X7.9.1 Manuals and schematics.

X7.9.2 Installation by vendor.

X7.9.3 Spare parts to be furnished or listed.

X7.9.4 Training.

X7.9.5 Servicing.

X7.10 *Special Requirements (Include if Necessary):*

X7.10.1 Alternative designs.

X7.10.2 List of exceptions to specification by vendor.

X7.10.3 Design information to be furnished with bid.

X7.10.4 Submission of design for purchaser's approval before construction.

X7.10.5 Jigs, facilities, etc., to be furnished by or to purchaser.

HEDIS 3.0

HEDIS 3.0 EXECUTIVE SUMMARY

HEDIS®* 3.0 represents a giant leap forward in the nation's effort to compare the performance of health plans in areas of critical importance to purchasers and consumers, and takes the gold standard in performance measurement to an even higher level. At a time of political gridlock and in an era of substantial discord, a committee representing diverse and often competing interests achieved consensus about what needs to be and what can be measured in managed care at this time. The product of these debates about plan performance accountability and measurement science—HEDIS 3.0—is a set of performance measures of unprecedented scope and reach. This version of HEDIS also sets up a process for its own continuing enhancement that involves the periodic, open, and rigorous solicitation and selection of new measures. This will give the public ever more comprehensive and meaningful information on plan performance as we move toward the 21st century.

What Is HEDIS and How Does It Serve Purchasers and Consumers?

HEDIS (Health Plan Employer Data and Information Set) is a set of standardized performance measures designed to ensure that purchasers and consumers have the information they need to reliably compare the performance of managed health care plans. It is sponsored, supported, and maintained by the National Committee for Quality Assurance (NCQA), a not-for-profit organization committed to evaluating and publicly reporting on the quality of managed care plans. HEDIS, in combination with information from NCQA's accreditation program (a rigorous and expert evaluation of how managed care plans are organized and how they operate), provides the most complete view of health plan quality available to guide choice among competing health plans. HEDIS 3.0, which will be widely implemented across the country next year, will provide purchasers and consumers with an unprecedented ability both to evaluate the quality of different health plans along a variety of important dimensions, and to make their plan decisions based on demonstrated value rather than simply on cost.

How Is HEDIS 3.0 Different than Earlier Versions?

HEDIS 3.0 is the third HEDIS set released by NCQA. In contrast to earlier efforts, HEDIS 3.0:

- *Is more outcomes, or results, oriented*—For the first time, health plans will be expected to measure how well their patients are able to function in their daily lives, in a way that will open a window on health plan success at improving functional health. For the first time, satisfaction results will be assessed with a single instrument, providing the ability to capture and compare members' experiences across different health plans. Yet HEDIS now, and will continue into the future, includes a mix of outcome and process measures, because both provide important information about a health plan's performance. Not only is it important, for example, for a health plan to measure results in cases of coronary artery bypass graft surgery, but it is equally important that health plans demonstrate that they do what they can to keep members from using tobacco and, therefore, getting heart disease in the first place.
- *Addresses the full spectrum of health care*—HEDIS 3.0 addresses the range of health care issues from prevention and early detection to acute and chronic care for children, adolescents, adults, and seniors and for conditions of high prevalence such as AIDS, breast cancer, smoking addiction, heart disease, and diabetes.
- *Brings private-sector and public-sector measurement efforts together*—For the first time, the same measurement standards will be applied to care provided to Medicaid beneficiaries, commercial enrollees, and Medicare risk populations. Bringing the private and public sectors together in this way not only increases the efficiency of measurement but creates the possibility of comparing care across populations as well as across health plans.
- *Standardizes measurement across the full range of issues*—HEDIS 3.0 addresses the range of issues that are important to purchasers and consumers when choosing a health plan, including clinical results, access to needed services, satisfaction with the experience of care, the cost of care, and other key dimensions.
- *Includes a process for its ongoing improvement*—HEDIS 3.0 is a unique structure that includes not only the national standards for performance reporting but additional measures in development, which are included as a testing set of measures. These measures are included to signal to managed care plans which measures may be required in the future and to create the opportunity for NCQA to work with researchers, consumers, purchasers, and health plans to refine these measures prior to their widespread implementation.

How Is HEDIS 3.0 Different than Other Performance Measurement Efforts?

While HEDIS is the national standard in performance measurement for health plans, other measurement efforts are

*HEDIS® is a registered trademark of the National Committee for Quality Assurance.

underway. HEDIS differs from those efforts in the following ways:

- *HEDIS measures have a track record and are widely reported.* Purchasers and consumers want to be confident that health plan measurements are statistically valid and reflect real differences in health care. HEDIS measures are precisely defined, validated, and have been successfully used by more than 330 managed care organizations to date. There is ample evidence that these measures permit consumers and purchasers to distinguish between plans, and that they can be used to successfully track improvement or decline in the performance of health plans over time. Furthermore, surveys suggest that a majority of large employers already request HEDIS data from all of their health plans.
- *HEDIS measures are specifically designed to help purchasers and consumers make comparisons.* While there are many valid reasons for measurement (e.g., supporting internal improvement, tracking performance over time), not all measures have the statistical properties needed to detect differences between health plans in order to guide choice—and no other set of measures is designed specifically with that purpose in mind. In addition, not all measures are designed to be relevant to purchasers and consumers, but this is an explicit objective of HEDIS 3.0.

How Was HEDIS Developed?

HEDIS 3.0 was developed by a broad-based committee—the Committee on Performance Measurement (CPM) —whose members were chosen to reflect the diversity of constituencies that performance measurement must serve: purchasers, both private and public (Medicare and Medicaid); consumers; organized labor; medical providers; public health officials; and health plans. In addition, a number of other individuals were asked to serve on the CPM. They brought other important perspectives as well as additional expertise in the areas of quality management and the science of measurement. The CPM and its related subcommittees were organized and staffed by NCQA; funding for the work came from a variety of public and private sources.

Throughout the course of its work, the CPM was able to draw on a broad base of expertise and knowledge. To help its members understand what information was important to purchasers and consumers, the CPM commissioned an expert subcommittee to prepare a report on the information needs of Medicare; it reviewed the work of NCQA's Medicaid Workgroup, which, with funding from the David and Lucile Packard Foundation, had produced Medicaid HEDIS; it commissioned a synthesis of available knowledge about how privately insured consumers make choices about health plans, and brought a number of experts in that field to its meetings; and, with support from The Commonwealth Fund, it commissioned focus groups to get consumer reaction to possible HEDIS 3.0 measures. To help CPM members understand the science and state of the art in performance measurement, the Committee organized a Technical Advisory Committee (TAC) and commissioned papers by leading experts that laid out pressing and fundamental issues in the field. These papers and the TAC brought the necessary levels of scientific rigor to the CPM's deliberations.

When the CPM was launched in September 1995, it was charged with moving HEDIS 2.5 (already the most widely used tool in health plan performance measurement) to the next level. The group defined its development platform as the existing HEDIS measurement sets that were already in widespread use—those developed for commercial enrollees (HEDIS 2.5) and those developed for the Medicaid program (Medicaid HEDIS). The CPM's strategy was to integrate these measures into a single, nonduplicative set and then to expand those measures (where feasible and appropriate) to include the Medicare risk population. This platform represents a historic first: the integration of public and private reporting requirements in health care.

Next, the CPM mapped out a strategy to develop additional measures—not only for HEDIS 3.0, but for future generations of HEDIS—in order to continue evolving the set to ever more relevant and comprehensive levels. The CPM decided that it could best accomplish this by tapping the collective knowledge and expertise of clinical and measurement experts across the country. As a result, it laid out an open process for developing measures: one that began with the CPM requesting, through a public call for measures, proposals and suggestions for new measures. At the same time, the CPM developed criteria to systematically and objectively guide the evaluation and selection of measures that were submitted.

What Kind of Measures Was the CPM Looking For?

As part of this Public Call for Measures, the CPM described the basic aspects of health plan performance that are important to purchasers and consumers. These defined the eight performance domains for which measures were sought:

1. *Effectiveness of care*—The Committee's objective here was to develop measures that assess how well the care delivered by a managed care plan is achieving the clinical results that it should. Interest in this domain reflects a desire to establish that the health plan is responding to the needs of those who are ill ("Does the health plan

make me better when I am sick?") and also to the needs of the well ("Does the health plan keep me well when I am healthy?"). It also reflects a desire to establish that the plan can provide excellent results, not only for the sort of care that "I know I will need," or even that "I expect I will need," but also for the sort of care that "I hope I won't need (but will need desperately if I do)."

2. *Access/availability of care*—The Committee's objective here was to develop measures that permit us to assess whether care is available to members, when they need it, in a timely and convenient manner. The desire for information about the accessibility of health care is not only an expression of a belief that accessibility is a precondition to effective care but also of a belief that the managed care plan has responsibility for managing care so that it is available to those who need it.
3. *Satisfaction with the experience of care*—These measures are intended to provide information about whether a health plan is able to satisfy the diverse needs of its members. The desire for information in this area recognizes that members tell us important things about the care they receive. It reflects the opinion that encounters with the health plan should occur in a manner that is responsive to and respectful of the preferences and interests of its members, and that its members' satisfaction is the most revealing summary of the extent to which this is so.
4. *Cost of care*—The Committee was seeking measures that would permit the comparison of health plans based on the value of the services they deliver. To some extent, we can do so by evaluating the results they achieve (above) against the premium collected. However—and particularly for members—the cost of care is not only the premium they pay, but the additional and rising costs they face (out of pocket) for services that are not covered, or for services that involve copayment and/or deductibles.
5. *Stability of the health plan*—Health plan stability is important, because consumers make enrollment decisions that generally bind them for a year. Should the plan's network of providers change significantly, or should the plan become insolvent, the member's health care could be badly disrupted. The CPM hoped to provide some measures to help consumers estimate how likely these problems might be.
6. *Informed health care choices*—The Committee believes that an important objective of a good managed care plan should be to help members become active partners in their health care decisions. To do so means that the health plan must equip members to make informed choices about their care. The Committee's objective in defining this domain was to develop measures that would assess how effectively health plans accomplished that result.
7. *Use of services*—How a health plan uses its resources is a signal of how efficiently care is managed and whether or not needed services are being delivered; it may also provide some information about where there are opportunities to improve both the effectiveness and efficiency of care. The Committee recognized that these may be important, especially to those who purchase care, who want to know how their health care dollars are being spent, and if employees are getting what they need. The Committee's objective in laying out this domain was to develop measures that would permit users to understand patterns of service use across different health plans.
8. *Health plan descriptive information*—Finally, there is clear interest in some of the attributes and operating characteristics of the health plan itself—in particular, in a variety of elements of plan management (including a description of selected network, clinical, utilization, and risk management activities). While these are not performance measures per se, they are bits of information that consistently have been of interest to purchasers and consumers. Their standardization (in previous versions of HEDIS) has greatly increased the value of such information.

In each of these domains, the CPM sought measures that would help purchasers and consumers compare health plans. With the assistance of the members of the TAC, the CPM laid out a series of criteria that defined the attributes considered important for measures to possess, both for HEDIS 3.0 and future generations of HEDIS. These attributes fell into three major categories:

1. *Relevance*—Measures had to be relevant to purchasers and/or consumers if they were to be considered for inclusion in HEDIS 3.0. Measures were relevant to the extent that they addressed issues that were known to significantly affect health outcomes, to the extent that those issues were controllable (or at least could significantly be influenced) by the health plan, and to the extent that there was evidence that purchasers and/or consumers would use that information in selecting a health plan.
2. *Scientific soundness*—Measures had to be scientifically sound for the CPM to have confidence that the information produced through measurement would lead to better decisions. To ensure soundness, the Committee sought measures that were reproducible (i.e., produce the same results when repeated in the same populations and setting), valid (i.e., make sense logically and relate to other measures looking at the same aspect of care), and accurate (i.e., measure what is actually happening). Measures also had to have sufficient statistical power to detect differences of the magnitude

expected between health plans (or the measures would not be useful for comparison) and had to include a strategy to adjust results for other factors (such as characteristics of the health plan population) that might lead to measured differences in health plan results.

3. *Feasibility*—The CPM was interested in producing a measurement set that was useful in 1996. While it was unwilling to be tightly bound by the limitations of current information systems—an explicit objective of the CPM was to use HEDIS measures to stimulate improvements in those information systems—it was also clear that those potential HEDIS measures that were easy to produce would be of most value in the short run. In order to be feasible, a measure needed to be precisely defined in order to collect data in the same way, it had to be possible to produce the measure at a reasonable cost, and the collection of data for the measurement could not threaten the confidentiality of any patient information.

The CPM recognized that few available measures would be likely to have all of these attributes to the fullest extent, but agreed that the longer term requirements for HEDIS measures should be established and communicated. More than that, the Committee used these attributes to guide its evaluation of potential HEDIS measures, and to identify issues that could be resolved empirically where measures fell far short. This, of course, was part of the genesis of the HEDIS 3.0 Testing Set.

The domains and attributes were summarized in the CPM's December 1995 Public Call for Measures. That solicitation went out to more than 1,700 organizations; by March 1996, 826 measures (in various stages of development) had been submitted to NCQA. The value of this approach is that we now have a very good sense of the scope and depth of existing performance measures, and it enabled the CPM to cull the best from that mix.

How Were Measures Evaluated and Selected?

Between April and June 1996, the submitted measures were evaluated by NCQA staff, by a multidisciplinary review team of 17 experts (including members of the CPM, TAC, individuals involved in the development of earlier versions of HEDIS, and experts from outside the process), and by the CPM itself. The review team (and a second special panel, constituted to review measures in the area of behavioral health) used multivoting processes to choose subsets of the most promising measures.

These measures were then exhaustively worked up by experts. Again, the CPM was fortunate to be able to draw on the very best resources, including the scientific resources of the U.S. Centers for Disease Control and Prevention (CDC), the Agency for Health Care Policy and Research (AHCPR), the Health Care Financing Administration (HCFA), and the Rand Corporation, as well as a number of individuals who are among the leaders in their fields. In addition, the HEDIS Users Group—primarily a group of health plans that have worked with NCQA to improve earlier HEDIS measures—provided invaluable assistance developing the detailed specifications for potential measures. Workups analyzed available evidence relevant to each of the attributes important to the CPM; these analyses were summarized in 10- to 30-page papers that were provided to CPM members before meetings.

At the final CPM meetings, measures were voted into HEDIS 3.0. No measures were perfect—the CPM had to decide whether available evidence and expert judgment established that a measure was good enough to warrant inclusion in the Reporting Set. New measures that addressed important areas of interest or concern, but for which available evidence and expert judgment raised significant issues, were voted into the Testing Set.

Levels of agreement among the CPM members were high; many votes were unanimous or very nearly so.

As the CPM considered the addition of new measures, it also considered whether measures from earlier versions of HEDIS were still necessary. In fact, several old measures were retired, either because clearly superior measures were identified, or because experience had established that these measures were not sound or not feasible, or because the marginal value associated with a measure was small relative to the burden associated with its reporting. The issue of burden became more compelling as the size of HEDIS 3.0 grew.

The CPM struggled with issues related to the resources required to produce HEDIS, particularly in light of the fact that sizable sectors of the health care industry (fee-for-service insurance and non-HMO forms of managed care) are not faced with analogous measurement and reporting requirements. During its deliberations, the CPM considered the costs associated with the Reporting Set measures and sought input during the review and comment period on how the cost burden may be further reduced.

Where Do We Go Next?

HEDIS 3.0 will remain the standard in performance measurement until at least 1998, the earliest date a significant revision might be released. But the CPM's process will outlive 3.0 to ensure that HEDIS continues to evolve and improve. As it has already, the CPM will periodically define the important issues for which we need information and will issue periodic calls for new measures to address those areas. It will evaluate those new measures as it has already done—systematically, scientifically, and in collaboration with outside experts. But the CPM will have available to it a richer universe from which to draw, for the Testing Set will be a resource to the CPM for measures that have been cultivated specifically for the purpose of health plan comparison. And, as NCQA works with others to stimulate the development of completely new measures in areas where there is currently nothing yet even for testing, the field from which to draw will grow even larger and richer. This process predicts that HEDIS® will continually improve and will remain responsive to purchasers and consumers of health care.

NCQA HEDIS COMPLIANCE AUDIT PROGRAM

BACKGROUND

The National Committee for Quality Assurance (NCQA) assumed responsibility for management of the evolution of the Health Plan Employer Data and Information Set (HEDIS®*) in 1992, with one clear goal: to devise a standardized set of performance measures that could be used by various constituencies to compare health plans and thus help drive quality improvement in the market. Since the release of HEDIS 2.0 in 1993, the demand for health plan performance data has grown dramatically. HEDIS has been embraced by employers, consumer organizations, state and federal regulators, consultants, and health plans as the performance measurement tool of choice, and surveys indicate that almost 90 percent of all health plans collect and report at least some HEDIS data.

To encourage widespread reporting, NCQA has worked with a broad-based committee of experts to develop and improve HEDIS in order to ensure that it meets the information needs of all affected stakeholders—employers, consumers, regulators, and health plans.

Although HEDIS itself has been widely praised as a meaningful and important tool for health plan assessment, there has been strong interest from employers and others in developing a means by which to validate data collected and reported by health plans. It is recognized that, despite the clear specifications defined in HEDIS, data collection and calculation methods employed by health plans may vary, and other errors may taint the results, diminishing the usefulness of HEDIS data for managed care organization (MCO) comparison. NCQA's analysis of HEDIS data collected as part of a national report card pilot project and the *Quality Compass*SM initiative, and experience with numerous state and local projects, confirm that these are justifiable concerns.

In order for HEDIS to reach its full potential, NCQA and others concluded that an independent audit of HEDIS collection and reporting processes, as well as an audit of the data manipulated by those processes, would be necessary in order to ensure that HEDIS specifications are met. Purchasers, regulators, and health plans have asked NCQA to develop a consistent audit methodology for use by all HEDIS auditors. In response, in 1996 NCQA convened the Audit Committee to develop such audit standards. The committee developed a precise, standardized methodology for verifying the integrity of HEDIS collection and calculation processes—the NCQA HEDIS Compliance Audit.TM† It is a two-part program consisting of an overall information systems capabilities assessment (IS standards) followed by an evaluation of the MCO's ability to comply with HEDIS specifications (HD standards). NCQA-certified auditors using standard audit methodologies will help enable purchasers to make more reliable apples-to-apples comparisons among health plans.

*HEDIS® is a registered trademark of the National Committee for Quality Assurance.

†HEDIS Compliance AuditTM is a trademark of the National Committee for Quality Assurance.

PROGRAM ADMINISTRATION AND OVERVIEW

NCQA will ultimately license organizations and certify members of their staffs to conduct these audits using NCQA's standardized audit methodology. This program will train individuals to become NCQA-certified auditors, who will then conduct HEDIS compliance audits based on a standardized methodology. Auditors will use the first half of the audit, the overall IS review, to identify data areas to focus on during the second half of the review (HEDIS Compliance Standards). This will allow for customization of each audit depending on the individual health plan's strengths and weaknesses. The audit will add a higher degree of integrity to HEDIS data and will enable MCOs to provide consumers and purchasers with consistent and comparable HEDIS reports.

THE AUDIT STANDARDS

The audit standards address all HEDIS 3.0 measurement domains except Informed Health Care Choices. They were designed to complement other verification activities that already occur within health plans. As a result, the standards do not address information audited by other organizations (e.g., financial/accounting firms or state regulatory agencies), or information based on narrative descriptions of programs that are addressed in the NCQA Accreditation Standards.

The NCQA HEDIS Compliance Audit indicates whether or not a managed care organization has adequate and sound capabilities for processing medical, member, and provider information as a foundation for accurate and automated performance measurement, including HEDIS reporting. The audit addresses the following functions in both the IS and HD categories:

- information practices and control procedures
- sampling methods and procedures
- data integrity
- compliance with HEDIS specifications
- analytic file production
- reporting and documentation

The audit is principally designed to verify the compliance of HEDIS production processes with specifications, not to establish the accuracy of HEDIS results. However, auditors will verify a sample of HEDIS measures to confirm that HEDIS results are based on accurate source information. The focus of the audit is on data management processes and algorithmic compliance (the translation of captured data into HEDIS statistics, according to the specifications defined by NCQA). Health plans may report additional information beyond the technical requirements of HEDIS. For example, plans may report comparisons to benchmarks, norms, or past HEDIS performance (trended data). Validating the use of such external data, however, is beyond the scope of the NCQA HEDIS Compliance Audit, which focuses on the technical aspects of how HEDIS data are produced.

continues

NCQA HEDIS Compliance Audit Program continued

Information System Capabilities Standards

The first part of each HEDIS Compliance Audit consists of a review of a health plan's overall information systems capabilities. Relevant standards address the basic capabilities a managed care organization has in place for collecting, storing, analyzing, and reporting health information. The managed care organization must have adequate capabilities for processing medical, member, and provider information as a foundation for accurate HEDIS reporting. The plan must also demonstrate the adequacy of its procedures, where manual processes are used, including medical record review processes. In short, a managed care organization must demonstrate effective systems, information practices, and control procedures for producing and using information in core business functions for auditors to have confidence in its HEDIS reporting.

Compliance with HEDIS Specifications Standards

The Standards and Guidelines for Assessing Specification Compliance assume that the auditor has completed the Information Systems Capabilities Assessment. Once the auditor has gained an understanding of the MCO information systems through this assessment, the auditor is able to design appropriate verification audit steps pertaining to specific HEDIS measures. In general, this section addresses compliance with conventional reporting practices and HEDIS specifications for the following domains:

- Effectiveness of Care
- Access/Availability of Care
- Use of Services
- Satisfaction with the Experience of Care—exclusively verification of third-party administration
- Health Plan Stability—select measures only
- Other Miscellaneous Measures (High-Cost DRGs, Board Certification)

Standards do *not* apply to most performance indicators in the Informed Health Care Choices, Cost of Care, and Health Plan Descriptive Information domains. The information reported in these areas is generally either based on narrative descriptions of programs that are not readily assessed by objective audit standards and validation methods, or is audited by independent certified public accountants for presentation in corporate financial statements and other publicly available information. Indicators of the managed care organization's financial and business position are audited by state regulators as well, and differ based on the requirements mandated by each state. These standards do not attempt to duplicate audit efforts and increase audit burden; rather, they attempt to cover measures that are generally not reviewed by others.

CERTIFICATION EXAMINATION AND PILOT TESTING

NCQA is currently developing a qualifying exam with the Chauncey Group, a division of the Educational Testing Service (ETS), which individuals must pass before being designated NCQA-certified auditors. The exam will consist, in part, of an audit of a hypothetical health plan's HEDIS processes against NCQA's standards. Auditors must take and pass the exam biannually in order to maintain certification. The first exam was administered by NCQA this past November.

Pilot testing was completed in August 1997, and will give NCQA a chance to fine-tune auditing methodologies. Following the conclusion of pilot testing, a Certification Methodologies Manual will be available for individuals going through the first round of training and examination for certification. At this time, NCQA will also begin licensing organizations to conduct HEDIS Compliance Audits. Individuals taking the certification exam must be employed by or contract with an NCQA-licensed organization and at the successful completion of the examination perform a minimum of two HEDIS Compliance Audits a year. Certification of individual auditors and licensing of qualified organizations will help ensure that standard auditing methodologies are used during all NCQA HEDIS Compliance Audits.

CONCLUSION

NCQA is committed to encouraging the broad use of HEDIS data by employers, consumers, and others to compare health plans. NCQA's HEDIS Compliance Audit™ Standards provide a national standard for auditing health plans' HEDIS® collection and reporting processes, thus allowing for accurate, apples-to-apples comparisons of performance data among plans. This will encourage value-based purchasing, which will, in turn, allow health plans to compete based on quality and value rather than on cost.

HEALTH LEVEL SEVEN (HL7)

OVERVIEW OF HEALTH LEVEL SEVEN (HL7)

BACKGROUND

HL7 was founded in 1987 to develop standards for the electronic interchange of clinical, financial, and administrative information among independent health care–oriented computer systems, e.g., hospital information systems, clinical laboratory systems, enterprise systems, and pharmacy systems.

In the last six years its membership has more than tripled to over 1,700 health industry members, including almost all of the major health care information systems consultants and vendors. The HL7 standard is supported by most health care information system vendors and used in the majority of large U.S. hospitals today. It is also used internationally in such countries as Australia, Austria, Belgium, Canada, Finland, Germany, Holland, Israel, Japan, New Zealand, and the United Kingdom. In fact, some countries have been so active with HL7 that they have formally launched local HL7 affiliate organizations, including HL7 Canada, HL7 Germany, HL7 Japan, HL7 New Zealand, HL7 The Netherlands, HL7 Finland, and HL7 Australia.

In June 1994, HL7 was designated by thc Amcrican National Standards Institute (ANSI) as an ANSI accredited standards developer. In February 1996, ANSI announced that the HL7 standard version 2.2 had been approved as an American National Standard. The HL7 standard version 2.3 was approved as an American National Standard in May 1997.

In late 1995 and throughout 1996 and 1997, HL7 dedicated resources to the acceleration of its version 3.0 standard. Such resources will enable HL7 to develop the version 3.0 standard in a much quicker time frame and still follow the ANSI balloting procedures.

HL7 TRANSACTIONS

The current standard (version 2.3) defines transactions for transmitting data about patient registration, admission, discharge and transfers, insurance, charges and payers, orders and results for laboratory tests, image studies, nursing and physician observations, diet orders, pharmacy orders, supply orders, master files, appointment scheduling, problem lists, clinical trial enrollments, patient permissions, voice dictations, advanced directives, and physiologic signals. Task forces in HL7 are also busy developing prototype transactions with new state-of-the-art technologies such as CORBA and Microsoft's OLE objects.

COOPERATION WITH OTHER STANDARDS-DEVELOPING ORGANIZATIONS

HL7 has a pure focus on health care informatics standards and cooperates closely with other standards developers such as American Society for Testing and Materials (ASTM), Accredited Standards Committee X12N (ASC X12N), American College of Radiology (ACR), National Electrical Manufacturers Association (NEMA), National Council for Prescription Drug Programs (NCPDP), and Institute of Electronics and Electrical Engineers (IEEE) directly and via the ANSI Health Informatics Standards Board, formerly the ANSI Health Informatics Planning Panel. Examples of such cooperative efforts include planning future joint (meetings with X12N, cross-copyrights with ASTM, and hosting joint working group meetings with IEEE, ACR, NEMA, and ASTM.

HL7 has pioneered the provision of its minutes and standard drafts at no cost through Internet FTP servers on the Internet (dumccss.mc.duke.edu) and supports a discussion group on the HL7@virginia.edu list server. We encourage other standards organizations to do the same.

HL7 also maintains two World Wide Web home pages on the Internet. The addresses are http:\\www.hl7.org and http://www.mcis.duke.edu/standards/HL7/hl7.htm

THE GOALS AND SCOPE OF HL7

What Is HL7?

HL7 is a standard for electronic data exchange in health care environments. It endeavors to standardize the format and protocol for the exchange of certain key sets of data among health care computer application systems. HL7 is accredited by ANSI to write these standards.

As with almost all United States standards, HL7 standards are voluntary consensus standards. There is no governmental mandate to use HL7, except in very limited circumstances. HL7 follows procedures that have been approved by ANSI for review and ballot to ensure that the standard represents a consensus view of a balance of users and producers of health care information systems.

HL7 is also the name of the group that publishes these standards.

What Is the Functional Scope of the HL7 Standard?

The standard currently addresses the interfaces among various systems that send or receive paticnt admissions/registration, discharge or transfer (ADT) data, queries, orders, results, clinical observations, billing, master file update information, health records, referrals, scheduling, and patient care. There are also HL7 standards for recording immunizations and drug reactions.

What Application Architecture Is HL7 Based On?

It tries not to assume a particular architecture with respect to the placement of data within applications. In particular, it is designed to support a central patient care system as well as a more

continues

Overview of Health Level Seven (HL7) continued

distributed environment where data reside in departmental systems. There is support for environments where there is no order entry system, a central order entry system, or multiple systems that can originate orders. There is support for environments where results data and observations reside on a single system or where they are distributed among several systems.

What Is Implied by the Phrase "Level Seven"?

The term *Level 7* refers to the highest level of the Open System Interconnection (OSI) model of the International Standards Organization (ISO). In the OSI conceptual model, the communications functions are separated into seven levels. Those developing the HL7 standard are primarily focused on the issues that occur within the seventh, or application, level. These are the definitions of the application data to be exchanged, the timing of the exchanges, and the communication of certain application-specific errors between the applications. Specifications at this level are referred to in the HL7 argot as *abstract message specifications.*

However, as a matter of pragmatic necessity, the HL7 specifications also define the presentation of the information, that is to say the strings of text that represent it. HL7 refers to these as the *encoding rules.* This represents Level 6 of the OSI conceptual framework. Most HL7 implementations use the HL7 encoding rules. However, there is an "out" in the current HL7 specifications. An implementation that follows the abstract message specifications but uses different encoding rules can claim to be HL7 conformant. There have been implementations using ASN.1 and LU6.2 to encode the data fields.

HL7 does not specify standards for communicating the character strings from one system to another. Several recommended lower-layer protocols were published as appendices to HL7 version 2.1. These can be used for implementing HL7 over serial lines and using TCP/IP. These will be republished, essentially unchanged, in the implementation guide for version 2.2. However, implementations using other lower layer protocols may claim HL7 compliance.

What Are the Goals of the HL7 Effort?

HL7's purpose is to facilitate communication in health care settings. The primary goal is to provide standards for the exchange of data among health care computer applications that eliminate or substantially reduce the custom interface programming and program maintenance that may otherwise be required. This primary goal can be delineated as a set of objectives.

- The standard should support exchanges among systems implemented in the widest variety of technical environments. Its implementation should be practical in a wide variety of programming languages and operating systems. It should also support communications in a wide variety of communications environments, ranging from a TCP/IP network stack to point-to-point RS-232C interconnections, as well as the transfer of data by batch media such as floppy disk and tape.
- Immediate transfer of single transactions should be supported along with bulk transfers of multiple transactions.
- The greatest possible degree of standardization should be achieved, consistent with site variations in the usage and format of certain data elements. The standard should accommodate necessary site-specific variations. This will include, at least, site-specific tables, code definitions, and possibly site-specific message segments.
- The standard must support evolutionary growth as new requirements are recognized. This includes support of the process of introducing extensions and new releases into existing operational environments.
- The standard should be built on the experience of existing production protocols and accepted industrywide standard protocols. It should not, however, favor the proprietary interests of specific companies to the detriment of other users of the standard.
- Initial versions of the standard focused on information systems within hospitals; versions 2.2 and 2.3 substantially expand coverage to define formats and protocols for computer applications in all health care environments.
- The very nature of the diverse business processes that exist within the health care delivery system prevents the development of either a universally agreed-on process or data model to support a definition of HL7's target environments. In addition, HL7 does not make a priori assumptions about the architecture of health care information systems nor does it attempt to resolve architectural differences between health care information systems. For these reasons, HL7 cannot be a true plug and play interface standard. These differences at HL7 sites will require site-negotiated agreements.
- The initial interest of the HL7 working group was to employ the standard as soon as possible. Having achieved this, HL7 has been approved by ANSI for recognition as an Accredited Standards Organization (ASO).
- Cooperation with related health care standards efforts (e.g., ACR/NEMA DICOM, ASC X12, ASTM, IEEE, NCPDP, etc.) has become a priority activity of HL7.

Source: Health Level Seven, Ann Arbor, Michigan.

ELECTRONIC DATA INTERCHANGE (EDI)

WORKGROUP FOR ELECTRONIC DATA INTERCHANGE (WEDi) GUIDING PRINCIPLES

WEDi's goal is to promote focused collaboration among the diverse community of health care industry stakeholders in a manner that achieves rapid implementation of electronic commerce utilizing appropriate cost-effective best practices. Guiding principles supporting this goal include

- stakeholder inclusiveness
- electronic data interchange (EDI) standards
- data protection
- administrative cost performance
- innovation

STAKEHOLDER INCLUSIVENESS

Electronic commerce should meet the needs of all stakeholders including consumers, employers, payers, providers, standards organizations, vendors, health insurers, and government agencies.

- Industrywide collaboration among health care stakeholders and their affiliated associations should be advanced through various forums to resolve impediments and to ensure the most effective use of electronic commerce.
- The scope of health care electronic commerce spans local, regional, national, and international community boundaries.
- Market competition should be valued as a means to achieve cost-effective electronic commerce.

ELECTRONIC DATA INTERCHANGE (EDI) STANDARDS

The creation, implementation, and continuous improvement of health care electronic commerce transactions useful to all stakeholders should be based on a recognized standards promulgation process conducted by appropriate standards-setting organizations.

- The standards development, version control, and testing processes should promote cost-effective best practices that facilitate rapid stakeholder adoption of the transaction protocols needed to take full advantage of electronic commerce.
- Beneficial use of EDI standards and implementation guides requires industrywide acceptance and adoption by all stakeholders.
- The benefits of EDI standards should be communicated to all stakeholders.

DATA PROTECTION

Federal preemptive legislation is required to preserve the confidentiality of health care information and to protect the data privacy of our citizens in the health care electronic commerce environment; therefore:

- Federal data privacy legislation should do the following:
  - Preempt state laws, except public health reporting laws, that inhibit the use of EDI for health care transactions.
  - Protect identifiable health care information wherever located and however obtained.
  - Designate an impartial entity to administer and enforce the law.
  - Be straightforward, provide for rapid implementation, and be easily enforced.
  - Provide appropriate civil and criminal penalties for violations.
- In addition, federal standards for privacy protection should guarantee a person's right to know that personal information is collected, stored, and processed and for what purpose it is used; ensure that the information is disclosed and used for a legitimate purpose; require persons to be notified of their privacy rights; and require implementation of standards and controls promulgated by the agency administering the law.

ADMINISTRATIVE COST PERFORMANCE

The urgency of the present should be a shared industrywide attitude that drives significant improvement in transaction processing cost performance for the many health care trading partners seeking full benefits from the use of electronic commerce.

- Establishing standard national identifiers for patients, providers, and payers is a priority that should be aggressively pursued so stakeholders can achieve maximum network transaction efficiencies and cost reduction.
- Adoption by stakeholders of industry best practices as they emerge from implementation of EDI standards is vital for the following transaction examples:
  - enrollment
  - eligibility verification and beneficiary plan coverage
  - appointment and managed care service authorization

continues

WEDi Guiding Principles continued

- claim submission
- payment remittance and electronic funds transfer
- materials management, orders, and payment

INNOVATION

The national information infrastructure needed for present and future generations of health care electronic commerce systems should have broad public and private stakeholder participation in its definition and development.

- Documented results of improved quality and administrative cost-effectiveness of new health information networks utilizing electronic commerce capabilities should be shared for the benefit of all stakeholders.
- Timely implementation of solutions to problems in electronic commerce should be added to the installed technology base where appropriate.
- Open hardware and software standards should be incorporated into new systems technology supporting electronic commerce.

JOINT COMMISSION STANDARDS/ REQUIREMENTS

1998 JOINT COMMISSION STANDARDS FOR INFORMATION MANAGEMENT

Management of Information

Overview

The **goal** of the information-management function* is to obtain, manage, and use information to improve patient outcomes and individual and hospital performance in patient care, governance, management, and support processes.

Delivering health care to patients is a complex endeavor that is highly dependent on information.[†] Hospitals rely on information about the science of care, individual patients, care provided, results of care, as well as its performance to provide, coordinate, and integrate services. Like human, material, and financial resources, information is a resource that must be managed effectively by the hospital's leaders.

To achieve this goal, the following processes are performed well:

- Identifying information needs;
- Designing the structure of the information-management system;
- Defining and capturing[‡] data[§] and information;
- Analyzing data and transforming[**] it into information;
- Transmitting[††] and reporting data and information; and
- Integrating and using information.

This chapter focus on the performance of these processes in managing

- patient-specific data and information;
- aggregate data and information;
- expert knowledge-based information[‡‡]; and
- comparative performance data and information.

The standards in this chapter focus on organizationwide information planning and management processes to meet the organization's internal and external information needs. They describe a vision for effectively and continuously improving information management in health care organizations. Achieving this vision involves

- ensuring timely and easy access to complete information throughout the hospital;
- improving data accuracy;
- balancing requirements of security[§§] and ease of access;

* **function** A goal-directed, interrelated series of processes, such continuum of care or management of information.

[†] **information** Interpreted set(s) of data that can assist in decision making.

[‡] **data capture** The acquisition or recording of data and information.

[§] **data** Uninterpreted material, facts, or clinical observations.

[**] **data transformation** The process of changing the form of data representation, for example, changing data into information using decision-analysis tools.

[††] **data transmission** The sending of data or information from one location to another.

[‡‡] **knowledge-based information** A collection of stored facts, models, and information found in the clinical, scientific, and management literature that can be used for designing and redesigning processes and for problem solving.

[§§] **data security** The protection of data from intentional or unintentional destruction, modification, or disclosure.

continues

1998 Joint Commission Standards for Information Management continued

- using aggregate* and comparative data to pursue opportunities for improvement;
- redesigning information-related processes to improve efficiency; and
- increasing collaboration and information sharing to enhance patient care.

While efficiency may be improved by computerization and other technologies, the principles of good information management apply to all methods, whether paper-based or electronic. These standards are designed to be equally compatible with noncomputerized systems and future technologies.

* **aggregate** To combine standardized data and information.

continues

1998 Joint Commission Standards for Information Management continued

Standards

The following is a list of all standards for this function. If you have a question about a term used here, please check the Glossary, pages 279 through 304. Terms that are critical to the understanding of the standard are defined in the margin adjacent to the term as it appears in the next section of this chapter.

IM.1 The hospital plans and designs information-management processes to meet internal and external information needs.

IM.1.1 Internal and external information-management processes are appropriate for the hospital's size and the complexity of its services.

IM.1.1.1 The hospital bases management, staffing, and material resource allocations for information management on the scope and complexity of services provided.

IM.1.1.2 Appropriate clinical and administrative staff participate in assessing the hospital's information needs, and in selecting, integrating, and using information-management technology.

IM.2 *Confidentiality, security, and integrity of data and information are maintained.*

IM.2.1 The hospital determines appropriate levels of security and confidentiality for data and information.

IM.2.2 Collection, storage, and retrieval systems are designed to allow timely and easy use of data and information without compromising its security and confidentiality.

IM.2.3 Records and information are protected against loss, destruction, tampering, and unauthorized access or use.

IM.3 *Uniform data definitions and data capture methods are used whenever possible.*

IM.3.1 Minimum data sets, data definitions, codes, classifications, and terminology are standardized whenever possible.

IM.3.2 The hospital collects data in a timely, economic, and efficient manner and with the degree of accuracy, completeness, and discrimination necessary for their intended use.

IM.3.2.1 Medical records are reviewed on an ongoing basis for completeness and timeliness of information, and action is taken to improve the quality and timeliness of documentation that impacts patient care.

IM.3.2.1.1 A representative sample of records is included in the review process.

IM.4 Decision makers and other appropriate staff members are educated and trained in the principles of information management.

continues

1998 Joint Commission Standards for Information Management continued

IM.5 Transmission of data and information is timely and accurate.

IM.5.1 The format and methods for disseminating data and information are standardized, whenever possible.

IM.6 Adequate integration and interpretation capabilities are provided.

IM.6.1 The hospital determines how long medical record information is retained, based on law and regulation and the information use for patient care, legal, research, and educational purposes.

IM.7 *The hospital defines, captures, analyzes, transforms, transmits, and reports patient-specific data and information related to care processes and outcomes.*

IM.7.1 The hospital initiates and maintains a medical record for every individual assessed or treated.

IM.7.1.1 Only authorized individuals make entries in medical records.

IM.7.2 The medical record contains sufficient information to identify the patient, support the diagnosis, justify the treatment, document the course and results, and promote continuity of care among health care providers.

IM.7.3 *The medical record thoroughly documents operative or other procedures and the use of anesthesia.*

IM.7.3.1 A preoperative diagnosis is recorded before surgery by the licensed independent practitioner responsible for the patient.

IM.7.3.2 Operative reports dictated or written immediately after surgery record the name of the primary surgeon and assistants, findings, technical procedures used, specimens removed, and postoperative diagnosis.

IM.7.3.2.1 The completed operative report is authenticated by the surgeon and filed in the medical record as soon as possible after surgery.

IM.7.3.2.2 When the operative report is not placed in the medical record immediately after surgery, a progress note is entered immediately.

IM.7.3.3 Postoperative documentation records the patient's vital signs and level of consciousness; medications (including intravenous fluids), blood, and blood components; any unusual events or postoperative complications; and management of such events.

IM.7.3.4 *Postoperative documentation records the patient's discharge from the postanesthesia care area by the responsible licensed independent practitioner or according to discharge criteria.*

continues

1998 Joint Commission Standards for Information Management continued

IM.7.3.4.1 Compliance with discharge criteria is fully documented in the patient's medical record.

IM.7.3.5 Postoperative documentation records the name of the licensed independent practitioner responsible for discharge.

IM.7.4 For patients receiving continuing ambulatory care services, the medical record contains a summary list of known significant diagnoses, conditions, procedures, drug allergies, and medications.

IM.7.4.1 The list is initiated for each patient by the third visit and maintained thereafter.

IM.7.5 When emergency, urgent, or immediate care is provided, the time and means of arrival are also documented in the medical record.

IM.7.5.1 The medical record notes when a patient receiving emergency, urgent, or immediate care left against medical advice.

IM.7.5.2 The medical record of a patient receiving emergency, urgent, or immediate care notes the conclusions at termination of treatment, including final disposition, condition at discharge, and instructions for follow-up care.

IM.7.5.3 When authorized by the patient or a legally authorized representative, a copy of the emergency services provided is available to the practitioner or medical organization providing follow-up care.

IM.7.6 Medical record data and information are managed in a timely manner.

IM.7.7 Verbal orders of authorized individuals are accepted and transcribed by qualified personnel who are identified by title or category in the medical staff rules and regulations.

IM.7.8 Every medical record entry is dated, its author identified, and, when necessary, authenticated.

IM.7.9 The hospital can quickly assemble and have access to all relevant information from components of a patient's record when the patient is admitted or is seen for ambulatory or emergency care.

IM.8 The hospital collects and analyzes aggregate data to support patient care and operations.

IM.9 The hospital provides systems, resources, and services to meet its needs for knowledge-based information in patient care, education, research, and management.

IM.9.1 The hospital's knowledge-based information resources are available, authoritative, and up to date.

continues

1998 Joint Commission Standards for Information Management continued

IM.9.2 The hospital's services, resources, and systems for knowledge-based information are based on a needs assessment.

IM.10 *Comparative performance data and information are defined, collected, analyzed, transmitted, reported, and used consistent with national and state guidelines for data set parity and connectivity.*

IM.10.1 The hospital uses external reference databases for comparative purposes.

IM.10.2 The hospital contributes to external reference databases when required by law or regulation or when appropriate to the hospital.

IM.10.3 The security and confidentiality of data and information are maintained when contributing to or using external databases.

continues

1998 Joint Commission Standards for Information Management continued

Standards and Intent Statements for Information Management Planning

Standard

IM.1 The hospital plans and designs information-management processes to meet internal and external information needs.

Intent of IM.1

A comprehensive needs assessment considers the following questions, as appropriate:

- What is the hospital's type, structure, size, and complexity?
- What are the needs of information users, including governance, leaders, clinical staff, inpatients, outpatients, patients' families, payers, purchasers, regulatory bodies, and accrediting bodies?
- What data and information does the hospital need to support planning?
- What data and information are needed for research and education?
- What are the relevant national and state guidelines for data set parity* and data connectivity† in interfacing information systems?
- What are the hospital's internal and external transmission requirements?
- What are the hospital's reporting needs over time (longitudinal reporting)?
- What data and information are needed for continuous performance improvement?
- What data and information does the hospital need to compare current performance with past performance? For benchmarking? For comparison with practice guidelines or parameters?
- What technology is appropriate?
- What technology is affordable?
- What does the hospital need to support customer and supplier relationships?
- What data and information does the hospital need to enhance cost-effectiveness (for example, to analyze resource use by patients with particular problems)?
- What data and information are needed to enhance work flow?
- What are the hospital's information requirements to support clinical and administrative decision making?
- Is the hospital planning to expand or redesign any services, such as library services, medical records, and computer services?
- What long-range plans are likely to affect the hospital's information needs?

The organization identifies its needs based on its

- mission;
- goals;
- services;
- personnel;
- mode(s) of service delivery (for example, hospital, home care facility, ambulatory);
- resources; and
- access to affordable technology.

* **data parity** The degree to which data are equivalent.

† **data connectivity** The ability to link data from different sources or systems.

continues

1998 Joint Commission Standards for Information Management continued

Standards

IM.1.1 Internal and external information-management processes are appropriate for the hospital's size and the complexity of its services.

IM.1.1.1 The hospital bases management, staffing, and material resource allocations for information management on the scope and complexity of services provided.

IM.1.1.2 Appropriate clinical and administrative staff participate in assessing the hospital's information needs, and in selecting, integrating, and using information-management technology.

Intent of IM.1.1 Through IM.1.1.2

Hospitals vary in size, complexity, governance, structure, decision-making processes, and resources. Information-management systems and processes vary accordingly. The hospital bases its information-management processes on a thorough analysis of internal and external information needs. The analysis considers what data and information are needed within and among departments, the medical staff, the administration, and the governing body, as well as information needed to support relationships with outside services, companies, and agencies. Leaders seek input from staff in a variety of areas and services. Appropriate individuals ensure that required data and information are provided efficiently for patient care, research, education, and management at every level.

Standards

IM.2 *Confidentiality,* security, and integrity† of data and information are maintained.*

IM.2.1 The hospital determines appropriate levels of security and confidentiality for data and information.

IM.2.2 Collection, storage, and retrieval systems are designed to allow timely and easy use of data and information without compromising its security and confidentiality.

IM.2.3 Records and information are protected against loss, destruction, tampering, and unauthorized access or use.

Intent of IM.2 Through IM.2.3

The hospital maintains the security and confidentiality of data and information, and is especially careful about preserving the confidentiality of sensitive data and information. The balance between data sharing and data confidentiality is addressed. The hospital determines the level of security and confidentiality maintained for different categories of information. Access to each category of information is based on need and defined by job title and function. An effective process defines

a. who has access to information;
b. the information to which an individual has access;
c. the user's obligation to keep information confidential;
d. when release of health information or removal of the medical record is permitted;

* **confidentiality** Restriction of access to data and information to individuals who have need, a reason, and permission for such access.

† **data integrity** The accuracy, consistency, and completeness of data.

continues

1998 Joint Commission Standards for Information Management continued

e. how information is protected against unauthorized intrusion, corruption, or damage; and
f. the process followed when confidentiality and security are violated.

Hospital policy establishes that medical records may be removed from the hospital's jurisdiction and safekeeping only under a court order, subpoena, or statute.

The hospital addresses items a through f whenever it implements any new data and information collection, storage, and retrieval system(s).

Standards

IM.3 *Uniform data definitions* and data capture methods are used whenever possible.*

IM.3.1 Minimum data sets,† data definitions, codes, classifications, and terminology are standardized whenever possible.

IM.3.2 The hospital collects data in a timely, economic, and efficient manner and with the degree of accuracy, completeness, and discrimination necessary for their intended use.

Intent of IM.3 Through IM.3.2

Standardizing terminology, definitions, vocabulary, and nomenclature facilitates comparison of data and information within and among organizations. Abbreviations and symbols are also standardized. Uniformly applied and accepted definitions, codes, classifications, and terminology support data aggregation and analysis and provide criteria for decision analysis. Quality control systems are used to monitor data content and collection activities, and to ensure timely and economical data collection. Standardization is consistent with recognized state and federal standards. The hospital minimizes bias‡ in the data and regularly assesses the data's reliability,§ validity,** and accuracy.††

Standards

IM.3.2.1 Medical records are reviewed on an ongoing basis for completeness and timeliness of information, and action is taken to improve the quality and timeliness of documentation that impacts patient care.

IM.3.2.1.1 A representative sample of records is included in the review process.

Intent of IM.3.2.1 Through IM.3.2.1.1

The review of medical records addresses the presence, timeliness, legibility, and authentication of the following data and information, as appropriate to the organization's needs:

* **data definition** The identification of the data to be used in analysis.

† **minimum data set** An agreed-on and accepted set of terms and definitions constituting a core of data; a collection of related data items.

‡ **bias** An influence on results that causes them to routinely depart from the true value.

§ **data reliability** The stability, repeatability, or precision of the data.

** **data validity** Verification of correctness; reflects the true situation.

†† **data accuracy** The extent to which data are free of errors.

continues

1998 Joint Commission Standards for Information Management continued

- Identification data;
- Medical history, including the chief complaint; details of the present illness; relevant past, social, and family histories (appropriate to the patient's age); and an inventory by body system;
- A summary of the patient's psychosocial needs, as appropriate to the patient's age;
- A report of relevant physical examinations;
- A statement on the conclusions or impressions drawn from the admission history and physical examination;
- A statement on the course of action planned for the patient for this episode of care and of its periodic review, as appropriate;
- Diagnostic and therapeutic orders;
- Evidence of appropriate informed consent;
- Clinical observations, including the results of therapy;
- Progress notes made by the medical staff and other authorized staff;
- Consultation reports;
- Reports of operative and other invasive procedures, tests, and their results;
- Reports of any diagnostic and therapeutic procedures, such as pathology and clinical laboratory examinations and radiology and nuclear medicine examinations or treatments;
- Records of donation and receipt of transplants or implants;
- Final diagnosis(es);
- Conclusions at termination of hospitalization;
- Clinical resumes and discharge summaries;
- Discharge instructions to the patient or family; and
- When performed, results of autopsy.

Medical record review is based on a representative sample (a sample representing the practitioners providing care and of the care provided). The review process is conducted by the medical staff, nursing, and other relevant clinical professionals. The focus of the review is on information available at the point of care.

It is expected that findings from the medical record review, as well as medical record completion statistics, will be available for at least quarterly review and are evident in the reports of this review function (for example, medical record committee minutes or medical executive committee minutes).

Standard

IM.4 Decision makers and other appropriate staff members are educated and trained in the principles of information management.

Intent of IM.4

Individuals in the organization who generate, collect, analyze, and use data and information are educated and trained to effectively participate in managing information. This education and training enable these individuals to

- understand security and confidentiality of data and information;
- use measurement instruments, statistical tools, and data analysis methods for transforming data into relevant information;
- collect unbiased data, gathered with a control for confounding or corrected on the basis of acceptable methodologies;
- assist in interpreting data;

continues

1998 Joint Commission Standards for Information Management continued

- use data and information to help in decision making;
- educate and support the participation of patients and family in care processes; and
- use indicators to assess and improve systems and processes over time.

Individuals are educated and trained as appropriate to their responsibilities, privileges, job descriptions, and data and information needs.

Standards

IM.5 Transmission of data and information is timely and accurate.

IM.5.1 The format and methods for disseminating data and information are standardized, whenever possible.

Intent of IM.5 and IM.5.1

Internally and externally generated data and information are accurately transmitted to users. The integrity of data and information is maintained, and there is adequate communication between data users and suppliers. The timing of transmission is appropriate to the data's intended use.

The format and methods of disseminating internal data and information are tailored to the needs of users and the hospital. Dissemination methods and formats provide for easy retrieval. The means by which data and information are exchanged is standardized whenever possible to facilitate interpretation.

Standards

IM.6 Adequate integration and interpretation capabilities are provided.

IM.6.1 The hospital determines how long medical record information is retained, based on law and regulation and the information use for patient care, legal, research, and educational purposes.

Intent of IM.6 and IM.6.1

The information-management process makes it possible to combine information from various sources and generate reports to support decision making. Specifically, the information-management process

a. coordinates collection of information;
b. makes information from one system available to another (for example, between clinical and organizational systems);
c. organizes data;
d. analyzes data;
e. interprets and clarifies data; and
f. generates and provides access to longitudinal data.

In addition, the information-management process provides the capability to link

g. patient care and nonpatient care data over time and among all care settings;
h. internal and external information sources;
i. patient care data and information from clinical literature; and
j. organizational data and management literature.

Data and information are retained for sufficient periods to comply with law and regulation and support patient care, management, legal documentation, research, and education.

continues

1998 Joint Commission Standards for Information Management continued

Standards and Intent Statements for Patient-Specific Data and Information

Standards

IM.7 *The hospital defines, captures, analyzes, transforms, transmits, and reports patient-specific data and information related to care processes and outcomes.*

IM.7.1 The hospital initiates and maintains a medical record for every individual assessed or treated.

IM.7.1.1 Only authorized individuals make entries in medical records.

IM.7.2 The medical record contains sufficient information to identify the patient, support the diagnosis, justify the treatment, document the course and results, and promote continuity of care among health care providers.

Intent of IM.7 Through IM.7.2

Information-management processes provide for the use of patient-specific data and information to

- facilitate patient care;
- serve as a financial and legal record;
- aid in clinical research;
- support decision analysis; and
- guide professional and organizational performance improvement.

To facilitate consistency and continuity in patient care, specific data and information are required. Administrative and direct patient care providers produce and use this information for professional and organization improvement. Medical records contain sufficient information to

- identify the patient;
- support the diagnosis;
- justify the treatment;
- document the course and results; and
- facilitate continuity of care.

The environment in which patient-specific information is provided supports timely, accurate, secure, and confidential recording and use of patient-specific information. The system recalls historical patient data and is able to furnish data about current encounters. To facilitate consistency and continuity in patient care, the medical record contains very specific data and information, including

a. the patient's name, address, date of birth, and the name of any legally authorized representative;
b. the legal status of patients receiving mental health services;
c. emergency care provided to the patient prior to arrival, if any;
d. the record and findings of the patient's assessment*;
e. conclusions or impressions drawn from the medical history and physical examination;
f. the diagnosis or diagnostic impression;
g. the reasons for admission or treatment;
h. the goals of treatment and the treatment plan;

* See the "Assessment of Patients" chapter.

continues

1998 Joint Commission Standards for Information Management continued

i. evidence of known advance directives;
j. evidence of informed consent, when required by hospital policy;
k. diagnostic and therapeutic orders, if any;
l. all diagnostic and therapeutic procedures and test results;
m. all operative and other invasive procedures performed, using acceptable disease and operative terminology that includes etiology, as appropriate;
n. progress notes made by the medical staff and other authorized individuals;
o. all reassessments and any revisions of the treatment plan;
p. clinical observations;
q. the patient's response to care;
r. consultation reports;
s. every medication ordered or prescribed for an inpatient;
t. every medication dispensed to an ambulatory patient or an inpatient on discharge;
u. every dose of medication administered and any adverse drug reaction;
v. all relevant diagnoses established during the course of care;
w. any referrals and communications made to external or internal care providers and to community agencies;
x. conclusions at termination of hospitalization;
y. discharge instructions to the patient and family; and
z. clinical resumes and discharge summaries, or a final progress note or transfer summary.

A concise clinical resume included in the medical record at discharge provides important information to other caregivers and facilitates continuity of care. For patients discharged to ambulatory (outpatient) care, the clinical resume summarizes previous levels of care. The discharge summary contains the following information:

- The reason for hospitalization;
- Significant findings;
- Procedures performed and treatment rendered;
- The patient's condition at discharge; and
- Instructions to the patient and family, if any.

For normal newborns with uncomplicated deliveries, or for patients hospitalized for less than 48 hours with only minor problems, a progress note may substitute for the clinical resume. The medical staff defines what problems and interventions may be considered minor. The progress note may be handwritten. It documents the patient's condition at discharge, discharge instructions, and follow-up care required.

When a patient is transferred within the same organization from one level of care to another (for example, from the hospital to residential care), and the caregivers change, a transfer summary may be substituted for the clinical resume. A transfer summary briefly describes the patient's condition at time of transfer, and the reason for the transfer. When the caregivers remain the same, a progress note may suffice.

Standards

IM.7.3 *The medical record thoroughly documents operative or other procedures* and the use of anesthesia.*

* **operative and other procedures** Includes operative, other invasive, and noninvasive procedures, such as radiotherapy, hyperbaric treatment, CAT scan, and MRI, that place the patient at risk. The focus is on procedures and is not meant to include medications that place the patient at risk.

continues

1998 Joint Commission Standards for Information Management continued

IM.7.3.1 A preoperative diagnosis is recorded before surgery by the licensed independent practitioner responsible for the patient.

IM.7.3.2 Operative reports dictated or written immediately after surgery record the name of the primary surgeon and assistants, findings, technical procedures used, specimens removed, and postoperative diagnosis.

IM.7.3.2.1 The completed operative report is authenticated* by the surgeon and filed in the medical record as soon as possible after surgery.

IM.7.3.2.2 When the operative report is not placed in the medical record immediately after surgery, a progress note is entered immediately.

IM.7.3.3 Postoperative documentation records the patient's vital signs and level of consciousness; medications (including intravenous fluids), blood, and blood components; any unusual events or postoperative complications; and management of such events.

IM.7.3.4 *Postoperative documentation records the patient's discharge from the postanesthesia care area by the responsible licensed independent practitioner or according to discharge criteria.*

IM.7.3.4.1 Compliance with discharge criteria is fully documented in the patient's medical record.

IM.7.3.5 Postoperative documentation records the name of the licensed independent practitioner responsible for discharge.

Intent of IM.7.3 Through IM.7.3.5

In addition to the information required in all medical records,† the hospital documents all aspects of a surgical patient's preoperative, operative, and postoperative care. The record includes the preoperative diagnosis, a complete description of the surgical procedure and findings, the names of all practitioners involved in the patient's care, the postoperative course, evidence of the patient's readiness for discharge from postanesthesia care, and details of the discharge.

Operative reports are consistently placed in the medical record consistent with hospital policies and procedures and state laws. This requirement applies to outpatients as well as inpatients, including donors and recipients of organs and tissues. When the operative report is not placed in the medical record immediately—for example, when there is a transcription or filing delay—an operative progress note is entered in the medical record immediately after surgery to provide pertinent information for anyone required to attend to the patient.

Postoperative documentation includes at least the following records:

- Vital signs and level of consciousness;
- Medications (including intravenous fluids) and blood and blood components;
- Any unusual events or postoperative complications, including blood transfusion reactions, and the management of those events;

* **authenticate** To verify that the process used to verify an entry is complete, accurate, and final.

† See IM.7 through IM.7.2

continues

1998 Joint Commission Standards for Information Management continued

- The names of providers of direct patient care nursing services, or the names of people who supervised that care if it was provided by someone other than a qualified registered nurse;
- The patient's discharge from the postanesthesia care, whether by a responsible licensed independent practitioner or by the use of relevant discharge criteria.

If discharge criteria are used, they are approved by the medical staff and rigorously applied to determine a patient's readiness for discharge. If the patient is discharged by a licensed independent practitioner, the practitioner's name is recorded in the postoperative documentation.

Standards

IM.7.4 For patients receiving continuing ambulatory care services, the medical record contains a summary list of known significant diagnoses, conditions, procedures, drug allergies, and medications.

IM.7.4.1 The list is initiated for each patient by the third visit and maintained thereafter.

Intent of IM.7.4 and IM.7.4.1

Patients sometimes receive ambulatory care services on a continuing basis, and often from more than one provider at the hospital. To promote continuity of care, both over time and among providers, the hospital maintains a record for any patient who is seen at three or more outpatient visits. The record, sometimes referred to as a "summary list," includes the following information:

- Known significant medical diagnoses and conditions;
- Known significant operative and invasive procedures;
- Known adverse and allergic drug reactions; and
- Medications known to be prescribed for or used by the patient.

"Known" refers to information gathered as part of the ambulatory care assessment and treatment.

This information is in the same location in all records, so that providers can find it quickly. If more than one clinic in the hospital keeps a record of the patient, each record notes that there is additional information elsewhere (see IM.7.9).

Standards

IM.7.5 When emergency, urgent, or immediate care is provided, the time and means of arrival are also documented in the medical record.

IM.7.5.1 The medical record notes when a patient receiving emergency, urgent, or immediate care left against medical advice.

IM.7.5.2 The medical record of a patient receiving emergency, urgent, or immediate care notes the conclusions at termination of treatment, including final disposition, condition at discharge, and instructions for follow-up care.

IM.7.5.3 When authorized by the patient or a legally authorized representative, a copy of the emergency services provided is available to the practitioner or medical organization providing follow-up care.

continues

1998 Joint Commission Standards for Information Management continued

Intent of IM.7.5 Through IM.7.5.3

The medical records of patients who have received emergency care contain not only the information required of all medical records, but additional information specific to the emergency visit. Such information is provided to the practitioner or organization responsible for follow-up care only when authorized by the patient or the legally authorized representative.

Standard

IM.7.6 Medical record data and information are managed in a timely manner.

Intent of IM.7.6

Timely entries are essential if a medical record is to be useful in a patient's care. A complete medical record is also important when a patient is discharged, since information in the record may be needed for clinical, legal, or performance-improvement purposes.

The hospital has a policy and procedures on the timely entry of all significant clinical information into the patient's medical record. Providers enter all such information accordingly.

Timely documentation of the patient's medical history, physical examination, and operative reports is especially important. A patient's medical record is complete when

- its contents reflect the patient's condition on arrival, diagnosis, test results, therapy, condition and in-hospital progress, and condition at discharge;
- its contents, including any required clinical resume or final progress notes, are assembled and authenticated; and
- all final diagnoses and complications are recorded without the use of symbols or abbreviations.

A medical record is considered delinquent when it has not been completed within a specific time following the patient's discharge. This time period is spelled out in the medical staff's rules and regulations and cannot exceed 30 days. The hospital measures medical record delinquency at regular intervals, no less frequently than every three months, and reports the data as part of medical record review function (IM.3.2).

Note: *If the average of the total number of records delinquent (for any reason) calculated from the last four quarterly measurements is equal to or exceeds twice the average monthly discharges, conditional accreditation will be recommended.*

Standard

IM.7.7 Verbal orders of authorized individuals are accepted and transcribed by qualified personnel who are identified by title or category in the medical staff rules and regulations.

Intent of IM.7.7

Practitioners often give orders verbally in the course of patient care. The quality of patient care may suffer if such orders are not received and recorded in a standard way. Each verbal order is dated and is identified by the names of the individuals who gave it and received it. And the record documents who implemented it. Individuals who receive verbal orders are qualified to do so and are authorized by the medical staff to do so as identified by title or category of personnel.

When required by state or federal law and regulation, verbal orders are authenticated within the specified time frame.

continues

1998 Joint Commission Standards for Information Management continued

Standard

IM.7.8 Every medical record entry is dated, its author identified, and, when necessary, authenticated.

Intent of IM.7.8

The hospital has a system in place to

- assure that only authorized individuals make entries into medical records;
- identify the date and author of every entry in the medical record; and
- enable the author to authenticate an entry to verify it is complete, accurate, and final.

The author authenticates those entries required by hospital policy. The hospital ensures that, at a minimum, entries of *histories and physical examinations, operative procedures, consultations*, and discharge summaries* are authenticated. Other entries are authenticated as specified by the hospital policy or medical staff bylaws or as required by state or federal law and regulation.

Hospitals establish policies and mechanisms to assure that only an author can authenticate his or her own entry. Indications of authentication can include written signatures or initials, rubber-stamps, or computer "signatures" (or sequence of keys). The medical staff rules and regulations or policies define what entries, if any, by house staff or nonphysicians must be countersigned by supervising physicians.

Standard

IM.7.9 The hospital can quickly assemble and have access to all relevant information from components of a patient's record when the patient is admitted or is seen for ambulatory or emergency care.

Intent of IM.7.9

Patients sometimes receive care in several areas of the hospital; as a result, records on the patient may exist in more than one location. To provide continuity of care, both over time and among providers, practitioners need ready access to all relevant information about the care a patient has received, regardless of where in the hospital that care was given.

The hospital uses a patient-information system to integrate all relevant information from a patient's record from various locations or makes available a summary of information relevant for patient care when the patient is seen. This applies when a patient

- is admitted to the hospital;
- is seen for a prescheduled ambulatory care visit;
- is seen for an unscheduled outpatient visit; and
- comes in for emergency services.

The medical record, computer system, or organization policy indicates when part of the record has been filed elsewhere. The patient information is provided in a timely manner by hard copy or screen display.

* The consultation report is a signed (authenticated) opinion of the consultant's findings for making a diagnosis for a specific patient or providing treatment advice on a specific patient. For the purpose of this standard, routine pathology and clinical laboratory reports and x-ray reports do not require authentication.

continues

1998 Joint Commission Standards for Information Management continued

Standard and Intent Statement for Aggregate Data and Information

Standard

IM.8 The hospital collects and analyzes aggregate data to support patient care and operations.

Intent of IM.8

The hospital aggregates and analyzes clinical and administrative data to support

- patient care;
- decision making;
- management and operations;
- analysis of trends over time;
- performance comparisons over time and with other organizations; and
- performance improvement.

The hospital is able to aggregate the following data and information:

a. Pharmacy transactions, as required by law and to control and account for all drugs;
b. Information about hazards and safety practices used to identify safety management issues to be addressed by the organization;
c. Records of radionuclides and radiopharmaceuticals, including the radionuclide's identity, the date received, method of receipt, activity, recipient's identity, date administered, and disposal;
d. Records of required reporting to authorities;
e. Performance measures of processes and outcomes;
f. Summaries of performance-improvement actions;
g. Practitioner-specific information*;
h. The ability to gather accurate, timely information for use in operational decision making and planning; and
i. Data and information to support clinical research.

Coding and retrieval systems are implemented for aggregating

j. medical record information about diagnoses and procedures;
k. patient demographic information; and
l. financial information.

Aggregate performance-improvement information includes information from risk management, utilization review, infection control, and safety management. Information about hazards and safety practices includes

m. summaries of the deficiencies, problems, failures, and user errors in safety management, life safety management, equipment management, and utilities management, as well as relevant published reports of hazards associated with any of these areas;
n. documented surveys, at least semiannually, of all areas of the facility to identify environmental hazards and unsafe practices; and
o. reports and investigations of all incidents involving property damage, occupational illness, or patient, personnel, or visitor injury.

* As defined in the "Medical Staff" chapter of this book.

continues

1998 Joint Commission Standards for Information Management continued

A continuously maintained control register for emergency and outpatient services* includes at least the following information for every individual seeking care:

p. Identification, such as name, age, and gender;
q. Date, time, and means of arrival;
r. Nature of complaint;
s. Disposition; and
t. Time of departure.

Standards and Intent Statements for Knowledge-Based Information

Standard

IM.9 The hospital provides systems, resources, and services to meet its needs for knowledge-based information in patient care, education, research, and management.

Intent of IM.9

Knowledge-based information, often referred to as "literature," includes journal literature, reference information, and research data. It may be found in a variety of forms, including articles, abstracts, or indexes in print or electronic format; recent editions of texts, periodicals, and other professional resources; and patient education materials that meet individual and organizational needs. Knowledge-based information is authoritative and up to date. It supports clinical and management decision making, performance-improvement activities, patient and family education, continuing education of staff, and research.

This standard addresses the hospital's ability to provide knowledge-based information to those who need it. A hospital's need for knowledge-based information can be met in a variety of ways, including an on-site library department or unit, the services of a qualified medical librarian on site, or a variety of other cooperative arrangements for providing similar services to effectively meet the knowledge-based information needs of the institutions. These services may be shared with other hospitals or community resources, as long as needed information is easily accessible to hospital staff.

Appropriate knowledge-based information is acquired, assembled, and transmitted to users. Knowledge-based information management consists of systems, resources, and services to

- help health professionals acquire and maintain the knowledge and skills they need to care for patients;
- support clinical and management decision making;
- support performance improvement;
- satisfy research-related needs; and
- educate patients and families.

* **outpatient services** Refers to a patient appointment system, and all the stated requirements do not apply.

continues

1998 Joint Commission Standards for Information Management continued

Standard

IM.9.1 The hospital's knowledge-based information resources are available, authoritative, and up to date.

Intent of IM.9.1

Knowledge-based resources are available and accessible to everyone in the hospital who needs them, including clinical and administrative staff, and patients and families when appropriate. These resources provide authoritative and up-to-date scientific, clinical, and managerial knowledge.

To be accessible, resources are in appropriate formats. For example, clinical and management literature may be available as paper or electronic journals, books, technical reports, and audiovisual media. Patient education material is often available in the form of brochures, articles, pamphlets, audiovisual materials, and models. Resources may also include externally produced databases and practice guidelines.

To select authoritative, up-to-date resources, the hospital may consult the

- *Selected List of Books and Journals for the Small Medical Library* (often called the Brandon-Hill list), published every other year by the Medical Library Association (MLA) in the *Bulletin of the MLA;*
- *Library for Internists,* published by the American College of Physicians every three years in the *Annals of Internal Medicine;*
- databases, publishing information, and reviews; and
- recommendations of resource users.

The hospital has a system for organizing knowledge-based information and providing it efficiently to users. Poison-control and formulary information is quickly and easily available when needed. A poison-control center hotline is usually the best source of up-to-date information on poisons.

Standard

IM.9.2 The hospital's services, resources, and systems for knowledge-based information are based on a needs assessment.

Intent of IM.9.2

When the hospital assesses its overall information needs, it looks at the need for knowledge-based information. The systems, resources, and services the hospital provides to meet these needs will depend on

- the services the hospital provides;
- the needs of those who will use the information.

Users include the medical and nursing staffs, administrators and managers, other health professional staff members, other hospital staff members, students, patients and their families, and researchers.

Specifically, the needs assessment addresses

- accessibility and timeliness;
- links with the hospital's internal information systems; and
- links with external databases and information networks.

Library and information services enable the hospital to

- respond to information requests from staff, patients, and families;
- anticipate information needs and systematically link literature to clinical and organizational processes; and

continues

1998 Joint Commission Standards for Information Management continued

- provide relevant, current, and accurate information within appropriate time frames and in formats appropriate to users' needs.

Information is accessible in one or more of the following locations:

- At the work site;
- In a shared central collection at the hospital (for example, a professional library);
- From outside sources (such as vendors or other institutions), with acceptable time delays.

The quality of the information service can be judged by the following criteria:

- Accuracy;
- Currency;
- Relevance to the request;
- Speed of response;
- Format (ease of use); and
- Validity of the information.

Standards and Intent Statements for Comparative Data and Information

Standards

IM.10 *Comparative performance data and information are defined, collected, analyzed, transmitted, reported, and used consistent with national and state guidelines for data set parity and connectivity.*

IM.10.1 The hospital uses external reference databases for comparative purposes.

IM.10.2 The hospital contributes to external reference databases when required by law or regulation or when appropriate to the hospital.

IM.10.3 The security and confidentiality of data and information are maintained when contributing to or using external databases.

Intent of IM.10 Through IM.10.3

These standards address the hospital's ability to use and contribute to collections of performance data from multiple institutions. As part of its information-management activities, the hospital exchanges clinical and knowledge-based data and information with other health care organizations. These activities help the hospital develop its future capabilities and goals.

The hospital uses external data and information to identify areas in which its own performance deviates from expected patterns. The hospital also contributes its own information to external reference databases. To ensure that the data is comparable across institutions, the hospital follows national and state guidelines on form and content.

PERFORMANCE MEASUREMENT SYSTEMS: EVALUATION AND SELECTION

Introduction

The next evolution in Joint Commission accreditation involves the integration of performance measurement into the accreditation process. Significant environmental factors have contributed to this evolution. As quality of care becomes an even more visible public issue, increased attention is being given to the effectiveness of current quality oversight processes and systems. The growing demand for objective, comparative information about the performance of health care organizations has created a need for a data-driven evaluation process that includes outcomes data. The Joint Commission's current triennial on-site survey process must evolve to include performance measurement data in order to continue assuring the public and other interested stakeholders that continuous attention is being given to the care provided by health care organizations. In addition, business coalitions, purchasers (employers), and payers (insurers) choosing among plans and providers are demanding objective evidence that they are buying good-quality care for a fair price. These demands assume access to useful outcomes data that permit comparison among providers.

To succeed in such an environment, accredited organizations require objective feedback about their own performance that they can use internally to support performance improvement activities and externally to demonstrate accountability to the public and other purchasers, payers, and stakeholders. Performance measurement activities provide scientifically valid, data-driven mechanisms that generate a continuous stream of performance information, enabling health care organizations to

- Have continuous access to objective data to support their claims of quality.
- Receive early warning of problems or conditions that could lead to serious errors.
- Verify the effectiveness of corrective actions.
- Identify areas of excellence within the organizations
- Compare their performance with that of peer organizations using the same measures within the same performance measurement system.

For the Joint Commission, performance measurement increases the value of accreditation by confirming the critical link between accreditation and outcomes of care. Integrating performance measures into the accreditation process will significantly enhance the accreditation decision by making it more credible, objective, consistent, and useful. In specific terms, it will

- Increase public- and private-sector reliance on Joint Commission accreditation, thereby building support for the consensus development and use of standards and performance measures, as well as reducing justification for duplicative evaluation activities.
- Provide the Joint Commission with performance data that it can use to
  - Monitor organization performance on a continuous basis.
  - Help organizations identify issues that require attention.
  - Focus triennial surveys on areas within an organization that represent the greatest potential opportunities for improvement.
- Help identify both exemplary performance and best practices to facilitate the provision of benchmarking services to health care organizations.
- Facilitate refinement of the Joint Commission's performance-based standards and the analysis and understanding of the relationships between standards and outcomes.

Such environmental factors led the Joint Commission to adopt new requirements that will initially affect hospitals and long-term care organizations participating in the accreditation process. Approved by the Joint Commission's Board of Commissioners in January 1997, these requirements relate to performance measurement activities and stipulate participation by accredited organizations in an acceptable performance measurement system. The following explains the new requirements, provides guidance for selecting a performance measurement system(s), and profiles measurement systems considered acceptable for inclusion in the accreditation process.

THE NEXT EVOLUTION IN JOINT COMMISSION ACCREDITATION

In determining the timetable for implementing performance measurement into the accreditation process, the Joint Commission conducted a field-readiness survey during the summer of 1996. Survey results showed that 69 percent of hospitals and 33 percent of long-term care organizations indicated that they currently participate in a performance measurement system. The majority of these organizations focus their use of the measurement system on clinical care for specific patient populations. Although the majority of these organizations submit data in some type of electronic format, a significant number submit data on paper.

Implementation of a more objective, data-driven accreditation process that includes outcomes data will be incremental over the next several years. Beginning in 1997, each accredited hospital and long-term care organization must

- Enroll in at least one performance measurement system chosen from a list published by the Joint Commission and select at least two clinical measures from the chosen system(s) that together address at least 20 percent of the organization's patient/resident population.
- Inform the Joint Commission of the system(s) it chooses and the measures it selects by December 31, 1997.

By March 31, 1999, hospitals and long-term care organizations will be required to submit third-quarter 1998 data from the chosen measurement system(s) for the selected measures. The Joint Commission expects that data will be submitted directly by the performance measurement system for the hospital or long-term care organization. Organization-level and system-level data must be submitted to the Joint Commission.

The new requirements and their timetable apply regardless of when the hospital or long-term care organization is due for its next triennial survey. Failure to meet these new requirements will result in a special type I recommendation. If not corrected, this type I recommendation could lead to conditional accreditation and ultimately to loss of accreditation.

Over the next several years, the Joint Commission will expand the scope of measurement expected in each hospital and long-term care organization and will phase in similar, incremental requirements in other accreditation programs. For example, current plans anticipate that accredited hospitals and long-term care organizations will be required to select two additional measures, for a total of four, by the end of 1998. Together, the four clinical measures should address at least 40 percent of the organization's patient/resident population. Similar increases in scope in subsequent years are also planned (for example, at least six clinical measures that together address 60 percent of the organization's patient/resident population), as are requirements for the use of health status and patient satisfaction measures. Ample notification about increased expectations will be provided to health care organizations to allow sufficient time for compliance.

Submission to the Joint Commission of third-quarter 1998 aggregate data for hospitals and long-term care organizations will begin no later than the first quarter of 1999. Following the data submission to the Joint Commission, Joint Commission staff will use criteria to review data trends and determine if contact with the health care organization is indicated (for example, a phone call, request for a written progress report, or an on-site survey). Such review will begin once enough data points are available, presumably by the end of 1999. Particular attention will be given to how the health care organization uses the data to analyze processes and improve care. In addition, a summary of organization performance data will be provided to surveyors for use during the regular on-site triennial survey.

THE JOINT COMMISSION'S LIST OF PERFORMANCE MEASUREMENT SYSTEMS

Hospitals and long-term care organizations must select a measurement system from the Joint Commission's list of acceptable performance measurement systems. The listings are based on information reported by the performance measurement systems about their compliance with initial screening criteria. Over time, the actual performance of these systems will be assessed against these criteria, and some of the systems may be found not to meet ongoing requirements. A health care organization using any system on this list, however, will be viewed as meeting current accreditation requirements for selection and participation in a measurement system.

The systems listed were evaluated against criteria defined by the Council on Performance Measurement, a panel of national experts in performance measurement convened by the Joint Commission. The criteria are listed in "The Joint Commission's Framework for the Selection of Performance Measurement Systems." The Council considered each applicant system's self-reported responses against these criteria. Although all listed systems meet the initial screening criteria, they will be required to meet several additional criteria in the future. These additional criteria are marked "Future compliance required." Listed systems have not yet been evaluated against these future criteria in the Framework. *Therefore, before you select a system, you are advised to carefully assess its current ability to meet, or plans to meet, these future criteria.*

Source: © *Comprehensive Accreditation Manual for Hospitals Special Update*, March 1997. Oakbrook Terrace, IL: Joint Commission on Accreditation of Healthcare Organizations, 1997, pp. PM-1–PM-6. Reprinted with permission.

THE JOINT COMMISSION'S FRAMEWORK FOR THE SELECTION OF PERFORMANCE MEASUREMENT SYSTEMS

The Council on Performance Measurement agreed that, to be useful within the Joint Commission's accreditation process, all qualifying performance measurement systems must include six elements called *attributes of conformance*. The six attributes specify that an acceptable performance measurement system

- includes appropriate performance measures focusing on organization performance or on patient care processes or outcomes
- has an automated, operational database
- ensures the accuracy and completeness of performance data
- uses risk adjustment or stratification methods to reduce or clarify the influence of confounding patient factors
- provides timely feedback of comparative data to participating organizations
- is useful and relevant to the accreditation process.

The Framework identifies the title of each attribute. Each of the six attributes is supported by 1 to 3 criteria, for a total of 13 criteria. Each criterion specifies how and when the systems must satisfy the requirement.

The Joint Commission does not expect all performance measurement systems to immediately and fully meet all 13 evaluation criteria before being approved for inclusion in the accreditation process. Therefore, five criteria and part of three others have been designated as requiring current compliance. These criteria are followed by the phrase "initial screening criteria" in parentheses. Five criteria and part of three others have been slated for future application. These criteria are followed by the phrase "future compliance required" in parentheses.

ATTRIBUTE 1: PERFORMANCE MEASURE

Performance Measure: A quantitative tool that provides an indication of a health care organization's performance in relation to a specified process or outcome.

Criterion A: The measurement system contains defined process or outcome performance measures that

- address at least one of the following performance categories: clinical, health status, satisfaction, administrative/financial (initial screening requirement)
- do not address individual practitioner performance exclusively (initial screening requirement)
- are related to at least one of the Joint Commission's accreditation programs (Ambulatory Health Care, Behavioral Health Care, Home Care, Hospital, Pathology and Clinical Laboratory Services, Long-Term Care, Health Care Network) (initial screening requirement)

Criterion B: Measures of performance targeted for potential use in the accreditation process are composed of specifications that are consistently applied across all participating health care organizations (for example, data element definitions, recommended data sources, population identification rules, calculation algorithms, sampling protocols). (future compliance required)

Criterion C: The measurement system has documented procedures for adding, modifying, maintaining, and deleting performance measures. (future compliance required)

ATTRIBUTE 2: DATABASE (MEASUREMENT SYSTEM TECHNICAL CAPABILITIES)

Database (Measurement System Technical Capabilities): The operational characteristics of measurement systems.

Criterion D: The measurement system

- contains one or more automated database(s) (initial screening requirement)
- is operational (initial screening requirement)
- is ongoing (that is, does not have a defined end date as in a demonstration project) (initial screening requirement)
- can link individual health care organizations or sites with their own data (initial screening requirement)
- receives and stores, or has access to, performance measure data at the level of individuals (for example, individual patient, enrollee, employee) for each measure targeted for potential use in the accreditation process (future compliance required)
- can electronically transmit, from a centralized source, aggregated health care organization specific performance measure data directly to the Joint Commission (that is, data transmission to the Joint Commission originates from the measurement system, not individual health care organizations) (initial screening requirement)
- can electronically transmit comparative (within and across participating health care organizations over time) performance measure data directly to the Joint Commission (initial screening requirement)

ATTRIBUTE 3: DATA QUALITY (PERFORMANCE MEASURE ACCURACY)

Data Quality (Performance Measure Accuracy): The extent to which performance measures correctly identify the events they were designed to identify.

Criterion E: The measurement system

- monitors and is accountable for the accuracy and completeness of the performance measure data elements received from participating health care organizations (initial screening requirement)
- has established that the algorithms used to calculate the performance measures targeted for potential use in the accreditation process are accurate (future compliance required)
- has established that the measures targeted for potential use in the accreditation process are able to consistently identify the events they were designed to identify across multiple

continues

The Joint Commission's Framework for the Selection of Performance Measurement Systems continued

individual participating health care organizations (future compliance required)

- uses the results of performance measure accuracy monitoring to continuously improve the measures (future compliance required)

Criterion F: The measurement system provides ongoing support to participating health care organizations to ensure that the accuracy of performance measure data elements is monitored by the organizations. (initial screening requirement)

ATTRIBUTE 4: RISK ADJUSTMENT/ STRATIFICATION

Risk Adjustment/Stratification: A process for reducing, removing, or clarifying the influences of confounding patient factors that differ among comparison groups.

Criterion G: The measurement system provides information on how it controls for the influences of confounding patient factors on performance measures targeted for potential use in the accreditation process. For performance measures that are currently risk adjusted, methodologies and techniques for reducing or removing the influences of confounding patient factors are described. For performance measures not currently risk adjusted, an explanation is provided for why the influences of confounding patient factors have not been addressed. (initial screening requirement) Examples of factors that patients might bright to an encounter, and for which risk adjustment might be utilized, include (but are not limited to)

- complications (conditions arising after the beginning of observation and treatment that modify the course of patient illness and the medical care required)
- comorbidities (preexisting diseases or conditions)
- severity of illness classification (for example, AJCC staging for oncology patients; ASA-PS classification for surgical patients)
- health status (for example, physical functioning, role disability due to physical health problems, bodily pain, general health perceptions, vitality, social functioning, role disability due to emotional problems, and general mental health)
- patient demographics (for example, age, ethnicity, and gender)

Criterion H: Performance measures targeted for potential use in the accreditation process are risk adjusted, as appropriate, to reduce or remove the influences of confounding patient factors so that valid and fair comparisons can be made across health care organizations. Each performance measure to which risk adjustment applies has a unique approach tailored to it. (future compliance required)

ATTRIBUTE 5

Performance Measure–Related Feedback: Performance measure–related information that is available, on a timely basis, to health care organizations participating in the measurement system for use in the organization's ongoing internal efforts to improve patient care and organizational performance.

Criterion I: The measurement system provides actively participating health care organizations access to comparative (across participating organizations within a system) performance measure–related feedback on measures targeted for potential use in the accreditation process. (initial screening requirement)

Criterion J: Performance measure–related feedback provided to health care organizations by the measurement system is

- updated at least once a year (the frequency of feedback on individual measures can vary due to the timing of data collection) (initial screening requirement)
- updated on a schedule that is consistent with the transmission of performance measure data by the measurement system to the Joint Commission (for example, quarterly) (future compliance required)

Criterion K: The measurement system makes educational resources available to help health care organizations understand and use performance measure data. (initial screening requirement)

ATTRIBUTE 6

Relevance for Accreditation: The extent to which performance measurement systems are useful and relevant in the accreditation process.

Criterion L: The measurement system can provide statistically valid comparisons across its participating organizations on each measure of performance targeted for potential use in the accreditation process. (future compliance required)

Criterion M: The measurement system is prepared to assist the Joint Commission with the development and implementation of research-based methodologies for conducting evaluative studies. These studies assess the extent to which the measurement system is useful and relevant to the accreditation process (for example, the degree to which performance measures are discriminatory; useful for developing probes for use by surveyors; and useful for reaching accreditation decisions). The measurement system will meet with Joint Commission staff, as necessary, to plan the approach for these assessments. (future compliance required)

Source: © *Comprehensive Accreditation Manual for Hospitals Special Update, March 1997.* Oakbrook Terrace, IL: Joint Commission on Accreditation of Healthcare Organizations, 1997, pp. PM-1–PM-6. Reprinted with permission.

3
Creation and Maintenance of the Clinical Database

Chapter 3

Creation and Maintenance of the Clinical Database

PATIENT IDENTIFICATION

PATIENT/CLIENT IDENTIFICATION SYSTEM: SAMPLE PROCESS

Comprehensive and Centralized System

The health record department shall provide and coordinate a centralized patient/client identification system. The system shall be comprehensive, based on two premises

1. There is a need to know the fact that an individual was brought to or presented self for care at this facility.
2. There is a need to know the disposition of each case.
   - *Admitted to care unit of this facility.* Such individuals are officially classified as a patient/client of this facility. An official health record/database is created, and an identifying number is assigned. Specifically, this includes inpatient, outpatient, newborn, and emergency services, including assessment and immediate transfer to another facility, and patients/ clients who complete the admission process and leave without being treated.
   - *Not admitted.* Specifically, these individuals include the following:
     - dead on arrival
     - patients/clients who choose to leave without completing the admission process
     - referred outpatients
     - stillborns

     No health record is created, and no identifying number is assigned. Information concerning stillborns is filed in the mother's health record. A notation is made in the master patient/client index that no health record was created (e.g., dead on arrival, left without completing admission process).

Purposes

This system has as its purposes the following:

- identification of the patient/client as a unique individual, distinguishable from all others with the same or similar name
- identification as a patient/client of this facility
- identification and linkage of documents relating to the care of each patient/client and coordination of these into a unit record
- provision of ready access to documentation for authorized use under the storage and retrieval functions
- provision of database for statistical information

Unit Number

Each patient/client shall receive an identifying number at the time of the initial admission to this facility for treatment in any of its treatment units. This number shall be retained and used for all subsequent admissions to any treatment unit.

Number Construction

The unit number shall be a six-digit number unique to this facility. The use of the social security number is prohibited, although this number may be collected and recorded as adjunct information.

Use of Prefixes and Suffixes

The use of prepays, suffixes, or other designations is permitted and encouraged in order to facilitate identification of a specific admission episode, billing information, or other special needs. However, the unit number is the official identifier, and documents/records shall be stored under the unit number.

Responsibility for Patient/Client Identification

The responsibility for patient/client identification shall be shared, with the primary control and responsibility resting with the health record department. This department shall designate the unit number to be used; control the central unit number assignment log; design the data gathering/face sheet form; carry out error detection, correction, and prevention; and maintain the central master file.

Intake/Admission Personnel

These units shall obtain full and accurate patient/client identification data and access the central master number assignment unit for unit number assignment for new admissions and verification and activation of unit number for readmissions. They shall forward to the central unit any error correction and/or update information associated with the process of patient/client identification.

Central Data Processing

This unit shall provide technical assistance in developing and implementing the computerized data system.

Intradepartmental Units

The discharge processing unit of the health record department shall routinely check the patient/client identification and unit number on health records. This shall be carried out as part of discharge processing, assembly, and chart completion. All other units noting an error, discrepancy, or omission shall refer the problem to the health record department for handling.

Control Register/Unit Number Inventory

A permanent unit number control register shall be maintained to show the following:

- unit number assigned
- name of patient/client
- date assigned
- date and reason any unit number is voided

A unit number shall be used only once. Voided unit numbers shall not be reissued. This control register is confidential; access is permitted only to authorized users.

Master Patient/Client Index

A permanent master patient/client index shall be maintained to show the following information:

- full name of patient/client
- date of birth
- sex
- address
- unit number assigned
- date of admission(s)
- date of discharge(s)
- attending physician

The mother's name for newborns and the name of both parents or guardians for minors shall also be added if necessary.

This index is confidential; access is permitted only to authorized users.

Continuous Update

Information shall be entered immediately when a new unit number is assigned. In the interest of accuracy and patient/client safety, information to update, clarify, or correct information shall be processed immediately if patient/client is in active treatment or within one workday for all other changes.

Updates shall be processed for the following:

- readmissions to any unit (inpatient or ambulatory)
- admission from outpatient or emergency to inpatient
- admission to outpatient or emergency from home care or hospice care
- name changes (marriage or other legal action)
- name clarifications (newborns, unconscious patients/clients, Jane Doe/John Doe patients/clients, aliases)
- clarification of any personal data (e.g., date of birth, seniority designations)
- other subsequent changes of personal information

Internal Arrangement of Index

The master patient/client index shall be arranged in a fixed order to permit easy and rapid access to the information. As far as possible, the index shall be computerized on an on-line system. Cross referencing shall be used as needed to facilitate access. The specific internal arrangement shall be as follows:

- *Alternative 1:* strict alphabetical index, using consistent rules of alphabetizing
- *Alternative 2:* the SOUNDEX® phonetic system, using the consistent rules of this phonetic system

Requests for Patient/Client Unit Number/ Identification

The master patient/client index is a confidential file with limited access. The following practices shall be implemented:

- *Manual systems.* Direct access to manual systems (card files, ledgers) shall be restricted to patient/client master file personnel. All requests for issuance, verification, and release of the unit number shall be processed by this unit.
- *Computerized on-line systems.* Direct access is permitted by authorized users to obtain the patient/client unit number. The internal security codes of the system shall be implemented in accordance with this limited access provision. Authorized access shall be given to direct patient/client care staff and administrative/support staff on a need-to-know basis (e.g., laboratories, radiology, release of information unit, storage and retrieval unit). No alteration of any kind shall be permitted by such staff. Updates, corrections, and additions shall be sent to the health record department for processing.

Related Processes

Provision of Off-Hours and Downtime Coverage

When the regular unit staff is not available (e.g., night shift hours), the health information management specialist shall designate the individual with authority to access the system and/or assign a unit number for new admissions. Computerized master patient/client indexes shall be developed with the appropriate backup systems to permit access to health records from the storage and retrieval system.

Forms Design and Procedural Instructions

Patient/client identification forms, such as the face sheet, application for treatment, and registration forms, shall be developed to permit easy entry of the necessary information. Particular attention shall be given to spacing on forms and the related instructions for designating clearly the patient's/client's given name, middle initial, surname, and date of birth.

Cross Indexing

Careful and thorough cross indexing shall be done with particular attention to name changes, aliases, newborn and mother linkage, and problem names.

Error Detection and Correction

A systematic program of error detection and correction shall be implemented.

A daily audit of the master patient/client index shall be carried out to check any data entered that workday. New unit numbers shall be issued and unit numbers or identification elements shall be updated and/or changed.

At least monthly, a sample of unit numbers and records shall be audited to detect errors. This shall be carried out using a sample size with a 95 percent confidence level. If the audit results show more than a 1 percent error rate, all the unit numbers issued that month shall be checked.

Error correction forms shall be developed and distributed for use in the department and selected units of the organization.

Error Prevention and Quality Control

The following are quality control/error prevention elements:

- limited access
- fixed responsibility
- restrictions on authority to change entries
- regular audit for error detection
- systematic update
- provision of backup system in case of computer failure or inadvertent erasure or destruction of data
- proper form design

There shall be regular (at least semiannual) training programs concerning information gathering from patients/clients so that adequate information is provided.

Patient/Client Identification Card

An embossed patient/client identification card shall be made at the time of admission and updated at each readmission. This card shall show the full identification and unit number for the patient/client. All data entries shall carry this consistent information. As an additional way of facilitating consistent patient/client identification as well as fostering comprehensive care, an identification card with computerized health record information shall be developed.

The prohibitions in federal regulations concerning identification of drug and alcohol treatment patients/clients shall be followed in implementing the patient/client identification card.

RULES FOR ALPHABETICAL FILING

The following principles of alphabetical filing of individual names shall be used in filing patient/client names in the master patient/client index or in filing any material in alphabetical sequence.

Strict alphabetical filing, letter by letter, shall be used. The usual order of name is *last name, first name, middle name or initial.*

Example	File As
Clement G. Whittaker	Whittaker, Clement G.
Mary Ann Braun	Braun, Mary Ann

The following guidelines and special considerations apply:

- **Abbreviations.** Spell out in full when the meaning is known.

Example	File As
St. John	Saint John
Sta. Assunta	Santa Assunta
Ste. Legere	Sainte Legere

- **Prefixes.** Consider these as part of the surname. Treat the surname as if it were one word even if it is spaced separately or written with capital letters.

Example	File As
Charles Bon Infante	Bon Infante, Charles
Sergio De Jesus	DeJesus, Sergio
Lisa del Valle	delValle, Lisa
M. de la Rigaudieri	delaRigaudieri, M.
Carl Di Cio	DiCio, Carl
Frances O'Neal	ONeal, Frances
Petra Van Orden	VanOrden, Petra
Eileen vanDer Kam	VanDerKam, Eileen
Sally Von Berg	VonBerg, Sally

Two alternatives are offered for filing names beginning with the prefixes *Mc* and *Mac*. One of the alternatives should be selected and used uniformly.

–*Alternative 1.* Treat the prefixes in strict alphabetical sequence.

Example	File in This Sequence
Irving Mac Donald	MacDonald, Irving
Joan McDonald	McDonald, Anne
Anne McDonald	McDonald, Joan

–*Alternative 2.* Treat all names as if the prefix were Mac.

Example	File in This Sequence
Irving MacDonald	McDonald, Anne
Joan McDonald	MacDonald, Irving
Anne McDonald	McDonald, Joan

- **Hyphenated names.** Treat as one continuous name.

Example	File As
Anna Stills-Meyer	StillsMeyer, Anna
Louis Goodman-Young	GoodmanYoung, Louis

- **Initials instead of full first name.** Initials precede a name beginning with that initial.

Example	File in This Sequence
G. Falk	Falk, G.
G. Norton Falk	Falk, G. Norton
George Norton Falk	Falk, George Norton

- **Surname only is given.**
  –*When a surname is used alone*, it precedes the same surname having an initial or a given name.

Example	File in This Sequence
Christopher Laurence	Laurence
Laurence	Laurence, A. C.
A. C. Laurence	Laurence, Christopher

–*When no given name is provided*, file by surname and date of birth; place in file chronologically, front to back.

Example	File in This Sequence
Baby Boy Ferris (10-08-86)	Ferris, Baby Boy (10-08-86)
Baby Boy Ferris (11-25-88)	Ferris, Baby Boy (11-25-88)

- Identical names.
  –*File by middle initial or name, if given.*

Example	File in This Sequence
Lelia A. Cass	Cass, Lelia A.
Lelia B. Cass	Cass, Lelia B.

–*If there is no middle name or initial*, file by date of birth, placing the oldest first.

Example	File in This Sequence
Lelia Cass (06-10-22)	Cass, Lelia (06-10-22)
Lelia Cass (02-08-40)	Cass, Lelia (02-08-40)

- **Seniority designations.** Designations such as senior, junior, or the third (III) are disregarded when placing names in alphabetical order. The information is entered in the file with the name as an additional element of identifying information.

Example	File in This Sequence
James Waters, Jr.	Waters, James (Junior)
James Waters, Sr.	Waters, James (Senior)
James Waters, III	Waters, James (Third)

- Titles.
  –*Title and given name only.* File exactly as given.

Example	File in This Sequence
Brother Francis	Brother Francis (under *B* in file)
Princess Maria Alessandra	Princess Maria Alessandra

–*Title and given name and surname.* Disregard the title; file by surname. Include the title in parentheses as an additional identifier.

Example	File As
Sister Patricia Kane	Kane, Patricia (Sister)
Doctor Ralph Vining	Vining, Ralph (Doctor)
The Hon. Elsa Bold	Bold, Elsa (The Hon.)
Major Clemson Golding	Golding, Clemson (Major)
Senator Clay Morris	Morris, Clay (Sen.)
Rabbi E. Weisel	Weisel, E. (Rabbi)

- **Aliases.** When an alternate name is used by the patient, file in usual alphabetical sequence. Place a cross reference to the legal name when it is known.

Example	File As
Harold Isele	Isele, Harold (see Pzerilechnowoski, Harold I.)

- **John Doe/Jane Doe designations.** When the patient's/client's name is not known at the time of treatment, a Jane or John Doe designation may be used. These are filed in chronological order by date of admission. The name is cross referenced to the legal name when it becomes known.

Example	File As
John Doe (adm. 06-06-73)	Doe, John (adm. 12-25-70)
John Doe (adm. 12-25-70)	Doe, John (adm. 06-06-73) (see also Biggs, Henry)

- **Brief form/shortened form/familiar name.** The shortened form of a given name is used only when the individual indicates that it is the legal name *and* is used in the signature. File the shortened form according to the usual alphabetical filing rules: *surname, given name, middle initial.*

Example	File As
Will Rogers	Rogers, Will

- **Married woman.** The legal name of a married woman includes her own first name. If the husband's first name is known, it may be placed in parentheses at the end of the name as an additional element of identification.

Example	File As
Gloria Sailman (Mrs. George Sailman)	Sailman, Gloria (Mrs. George)

- **Native American names.**
  –*File by tribal name as surname when a given name and tribal name are provided.*

Example	File As
Joseph Silver Wolf	Silver Wolf, Joseph

–*File tribal name exactly as given when only the tribal name is provided/used.*

Example	File As
Silver Wolf	Silver Wolf

- **Hispanic Names.** These commonly consist of both the father's and mother's surname. File in strict alphabetical order, starting with the full surname of the patient/client.

Example	File As
Sergio Alvarez Guedes	Alvarez Guedes, Sergio
Arnaldo Andre Velez Medina	Velez Medina, Arnaldo Andre
Maria Hermina Bazar Acevedo	Bazar Acevedo, Maria Hermina
Odessa Sierra Morena	Sierra Morena, Odessa

- **Surname not readily determined; custom in name usage does not conform to anglicized practices.**
  –*If no part can be recognized as a given name, middle name, and surname,* file as a whole, exactly as given.

Example	File As
Yang Seung	Yang Seung
Chen Bor Kuan	Chen Bor Kuan
Yang Shiao-Hong	Yang Shiao-Hong
Pak Siu	Pak Siu
Pak Koon	Pak Koon

–*If a surname and given name can be differentiated,* file in usual alphabetical sequence of surname, given name, and middle initial.

Example	File As
Clement Chen Hung Yang	Chen Hung Yang, Clement
Rose Pak Siu	Pak Sui, Rose
Joseph Chen Bor Kuan	Chen Bor Kuan, Joseph

The filing sequence for the names given in this set of examples is:

Chen Bor Kuan
Chen Bor Kuan, Joseph
Chen Hung Yang, Clement
Pak Koon
Pak Siu
Pak Siu, Rose
Yang Seung
Yang Shiao-Hong

Source: Joan Gratto Liebler, *Medical Records: Policies and Guidelines*, Aspen Publishers, Inc., © 1995.

DATA SETS

STANDARD CORE DATA SETS

Medicare and other agencies require uniform compilation of data for assessment and measurement of patient outcomes. In compiling a data dictionary for the organization, or in developing hard copy or electronic data capture, the health information management specialist needs to reflect these mandated data elements in any such undertaking. The current versions of standard core data sets are discussed below.

Uniform Billing-92

The six points are as follows:

1. Issued by Health Care Financing Administration (HCFA)
2. Latest version: 1992
3. Originally developed in 1982 by the National Uniform Billing Committee (NUBC)
4. For use in billing any third-party payer
5. May be modified to meet the needs of the individual health care facility for coordination with its various third-party payers
6. Detailed instructions are provided in the UB-92 manual from HCFA and NUBC

Uniform Hospital Discharge Data Set

The six key points are as follows:

1. Issued by the Department of Health and Human Services (formerly the Department of Health, Education and Welfare)
2. Latest revision: 1993
3. Original version and revisions: 1974, revised 1985, and 1992
4. For use in acute care facilities—inpatient services
5. Defines 14 specific elements to be collected
6. *See* also the 1996 Core Health Data Elements (*see* "Core Health Data Elements Proposed for Standardization" and Uniform Billing-92). *See* "Uniform Hospital Discharge Data Set."

Acute Care—Core Health Data Elements

The five key points are as follows:

1. Issued by the National Committee on Vital and Health Statistics (NCVHS)
2. Latest version: January 1, 1996, and January 16, 1996
3. For use in both inpatient and ambulatory care services
4. For the first 12 elements, with the exception of unique identifiers, information may not need to be collected at each encounter. Updates are recommended at least annually.
5. For complete background information about the history and details of the data set, plus future plans for further modifications, the reader is referred to: National Committee on Vital and Health Statistics, Executive Summary: Core Health Data Elements Report, August 1996 (Washington, D.C., Health Care Financing Administration).

For further information, *see* "Core Health Data Elements Proposed for Standardization."

Uniform Ambulatory Care—Data Set

The five key points are as follows:

1. Issued by the National Committee on Vital and Health Statistics (NCVHS)
2. Latest version June 1989
3. For use in all ambulatory care facilities
4. Use is recommended, not required
5. For further information, the reader is referred to two additional references:
   a. National Committee on Vital and Health Statistics, Report of the NCVHS Subcommittee on Ambulatory Care Statistics and the Interagency Task Force

on the Uniform Ambulatory Care Data Set (Health Care Financing Administration, June 1989).

b. Laura K. Feste, *Ambulatory Care Documentation*, American Medical Record Association, 1989. (now titled American Health Information Management Association).

Minimum Data Set for Nursing Home Resident Assessment and Care Screening (Skilled and Intermediate Care)

The six key points are as follows:

1. Issued by Health Care Financing Administration
2. Latest version: November 1991
3. Originally developed in 1980 by the National Committee on Vital and Health Statistics
4. For use in nursing care facilities (regardless of sponsorship and organizational placement [e.g., subacute care facility])
5. *NOTE:* Individual states may add supplementary items for use within their jurisdiction. Consult the specific state's Department of Health and/or Welfare for detailed provision relating to that state's requirements.
6. For further information, the reader is referred to: Health Care Financing Administration, Resident Assessment Instrument Manual (RAI Manual), December, 1990.

Uniform Data Set for Home Care and Hospice

The six key points are as follows:

1. For use in home care and hospice care settings for both children and adult patients
2. Revised September 1995
3. Developed by the National Association for Home Care
4. Use of this data set is optional but highly recommended
5. Should be used in concert with the Health Care Financing Administration Outcome Assessment Information Set (OASIS) data elements
6. For additional information about incorporating the data set into patient record, the reader is referred to the following publication: Susan B. Miller, *Documentation and Information Management in Home Care and Hospice Programs*, American Health Information Management Association, Chicago, IL.

Home Health Care Outcome and Assessment Information Set (Medicare—OASIS-B)

The five key points of the March 10, 1997, narrative background (*Federal Register*) are as follows:

1. The data set is intended for evaluation of adult, nonmaternity patients in home health agency programs.
2. The data set is for use in developing, implementing, and managing an outcome-based quality assessment and performance improvement program.
3. The process is to gather and study data at the start of care and at follow-up points concluding with discharge.
4. Health Care Financing Administration intends that the OASIS be used exactly as specified in order to build validity, although the home health agency can rearrange and/or distribute the OASIS items within the agency's comprehensive assessment system as long as the items themselves remain exactly as written and specified by the Secretary of the U.S. Department of Health and Human Services.
5. Home health agencies should plan to carry out two types of data accuracy checks:
    - Check completeness of data (i.e., whether all OASIS items have been completed).
    - Examine data for logical inconsistencies in the documentation.

Source: Joan Gratto Liebler, *Medical Records: Policies and Guidelines*, Aspen Publishers, Inc. © 1997.

UNIFORM HOSPITAL DISCHARGE DATA SET

Number 1 — **Personal Identification**—The unique number assigned to each patient within a hospital that distinguishes the patient and his or her health record from all others in that institution.

Number 2 — **Date of Birth**—Month, date, and year of birth.

Number 3 — **Sex**—Male or female.

Number 4a — **Race**—White, Black, Asian or Pacific Islander, American Indian/Eskimo/Aleut, Other.

Number 4b — **Ethnicity**—Spanish origin/Hispanic, Non-Spanish origin/Non-Hispanic.

Number 5 — **Residence**—ZIP Code, code for foreign residence.

Number 6 — **Hospital Identification**—A unique institutional number within a data collection system.

Numbers 7–8 — **Admission and Discharge Dates**—Month, day, and year of both admission and discharge.

Numbers 9–10 — **Physician Identification**—Each physician must have a unique identification number within the hospital. The attending physician and the operating physician (if applicable) are to be identified.

Number 11 — **Diagnoses**—All diagnoses that affect the current hospital stay.

- Principal diagnosis is designated and defined as: The condition established after study to be chiefly responsible for occasioning the admission of the patient to the hospital for care.
- Other diagnoses are designated and defined as all conditions that coexist at the time of admission, that develop subsequently, or that affect the treatment received and/or the length of stay. Diagnoses that related to an earlier episode that have no bearing on the current hospital stay are excluded.

Number 12 — **Procedures and Date**—All significant procedures are to be reported.

- A significant procedure is one that is:
  1. Surgical in nature, or
  2. Carries a procedural risk, or
  3. Carries an anesthetic risk, or
  4. Requires specialized training.
- For significant procedures, the identity (by unique number within the hospital) of the person performing the procedure and the date must be reported.
- When more than one procedure is reported, the principal procedure is to be designated. In determining which of several procedures is principal, the following criteria apply:

  The principal procedure is one that was performed for definitive treatment rather than one performed for diagnostic or exploratory purposes, or was necessary to take care of a complication. If there appear to be two procedures that are principal, then the one most related to the principal diagnosis is selected as the principal procedure.

continues

Uniform Hospital Discharge Data Set continued

Number 13 **Disposition of Patient**

- Discharged to home (routine discharge).
- Left health care facility against medical advice.
- Discharged to another short-term hospital.
- Discharged to a long-term care institution.
- Died.
- Other.

Number 14 **Expected Payer for Most of This Bill**—Single major source that the patient expects will pay for his or her bill.

- Blue Cross
- Other insurance companies
- Medicare
- Medicaid
- Workers' compensation
- Other government payers
- Self-pay
- No charge (free, charity, special research, or teaching)
- Other

Source: Reprinted from Health Care Financing Administration.

CORE HEALTH DATA ELEMENTS PROPOSED FOR STANDARDIZATION

CORE HEALTH DATA ELEMENTS

1. Personal/Unique Identifier**
2. Date of Birth
3. Gender
4. Race and Ethnicity
5. Residence
6. Marital Status
7. Living/Residential Arrangement*
8. Self-Reported Health Status**
9. Functional Status*
10. Years of Schooling
11. Patient's Relationship to Subscriber/Person Eligible for Entitlement
12. Current or Most Recent Occupation and Industry**
13. Type of Encounter**
14. Admission Date (inpatient)
15. Discharge Date (inpatient)
16. Date of Encounter (outpatient and physician services)
17. Facility Identification*
18. Type of Facility/Place of Encounter*
19. Health Care Practitioner Identification (outpatient)*
20. Provider Location or Address of Encounter (outpatient)
21. Attending Physician Identification (inpatient)*
22. Operating Clinician Identification*
23. Health Care Practitioner Specialty*
24. Principal Diagnosis (inpatient)
25. Primary Diagnosis (inpatient)
26. Other Diagnoses (inpatient)
27. Qualifier for Other Diagnoses (inpatient)
28. Patient's Stated Reason for Visit or Chief Complaint (outpatient)**
29. Diagnosis Chiefly Responsible for Services Provided (outpatient)
30. Other Diagnoses (outpatient)
31. External Cause of Injury
32. Birth Weight of Newborn (inpatient)
33. Principal Procedure (inpatient)
34. Other Procedures (inpatient)
35. Dates of Procedures (inpatient)
36. Procedures and Services (outpatient)
37. Medications Prescribed
38. Disposition of Patient (inpatient)*
39. Disposition of Patient (outpatient)
40. Patient's Expected Sources of Payment*
41. Injury Related to Employment
42. Total Billed Charges*

*Element for which substantial agreement has been reached, but for which some amount of additional work is needed.

**Element that has been recognized as significant but for which considerable work remains to be undertaken.

A lack of asterisk indicates that these elements are ready for implementation.

PERSON/ENROLLMENT DATA

The elements described in this section refer to information collected on enrollment or at an initial visit to a health care provider or institution. It is anticipated that these elements will be collected on a one-time basis or updated on an annual basis. **With the exception of the personal/unique identifier**, they do not need to be collected at each encounter.

1. Personal/Unique Identifier—the unique name or numeric identifier that will set apart information for an individual person for research and administrative purposes.

- Name—last name, first name, middle initial, suffix (e.g., Jr., III, etc.)
- Numerical identifier

The personal/unique identifier is the element that is the most critical element to be collected uniformly. The National Committee on Vital and Health Statistics (NCVHS) recommends the use of the Social Security Number (SSN) with a check item such as date of birth, while at the same time undertaking the study and evaluation needed to confirm this use or the recommendation of another identifier. More emphasis on the confidential use of SSN is essential. Standards groups should be consulted regarding setting criteria for recording of names.

Rationale and Discussion

Without a universal unique identifier or a set of data items that can form a unique identifier, it will be impossible to link data across the myriad health care locations and arrangements. In the 1992 revision of the Uniform Hospital Discharge Data Set (UHDDS), the NCVHS recommended "using the Social Security Number with a modifier as necessary, as the best option currently available for this unique and universal patient identifier." However, recent testimony has led the Committee to investigate this issue further, in light of perceived inadequacies of the SSN (e.g., lack of a check digit, multiple SSNs, etc.), particularly when used alone, and impediments (legal and otherwise) to its use. Other potential problems include lack of numbers for newborns, legal and illegal noncitizens, and persons who wish to hide their identity, as well as a recommendation that a system would need to be established to assign and track dummy numbers.

New York State presented testimony that indicated that the last four digits of the SSN combined with the birth date were capable of linking data to a very high degree of probability. The State of California has tested the use of a series of data items that are readily known by individuals and that can be combined to link data. By January 1998, all California State Department of Health databases will contain five data items to facilitate linkage. These data items include birth name, date of birth, place of birth, gender, and mother's first name. Seven confirmatory data items (including SSN) should also be collected when possible.

continues

Core Health Data Elements Proposed for Standardization continued

Those present at the November and December 1995 NCVHS regional meetings agreed that the establishment of a unique identifier is the most important core data item. A unique identifier such as the SSN in conjunction with at least one other data item or, alternatively, an identifier drawn from another distinct set of data items routinely collected presently would seem the most viable. Whichever number is chosen, attention must be paid to which data linkages will be permitted and for what purposes.

Development of a unique identifier does not necessarily mean that the individual is identifiable to users. The NCVHS recognizes the vital importance of maintaining confidentiality and emphasizes that any public use of a unique identifier should be in an encrypted form. The unique identifier must be developed and protected in such a way that the American public is assured that their privacy will be protected.

2. Date of Birth—year, month, and day—as recommended by the UHDDS and the Uniform Ambulatory Care Data Set (UACDS). It is recommended that the year of birth be recorded in four digits to make the data element more reliable for the increasing number of persons of 100 years and older. It will also serve as a quality check as the date of birth approaches the new century mark.

3. Gender—as recommended by the UHDDS and the UACDS.

- Male
- Female
- Unknown/not stated

4. Race and Ethnicity—The collection of race and ethnicity data has been recommended by the UHDDS and the UACDS, and these elements have a required definition for federal data collection in Office of Management and Budget (OMB) Directive 15. The definition has been expanded slightly from the OMB requirement

- Race
  - –American Indian/Eskimo/Aleut
  - –Asian or Pacific Islander (specify)
  - –Black
  - –White
  - –Other (specify)
  - –Unknown/not stated
- Ethnicity
  - –Hispanic Origin (specify)
  - –Other (specify)
  - –Unknown/not stated

It is recommended that this item be self-reported, not based on visual judgment or surnames. Whenever possible, the Committee and participants recommended collecting more detailed information on Asian and Pacific Islanders, as well as persons of Hispanic origin.

Rationale and Discussion

The collection of this element allows for the investigation of issues surrounding health and health care by a person's race and ethnic background. Although it is best understood in conjunction with a socioeconomic indicator, researchers may gain a better understanding of the trends and impact of care on racial/ethnic minorities in the United States. It remains unclear whether or not the modest health gains seen in low-income and racial/ethnic minority populations in the last 30 years will continue, considering the changes in the U.S. health care system. These data assist in the examination of disparities in stage of illness, care, and outcome, some of which have been documented in the past among racial and ethnic groups.

OMB is currently investigating the possibility of changes to this classification, and the Committee will await the OMB recommendations. The Committee is concerned about the possible inclusion of a "multiracial" category, without an additional element requesting specific racial detail and/or primary racial identification, because of its anticipated impact on trend data and loss of specificity.

The National Association of Health Data Organizations has also opposed such an inclusion. A recent Bureau of Labor Statistics study found that only 1.5 percent of respondents will choose the multiracial category. The study also found that with the multiracial option there was a considerable decline in percentage terms (approximately 29 percent) of respondents choosing American Indian, Eskimo, or Aleut. However, there is some evidence that the number of interracial marriages is accelerating.

5. Residence—Full address and ZIP code (nine-digit ZIP code, if available) of the individual's usual residence

Rationale and Discussion

This recommendation is in accord with the 1992 UHDDS and the UACDS, as well as recommendations by the NCVHS Subcommittee on State and Community Health Statistics. The Subcommittee determined that residential street address has the advantage of enabling researchers to aggregate the data to any level of geographic detail (block, census tract, ZIP code, county, etc.) and is the best alternative to ensure the availability of small area data. In addition, home address will allow the application of GIS (Geographic Information Systems) technology to the analysis of health issues. Some thought needs to be given to completing this item for persons with no known residence or persons whose residence is outside of the United States. Because the full residential address could serve as a proxy personal identifier, confidentiality of the complete information must be safeguarded in public use of the data.

6. Marital Status—The following definitions, as recommended by the NCVHS, should be used.

continues

Core Health Data Elements Proposed for Standardization continued

- Married
  A person currently married. Classify common-law marriage as married.
  –living together
  –not living together
- Never married
  A person who has never been married or whose only marriages have been annulled.
- Widowed
  A person widowed and not remarried.
- Divorced
  A person divorced and not remarried.
- Separated
  A person legally separated.
- Unknown/not stated

Rationale and Discussion

The Committee recognizes that a person's social support system can be an important determinant of his or her health status, access to health care services, and use of services. Marital status is one element that is sometimes used as a surrogate for the social support system available to an individual and can be important for program design, targeting of services, utilization and outcome studies, and other research and development purposes. It also may be required to verify benefits.

7. Living/Residential Arrangement—The following definitions are recommended by the NCVHS:

- Living arrangement
  –Alone
  –With spouse
  –With significant other/life partner
  –With children
  –With parent or guardian
  –With relatives other than spouse, children, or parents
  –With nonrelatives
  –Unknown/not stated

  Multiple responses to this item are possible. This element refers to living arrangements only. Marital status is discussed in 6. Marital Status.

- Residential arrangement
  –Own home or apartment
  –Residence where health, disability, or aging-related services or supervision are available
  –Other residential setting where no services are provided
  –Nursing home or other health facility
  –Other institutional setting (e.g., prison)
  –Homeless or homeless shelter
  –Unknown/not stated

Rationale and Discussion

The usual living/residential arrangement of an individual is important for understanding the health status of the person as well as the person's follow-up needs when seen in a health care setting. Together with marital status, this element provides a picture of potential formal/informal resources available to the person. The element also provides information on patient origin for health resource planning, and for use as an indirect measure of socioeconomic status.

A key distinction to be ascertained in "residential arrangement" is whether organized caregiving services are being provided where the patient lives. The Committee encourages the use of the above definition, while continuing to study and evaluate other residential categories, such as those used by the Bureau of the Census.

8. Self-Reported Health Status—There was much interest in documenting health status, one element that can precipitate the demand for health care and help determine the prognosis, although there was no consensus on how its definition should be standardized. A commonly used measure is the person's rating of his or her own general health, as in the five-category classification, "excellent, very good, good, fair, or poor." Used in the National Health Interview Survey and many other studies, this item has been shown to be predictive of morbidity, mortality, and future health care use, when collected in a general interview type of setting. This item would be collected at first clinical visit and periodically updated, at least annually. Additional evaluation and testing are needed on standardizing the health status element. At the present time, standards-setting organizations should assign place holder(s) for this element.

9. Functional Status—The functional status of a person is an increasingly important health measure that has been shown to be strongly related to medical care utilization rates. A number of scales have been developed that include both self-report measures, such as the listings of limitations of Activities of Daily Living (ADL) and Instrumental Activities of Daily Living (IADL) and the National Health Interview Survey age-specific summary evaluation of activity limitations, and clinical assessments, such as the International Classification of Impairments, Disabilities, and Handicaps (ICIDH) and the Resident Assessment Instrument (RAI) (widely used in nursing homes). In addition, there are some disabilities, such as severe mental illness or blindness, where ADLs and IADLs are not sufficient measures. Self-report and clinician measurements are each valuable, and having both available is especially informative. Whichever method is used should be designated. Particular scales are more appropriate for measuring different functions or disabilities and should be selected on the basis of the needs of the patient population (such as, use of social functioning scales for those with mental disorders and substance abuse). Functional assessment scales must also be age-appropriate. At present, there is no widely recognized instrument for measuring the functional status of children. Periodicity of assessment also is an issue.

Consideration of these various issues and additional study and evaluation are needed before recommendations can be made for standardizing functional status measurement. Work on this topic is currently ongoing in the NCVHS Disability and Long-Term

continues

Core Health Data Elements Proposed for Standardization continued

Care Statistics Subcommittee. It is possible that the description of functional status may entail more than a single measure, thus needing space for more than one measure and/or an additional element to document the scale used. At the current time, however, it is crucial that standards-settings organizations set aside place holder(s) for this element.

10. Years of Schooling—highest grade of schooling completed by the enrollee/patient. For children under the age of 18, the mother's highest grade of schooling completed should be obtained.

Rationale and Discussion

Collection of years of schooling has been recommended by the NCVHS and others as a proxy for socioeconomic status (SES). Years of schooling has been found to be highly predictive of health status and health care use.

Ideally, one would also collect income to more fully define socioeconomic status. However, income questions are often considered intrusive, whereas years of schooling are more acceptable to respondents. The NCVHS Subcommittee on Ambulatory and Hospital Care Statistics commented in the 1994 UACDS revision that years of schooling completed is the most feasible socioeconomic element to collect in the UACDS.

11. Patient's Relationship to Subscriber/Person Eligible for Entitlement—

- Self
- Spouse
- Child
- Other (specify)

Rationale and Discussion

This relationship (i.e., self, spouse, or child of subscriber) is often obtained and can be of importance for payment and research purposes.

12. Current or Most Recent Occupation and Industry—This data item is very useful in tracking occupational diseases as well as better defining socioeconomic status. Standardized coding schemes, such as the Census Bureau's Alphabetical Listing of Occupation and Industry and the Standardized Occupation and Industry Coding (SOIC) software developed by the National Institute for Occupational Safety and Health, should be reviewed. In some situations, it is possible to collect a free-form narrative in place of the codes, to be coded at a later point.

The Committee feels that, over time, there will be increasing attention focused on this item and reaffirms its recommendations in the 1994 revisions to the UACDS that additional study and evaluation be conducted on the feasibility and utility of collecting and periodically updating information on a person's occupation and industry. In addition, the usefulness of both current/most recent occupation and industry as well as the addition of usual or longest held occupation and industry must be evaluated. All have significant value and could result in the collection of four separate data elements.

ENCOUNTER DATA

The elements described in this section refer to information related to a specific health care encounter and are collected at the time of each encounter.

13. Type of Encounter—This element is critical to the placement of an encounter of care within its correct location (i.e., hospital inpatient, outpatient, emergency department, observation, etc.). However, there was no clear-cut listing of mutually exclusive encounter locations or definitions to draw upon. This term is one that needs study and evaluation before it can be implemented. However, a place holder for this element is recommended to the standards-setting organizations.

14. Admission Date (inpatient)—year, month, and day of admission as currently recommended in the UHDDS and by ANSI ASC X12. An inpatient admission begins with the formal acceptance by a hospital of a patient who is to receive health care practitioner or other services while receiving room, board, and continuous nursing services. It is recommended that the year of admission contain four digits to accommodate problems surrounding the turn of the century.

15. Discharge Date (inpatient)—year, month, and day of discharge as currently recommended in the UHDDS and by ANSI ASC X12. An inpatient discharge occurs with the termination of the room, board, and continuous nursing services, and the formal release of an inpatient by the hospital. Four digits are recommended for the discharge year.

16. Date of Encounter (outpatient and physician services)—year, month, and day of encounter, visit, or other health care encounter, as recommended by the UACDS and ANSI ASC X12. Each encounter generates a date of service that can be used to link encounters for the same patient over time. Grouping of similar services provided on different dates, as is often the case under batch billing, can be problematic if specificity of data elements is lost; the objective is to encourage identifying a unique date of record for each encounter. However, for services billed on a batch basis, two dates would be required to encompass the range of dates from the beginning of all treatments included under the batch (global) code to the end, with a check box to indicate that this is a batch-based encounter.

17–23. Health Care Facility and Practitioner Identifiers—Each provider should have a universal unique number across data systems. The National Provider Identifier and National Provider File (NPI/NPF), currently under development by the Health Care Financing Administration (HCFA) and intended for implementation in 1997, could and should meet this need, if all providers are included. The NPI/NPF will provide a common means of uniquely identifying health care providers, including institutions, individuals, and group practices, both Medicare providers and those in other programs. Participation in the sys-

continues

Core Health Data Elements Proposed for Standardization continued

tem will be voluntary for non-HCFA providers at first. Currently some states are using state facility identifiers, but the Committee recommends that these identifiers be superseded by the NPI/NPF.

The immediate goal of the NPI/NPF project is to support HCFA's Medicare Transaction System initiative by providing a single, universal method for enumerating the providers who serve Medicare beneficiaries. It will do so by assigning a unique identifier to each provider. In the future, the system will integrate non-HCFA subscribers. It is planned that enumeration of Medicare providers will begin in calendar year 1996. The draft systems requirement definition was issued in January 1995. It is recommended that the NPF be the source of all unique provider identifiers, for institutions and individuals. Systems may also choose to collect other identifiers (e.g., tax number), which they can link to the NPI. Items shown below with an asterisk (*) indicate that this type of information can be obtained from linking the NPI with the National Provider File and may not need separate collection. The Committee recognizes that all practitioners may not be included initially in this system but ultimately all should be included.

17. Facility Identification—the unique HCFA identifier, as described above. This identifier includes hospitals, ambulatory surgery centers, nursing homes, hospices, etc. If the HCFA system does not have separate identification numbers for parts of a hospital (i.e., Emergency Department, Outpatient Department), an additional element (such as element 13) will need to be collected along with the facility ID to differentiate these settings. The Committee recommends that the HCFA identifier be adopted when completed.

18. Type of Facility/Place of Encounter*—As part of the NPI/NPF system, described above, HCFA is defining a taxonomy for type of facility. This taxonomy builds on previous NCVHS and departmental work and should be reviewed by the NCVHS and standards organizations. The Committee encourages the development of one taxonomy and will monitor progress.

19. Health Care Practitioner Identification (outpatient)—the unique national identification number assigned to the health care practitioner of record for each encounter. There may be more than one health care provider identified

- The health care practitioner professionally responsible for the services, including ambulatory procedures, delivered to the patient (health care practitioner of record)
- The health care practitioner for each clinical service received by the patient, including ambulatory procedures

Initial enumeration by HCFA will focus on individual providers covered by Medicare and Medicaid; however, the system will enable enumeration of other health care practitioners, as identified by system users. The Committee recommends that the HCFA identifier be adopted when completed.

20. Provider Location or Address of Encounter (outpatient)—the full address and ZIP code (nine digits preferred) for the location at which care was received from the health care practitioner of record (see 19). As recommended by the UACDS, address should be in sufficient detail (street name and number, city or town, county, state, and ZIP code) to allow for the computation of county and metropolitan statistical area.

21. Attending Physician Identification (inpatient)—the unique national identification number assigned to the clinician of record at discharge who is responsible for the discharge summary, as recommended by the 1992 UHDDS.

22. Operating Clinician Identification—the unique national identification number assigned to the clinician who performed the principal procedure, as recommended by the UHDDS.

23. Health Care Practitioner Specialty*—As part of the NPI/NPF system, HCFA has identified a very detailed list of specialties for health care practitioners. This listing should be reviewed by the NCVHS and standards organizations and, if found acceptable, recommended for use.

24. Principal Diagnosis (inpatient)—As recommended by the UHDDS, the condition established after study to be chiefly responsible for occasioning the admission of the patient to the hospital or nursing home for care. The currently recommended coding instrument is the ICD-9-CM.

Rationale and Discussion

Principal diagnosis is required by most systems for inpatient reporting. The Committee acknowledges that there are differences in coding guidelines for reporting diagnosis in inpatient and outpatient settings, and this may result in a lack of comparability in data between the two settings. It is recommended that convergence of these guidelines be investigated.

25. Primary Diagnosis (inpatient)—The diagnosis that is responsible for the majority of the care given to the patient or resources used in the care of the patient. The currently recommended coding instrument is the ICD-9-CM.

Rationale and Discussion

The primary diagnosis is not part of the UHDDS, and in most diagnostic situations the principal and primary diagnoses will be identical. Respondents have indicated a mixed use of this item for inpatients. There is also concern that medical personnel may be confusing the definitions/uses of principal versus primary diagnosis. Some respondents incorrectly interpreted this item as a means of classifying primary site for cancer, utilizing ICD-O (oncology). The NCVHS notes that the Department of Veterans Affairs routinely collects this element, and thus approves the continued inclusion in this core list, pending a review of uses and users of this element.

26. Other Diagnoses (inpatient)—As recommended by the UHDDS, all conditions that coexist at the time of admission, or develop subsequently, that affect the treatment received and/or

continues

Core Health Data Elements Proposed for Standardization continued

the length of stay. Diagnoses that refer to an earlier episode that have no bearing on the current hospital or nursing home stay are to be excluded. Conditions should be coded that affect patient care in terms of requiring clinical evaluation, therapeutic treatment, diagnostic procedures, extended length of hospital or nursing home stay, or increased nursing care and/or monitoring. The currently recommended coding instrument is the ICD-9-CM.

27. Qualifier for Other Diagnoses (inpatient)—The following qualifier should be applied to each diagnosis coded under "other diagnoses," as was recommended in the 1992 revision of the UHDDS:

Onset prior to admission

- Yes
- No

Rationale and Discussion

This element is currently being collected by California and New York hospital discharge data systems. There is an indication that use of this qualifier can contribute significantly to quality assurance monitoring, risk-adjusted outcome studies, and reimbursement strategies.

28–31. Ambulatory Conditions—The elements for ambulatory conditions contain information on the Patient's Stated Reason for Visit and the Problems, Diagnosis, or Assessment, both of which were recommended by the UACDS. The latter element, which describes all conditions requiring evaluation and/or treatment or management at the time of the encounter as designated by the health care practitioner, has been divided into two elements: (1) the diagnosis chiefly responsible for services provided, and (2) other diagnoses.

28. Patient's Stated Reason for Visit or Chief Complaint (outpatient)—Includes the patient's stated reason at the time of the encounter for seeking attention or care. This item attempts to define what actually motivated the patient to seek care and has utility for analyzing the demand for health care services, evaluating quality of care, and performing risk adjustment. The NCVHS recommended this as an optional item in the UACDS but noted that high priority should be given to conducting additional study as to the feasibility, ease, and practical utility of collecting the patient's reason for encounter, in as close to the patient's words as possible. There is not one agreed-upon coding system for this item; the International Classification of Primary Care and the Reason For Visit Classification used by the National Ambulatory Medical Care Survey are two such systems. Additional evaluation and testing are warranted for this important information.

29–30. Problem, Diagnosis, or Assessment (outpatient)

29. Diagnosis Chiefly Responsible for Services Provided (outpatient)—The diagnosis, condition, problem, or the reason for encounter/visit chiefly responsible for the services provided. Condition should be recorded to the highest documented level of specificity, such as symptoms, signs, abnormal test results, or other reason for visit, if a definitive diagnosis has not been established at the end of the visit/encounter. The currently recommended coding instrument is the ICD-9-CM.

Rationale and Discussion

Information on all patient problems and diagnoses requiring attention at the encounter are needed to assess the quality of care delivered, to determine what types of health problems are being seen and treated in the different types of ambulatory care facilities, and for assessing the appropriateness of the setting used to perform the services. During the NCVHS review of core health data elements, discussion arose regarding the specificity of diagnoses reported. The official national outpatient/physician coding and reporting guidelines provide instruction that a suspected or rule-out condition not be reported as though it is a confirmed diagnosis. The instruction clarifies that only what is known to the highest level of specificity should be reported. In some instances this may be a symptom or an abnormal finding. Medicare and many other payers adhere to these guidelines. Some third-party payers, however, have ignored the guidelines and required facilities and health care practitioners to report a diagnosis that justifies the performance of services being provided. This has resulted in inconsistent data found in many outpatient databases and has skewed patient outcome studies. It is anticipated that the introduction of ICD-10 will alleviate this problem. The NCVHS recommends continued monitoring of provider practices with regard to coding and revision of these recommendations if current guidelines continue to be ignored.

30. Other Diagnoses (outpatient)—The additional code(s) that describes any coexisting conditions (chronic conditions or all documented conditions that coexist at the time of the encounter/visit, and require or affect patient management). Condition(s) should be recorded to the highest documented level of specificity. The ICD-9-CM is the recommended coding convention.

Rationale and Discussion

Information on multiple diagnoses is important for developing severity indexes and assessing resource requirements and use.

31. External Cause of Injury—This item should be completed whenever there is a diagnosis of an injury, poisoning, or adverse effect. The currently recommended coding instrument is the ICD-9-CM. The priorities for recording an External Cause-of-injury code (E-code) are

1. Principal diagnosis of an injury or poisoning.
2. Other diagnosis of an injury, poisoning, or adverse effect directly related to the principal diagnosis.
3. Other diagnosis with an external cause.

continues

Core Health Data Elements Proposed for Standardization continued

Rationale and Discussion

The collection of this element has been recommended by the UHDDS and the UACDS, and a separate element for its collection is included on the UB-92. The information that this element provides on the causes of patients' injuries or adverse effects is considered essential for the development of intervention, prevention, and control strategies. Compelling evidence presented by the Indian Health Service, states, and nonprofit organizations demonstrates that effective intervention strategies can be implemented in response to available data on external causes of injury.

32. Birth Weight of Newborn (inpatient)—The specific birth weight of the newborn, recorded in grams.

Rationale and Discussion

Birth weight of newborn is readily available in the health record and has singular importance for risk-adjustment outcome studies and health policy development related to maternal and infant health.

33–35. Procedures (inpatient)—All significant procedures, and dates performed, are to be reported. A significant procedure is one that is

- Surgical in nature, or
- Carries a procedural risk, or
- Carries an anesthetic risk, or
- Requires specialized training.

Surgery includes incision, excision, amputation, introduction, endoscopy, repair, destruction, suture, and manipulation. A qualifier element is recommended to indicate the type of coding structure used (i.e., ICD, CPT, etc.).

33. Principal Procedure (inpatient)—As recommended by the UHDDS, the principal procedure is one that was performed for definitive treatment rather than one performed for diagnostic or exploratory purposes, or was necessary to take care of a complication. If there appear to be two procedures that are principal, then the one most related to the principal diagnosis should be selected as the principal procedure. ICD-9-CM Vol. 3 is required; however, NCVHS strongly advocates a single procedure classification for inpatient and ambulatory care.

34. Other Procedures (inpatient)—all other procedures that meet the criteria described in element 33.

35. Dates of Procedures (inpatient)—year, month, and day, as recommended in the UHDDS and by ANSI ASC X12, of each significant procedure.

36. Procedures and Services (outpatient)—As recommended by the UACDS, describe all diagnostic procedures and services of any type including history, physical examination, laboratory, X-ray or radiograph, and others that are performed pertinent to the patient's reasons for the encounter; all therapeutic services performed at the time of the encounter; and all preventive services and procedures performed at the time of the encounter. Also, describe, to the extent possible, the provision of drugs and biologicals, supplies, appliances, and equipment. The HCFA Common Procedure Coding System (HCPCS), based on CPT-4, is required for physician (ambulatory and inpatient), hospital outpatient department, and free-standing ambulatory surgical facility bills; however, NCVHS strongly advocates a single procedure classification for inpatient and ambulatory care. The Committee recognizes the importance and desirability of linking services with diagnoses wherever feasible.

37. Medications Prescribed—Describe all medications prescribed or provided by the health care practitioner at the encounter (for outpatients) or given on discharge to the patient (for inpatients), including, where possible, National Drug Code, dosage, strength, and total amount prescribed.

Rationale and Discussion

The collection of information on medications is crucial to understanding the health care encounter and the services provided to a patient. The Committee recognizes that not all providers are obtaining this detail, but it is anticipated that these data will be more frequently collected in the near future with the growth of computerized prescription information.

38. Disposition of Patient (inpatient)—as by the UB-92 and as an expansion of the 1992–93 UHDDS data element

- Discharged Alive
  - Discharged to home or self-care (routine discharge)
  - Discharged/transferred to another short-term general hospital for inpatient care
  - Discharged/transferred to skilled nursing facility (SNF)
  - Discharged/transferred to an intermediate care facility (ICE)
  - Discharged/transferred to another type of institution for inpatient care or referred for outpatient services to another institution
  - Discharged/transferred to home under care of organized home health service organization
  - Discharged/transferred to home under care of a Home IV provider
  - Left against medical advice or discontinued care
- Expired
- Status not stated

Rationale and Discussion

In addition to documenting whether the patient was discharged alive or died during the hospitalization, the patient disposition is an indicator of the patient's health status at the time of discharge and need for additional services.

39. Disposition of Patient (outpatient)—the health care practitioner's statement of the next step(s) in the care of the patient. Multiple responses are possible. At a minimum, the following classification is suggested:

- No follow-up planned (return if needed, PRN)
- Follow-up planned or scheduled

continues

Core Health Data Elements Proposed for Standardization continued

- Referred elsewhere (including to hospital)
- Expired

Rationale and Discussion

The critical distinction here is whether follow-up is planned or scheduled, as an indicator of continuing health problems and continuity of care. "Expired" has been added because the outpatient setting includes a wide range of sites, including Emergency Departments and ambulatory surgery centers.

40. Patient's Expected Sources of Payment—The following categories are recommended for primary and secondary sources of payment:

- *Primary Source*—The primary source that is expected to be responsible for the largest percentage of the patient's current bill.
- *Secondary Source*—The secondary source, if any, that will be responsible for the next largest percentage of the patient's current bill.
  - Self-pay
  - Workers' compensation
  - Medicare
  - Medicaid
  - Maternal and Child Health
  - Other government payments
  - Blue Cross
  - Insurance companies
  - No charge (free, charity, special research, or teaching)
  - Other
  - Unknown/not stated

Rationale and Discussion

The categories in this element were recommended by the UHDDS for primary and secondary sources of payment. The Committee recognizes the ongoing discussion of discrepancies between "expected" and "actual" sources of payment. Source of payment categories, as recommended in the past, are no longer sufficient. The continuing expansion of types of payments and the combination of payments within groups is ever changing. However, the information is still considered useful to collect for trend purposes and for some indication of patients' coverage by third-party payers.

HCFA is developing a new system, called the HCFA PAYERID project, which will assign a unique identifier to every payer of health care claims in the United States. Participation is voluntary and HCFA, which is funding its development, has been working to get consensus about the kind of system that would be useful. The database will contain payer names, billing addresses, and business information. The information, which is already in the public domain, will be accessible by names and ID numbers and available in several formats. Who will have access to the database for research purposes, and to what data, has yet to be determined. "Payers" are defined as public and private entities that have contract responsibility for health care payment.

Medicare decided a PAYERID was needed because of the difficulty its contractors were having in transferring claims to other insurance companies due to incomplete information or multiple names for payers. It is hoped that the system will improve the coordination of benefits as well as provide access to information about health insurance and make it easier to track third-party liability situations. HCFA, however, has estimated that there are approximately 30,000 individual payers in the United States. They currently are not developing a system of categories to accompany the IDs. Such a system would be helpful to the extent that it is feasible in the current highly dynamic market.

Because the PAYERID system is still being developed, and because HCFA currently has no plans to categorize payers, the Committee recommends the current UHDDS categories while encouraging continued study and evaluation of categories used by other data collectors.

41. Injury Related to Employment—Yes, No.

Rationale and Discussion

Whether an injury is work-related or not can be of significant importance both in the area of injury prevention and in medical care payment. During the discussion on including External Cause of Injury in the 1994 revision to the UACDS, CDC and labor and business groups urged collection of whether or not an injury occurred at work or was work-related. This element is currently collected on the HCFA 1500 form.

42. Total Billed Charges—All charges for procedures and services rendered to the patient during a hospitalization or encounter.

Rationale and Discussion

The UHDDS and UACDS have recommended the collection of all charges for procedures and services rendered to the patient during a hospitalization or encounter. This item already is collected by most state health data organizations collecting hospital discharge information and offers the only readily available information on the fiscal dimensions of care and the relative costs of different types of care. Although there is agreement that "payments" or "costs" are needed, most participants agreed that it is virtually impossible to collect these items consistently across time and locations. Moreover, in the electronic format, in most instances, payments would not be available at the time that patient and medical data are entered. It might not be feasible to expect the record to be updated to include payment data when it becomes available. Therefore, billed charges should be collected, at a minimum.

Source: Health Care Financing Administration, Core Health Data Elements: Report of the National Committee on Vital and Health Statistics, August 1996. http://aspe.os.dhhs.gov/ncvhs/ncvhsr1.htm.

STATISTICS, DATA COLLECTION, INDEXES, REGISTERS, AND REPORTS

POLICIES AND PROCEDURES FOR UTILIZING STATISTICS, DATA COLLECTION, INDEXES, REGISTERS, AND REPORTS

Centralized and Comprehensive System

The health record department shall develop and maintain a central, comprehensive system of data collection, statistical analysis, indexes, registers, and reports. This comprehensive database shall be developed and maintained for the following purposes:

- satisfaction of legal, regulatory, and accrediting mandates
- review of reimbursement-related information under third-party payer provisions
- administrative planning
- risk management review
- patient care evaluation
- professional staff uses (e.g., individual analysis of practice, professional staff committee activities)
- research and education

Scope of Data Collection

Statistical profiles and diagnostic information, indexes, and registers, and reports derived from them, shall reflect information about the following:

- inpatients
- outpatient clinics and same-day surgery units
- emergency medical services
- facility-sponsored home care and hospice care

Under terms of specific contractual arrangements, with an appropriate fee paid to the facility, similar services will be provided to private practitioners and group practices that are associated with the facility. The approval of the chief executive officer shall be obtained for such arrangements.

Ethical Considerations

Functions associated with data collection and processing shall be carried out in accordance with strict ethical practices:

- Data shall be drawn from documented patient/client care.
- The privacy of patients/clients and practitioners shall be protected.

Access to and Distribution of Data and Reports

Classification of Data

Access to the database shall be strictly controlled in order to achieve the following:

- protect the confidentiality of the data
- safeguard the privacy of the patient/client and practitioner
- foster data integrity by protecting them from loss, destruction, or tampering

For the purposes of this policy, data are classified as one of two types:

1. *privileged:* patient/client or practitioner identifiable
2. *aggregate data, nonprivileged:* patient/client or practitioner not identifiable

Authorized Access Levels

In consultation with the administrative and medical staffs, the director of health records shall determine the content, schedule of production, and distribution of routine reports.

In determining the distribution of routine reports and the processing of requests for data of a nonroutine nature, authorized users are defined in the following three categories:

1. restricted access
    - board of trustees and chief executive officer or designee
    - medical staff (individual staff member for information pertaining to self, members of designated committees and review boards carrying out a specific function)
2. access to routine reports/aggregate data for purposes of carrying out a specific responsibility (e.g., committee functions, review board activities, or approved projects)
    - intraorganizational personnel
        - board of trustees and chief executive officer or designee
        - risk management, utilization review, and QA coordinators and committee members
        - medical staff committees and review boards carrying out specific functions

  - professional practitioners carrying out specific committee or review functions
  - researchers who have obtained institutional approval for a specific project
  - students in an approved educational program sponsored by the facility who have received approval for a specific project; approval must be obtained from the director of the program and designated official of this facility
- external agencies or individuals
  - licensing and accrediting bodies and third-party payers in a contractual relationship with the facility (e.g., Blue Cross, health maintenance organizations)
  - federal-mandated or state-mandated agencies within their defined jurisdiction (e.g., Peer Review Organization, Health Care Cost Containment Council, areawide planning agency)

3. special authorization required
   - students assigned to the facility under a formal affiliation agreement need the approval of the director of the program *and* the director of the clinical affiliation at the facility; medical staff approval will be required as needed
   - outside researchers need the approval of the chief executive officer and medical staff

Requests and Priority Determinations for Reports

All requests for reports shall be made in writing and submitted in a timely manner, giving the department at least three workdays to process the request. The department shall prioritize requests based on internally and externally mandated functions, the research mandate of the facility, and similar considerations.

Requests for reports shall be submitted on official forms and shall include the following:

- specific data requested
- purpose of study
- approval signatures when required

Nomenclature

Uniform terminology shall be used to describe all diseases, operations, symptoms, and procedures. The nomenclature used shall be compatible with the classification system, meet mandated requirements (e.g., Medicare billing), and be approved by the medical staff.

Accordingly, the nomenclature found in the following shall be used:

- *Current Medical Information and Terminology* (current edition)—for acute care
- *Current Procedural Terminology* (current edition)—for ambulatory care
- *Diagnostic and Statistical Manual of Mental Disorders* (current edition)—for psychiatric care
- *Systemized Nomenclature of Pathology* (current edition)—for pathology specimens

Classification System

Uniform classification shall be used to reflect all diseases, operations, symptoms, and procedures. The classification system shall be compatible with international classification systems, meet mandated requirements (e.g., DRG assignment under Medicare), and be approved by the medical staff.

Accordingly, the classification system of the *International Classification System, Clinical Modification* (current edition) shall be used. In addition, *Current Procedural Terminology* (current edition) and the *Diagnostic and Statistical Manual of Mental Disorders* (current edition) shall be used as necessitated by the particular needs of ambulatory and psychiatric care.

Diagnostic and procedural coding shall be assigned for all inpatients and outpatients. Appropriate processing of DRG assignment and related procurement of attestation statements from physicians shall be carried out by health record personnel. Coding shall be based on clinically complete medical records.

The sequencing of diagnoses shall be in accordance with the Uniform Hospital Discharge Data Set provisions. The assignment of diagnoses is a physician responsibility. Health record personnel shall bring to the attention of the physician any entries that should be reflected in diagnostic statements.

Statistical Compilations and Reports

Statistical information shall be compiled for inpatient adults and children, newborns, facility-based ambulatory care, and programs such as home care and hospice care. Data shall be collected on a routine basis in accordance with consistent definitions, consistent units of measure, and uniform methods of collection.

Statistical reports shall be prepared as needed for use by the medical and administrative staffs and as required by accrediting and regulatory agencies. The health information management specialist shall meet with the appropriate representatives of the medical and administrative staffs to determine the specific time frames for the compilation of statistical reports.

Individual Statistical Profiles

The basic data elements for each patient/client shall be consistent with the Uniform Hospital Discharge Data Set for inpatients and the Uniform Ambulatory Medical Care Data Set for ambulatory patients.

The following statistical information shall be available reflecting inpatient care:

- inpatient census
  - service days
  - average daily census
- length of stay
  - individual
  - average
- occupancy rate
  - percentage of occupancy
  - bed turnover rate
- morbidity rate
  - gross infection rate
  - net infection rate
  - gross maternal infection rate
  - net maternal infection rate
  - postoperative infection rate
- mortality rate
  - gross
  - net
  - maternal
  - postoperative
  - anesthesia
- autopsy rate
  - gross
  - net
  - facility (adjusted)
- Caesarean section rate

The following statistical information shall be available reflecting newborn care:

- newborn census
- length of stay
  - individual
  - average
- mortality rate
  - infant
  - neonatal
  - perinatal
  - fetal

The following statistical information shall be available reflecting ambulatory care:

- occasion of service
- episode of care
- encounters

Special Statistical Reports

Special statistical reports may be compiled from the routinely gathered data:

- source of referral patterns
- consultation patterns
- time and day of week admission patterns
- time and day of week discharge patterns
- preoperative and postoperative length of stay analysis
- age distributions

Required Reports to External Agencies

A comprehensive system for preparing and processing required reports to external agencies shall be developed and implemented in cooperation with the medical and professional staffs. This system shall foster timely and accurate compliance with the regulatory provisions of local, state, and federal agencies. Specific report preparation and processing by this unit include the following:

- communicable diseases
- inborn metabolic error
- inheritable disorders and diseases
- sickle cell anemia and sickle cell trait
- cancer
- adverse drug and chemical reactions
- adverse events following immunization
- dementias
- lead poisoning
- vaccine injury

Assistance in report preparation and processing shall be provided to the medical and professional staffs in their efforts to comply with the following mandated reporting:

- suspected child abuse
- suspected older adult abuse
- firearms and criminally afflicted injuries
- data for National Practitioners Data Bank under the Health Care Quality Improvement Act of 1986
- cardiac pacemaker registry information

Vital Statistics

Birth and death certificates shall be prepared and processed in strict conformity with the guidelines and regulations prepared by the National Center for Health Statistics and the state's division of vital statistics.

In cooperation with the medical and nursing staffs, the health record department shall process the demographic information. Medical and nursing personnel shall supply the clinical information.

Birth Certificates. Particular care shall be taken to conform to regulations concerning special situations such as

- acknowledgment of paternity statements
- registration other than as child of mother's husband
- registration of child of an unmarried woman
- use of multiple surnames

Information about the legal implications of naming a child, acknowledgment of paternity, and similar considerations shall be provided to the mother, father, and/or husband by qualified personnel. Health record personnel shall refer the patient/client to the designated personnel should such questions arise.

A copy of the worksheet shall be signed by the mother to indicate her approval of the information as correct and satisfactory for submission on the birth certificate. This copy shall be placed in the health record of the newborn.

Death Certificates. Particular care shall be taken to conform to regulations concerning special definitions and circumstances including

- requirements of state's abortion control act
- fetal death
- cause of death (underlying cause, immediate cause, intervening cause)

The health record department shall cooperate with the medical staff in providing inservice education to house staff and other medical staff members concerning proper completion of death certificates.

Releasing Copies of Certificates. In accordance with state regulations, no copies of birth or death certificates shall be made for release to the patient/client or next of kin. All requests for vital statistic information shall be directed to the appropriate state agency.

NOTE: Consult current interpretation of state law concerning permissibility of retaining a copy of birth or death certificates. Consult hospital legal counsel to determine what restrictions to its access should be placed if a copy is retained (when permissible by state law).

AIDS and ARC Reports and Statistical Data

The specific provisions of state and federal regulatory agencies shall be adhered to. The responsibility for reporting such required data shall be coordinated with the facility's laboratory staff, medical staff, and health record department. Specific areas of report initiation, verification, and submission shall be outlined in the procedures relating to this policy.

No separate statistical log or register shall be developed. Relevant information shall be entered in the usual disease and operation indexes.

As far as possible, the American Medical Record Association's "Guidelines for Handling Health Data on Individuals Tested or Treated for the HIV Virus" shall be adopted for use.

Indexes and Registers

Indexes and registers shall be developed and maintained by the health record department within its assigned jurisdiction. The health record department shall assist other departments charged with the responsibility for maintaining special registers (*see* "Special Indexes and Registers").

Key Points

The following are the key points for each register or index:

• **Index or register**	Specific name of index or register
• **Responsibility**	A function of the health record department *or* provision of assistance to another department having responsibility
• **Content**	Detailed specifications of required and optional content
• **External agency requirement or standard**	Specific agency having guidelines or regulations; these are in addition to the usual regulations and accrediting requirements for the facility
• **Form**	Any consideration about manual system, automated system, and/or use of microimage. User of sample policy must specify for facility.
• **Retention**	Permanent where applicable is noted. If retained for only a period of years, specify. *NOTE:* American Medical Record Association guidelines recommend 10-year retention period in the absence of any other requirement.
• **Access and special considerations**	This is keyed to the policy statement that outlines the categories of access.

Source: Joan Gratto Liebler, *Medical Records: Policies and Guidelines*, Aspen Publishers, Inc. © 1990.

SPECIAL INDEXES AND REGISTERS

INDEX OR REGISTER	Admission Register
HEALTH RECORD DEPARTMENT RESPONSIBILITY	Maintain, update, and control
CONTENT	Chronological entry for each patient/client *Detailed information:* • Patient/client name • Date of birth • Sex • Date and time of admission • Unit number • Attending physician
EXTERNAL AGENCY REQUIREMENT OR STANDARDS	
FORM	*NOTE:* Specify whether automated or manual system is used.
RETENTION	Permanent
ACCESS/SPECIAL CONSIDERATIONS	Restricted

INDEX OR REGISTER	Discharge Register
HEALTH RECORD DEPARTMENT RESPONSIBILITY	Maintain, update, and control
CONTENT	Chronological entry for each patient/client *Detailed information:* • Patient/client name • Identifying number • Date and time discharged • Attending physician
EXTERNAL AGENCY REQUIREMENT OR STANDARDS	
FORM	*NOTE:* Specify whether automated or manual system is used.
RETENTION	Permanent
ACCESS/SPECIAL CONSIDERATIONS	Restricted

INDEX OR REGISTER	Emergency Department Register
HEALTH RECORD DEPARTMENT RESPONSIBILITY	Assist designated department in developing, maintaining, and controlling
CONTENT	• Patient/client identification • Time and means of arrival • Nature of complaint • Disposition • Time of departure • Time in observation unit if applicable Dead-on-arrival cases should be entered in this register.
EXTERNAL AGENCY REQUIREMENT OR STANDARDS	
FORM	*NOTE:* Specify whether automated or manual system is used.
RETENTION	Permanent
ACCESS/SPECIAL CONSIDERATIONS	Restricted

continues

Special Indexes and Registers continued

INDEX OR REGISTER	Operating Room Register
HEALTH RECORD DEPARTMENT RESPONSIBILITY	Assist designated department in developing, maintaining, and controlling
CONTENT	• Patient/client identification • Operations and procedures • Date • Surgeon and assistants • Service on which patient was hospitalized • End results of the hospitalization • Date of admission and/or discharge and/or length of stay • Associated diseases and operations
EXTERNAL AGENCY REQUIREMENT OR STANDARDS	American College of Surgeons
FORM	*NOTE:* Specify whether automated or manual system is used.
RETENTION	[Number of] years
ACCESS/SPECIAL CONSIDERATIONS	Restricted

INDEX OR REGISTER	Disease and Operations Index
HEALTH RECORD DEPARTMENT RESPONSIBILITY	Maintain, update, and control
CONTENT	• Patient/client unit number • Sex • Age • Race • Attending physician or surgeon • Department • End results (discharge, death) • Autopsy as applicable • Diagnoses • Operations
EXTERNAL AGENCY REQUIREMENT OR STANDARDS	
FORM	*NOTE:* Specify whether automated or manual system is used.
RETENTION	10 years (nonresearch facility) 25 years (research facility)
ACCESS/SPECIAL CONSIDERATIONS	Restricted

INDEX OR REGISTER	Physician Index
HEALTH RECORD DEPARTMENT RESPONSIBILITY	Maintain, update, and control
CONTENT	Indexed by physician name Includes • Patient/client name • Unit number • Length of stay • End result (discharge, death)
EXTERNAL AGENCY REQUIREMENT OR STANDARDS	Specialty boards
FORM	*NOTE:* Specify whether automated or manual system is used.
RETENTION	[Number of] years
ACCESS/SPECIAL CONSIDERATIONS	This index is subject to subpoena.

continues

Special Indexes and Registers continued

INDEX OR REGISTER	Birth Register
HEALTH RECORD DEPARTMENT RESPONSIBILITY	Maintain, update, and control
CONTENT	• Baby's name • Mother's name • Father's name • Date and time of birth • Sex • Address
EXTERNAL AGENCY REQUIREMENT OR STANDARDS	Department of Vital Statistics National Center for Health Statistics
FORM	*NOTE:* Specify whether automated or manual system is used.
RETENTION	Permanent
ACCESS/SPECIAL CONSIDERATIONS	Restricted

INDEX OR REGISTER	Death Register
HEALTH RECORD DEPARTMENT RESPONSIBILITY	Maintain, update, and control
CONTENT	• Patient/client name, sex, and race • Date of birth • Address • Date and time of death • 48-hours-and-under designation • Fetal death designation • Cause of death • Autopsy or coroner's case • Attending physician • Funeral home
EXTERNAL AGENCY REQUIREMENT OR STANDARDS	Department of Vital Statistics National Center for Health Statistics
FORM	*NOTE:* Specify whether automated or manual system is used.
RETENTION	Permanent
ACCESS/SPECIAL CONSIDERATIONS	Restricted

INDEX OR REGISTER	Trauma Register
HEALTH RECORD DEPARTMENT RESPONSIBILITY	Maintain, update, and control
CONTENT	As stipulated in accrediting agency requirements, including • Severity of injury • Probability of dying • Anatomic site of injury • Nature of injury • Mechanism of injury • Classification of patient/client injuries • Demographic information • Outcome
EXTERNAL AGENCY REQUIREMENT OR STANDARDS	Statewide or areawide trauma system agency Accrediting agency
FORM	*NOTE:* Specify whether automated or manual system is used.
RETENTION	[Number of] years
ACCESS/SPECIAL CONSIDERATIONS	Routine authorization

continues

Special Indexes and Registers continued

INDEX OR REGISTER	Cancer Register
HEALTH RECORD DEPARTMENT RESPONSIBILITY	Maintain, update, and control
CONTENT	As detailed in American College of Surgeons' Cancer Program Guidelines and in state cancer registry regulations
EXTERNAL AGENCY REQUIREMENT OR STANDARDS	American College of Surgeons State department of health regulations
FORM	*NOTE:* Specify whether automated or manual system is used.
RETENTION	[Number of] years
ACCESS/SPECIAL CONSIDERATIONS	Restricted

INDEX OR REGISTER	Organ Transplant Register
HEALTH RECORD DEPARTMENT RESPONSIBILITY	Assist designated department in developing, maintaining, and controlling
CONTENT	• Medical condition • Blood type • Tissue type • Genetic information • Laboratory results re: organ function studies • Length of time recipient has been waiting for organ donation
EXTERNAL AGENCY REQUIREMENT OR STANDARDS	Federal and state laws require transplant forms be in the medical record with consent from next of kin of the deceased for organ removal.
FORM	*NOTE:* Specify whether automated or manual system is used.
RETENTION	[Number of] years
ACCESS/SPECIAL CONSIDERATIONS	Restricted

INDEX OR REGISTER	Eye Bank Register
HEALTH RECORD DEPARTMENT RESPONSIBILITY	Assist designated department in developing, maintaining, and controlling
CONTENT	• Recipient form: name of the patient who received the eye, patient's age, reason for transplant, diagnosis, physician number, donor age, date of donor's death • Donor information: patient name, address, age, and sex; cause and time of death; time of harvesting of the eye, time of preservation
EXTERNAL AGENCY REQUIREMENT OR STANDARDS	Eye Bank Association of America
FORM	*NOTE:* Specify whether automated or manual system is used.
RETENTION	[Number of] years
ACCESS/SPECIAL CONSIDERATIONS	Restricted

Source: Joan Gratto Liebler, *Medical Records: Policies and Guidelines*, Aspen Publishers, Inc., © 1990.

4
Creation and Maintenance of the Health Record

Chapter 4

Creation and Maintenance of the Health Record

CONTENT OF THE HEALTH RECORD

PATIENT/CLIENT HEALTH RECORD: POLICIES AND PROCEDURES

Definition and Creation

Health record documentation shall be developed and maintained for each patient/client who receives assessment and/or treatment in any component of this health care facility. All documentation for each individual shall be assembled and located in one central record, unique to that patient/client, thereby constituting a unit record. Documentation with the unit record shall be maintained in the standardized format and arranged in the standardized sequence. This unit record shall be processed and located in the health record department.

The following three operational definitions are used in this policy statement:

1. *Health care facility:* the corporate entity as a whole, whether in a centralized or decentralized physical location, legally titled [*corporate name of facility*]; including all departments and programs directed and staffed by physicians on the active medical staff, nurses, and allied health practitioners as defined by the health care facility bylaws. Specifically included are
   - inpatient services
   - short-stay services
   - outpatient clinics (exclusive of private group practice)
   - emergency care services/urgent care services
   - health care facility/hospital based home care and/or hospice programs
   - health maintenance organizations (facility sponsored)

   Specifically excluded are
   - private physician care rendered in a private office (even if located on health care facility property)
   - group practice care rendered in a private office under a private group practice contract among physicians and patients/clients
   - referred outpatient (i.e., an individual who is admitted exclusively to a special diagnostic or therapeutic department of the facility for diagnosis and/or treatment on an ambulatory basis); the referring physician is responsible for this individual.
2. *Patient/client:* any individual receiving assessment and/or treatment in any component or department of the health care facility.
   Employees of the facility who receive health care at the facility shall be classified as patients, with all the safe-

guards for record access provided for any other patient. Additional access safeguards may be instituted as appropriate.

3. *Health record:* confidential document and/or combination of documents created in the normal course of patient/client care, from initial assessment through conclusion of treatment. This document, created in the sequence of events as they occur, should be sufficiently comprehensive to support the diagnoses, course of treatment, and outcome.

Purposes of Health Record and Database

Complete and accurate health record documentation shall be developed and maintained for the primary purpose of fostering continuity of patient/client care by maintaining a means of communication among the health care practitioners treating a patient now and in the future.

Such documentation shall also be developed and maintained in light of the related purposes that are derived from and associated with this primary purpose:

- *Use for patient/client:* to provide information for continuity of care, evidence in support of insurance and reimbursement claims, proof of illness, and legal defense
- *Use by health care provider/practitioner:* to provide a basis for quality assurance and education review of care rendered by an individual practitioner as a member of a professional health care team; proof of care rendered; and legal defense
- *Use for research:* to provide a basis for comparative studies to advance the knowledge and practice of effective patient care interventions
- *Use by institution, managers, and administration:* to provide a basis for programwide quality assurance and utilization review processes; proof of care rendered; analysis of costs; risk management review; legal defense; compliance with legal and regulatory mandates and professional and accrediting agency standards; long-range planning; and educational programs for physicians, nursing personnel, allied health practitioners, and students in these various health care disciplines
- *Use by the community as a whole/public at large:* through properly designated public health agencies and officials, to provide information for the development of material relating to public health profiles, studies, vital statistics, and preventive medicine

All related policies, practices, and procedures shall be developed in a manner consistent with these purposes.

Responsibility for Documentation and Authentication

The health care physician/practitioner who treats a patient/client shall have the responsibility for documenting and authenticating the care rendered. Such documentation shall be in accordance with

- generally accepted professional standards of documentation
- specifically mandated regulatory, legal, and/or accrediting standards
- documentation guidelines developed in concert with this policy statement and approved by the medical staff
- health record content policy of this facility

The following health care practitioners are included in this designation of responsibility:

- medical staff
- licensed nurses
- physician assistants
- medical students
- psychologists
- social workers
- allied health practitioners
- chaplains

[*NOTE:* See institutional bylaws for specific designation; this policy provision must conform to bylaws statement.]

Proper Authentication

Proper authentication shall be added at the conclusion of each entry and shall consist of the practitioner's name and professional title or initials indicating the professional credential. The use of a rubber stamp or any other device for authentication (e.g., computerized security and authentication code) shall be specifically approved in writing by the president of the medical staff and the chief executive officer. This document, which shall include a statement that use of the rubber stamp or device shall be limited to the individual and shall remain under the individual's direct control, shall remain on file in the office of the chief executive officer. Copies or listings of such approvals shall be provided to the health record staff involved in processing the health record/database.

No other individual (clerical or administrative staff) shall be authorized to enter, delete, change, sign, or authenticate material in the health record/database. This provision is not intended to prohibit assistance in preparing material for direct entry and authentication by a responsible, professional practitioner or member of the medical staff.

If the process of countersignatures is not used by the medical staff to signify review and supervision of the care being given, a suitable entry shall be made in the progress note section stating that the attending physician is in agreement with the orders, evaluation, or specific treatment noted.

Ownership of Health Record

The health record shall be considered the property of the health care facility, which shall seek to safeguard it from unauthorized use, access, loss, and destruction. The patient/client's legally recognized interest in the content of the health record shall be noted and honored by the development of appropriate access and release of information practices. Material shall not be accessed or released without the appropriate patient/client consent.

The health record document(s) shall not be removed from the premises except as required by specific subpoena or court order and approved by the chief executive officer or designee. Further, the documents shall not be placed in areas, work spaces, personal lockers, or briefcases where they are inaccessible for use by all authorized users.

Guidelines for Health Record Entries

Entries in the health record shall be made to reflect each patient/client event of care. These entries shall be characterized by generally accepted documentation features, including the following:

- unique identification for each patient/client
  - name and identification number and date of birth on each page, front and reverse sides
  - no preprinted or pretyped (canned) reports or entries
- original document in unit record
- factualness and objectivity
  - preliminary findings and observations noted as such
  - results of studies, tests and evaluations, and actions taken properly noted
  - freedom from negative comments about any individual, including patient or family member
- accuracy
  - legible handwriting; typed entries if possible
  - no misfiles
- creation in normal course of patient care
  - entries made according to standard content
  - entries made on approved forms
  - abbreviations limited to those listed on approved abbreviation list
- timeliness
  - documented as close to the time of the actual event as feasible
  - late entries and addenda so noted; reason for late entry or addenda given
  - identifiable and clearly noted date and time (month, day, year, A.M. or P.M.)
  - no charting ahead in anticipation of actually rendering the care
- freedom from inadvertent or intentional alterations and potential for such altering
  - continuous entries, with no blank pages, lines, or spaces; line drawn to end of page when entries do not fill page
  - written in pen with permanent blue or black ink
  - error corrections done in a manner that does not obliterate original entry; error so marked; correction note indicated; date and signature of individual making correction entered
- authentication
  - signature (first and last name) on each entry
  - initials or title indicating professional credential
- internal consistency
  - data entries reflect similar observations of fact as recorded by different disciplines; when there is a difference of observation and/or interpretation, it is noted

Videotape Recordings

Videotape Recordings of Individual Patients

Videotape recordings of patient care transactions for an individual patient are a part of the official health record for that patient when, in the judgment of the patient care provider, they are the best means of documenting the patient care transaction (e.g., rehabilitation evaluation, gait training progress). Videotaped entries shall be characterized by the same level of detail as required for all other entries: clear patient identification, date, and visual identification of provider. This information shall be contained within the videotape itself and also be placed on the external label.

A written, signed, and dated entry shall be placed in the hard-copy health record to indicate the existence of the videotape. The usual periodic summaries of such care shall be entered.

The videotape is stored in the permanent storage and retrieval area of the central health record department. It is subject to the same conditions and requirements for retention and access as other records.

Videotape Recordings of Groups of Patients

Videotape recordings of patient care transactions for a group of patients shall be summarized in written form by the patient care provider. The tape is then erased or destroyed. Tapes that include transactions among several patients are not incorporated into the official health record because this would violate the privacy and confidentiality requirements for individual patients.

Consents for Videotaping

A specific consent shall be obtained to permit the videotaping of patient care transactions. This consent shall be dated and signed and shall include the purpose of the videotaping

- patient care only
- education and research only, for use within the facility
- education and research, including external use
- a combination of any of these purposes

The consent form shall be filed in the permanent health record.

Videotapes for Education and Research Only

When videotapes are produced, with proper patient consent, for the sole purpose of education and research, they are not part of the official health record. The consent form shall be filed in the permanent health record. The videotapes are stored in the educational or research unit that created the videotape.

Facsimile Transmissions

Selected information shall be processed by facsimile transmission when this procedure is in the best interests of fostering immediate patient care. The documents are then incorporated into the permanent health record of the patient. The usual conditions for release of information apply to the request for the release of such information. Only certain material should be transmitted, and specific procedures must be followed to safeguard the confidentiality of the material and preserve the integrity of the data as information processed during the normal course of business.

Examples of Permitted Transmissions

- Physician orders when the usual conditions required for verbal orders are met. The orders must be dated and signed on the original form being transmitted. Countersignatures are required as specified in state regulations for the facility and state laws of evidence. According to the June 1990 advisory letter (no. 90-25) of the Health Care Financing Administration, physician orders, if properly signed on the transmitted original, need not be countersigned at a later date.
- Diagnostic and laboratory studies (except those related to human immunodeficiency virus [HIV] and acquired immune deficiency syndrome [AIDS]), when such transmittal would permit more immediate and comprehensive diagnosis.
- Fetal heart monitoring tracings.
- Patient authorization for release of information, provided the authorization includes:
  - a statement that the patient understands the risks involved in such transmission processes
  - a statement that a faxed copy may be deemed as having the same force and effect as an original
- Next-of-kin or guardian consents in emergency situations, with the stipulation that a written consent will be sent immediately.

Examples of Prohibited Transmissions

- Any patient care document reflecting any of these conditions or diagnoses
  - AIDS/HIV-related conditions
  - sexually transmitted diseases
  - drug or alcohol abuse
  - psychiatric conditions
- Any document reflecting peer review or risk management information.
- Health record information in response to requests from anyone other than direct patient care providers. This prohibition includes requests from insurance companies, attorneys, and employers.

Administrative Policies and Procedures

Transmittal and receipt of facsimile materials shall be processed in a timely, consistent manner as set forth in the policies and procedures listed below.

Selection of Equipment. Plain paper facsimile equipment shall be used, if possible. When thermal process equipment must be used, a photocopy of the transmittal is made immediately onto paper that meets record-retention standards. The thermal paper copy is immediately destroyed by shredding.

Location of Equipment. Facsimile equipment shall be located in areas where the security of the data is ensured

- *patient care units:* in restricted area of nursing station
- *health record department:* in release of information section

Designated Key Operators. Specific personnel in each unit shall be designated as having responsibility for carrying out the procedures relating to the transmission and receipt of facsimile transmissions. Job descriptions shall include this designated responsibility. Training programs for designated key operators shall contain a unit on the required procedural safeguards.

Pretransmittal Preparation

- Verify the fax number of the intended recipient.
- Verify that fax equipment is located in a secure area.

OR

- Verify that there is immediate availability of an authorized recipient on standby to receive the transmission.
- Prepare a Telephone Inquiry: Emergency Request form.
- Prepare a transmittal cover sheet.

Post-Transmittal Follow-Up

- Receive acknowledgment of receipt of transmission.
- Place copy of cover sheet, emergency request form, and receipt of transmittal acknowledgment in the designated area for filing in the permanent health record.
- Complete the transmittal log showing:
  - –patient's name
  - –date of transmittal
  - –requestor's name, address, and facsimile number
  - –number of pages sent

Receipt of Facsimile Transmission

- Remove material from transmittal equipment immediately.
- Count the number of pages received.
- Check for accuracy of the patient identification to be sure that all the documents received are intended from receipt by the facility.
- Send verification of receipt of the information if this has been requested by the sender.
- Place material in a sealed envelope with proper patient identification on the outside; place the envelope in a designated area for pickup.
- Notify the intended receiver that material has arrived and is ready for pickup, or deliver it to the designated location.

Misdirected Facsimile Transmission

- Receipt of misdirected transmission: notify sender of the inadvertent misdirection; destroy the material by shredding.
- Transmittal of material that inadvertently becomes misdirected.
  - –Obtain the fax number of the unintended receiver. (This information is usually available in the internal logging system of the equipment.)
  - –Immediately transmit a request to this unintended receiver and ask that the material be destroyed immediately or returned by mail or delivery service.
  - –Complete an incident report and process it according to the usual risk management procedures.
  - –Check the fax number of the intended recipient and complete the transmittal process after a test run has been made.

Source: Joan Gratto Liebler, *Medical Records: Policies and Guidelines*, Aspen Publishers, Inc., © 1995.

CONTENT AND SEQUENCE OF THE HEALTH RECORD/DATABASE: POLICIES AND PROCEDURES

General Premises

The content of the health record/database for each patient/client shall be sufficiently comprehensive and detailed to achieve the following:

- foster high quality and continuity of patient/client care
- meet the requirements of the legal and regulatory agencies with jurisdiction over the facility and the accrediting standards of agencies in whose accreditation programs the facility participates
- supply a database for all other uses of the document(s)
- reflect the assessment and care of the patient/client including diagnoses, details of diagnostic studies, treatments rendered, and outcome and disposition

General Delineation of Content

The content of the health record/database shall include but not be limited to

- identification of patient/client as an individual and as a patient/client
- consents, permissions, and refusals for treatment and related legal documents
- clinical database, which includes
  - – assessments, examinations, diagnostic studies, and evaluations
  - – treatments rendered
  - – continuing observations and notes
  - – outcome, disposition, provision for after-care, and patient/family instruction and/or education concerning follow-up care
  - – administrative and nondirect patient care data

Standardized Format

Standardized forms shall be developed for each type of health record document in order to achieve the following:

- foster ease of access to the information
- routinize the placement of information within the health record
- reduce the possibility of error by the practitioner when adding to data and accessing and using information
- foster ease of distribution/dissemination of information through a multiple-copy format when more than one immediate user of the information is involved

- provide for uniform entry of patient/client identification, assessment, and treatment data

The standard forms used in the health record shall be designed to meet computerization requirements and archival specifications for record retention.

Forms Control Committee

The responsibility for forms design and control shall rest with a facilitywide forms committee that shall include members of the administrative and direct patient care departments as needed. The chairperson of the committee shall be the health information management specialist. Documents relating to legal consents, refusal for treatment, and similar data entries shall be cleared with legal counsel and/or risk management staff. The duties of the committee shall be to review and approve all new forms, periodically review and revise existing forms, and oversee the forms control process.

Forms Control Register and Inventory

The health information management specialist shall maintain a forms control register and inventory log showing the following:

- form title
- form number
- date approved by medical staff and administrative officials or the forms design committee
- date revised (latest revision)
- history of form
  - date of initial inception
  - date and copy of original form
  - date and copy of all subsequent revisions
  - working notes reflecting rationale for changes
- listing of distribution of copies for multiple-copy forms
- cost specifications and source for ordering (internal supply source or external vendor)
- inventory of current supply

Ordering and Purchasing Forms

In order to maintain inventory control and take advantage of cost-effective measures relating to forms procurement, and ensure that the most recent version of each approved form is used, all orders for forms, both internal and external, shall be routed through the health record department for approval before processing by the internal supply source or external vendors.

Standardized Abbreviations and Symbols

In order to reduce error and foster clarity of written communication, only approved abbreviations and symbols shall be used in making data entries in the health record. Each approved abbreviation and symbol shall have *only one* meaning. The standardized abbreviations and symbols listing shall be approved by the pharmacy and therapeutics committee and the health record committee of the medical staff, who shall review and revise the list at least annually. The health information management specialist shall initiate and participate in this review.

NOTE: Each facility must adapt this list, selecting the meaning that will be used for abbreviations and symbols having more than one meaning and eliminating the other meanings to avoid confusion.

Health Record/Chart Organization

The health record content shall be placed in a standardized sequence within the record of each patient in order to foster ease of access to the material for all subsequent use. The underlying principle for the grouping of material is derived from the fact that documents are generated in the normal course of business.

Material placed in the health record folder shall be filed in two major sections: (1) inpatient admissions and (2) emergency service, resulting in inpatient admission documents on the right side and documents for outpatient and emergency care not resulting in immediate inpatient admission on the left side.

All information (clinical, legal, and administrative) relating to an episode of care shall be grouped together, as this set of information was the basis on which the care was initiated and carried out. Documents for the most recent episode of care shall be placed on top of documents for previous episodes for ready access to the most current health status of the patient/client.

Documents for each episode of care shall be identified and separated from documents for other episodes by dividers.

Source-Oriented Format

Within each segment of the record, the material for the episode of care shall be placed in source-oriented groupings: by clinical department and/or the health care practitioner specialty providing the care. Material shall be placed in chronological order within each grouping by health record personnel at the time of chart analysis and review for completion, which is done at the conclusion of the episode of care.

During the inpatient stay, materials shall be arranged in a similar order, except as determined by the director of nursing and the medical director, in consultation with the health information management specialist. The need for ready access to critical data during the immediate care of the patient/client shall be honored. Within each department, a uniform arrangement shall be determined and followed. The placement of materials in the designated order during the inpatient stay is the responsibility of unit clerical staff, under the direct supervision of the director of nursing. [*Alternate policy statement:* The placement of materials in the designated order during the inpatient stay is the responsibility of health record personnel, under the direct supervision of the health information management specialist.]

Alternate Format: Automated Patient Record of Care

To foster consistency and uniformity of data and to facilitate the electronic exchange of data, the format, content, and structure of the computer-based health record shall be consistent with the ASTM Standards.[1] (*See* "The Overall Structure of the Computer-Based Patient Record" in the "American Society for Testing and Materials" section in Chapter 2.)

Detailed Sequence of Health Record Content

NOTE: The following sequence must be adapted to conform to the finalized chart content set forth in the facility's policy on chart content.

The sequence of placement at discharge shall be as shown in the following outline.

I. Identification/Demographic Information
   A. Admission/discharge sheet or face sheet
   B. Registration form

II. Legal and Administrative Documents
   A. Notice of Patient Bill of Rights
   B. Consents:
      1. consent to treatment signed at admission
      2. updates to consent
      3. special consents (e.g., organ donation, blood transfusion, radiology, experimental drug or treatment, research subject, photograph or videotape, presentation/appearance at special teaching or clinical case conference session)
      4. operation and procedure consents
      5. anesthesia consent
      6. refusal of blood transfusion
      7. refusal of specified treatment
      8. waivers and releases
      9. departures against medical advice
      10. living will documents
   C. Power of attorney or conservatorship
   D. Psychiatric commitments/authorization to hold patient/client court orders
   E. Billing and insurance information data sheet
   F. Conditions/agreement for admission
   G. Medicare and Medicaid certifications
   H. Patient's/client's possessions at time of admission
   I. Patient's/client's possessions at time of discharge
   J. Release of information and requests for access to record consent/release/request forms, court orders, and subpoenas
   K. Listing of release of information and/or access to health record; listing of material actually released

III. Discharge Data
   A. Discharge summary including discharge instructions and after-care instructions
   B. Interagency referral forms sent to receiving facility
   C. Documentation associated with death of patient/client
      1. danger/critical list notice
      2. notification of family
      3. information compiled for completion of death certificate
      4. copy of death certificate if permitted by state regulations
      5. next-of-kin directives regarding mortuary services
      6. release of body/mortuary record
      7. autopsy consent
      8. autopsy report (preliminary report, provisional diagnoses, and full protocol)

IV. Physician Orders and Medication Records
   A. Allergic reaction notices
   B. Physician orders
   C. Pharmacist review of medication orders
   D. Record of medications given
   E. Anticoagulant record

V. Clinical Assessment/Clinical Database
   A. Preadmission assessments and studies
   B. Interagency or physician referral form
   C. Emergency department form when patient/client sent directly to inpatient unit
   D. Ambulance/emergency transport summary
   E. Materials abstracted from hospital or clinic chart sent by referring agent or requested by practitioners
   F. History and physical examination
   G. Interval notc/update of history and physical examination
   H. Consultations and special assessments
   I. Clinical laboratory studies
   J. Diagnostic tests and studies: requests and interpretations (e.g., radiology, electroencephalograms, electrocardiograms, nuclear medicine scans, pulmonary function studies, radioisotope studies, electromyograms)
   K. Biopsy reports, surgical pathology reports, and disposition of body parts

[1] *Standard Guide for Content and Structure of the Computer-Based Patient Record,* 1384–96. American Society for Testing and Materials, Philadelphia, PA, 1996.

VI. Course of Treatment Documentation
   A. Patient/client care plan
   B. Discharge plan
   C. Physician notes
   D. Notes by health care disciplines except nursing (separate section)
      1. dietary/nutrition
      2. social service
      3. clinical psychology
      4. chaplaincy
      5. physical medicine and rehabilitation (e.g., physical therapy, occupational therapy, vocational rehabilitation, respiratory therapy, audiology, and speech therapy)
      6. dentistry
   E. Additional material concerning specialized aspects of care

VII. Nursing Documentation
   A. Nursing assessment
   B. Nursing plan of care
   C Tracking and flow sheets (e.g., intake/output, weight, bowel and bladder function, vital signs, critical care)
   D. Nurses' notes
   E. Interward transfer record

In addition to these documents, certain admissions shall have specialized forms reflecting particular aspects of the care (see VI.E in outline above):

- surgical care documentation
  - preanesthesia evaluations
  - anesthesia record
  - postanesthesia evaluation
  - operative report
  - blood transfusion record during surgery
  - intravenous infusion record during surgery
  - recovery room observations
  - tissue/pathology reports: any removal of body parts
- obstetrical care documentation
  - discharge summary: undelivered; complicated delivery
  - prenatal care summary
  - labor progress chart
  - labor and delivery summary with notation of outcome
  - analgesia and anesthesia evaluation
  - analgesia and anesthesia record
  - operation or procedure related to delivery
  - intravenous infusion record
  - postpartum record
  - toxemia monitoring
  - cross reference to newborn
  - pathology reports for tubal ligation or hysterectomy
  - consultations/physician review (e.g., Caesarean section, sterilization, abortion)
  - consents (e.g., sterilization, Caesarean section, abortion, disposal of stillborn, release for adoption)
  - fetal monitoring data
  - court orders and special decrees (e.g., refusal of parent[s] to allow transfusions or certain treatments)
- newborns
  - footprint and identification verification
  - signed release for removal of infant by parent or designated agent of parent
  - birth certificate information (copy of certificate if permitted by state regulations)
  - cross reference to mother's chart including, as needed, prenatal care summary and fetal monitoring summary
  - discharge summary (e.g., complicated or premature births, neonate intensive care, prolonged stay)
  - summary of delivery
  - evaluation at birth
  - growth and development/pediatric assessment and/or low birth weight graphic chart
  - circumcision (e.g., consent, procedure summary)
  - neonate intensive care graphic records and notes
- pediatric chart
  - release of child to parent or designated agent of parent
  - clear notation of source of information/informant
  - history of childhood diseases
  - immunization record
  - growth and development comparative graphic records
  - court orders and special decrees (e.g., refusal of parent[s] to allow transfusions or certain treatments)
- emergency department (usually one composite form)
  - emergency department report
  - disposition note: discharged from emergency care, *or* admitted to inpatient care, *or* transferred to other health care facility
  - addendum notes (e.g., major trauma, infection, chest pain)
  - summary received from paramedics or emergency transport service personnel
- outpatient clinic
  - identification section
  - legal and administrative documents (e.g., consents for care; refusals of treatment; follow-up notes/attempts to reach patient/client who does not return for care, suture removal, or similar situations)
  - assessment, history, and physical examinations
  - treatment notes
  - concluding note showing disposition of patient/client and clear statement of end of episode of care
  - "fit for work" or health clearance forms
  - transfer forms (referral to other health care setting)

Source: Joan Gratto Liebler, *Medical Records: Policies and Guidelines*, Aspen Publishers, Inc., © 1992.

TIMELINESS OF HEALTH RECORD DOCUMENTATION—POLICY AND PROCEDURE

	Issued By:	Policy #:
	Prepared By:	Revision #:
	Approved By:	Effective Date:
Subject: Timeliness of Health Record Documentation		Page of

Purpose:
- To ensure timely and complete health record documentation as it occurs to support ongoing quality patient care
- To meet the regulatory requirements of accrediting agencies and the documentation requirements for reimbursement by third-party payers
- To reduce risk to the patient and hospital

Policy: Health record documentation will be written within the time frames as stated in the standards and hospital policy. Health record documentation will adhere to completion guidelines as stipulated in the health record handbook.

Standards:
1. The history and physical (H & P) must be written within 24 hours of admission and, except in emergency situations, always prior to the performance of surgery.
2. Informed consent to surgery and invasive procedures will be obtained and signed prior to the performance of the procedure except in emergencies.
3. Telephone/verbal orders of authorized individuals are accepted and transcribed by qualified individuals who are identified by title or category in the medical staff rules and regulations.
4. Operative reports/surgical dictations must be dictated directly following surgery.
5. All medical documentation, content, and signature requirements must be kept concurrent with the inpatient stay.
6. Hospital staff physicians shall complete records delivered to their office within five days of delivery.
7. Discharge summaries must be dictated on the unit on the day of discharge.
8. The discharge report and discharge instructions must be completed in their entirety at the time of discharge. The discharge report for expired patients must be completed and signed at the time that the death certificate is completed.
9. The provisional anatomical diagnosis shall be recorded in the medical record within 48 hours after an autopsy has been performed.
10. The DRG data summary must be verified and signed immediately on the day of delivery to the physician.
11. The entire health record, including signatures, must be completed within 30 days of discharge.
12. Progress notes must be entered daily and must include the name and credentials of the individual making the entry, the department/service of the individual making the entry, and signature. Cosignatures by senior staff, in the case of supervision of resident involvement in the care of the patient, must be completed during rounds.

Procedure:
1. Place all appropriate initial documentation forms in the chart for practitioners' use when the floor chart is created.
2. Practitioner will complete appropriate service-specific forms and sign all entries as noted in the standards.

References: JCAHO Manual for Hospital Accreditation 1998
Henry Ford Hospital Handbook
Federal, state, and local regulations
Third Party Payer Requirements

Courtesy of Henry Ford Health System, Detroit, Michigan.

ADMISSION RECORD

Admission Record

Patient's Name	Admission Date & Time	☐ A.M. ☐ P.M.

Present Address

Home Address If Different From Above	Church Affiliation

Birth Date	Sex	Marital Status	Race	Social Security No.	Welfare Claim No.

Attending Physician	Address	Phone
Alternate Physician	Address	Phone
Name of Dentist	Address	Phone
Name of Pharmacist	Address	Phone
Mortician	Address	Phone

Expenses Paid By: Family	Insurance	Medicare / Welfare / Social Security

Admitting Diagnosis:

Admitting Service	Date of Last Admission

Allergies:

Rehabilitation Potential:

Hospital Insurance	Address	Policy No.
Burial Insurance	Address	Policy No.
Next of Kin or Legal Representative	Address	Phone

Hospital Preference

This patient has been informed of his physical and mental condition and plan of treatment. ☐ Yes ☐ No

If no, explain: __________

*Physician's Signature __________ (date)

*If this section is not signed by the physician this summary information has been transcribed from document(s) contained in this patient's clinical record which appropriately bear the physician's signature. Signature of Transcribing Nurse: __________ Date __________

In Case Of Emergency
(Relative or Friend)

Name	Address	Relationship / Phone
Name	Address	Relationship / Phone
Name	Address	Relationship / Phone

Reprinted with permission of Briggs Corporation, Des Moines, Iowa 50306, 800-247-2343.

HISTORY AND PHYSICAL

HISTORY AND PHYSICAL

Chief Complaint:

Past History:

Family History:

Allergies:

Operations—Minor:

Major:

Physical Findings: BP Temp. Pulse Resp. Wt.

Head

Neck

Chest

Cardio-Vascular

Abdominal

Genito-Urinary

Skin

Bones and Joints

Glandular

Neuromuscular

Working Diagnosis:

REHAB. POTENTIAL:

PATIENT INFORMED OF MEDICAL CONDITION ____YES ____NO IF NO, REASON:

DATE: ________________ ATTENDING PHYSICIAN'S SIGNATURE ________________

NAME—LAST	FIRST	MIDDLE	ROOM NO.	ATTENDING PHYSICIAN	HOSP. NO.

DISCHARGE INSTRUCTIONS

Discharge Instructions

Patient Name	Physician	Room #	Hosp. #

Dismissal date ____________________

Dismissal time ____________________

Patient left via ____________________ Accompanied by ____________________

Patient condition upon discharge and summary of significant data of hospitalization.

Patient Instructions

Doctor's appointment: ____________________

Diet: ____________________

Activity: ____________________

Treatment: ____________________

Medication: ____________________

Name

Hosp. #

Room #

Physician

I have received and understand the above instructions:

Patient Signature (or person receiving instruction)

Nurse's Signature

Reprinted with permission of Briggs Corporation, Des Moines, Iowa 50306, 800-247-2343.

PROCESSING, ANALYSIS, AND REVIEW OF THE HEALTH RECORD

DISCHARGE PROCESSING, ANALYSIS, AND REVIEW FOR COMPLETENESS: POLICIES AND PROCEDURES

Comprehensive and Coordinated System

The health record department shall provide and coordinate a centralized system for the routine and timely receipt and processing of the health record of each patient/client at the following times:

- discharge from inpatient stay
- conclusion of any episode of care in the ambulatory care departments, emergency department, home care, hospice, or any other unit of care sponsored by this facility

The process of discharge analysis/completeness review shall be augmented by concurrent review processes carried out by health record personnel.

The major components of this system are the following activities, which shall be carried out by health record personnel:

- prompt receipt and entry of the record into the system at discharge from inpatient status or conclusion of ambulatory care
- verification check (reviewing each document for presence and correctness of patient/client identification and proper unit number assignment)
- review and correction of misfiles
- processing of documents according to prescribed order
- initial review for completeness
- monitoring notification process for completeness
- preparation of reports for clinicians' qualitative review
- provision of access to authorized users
- appropriate coordination of functions with other functions in the department and in the facility
- preparation of reports for administrative and professional staff

Purposes

The processes shall be developed to achieve the following:

- support continuity of care through the provision of complete and accurate health information for each patient/client
- promote timely and accurate entries in the health record/database
- foster compliance with applicable legal, regulatory, and accrediting agency mandates
- assist patient/client care providers in meeting their obligations to document care
- assist patient/client care providers in meeting their obligation to review quality of care as documented
- assist administrative officers in protecting the facility against charges of malpractice
- foster timely provision of information for billing and financial management purposes
- provide a preliminary assessment of potential risk management concerns, billing disputes, or unusual situations

Responsibility

Quantitative and qualitative analysis and timely completion of health records shall be shared by the individual health care providers, the medical staff as a whole, the administrative officers of the facility, and the health record department. These responsibilities specifically include the following:

- *health care provider:* has a primary responsibility for accurate, complete, and timely entries for care provided by him or her
- *clinical department chair/chief of service:* receives and acts on reports concerning patterns of record deficiencies in the department or service; enforces approved penalty system
- *medical staff as a whole:*
  - adopts standards for health record content and time frame for completion
  - incorporates these into binding rules and regulations for the clinical staff
  - adopts a review process, such as a committee activity, to monitor compliance and review quality of documentation
  - adopts a penalty system for noncompliance
- *health record committee:*
  - develops an approved set of guidelines for completeness and approves the deficiency review list to be used by health record personnel in performing quantitative analysis
  - carries out quality review of documentation
  - coordinates quality review activities and problem findings with other quality assurance reviews carried out by the medical staff
  - retires health records that remain permanently incomplete because of extenuating circumstances
- *administration:* provides administrative support and enforcement of sanctions established by the medical staff

- *health record department:*
  - carries out quantitative analysis based on approved guidelines developed by the medical staff
  - maintains a system of record monitoring and reporting of completeness status
  - prepares reports concerning compliance/noncompliance with record completeness standards for medical staff or administrative action
  - prepares reports for administrative review, including risk management and potential billing problems

Criteria for Completeness

Each record shall contain the specific information needed to justify the diagnosis and course of treatment. Therefore, a health record shall be considered complete when it contains the following:

- documentation appropriate to the particular episode of care
- proper authentication of all entries
- complete and consistent diagnosis
- signed attestation (DRG) statement if Medicare patient

Deficiency/review lists for each category of care (inpatient, outpatient, etc.) shall be developed by the health information management specialist and approved by the appropriate committee of the medical staff.

Exceptions and Permanent Incomplete Records

In circumstances in which the health care provider is unable to complete the required health record entries, the matter shall be referred to the appropriate medical staff committee. This committee shall prepare a statement noting the reason for the permanent incompleteness (e.g., death or incapacity of practitioner, practitioner no longer employed/available to complete data entries). This statement shall be filed in the health record, which shall then be placed in the permanent file.

Stages of Review for Completeness

A combination of concurrent and postdischarge reviews shall be carried out to foster timely completion of documentation.

Concurrent Review

In order to contribute to improved patient/client care and expedite the availability of accurate medical information for patient/client care and reimbursement purposes (particularly DRG assignment), a system of concurrent health record review shall be implemented. Health record personnel shall review the health records of all inpatients at the following two intervals:

1. two days following admission
2. at the end of every two-day period thereafter

The review shall focus on the following:

- presence, agreement, and updates of diagnostic statements
- presence of complete history and physical examination findings
- signature on all entries, with particular attention to verbal/telephone orders
- completion of certifications
- receipt of test results from ancillary departments
- progress notes and statements of patient/client condition
- required consents and documents associated with surgery

Home care and hospice care records shall be reviewed at the end of the first seven days and at two-week intervals thereafter. Particular attention shall be given to the documentation and updates of patient/client care plans and discharge plans.

Concurrent Chart Review

Prolonged Stay Patients. For patients whose program of care requires prolonged stay (e.g., skilled nursing care; psychiatric inpatient care), a process of periodic, concurrent chart review fosters timeliness and accuracy of documentation. The forms that follow are customized to reflect the usual documentation for specific periods of care:

- first week of admission
- monthly/quarterly
- annual
- special circumstances
- discharge

These forms are for administrative use, maintained on a continuing basis for each patient. They are not a part of the health record proper, but are kept in an administrative file by patient name for repeat use from admission through discharge.

Quantitative Review

At the time of discharge from inpatient status or at the conclusion of a department's or unit's care, a detailed analysis of the record shall be done by health record personnel. The approved record deficiency list will be used.

Clinical Staff Review

Clinical staff review shall be carried out by the designated review committee. Its focus shall be the review of medical documentation for clinical pertinence with particular attention given to the following:

- inclusion of all positive and negative findings appropriate to the case
- discrepancies, errors, omissions, and inaccuracies
- timeliness of documentation

Compliance with the facility's stated policies of documentation, including time frames, shall be emphasized.

Nursing and allied health practitioners shall participate in this review as appropriate.

Time Frames and Penalties

Time Frames

As far as possible, health record documentation shall be completed in an ongoing manner throughout the stay. When data entries are not completed by the time of discharge, the following time frames and definitions shall apply:

- *incomplete status:* any record not complete within 15 days of discharge
- *delinquent status:* any record not complete beyond the initial 15 days

Health record personnel shall obtain the health records of discharged and ambulatory care patients/clients on the day of discharge and/or the clinic visit. Assembly and quantitative review will be carried out in a timely manner so that the record is available by 10 A.M. the following workday. Any day during which the record is unavailable to the responsible practitioner for record completion will be omitted from the count of days when incomplete or delinquent status is determined.

Penalties

Physicians will be subject to suspension of privileges, except for the ability to care for patients/clients already admitted. The time period for such suspensions is as follows:

- *effective date:* seven workdays after notification that records are incomplete
- *in effect:* until records are complete

Residents and clinicians in training shall carry out all responsibilities before certificates of completion or similar documentation is issued.

The source of authority for these penalties is their adoption by the medical staff. The responsibility for enforcement rests with the president of the medical staff.

No payment to physicians as an inducement for record completion shall be made. Completion of documentation is a legal and ethical responsibility.

Monitoring and Notification System

A monitoring system shall be implemented to track the completion process. Monitoring shall be performed at least daily to reflect the following:

- reports received after initial record assembly
- reports received from the dictation/transcription unit
- reports completed and/or signed

The record deficiency list and suspension list shall be updated accordingly.

A regular, weekly system of record counting and notification shall be implemented. Notification processes shall include the following:

- notice to physician
  - number of records incomplete
  - number of records delinquent
  - number of days each record is delinquent
  - reminder of suspension process
- notice of suspension
  - notice given to physician
  - number of records delinquent
  - number of days each record is delinquent
  - notice to head of clinical service
  - notice to admissions department
  - notice to president of medical staff

Use of and Access to Incomplete Records

The use of and access to records during the completion process shall be restricted to permit timely completion. Use of the records for direct patient/client care needs shall be accommodated in every instance. Appropriate procedures shall be developed for timely delivery and return of incomplete records needed for direct patient/client care. The following are considerations associated with common categories of requests for records:

- category of request
- authorized users
- location during use
- retrieval priority and time frame

- time period for use
- special considerations

Storage and Retrieval of Incomplete Records

Incomplete records shall be located in the health record department in suitable storage space that permits easy retrieval for use during incomplete processing. All the policies and practices to safeguard permanent records shall apply to incomplete record storage. The incomplete record storage and retrieval system shall be coordinated with the permanent storage and retrieval system. The following factors shall be taken into account in determining the specific location in the department of the incomplete records:

- frequency of access during incomplete phase for use in postdischarge follow up in ambulatory care departments
- need for access by more than one clinical care provider

The tracking system, filing of continuing care and late reports, and requests for records procedures shall be modified to meet the needs imposed by the chosen method.

Alternative 1

Incomplete records shall be placed in a separate file area in the discharge processing unit of the department. Records shall be filed by the terminal digit method.

Alternative 2

Incomplete records shall be placed in a separate file area in the discharge processing unit of the department. Records shall be filed by name of physician practitioner.

Alternative 3

Incomplete records shall be interfiled with completed records in the main storage and retrieval area because of the heavy demand for direct patient/client care use during the immediate postdischarge period and because of the frequency of outpatient visits.

Special Reviews and Reports

The health record department shall maintain a review process to support the facility's overall efforts in quality assurance, risk management, and education. To this end, specific reports shall be compiled on a routine basis.

Medical Staff Committee Reports

Periodic reports, at least quarterly, shall be provided to the medical staff committee charged with oversight of quality of patient/client care documentation. The report will have as its focus the degree of compliance with the documentation policies of this facility. The format and content of this report will be developed jointly by the health information management specialist and the appropriate medical staff committee. These reports will omit all identification of individual patients/clients.

Risk Management Reports

These reports shall consist of two types:

1. periodic report (at least quarterly) concerning general quality of documentation and degree of compliance with documentation policies of this facility (reports shall omit all identification of individual patients/clients)
2. preliminary screening of problem occurrences
   - death
   - cardiac or respiratory arrest
   - acute myocardial infarction during or following surgery
   - admission as inpatient within 72 hours of treatment in this facility's emergency or outpatient department
   - readmission to inpatient care within 72 hours of discharge
   - departures against medical advice
   - refusal to consent/refusal of treatment
   - surgery without required presurgical consultations
   - consent form discrepancies (date of consent inconsistent with date of treatment or operation, operation consented to different than operation performed)
   - return to operating room for complication resulting from previous operation
   - adverse drug reaction

The format and specific content of the occurrence screening profile shall be developed jointly by the director of medical records, the risk manager, and legal counsel.

Billing Audit

In coordination with the chief financial officer and billing department, preliminary preparation of the billing audit profiles on a selected sample of records shall be completed at least quarterly and on individual records on a demand basis. The format and specific content shall be developed jointly by the health information management specialist and the chief financial officer.

Source: Joan Gratto Liebler, *Medical Records: Policies and Guidelines*, Aspen Publishers, Inc., © 1995.

PHYSICIAN HEALTH RECORD COMPLETION RESPONSIBILITIES—INPATIENT ADMISSIONS

Document	Responsible Provider	Completion Time	Components of Document Required
History & Physical	Admitting Physician	Within 24 Hours of Admission; By 4:00 P.M. the Day Prior to Surgery	Initial Assessment/screening of physical, psychological, and social status to determine the need for care or treatment, the type of care or treatment to be provided, and the need for further assessment. Components should include chief complaint, history of present and past illness, family history, social history, systems review, metabolic status, habits, allergies, current medications.
Operative Report	Surgeon	Immediately Following Surgery	Description of the findings, the technical procedures used, the specimen removed, the postoperative diagnosis, and the name of the primary surgeon and any assistants participating in the surgery.
Consultation	Consulting Physician	Within 24 Hours	Findings of consultation.
Verbal Orders	Ordering Physician	Within 24 Hours	
Discharge Diagnoses	Attending Physician	On Discharge	Complete listing of all final diagnoses including complications and comorbidities.
Discharge Summary	Attending Physician	Within 15 Days of Discharge	Summary of the reason for hospitalization, the significant findings, the procedures performed and treatment rendered, the patient's condition on discharge, and any specific instructions given to the patient and/or family, as pertinent (information on DISCHARGE ORDER pertinent).
Attestation Statement	Attending Physician	Upon Completion of Coding	

Admitting Physician: The physician who either makes the decision to admit the patient or accept the patient to his/her service; this will rarely be the ER physician.

Attending Physician: The physician who provides and maintains primary responsibility for the patient's care during the inpatient admission; this may be the admitting physician and/or the surgeon.

- This physician will be responsible for the majority of physician orders/progress notes in the record.
- This physician is not necessarily the discharging physician.

Courtesy of Door County Memorial Hospital, Sturgeon Bay, Wisconsin.

PHYSICIAN HEALTH RECORD COMPLETION RESPONSIBILITIES—OUTPATIENT/ AMBULATORY SURGERY

Document	No Anesthesia/Topical/Local/ Regional Block	IV Sedation	General, Spinal, or Epidural Anesthesia
History	Minimal documentation must include: • indications/symptoms for procedure • current medications and dosages • any known allergies • existing comorbid conditions, if any	Minimal documentation must include: • indications/symptoms for procedure • current medications and dosages • any known allergies • existing comorbid conditions, if any	Minimal documentation must include: • indications/symptoms for procedure • current medications and dosages • any known allergies • existing comorbid conditions, if any
Physical Examination	Minimal documentation must include: • mental status assessment • examination specific to the proposed procedure and any comorbid conditions	Minimal documentation must include: • mental status assessment • exam specific to the proposed procedure and any comorbid conditions • examination of the heart and lungs by auscultation	Minimal documentation must include: • mental status assessment • exam specific to the proposed procedure and any comorbid conditions • examination of the heart and lungs by auscultation • assessment and written statement about the patient's general condition
Preprocedure Note	A note on the day of surgery that evaluates the patient's current status for surgery. • The note can be written by a physician, operating practitioner, or individual qualified to administer anesthesia. • A note is not required when the history and physical are written on the day of surgery.	A note on the day of surgery that evaluates the patient's current status for surgery. • The note can be written by a physician, operating practitioner, or individual qualified to administer anesthesia. • A note is not required when the history and physical are written on the day of surgery.	A note on the day of surgery that evaluates the patient's current status for surgery. • The note can be written by a physician, operating practitioner, or individual qualified to administer anesthesia. • A note is not required when the history and physical are written on the day of surgery. • For patients undergoing general or spinal anesthesia, the note must include an anesthesia history and risk assessment by a person qualified to administer anesthesia.

Courtesy of Door County Memorial Hospital, Sturgeon Bay, Wisconsin.

DICTATION AND TRANSCRIPTION

DICTATION/TRANSCRIPTION SYSTEM: SAMPLE PROCESS

Purpose

The health record department shall provide and coordinate a centralized dictation/transcription system to support the documentation process associated with quality patient/client care. This service shall be provided in order to achieve the following:

- support continuity of care by expediting the transmittal of information on a priority basis
- promote timely and accurate entries into the health record
- facilitate compliance with standards of documentation mandated by state and federal regulatory agencies and voluntary accrediting agencies
- foster legible, uniform, and complete health record documentation

Reports dictated and transcribed reflect the development of documentation in the normal course of business and shall routinely carry the following information:

- name of facility
- type of report
- identification of patient/client
- dates of admission and discharge
- date dictated
- date transcribed
- initials of transcriptionist
- signature of authenticator, who shall be the originator of the documented content of the report except in extraordinary cases noted by the health record committee or executive committee of the medical staff

Scope of Service

The following entries in the health record shall be processed on a routine basis through the dictation/transcription service:

- history and physical examination
- discharge summary
- consultation
- operative report
- autopsy protocols
- emergency department summaries
- radiology reports
- electroencephalogram reports
- electrocardiogram reports
- correspondence, progress notes, and consultations generated by approved members of group practices and private practitioners who enter into a contractual arrangement with the health record department for payment for this service

Authorized Users and Authorized Access

The physicians and allied health professionals responsible for documenting reports shall be authorized to access the dictation system. Such practitioners will be provided with an individual access code as well as general instructions for using the system. These general instructions will include the following:

- standard formats to be used for reports
- standard abbreviations and symbols approved by the medical staff
- detailed instructions concerning access to the dictating system

Access to material dictated but not transcribed is limited to the following:

- the originator
- other health care providers for the purpose of decision making/emergency action in the process of continuity of care
- personnel in the health record department who process materials essential to the billing function mandated under federal and/or state regulations

Processing Time and Priority Designation

As far as possible, all material entered into the dictation system shall be transcribed and placed in the appropriate health record by health record personnel within the time frames noted here. These processing times are established in recognition of the time-sensitive value of health record entries. Routine dictation shall be processed within these time frames:

History and physical examinations	24 hours
Discharge summaries	48 hours
Operative reports	24 hours
Consultations	24 hours
Emergency service summaries	24 hours
Autopsy protocols	
Preliminary findings	7 workdays
Complete protocol	21 workdays
Radiology reports	24 hours
Electroencephalogram reports	24 hours

Electrocardiogram reports	24 hours
Materials received from group practices under contractual arrangements	As negotiated in contract

STAT reports shall be dictated on a special access line (or channel) for immediate and continual processing during the day and evening shifts (8 A.M. to 9 P.M.). STAT reports dictated during the night shift will be processed immediately at the beginning of the next workday. The usual turnaround time for STAT work is three work hours. The following is considered STAT work:

- discharge summaries for patients/clients being transferred
- history and physical examinations for patients/clients scheduled for surgery
- operative reports for patients/clients requiring additional surgery after the initial surgery has been completed
- emergency department notes for patients/clients admitted directly from emergency care to an inpatient unit
- any report such as a consultation, radiology, or similar note associated with decisions relating to surgical interventions

When transcription of STAT material is processed at an off-site location, a facsimile reproduction shall be placed on the health record and replaced with the original report when it is delivered to the facility.

Access and Location of Dictation Facilities

Dictation facilities shall be provided on a continuous basis (i.e., 24 hours a day/7 days a week) via direct telephone access. Such telephone units shall be made available in designated areas throughout the facility to permit easy access by authorized users of the system. At a minimum, such telephone access units shall be placed at the following locations:

- all nursing stations, both inpatient and outpatient
- physicians' lounge
- emergency department
- health record department
- operating room

Provisions for privacy during the dictation transaction shall be made, with particular attention given to those areas of the facility where patients and the general public are within hearing distance of the access unit.

Access through off-site telephone lines in physicians' private offices shall be available as an additional convenience.

There shall be sufficient telephone lines to the central receiving unit to avoid access collision during peak dictation periods. There shall be automatic transfer to the next available unit without delay to the practitioner who wishes to dictate.

Staffing and Use of Contractual Services

Staffing

The health information management specialist shall develop a staffing pattern for the medical transcription unit consistent with the purposes and deadlines outlined in this policy. The transcription function shall be staffed, as appropriate, by a combination of full-time and part-time employees, augmented with the services of individual contractual agents and/or transcription services. Employees of the facility shall be governed by the personnel policies of the department and the facility. Contractual agents shall be governed by detailed provisions in the contract made with them.

When facility employees work at off-site, home-based transcription units, care shall be taken to ensure that all laws and regulations concerning health and safety are followed. Such arrangements shall be cleared with the personnel/labor relations department.

Use of Contractual Services

Contract provisions with individual independent contractors shall be similar to the provisions for incorporated transcription services. In addition, care will be taken to include provisions relating to health and safety laws and regulations. Further, special provisions shall be included to ensure the confidentiality of materials during the off-site processing time, including the designation of restricted space that is free from household/family access. The loaning of equipment and its maintenance shall be done in a manner consistent with the facility's inventory provisions.

Standard Format

All reports shall be transcribed in the standard format shown for ease of reference and efficiency of processing.

Facility Logo	Name of Report	Patient/Client Name Patient/Client Unit Number

The use of canned reports or preprinted/pretyped reports is prohibited. The guidelines and directives of accrediting and regulatory agencies shall be followed regarding the prohibition of such practices.

Quality Controls

Both routine and periodic audits of dictated/transcribed reports shall be carried out to monitor and enhance the quality of the materials produced in this process. Each report shall be routinely reviewed for the following:

- proper patient/client identification
- adherence to standard format
- proper use of abbreviations and symbols
- correction of typographic errors, spelling errors, and mistakes in medical terminology
- general appearance

Periodic assessment will be made concerning the following aspects of the dictation/transcription system:

- adherence to processing times and designated priorities
- need to review and update the abbreviations and symbols list
- adherence to policies relating to distribution of copies
- downtime and equipment malfunction time

Intradepartmental Coordination and Distribution of Copies

The processes and procedures of the dictation/transcription unit shall be coordinated with other departmental functions to foster the timely distribution of reports into the health record. Close coordination shall be maintained with other units of the department that need information included in or derived from the dictated/transcribed reports:

- *Storage and retrieval.* This unit shall be staffed to provide immediate and timely placement of the transcribed reports in inpatient health records and outpatient care units.
- *Incomplete records.* This unit shall update the information concerning the status of required reports for purposes of report completion and shall file reports in the incomplete health records held in the unit.
- *Coding and billing.* This unit shall be provided with information necessary for the timely provision of required billing data.
- *Release of information.* All requests for release of information (except for copies of transcribed reports distributed by the transcription unit) shall be processed through this unit so that compliance with patient/client privacy and confidentiality provisions may be maintained.

The staff of the transcription unit shall distribute copies of transcribed reports as follows:

- one copy to the originator of the report
- one copy to the attending physician if this practitioner is not the originator of the report
- one copy to the physician or facility designated by the attending physician as the next provider of care

Normally, only edited and signed copies of reports shall be distributed. Only upon written, explicit direction from the originator shall an unedited, unsigned report be released. Such a report shall carry on each page, in large print, the phrase *Draft/Unedited/Unsigned/Preliminary Copy.*

Source: Joan Gratto Liebler, *Medical Records: Policies and Guidelines*, Aspen Publishers, Inc., © 1990.

WORKSHEET FOR CUSTOMIZING DICTATION/TRANSCRIPTION POLICIES

Policy Elements	Special Considerations
Date dictated and date typed	Clear with risk management and legal counsel.
Scope of service	Determine which reports will be processed by the health record department; wholly centralized, reflecting work of all units of the facility, or partially centralized, reflecting work of inpatient units only. Determine desirability of doing work for related units (e.g., group practices or private practitioners) as an income-generating function. Clear this with chief executive officer because of tax-exempt status considerations and other contractual aspects.
Use of independent contractors and use of employees off site/at home	Check with personnel/labor relations to determine applicability of any state or federal law regarding working conditions, health and safety factors, and similar considerations. Check with personnel/labor relations for consistency with collective bargaining agreements or employee work rules.
Distribution of reports and intradepartmental coordination	Cross reference with policies and procedures for closely related practices.
Distribution of draft/unedited material	Check with risk management. Check with medical staff.
Incentive wage	Develop valid work standards based on specific procedures. Clear with personnel/labor relations.
Priority and definition of STAT work	Check chart completion deadlines in state department of health regulations, federal Conditions of Participation for Medicare, and accrediting agency standards. Define STAT reports with medical staff.
Location and type of dictation facilities	Check telephone line capacity. Check special needs of facility that stem from architectural layout.
Staffing patterns	Check with personnel/labor relations concerning off-site/at-home work arrangements.
Use of contractual services	Consult with controller (purchasing and contracts division) for required aspects of bidding and contract specifications.

Source: Joan Gratto Liebler, *Medical Records: Policies and Guidelines*, Aspen Publishers, Inc., © 1990.

MINIMUM ELEMENTS OF CONTRACTS WITH INCORPORATED TRANSCRIPTION SERVICES

- **Data security and patient data confidentiality.**
  - Pick up and delivery of dictated or transcribed material shall be by bonded courier.
  - Material shall be transported in locked storage boxes.
  - All employees of the transcription service shall sign the confidentiality statement.
- **Dictation access.**
  - Dictation access shall be available on a continuous basis (i.e., 24 hours a day/7 days a week) via direct wire telephone service.
  - Sufficient telephone receiving lines shall be available to avoid access collision during peak dictation periods.
  - Automatic transfer to the next available unit without delay shall be available to practitioners who wish to dictate.
- **Compatibility of equipment.**
  - The telephone wire and system for receipt of dictation from the facility's lines and physicians' private offices shall be compatible with that of the facility.
  - Word processing units with compatible printout capability for an on-site printing process shall be used.
  - Equipment for transmission of facsimile documents to the facility shall be compatible with that used by the facility.
- **Use of preprinted or pretaped material.** Documents shall not be preprinted or pretaped.
- **Turnaround time.** Compliance with turnaround times established by the facility in its directives concerning STAT work and routine reports shall be maintained.
- **Abbreviations and symbols.** The facility's approved abbreviation and symbol list shall be used.
- **Format and forms.** Compliance with the use of the facility's standard format and use of standardized forms provided by the facility shall be maintained.
- **Other materials.** Provision of all other materials such as paper, equipment, and supplies shall be by the contractual agency.
- **Copies of records.** Provision of additional copies shall be restricted to distribution by the facility according to its policies. Distribution of copies by the contractual agency is strictly prohibited.
- **Storage of material on disks.** Material on disk shall be stored for 90 workdays after the material is initially transcribed and forwarded to the facility.
- **Transmission of records.** Material shall be transmitted to the facility for printing at specified times:

8 A.M.	2 P.M.
10 A.M.	4 P.M.
noon	6 P.M.

  STAT material shall be transmitted continuously throughout the workday.
- **Billing.**
  - The basis of billing shall be established on the following standard of transcribed material: ($0.00) per line (a line of typing is defined as containing 12 words on average). [*Alternate basis of billing:* The basis of billing shall be established on the following standard of dictated material: ($0.00) per hour of dictation exclusive of blank spaces on dictation medium.]
  - Any work deemed unacceptable because of spelling errors, faulty general appearance, or failure to adhere to standard formats shall not be billed.
  - Transcription of work that needs to be reprocessed because of the unacceptability of the original transcription shall be done at no cost.
  - The frequency and form of billing and expectations concerning date of payment after receipt of bill shall be established.
- **Tracking system.** The contractual agent shall maintain the capacity for advising the facility of the status of work in progress. This capacity shall include advisement on a demand basis during normal work hours (8 A.M. to 6 P.M.).
- **Discontinuance of contractual arrangement.** A notification of at least 60 workdays by either party shall be required in order to terminate the contractual arrangement between the agency and the facility.

Source: Joan Gratto Liebler, *Medical Records: Policies and Guidelines*, Aspen Publishers, Inc., © 1990.

HEALTH RECORD FORMAT

FORMS DEVELOPMENT AND APPROVAL—ADMINISTRATIVE POLICY

PURPOSE

To provide guidelines to the staff on the appropriate process for the development and approval of all forms that are to be maintained *permanently* in the patient health record.

POLICY STATEMENTS

1. All new health record forms, stickers, and inserts should be reviewed by the health information management specialist and must be approved by an administrative director and/or the Medical Executive Committee prior to implementation.
2. All revisions of existing health record forms should be reviewed by the health information management specialist and must be reviewed and/or approved by an administrative director and/or the Medical Executive Committee prior to implementation.
3. The chief of staff and/or the administrator can provisionally approve a form to be used prior to the Medical Executive Committee meeting; however, the form will still be subject to final committee approval.
4. All forms must meet basic format guidelines.
5. Consent forms will be subject to review by hospital legal counsel prior to approval.

BASIC FORM GUIDELINES

1. Forms should be printed on 8½ x 11–inch paper with margins as follows:
   - *Vertical forms:* Left, right, and bottom margins of ½ inch. A top margin of 1 inch should be allowed for binding purposes. Forms that are double-sided should allow for a 1-inch margin on both the top and the bottom.
   - *Horizontal forms:* Top, right, and bottom margins of ½ inch. A left margin of 1 inch should be allowed for binding purposes. Forms that are double-sided should allow for a 1-inch margin on both the right and left edges.
2. Forms should include hospital identification, the title of the form, and the sponsoring department if applicable. A form number shall be assigned and located under the identification. The number will provide a history of when the form was developed and allow for ease in ordering.
   - *Vertical forms.* Located in the left lower corner.
   - *Horizontal forms.* Located in the left lower corner.
3. Forms shall include adequate space allowance for patient identification (adhesive label).
   - Vertical forms. Located in the right lower corner.
   - Horizontal forms. Located in the left lower corner.
4. Multiple-part forms should clearly delineate the routing instructions for each part (original—chart; yellow—department; pink—physician).

PROCESS

1. Once a form has been designed or revised, a copy of the form, along with a written or verbal explanation of its use, shall be forwarded to the health information management specialist. A Health Record Forms Justification should be completed.
2. The form will be reviewed and, if it is a medical staff form, forwarded to the Medical Executive Committee to be included in the agenda packet for review and approval at the next meeting.
   - Forms should be approved at the affected medical staff department level prior to referral to the Medical Executive Committee.
     - –Medical staff forms should be approved at the medical staff department level.
     - –Ancillary department forms should be approved at the division level.
     - –Multidisciplinary forms should be approved at all levels noted above.
   - If the form is to be tested prior to permanent usage, this should be indicated on the Forms Justification, along with the trial period dates.
   - The manager/staffperson requesting approval may be asked to make a presentation to the Medical Executive Committee.
3. The health information management specialist will communicate the decision of the Medical Executive Committee to the staffperson requesting approval. The staffperson will be responsible for facilitating the subsequent education, printing, and circulation process if approved or making the appropriate changes to the form if not approved.
4. A record of forms approval will be maintained as a permanent part of the Medical Executive Committee meeting minutes.

Courtesy of Door County Memorial Hospital, Sturgeon Bay, Wisconsin.

FORMS FORMAT DESIGN GUIDE FOR COMPUTER-GENERATED FORMS

DATE SUBMITTED		☐ NEW ☐ REVISED IF REVISION, DOES IT REPLACE EXISTING FORM? ☐ YES ☐ NO
FORM NAME	FORM NUMBER	FORM NUMBER OF FORM REPLACED
		NAME OF FORM REPLACED

1. All appropriate Committee/Director/Vice President approvals must appear on this form.
2. Policy and Procedure relevant to form presented must be submitted with form and this guide.
3. All abbreviations must conform to the master abbreviation list.
4. Personal names shall not appear on forms.
5. When approved, the person submitting the form will be responsible for inservicing the form.
6. If form is a revision and not a permanent part of patient's chart, submit the original proposed form along with this completed guide and the form(s) it replaces to Medical Education.
7. If form is a new or revised health record form and is a permanent part of the patient's chart, submit the original of your proposed form along with this completed guide to the health information management specialist.
8. If form is for patient education, send proposed form, along with this completed guide, to Medical Education for review by Consumer Health Education Committee.

USAGE		ADDITIONAL INFORMATION
ESTIMATE NUMBER OF FORMS USED YEARLY	WILL FORM REMAIN PERMANENT PART OF RECORD ☐ YES ☐ NO	
WILL FORM REMAIN PART OF PATIENT'S PERMANENT RECORD? ☐ YES ☐ NO		
DEPARTMENT(S) UTILIZING THIS FORM		
	COST CENTER NUMBER	
JUSTIFICATION FOR NEED FOR FORM		
NAME OF PERSON SUBMITTING FORM	TELEPHONE NUMBER	
DO YOU WISH TO PRESENT THIS FORM IN PERSON?	☐ YES ☐ NO	
IF FORM(S) USED SOLELY IN YOUR DEPARTMENT, ARE YOU WILLING TO BE RESPONSIBLE FOR STORAGE, INVENTORY, AND REORDERING?	☐ YES ☐ NO	
IS A TRIAL PERIOD REQUIRED FOR FORM?	☐ YES ☐ NO	
IF FORM IS A REVISION OF AN EXISTING FORM		
ARE YOU WILLING TO USE OLD FORMS IN STOCK?	☐ YES ☐ NO	
STOCK ON HAND	DATE	
DISPOSITION OF OLD STOCK (ANY UNUSED STOCK WILL BE CHARGED TO REQUESTING DEPT.)		

COMMITTEE(S) THAT REQUIRE APPROVAL OF THIS FORM	APPROVED/DATE	DENIED/DATE	N/A
	☐	☐	☐
	☐	☐	☐
	☐	☐	☐

SIGNATURE(S) OF DIRECTOR OR COMMITTEE CHAIRMEN APPROVING THIS FORM		
X	X	VICE PRESIDENT'S APPROVAL
X	X	

☐ DESIGN APPROVED, PROCEED ☐ DESIGN DENIED, DO NOT PROCEED	AUTHORIZED SIGNATURE	DATE SIGNED

Courtesy of Bay Medical Center, Bay City, Michigan.

HEALTH RECORD FORM REQUEST AND JUSTIFICATION

Date Submitted:	Submitted By:
Form Title:	Number

☐ New Form Will There be a Trial Period? If so, Dates: ______

☐ Revision of Form Number ______ (Attach Copy of Original Form)

Instructions:
Complete this form and attach a rough draft of the new form or revision. Route the form to the health information management specialist for review and/or inclusion on the next agenda for medical staff approval along with this completed form.

Justification for Usage:

Completion Responsibilities:

☐ Nursing
☐ Medical Staff
☐ Other: ______

To be located in what section of the completed medical record: ______

☐ Indicate if form requires tagging for deficiency if not complete on discharge.

REVIEWED/APPROVED BY

Health Information Management Specialist	Division Director	Medical Executive Committee
Date:	Date:	Date:

PRINTING INFORMATION

Paper Color	Paper Size	Paper Style/Set Up	Collated	Punched	Other
☐ White ☐ Buff ☐ Yellow ☐ Pink ☐ Green ☐ Goldenrod ☐ Blue ☐ Other	☐ $8^1/_2$ by 11—Vertical ☐ $8^1/_2$ by 11—Horizontal ☐ Other:	☐ One Side ☐ Two Sides (Head to Head) ☐ Two Sides (Head to Foot) ☐ NCR	☐ Yes ☐ No	Number of Holes: ______ Position: ☐ Top ☐ Left ☐ Other:	Overall Size: ______ Number to Be Printed

Other Instructions:

Courtesy of Door County Memorial Hospital, Sturgeon Bay, Wisconsin.

5
Legal Considerations and Risk Management Factors

Chapter 5

Legal Considerations and Risk Management Factors

CONFIDENTIALITY AND SECURITY CONCERNS

OVERVIEW OF NATIONAL RESEARCH COUNCIL REPORT—*FOR THE RECORD: PROTECTING ELECTRONIC HEALTH INFORMATION*

The National Research Council (NRC) released *For the Record: Protecting Electronic Health Information* on March 5, 1997, at a press conference in Washington, DC. The report stressed that "Industry standards, regulatory action, and pressure from consumers all are needed to bolster the privacy and security of patient records."

In October 1995, the Computer Science and Telecommunications Board (CSTB) of the NRC answered a request from the National Library of Medicine (NLM) to look into the issue of "maintaining privacy and security in health care applications of the national information infrastructure." With funding and support from the NLM, the Warren Grant Magnuson Clinical Center of the National Institutes of Health (NIH) and the Massachusetts Health Data Consortium, the CSTB formed the 15-member Committee on Maintaining Privacy in Health Care Applications of the National Information Infrastructure (NII). According to the NRC, committee members were to maintain expertise in "computer and information security, health informatics, health information management, health care privacy, law, medical sociology, and health information systems." Two American Health Information Management Association (AHIMA) members participated on the committee: Kathleen A. Frawley, JD, MS, RRA, AHIMA's vice president of legislative and public policy services, and Susan P. Dowell, executive vice president and chief operating officer, Medicus Systems Corporation.

The committee was charged to "Observe and assess existing technical and nontechnical mechanisms for protecting the privacy and maintaining the security of health care information systems, identify other mechanisms worthy of testing in a health care environment, and outline promising areas for further research." In executing its charge, the committee was instructed to address numerous questions in the following areas:

- threats to health care information
- adequacy of existing privacy and security measures
- future mechanisms and best practices
- barriers to adoption

In developing its conclusions and recommendations, the committee conducted six site visits to various organizations and held five committee meetings with a multitude of participants in the health care system, briefings, work plan development sessions, and deliberations on findings and recommendations. To ensure that committee members maintained analytical consistency when participating in site visits, a standard site visit protocol was developed.

Recommendations

The committee developed recommendations in five separate areas: (1) improving privacy and security practices, (2) creating an industrywide security infrastructure, (3) addressing systemic concerns related to privacy and security, (4) developing patient identifiers, and (5) meeting future technological needs.

Improving Privacy and Security Practices

The report recommends that all organizations that handle patient-identifiable health care information adopt a set of technical and organizational policies, practices, and procedures to protect such information. Technical practices and procedures that the committee believes organizations should now adopt include

- individual authentication of users
- access controls
- audit trails
- physical security and disaster recovery
- protections of remote access points
- protection of external electronic communications
- software discipline
- system assessment

Practices that the committee believes organizations can now implement include

- establishment of security and confidentiality policies
- establishment of security and confidentiality committees
- identification of information security officers
- establishment of education and training programs
- development of sanctions for violations of confidentiality and security policies
- improvement of authorization forms
- permission for patient access to audit logs

Practices recommended for future implementation include

- implementation of strong authentication
- development of enterprisewide authentication
- use of access validation tools or software
- implementation of expanded audit trails
- use of technologies for electronic authentication of electronic records

Creating an Industrywide Security Infrastructure

The second recommendation of the committee called for the government and the health care industry to create the infrastructure necessary to support the privacy and security of electronic health information. As a part of this recommendation, the committee identified the following actions:

- The Secretary of Health and Human Services (HHS) establishes a standing health information security standards committee within the National Center for Vital and Health Statistics to develop and update privacy and security standards for all users of health information. Membership on the committee would be drawn from existing organizations that represent the broad spectrum of users and subjects of health information.
- Congress provides initial funding for an organization for the health care industry to promote greater sharing of information about security threats, incidents, and solutions.

Addressing Systemic Concerns Related to Privacy and Security

This section recommends that the federal government work with industry to promote and encourage an informed public debate to determine an appropriate balance between the privacy concerns of patients and the information needs of various users of health information. The committee sees the debate's objective as developing "a consensus about the ways in which privacy concerns can be balanced against the legitimate needs of other users for patient-identifiable health information." To achieve this goal, further recommendations are included

- Organizations that collect, analyze, or disseminate health information should adopt a set of fair information practices similar to those contained in the federal Privacy Act of 1974.
- The Department of HHS should work with state and local governments, health care researchers, and the health care industry to establish a program to promote consumer awareness of health privacy issues and the value of health information for patient care, administration, and research. It should also conduct studies that will develop a series of recommendations for improving the level of consumer awareness of health data flows.
- Professional societies and industry groups should continue and expand their leadership roles in educating members about privacy and security issues in their conference discussions and publications.
- The Department of HHS should conduct studies to determine the extent to which, and the conditions under which, users of health information need data containing patient identities.
- The Department of HHS should work with the U.S. Office of Consumer Affairs to determine appropriate ways to provide consumers with a visible, centralized point of contact regarding privacy issues (privacy ombudsman).

Developing Patient Identifiers

One of the most contentious issues in the privacy and confidentiality debate concerns universal patient identifiers. The committee recommends that any effort to develop a universal patient identifier should weigh the presumed advantages of such an identifier against potential privacy concerns.

The committee did not recommend for or against the use of the Social Security Number (SSN) or any other number or proposal for a universal patient identifier. Doing so would have been outside of its original charge. Whether a universal patient identifier is the SSN or some other notation, the privacy concerns remain the same.

Meeting Future Technological Needs

The committee's report recognizes that technology will advance and threats to privacy will continue to become more sophisticated. To help combat future threats to health information privacy, the committee recommends that the federal government take steps to improve information security technologies for health care applications. The committee outlined the following steps to adhere to this recommendation:

1. To facilitate the exchange of technical knowledge on information security and the transfer of information security technology, the Department of HHS should establish formal liaisons with relevant government and industry working groups.
2. The Department of HHS should support research in those areas that are of particular importance to the health care industry, but that might not otherwise be pursued. These areas include identification and linking of patient records, anonymous care and pseudonyms, audit tools, and tools for rights enforcement and management.
3. The Department of HHS should fund experimental testbeds that explore different approaches to access control that hold promise for being inexpensive and easy to incorporate into existing operations and that allow access during emergency circumstances.

Source: Kathleen A. Frawley and Donald Asmonga, "National Research Council Releases Report on Protecting Electronic Health Information," *Journal of AHIMA*, Vol. 68:5, American Health Information Management Association, © 1997.

ELECTRONIC HEALTH RECORDS AND THE LAW

Introduction

Use of automated health records and record systems presents new legal questions concerning providers' relationships with regulators and with patients. When a provider is contemplating installation or modification of a fully automated record system, it is important to ascertain whether the system will comply with applicable licensure laws and regulations, with Medicare requirements, and with applicable accreditation requirements. In addition, preserving the confidentiality and integrity, accessibility, accuracy, and durability of health records on an automated system presents special problems. Computerized health records present unique security concerns because of their vulnerability to computer viruses and other sabotage. Courts have not yet dealt with the liability and damages issues relating to patient injuries caused by computer viruses and other forms of sabotage committed against a computerized health record system. Finally, it is vital that computerized health record systems be designed, installed, and maintained in a manner that preserves the reliability of records created and stored on such systems so that these records will be admissible as evidence in court and will be credible as evidence.

Confidentiality and Integrity Issues

A computerized health record system must be designed, installed, and maintained to preserve both the confidentiality and the integrity of patient health information. A report issued in 1993 by the Office of Technology Assessment defined confidentiality and integrity as follows:

- *Confidentiality* involves control over who has access to information.
- *Integrity* means that information and programs are changed only in a specified and authorized manner, that the computer resources operate correctly, and that the data in them are not subject to unauthorized changes.

The Joint Commission on Accreditation of Healthcare Organizations (Joint Commission) has promulgated standards relating to information confidentiality and integrity, requiring that hospitals have a functioning mechanism to preserve confidentiality and to safeguard health records against loss, destruction, and unauthorized access or use. Significant legal risks directly associated with computer-based health record systems relate to the failure to preserve the confidentiality or integrity of data.

The legal obligation to protect the confidentiality of patient health information derives from various sources, but is primarily based on state statutes and the common law. Other sources of health care providers' duty to maintain the confidentiality of patient health care information include federal statutes and regulations, such as those concerning alcohol and drug abuse patient records, Medicare regulations, accreditation standards, and ethical standards promulgated by various health care trade and professional associations. In addition, the function of health records as evidence in trials and administrative hearings requires a provider to protect its records from unauthorized access.

Legal confidentiality obligations do not vary with the medium on which health records are stored. The same confidentiality requirements apply to paper records and computer-based health records, even though special safeguards may be legally mandated to preserve the confidentiality of computer-based health records. Confidentiality obligations do, however, vary from state to state. They may also vary depending on the nature of the recordkeeper and the type of information recorded. In some instances, health record confidentiality requirements also vary according to the type of information transaction involved or the purpose of a particular disclosure of information. When individual health care data are transmitted across state lines, it may not always be clear which state's law applies or which court will have jurisdiction if a dispute arises over disclosure of an individual's health information.

Computerization of patient information increases the risk of unauthorized disclosure of personal medical information, thereby necessitating special safeguards to keep the information confidential. The ease with which personal health information can be collected, stored, and accessed on a computer-based record system means that, generally, more information is included in a computer-based record than in a paper record. The detailed and sophisticated health information often found in computer-based records and the trend toward use of this information for nonhealth purposes makes computerized health records attractive targets. A single breach of a computerized record system's security can lead to disclosure of hundreds or even thousands of records and to potentially catastrophic liability for such disclosure, because computers are capable of accessing, copying, and transmitting large numbers of records within a very short time span.

Because of the complexity of health care delivery and the increasing specialization of health care providers, many individuals are involved in creating or using computerized patient records in institutions or group practice settings. This often means that a record can be accessed from numerous locations. Communications technology also makes possible offsite access to health records. This stands in sharp contrast to paper records, which generally can be accessed from only a single location.

Automation of the information distribution process, and computer and communication linkages, allow widespread access to health records, not only by the parties involved in providing care but also by secondary users of the information. Secondary users of health record information include life, health, and disability insurers; employee health benefit plans and support organizations; educational institutions; both the civil and criminal justice systems; rehabilitation and social welfare programs; credit agencies and banking centers; public health agencies; and researchers. Accordingly, confidentiality must be maintained, and unauthorized access to patient records must be prevented both by inside and outside users of computerized health record systems and by primary and secondary users of individual health information.

Unauthorized disclosure of health record information can lead to various forms of liability. Briefly, state legislation imposes both criminal and civil penalties for breaches of the duty of confidentiality. Many jurisdictions also grant statutory private rights of action to patients who are injured by the unauthorized disclosure of confidential medical information. Licensure statutes and regulations frequently contain sanctions for improper disclosure of health record information. Under the common law, several legal theories can also support a finding of liability for improper disclosure of personal health information. These theories include invasion of privacy, breach of confidentiality, breach of implied contract, defamation, and intentional infliction of emotional distress. In addition, federal statutes, such as those governing release of alcohol and drug abuse records, provide penalties for the improper release of information.

System Security Measures

Because the potential for large-scale breaches of data security is much greater in a computerized health record system, and because a provider bears the greatest risk of liability for unauthorized disclosure, a provider who implements such a system must be sure that it adequately protects confidentiality with respect to both internal and external users of the system. Computer system security must, therefore, balance the need for ready access to patient information by those involved in patient care with the need to protect against unauthorized access. This may require some delicate balancing among conflicting objectives. A provider may be liable when its records are so highly guarded that medical information is not readily available to those caring for a patient; on the other hand, the provider can be liable for breaches of confidentiality that result from permitting easy access to health records by unauthorized personnel.

The level of system security required by law for systems containing health records is not clear. Under general principles of negligence liability, however, it is clear that security must be reasonable at a minimum. Because what is considered reasonable security changes over time, it is important that system security be periodically reviewed and updated.

To comply with legal requirements, a health record system must provide for both system and data security. Data security exists when data are protected from improper disclosure or unauthorized or unintended alteration. System security implies that a defined system functions in a defined operational environment, serves a defined set of users, contains prescribed data and operational programs, has defined network connections and interactions with other systems, and incorporates safeguards to protect the system against defined threats to the system and its resources and data.

Appropriate computer security can generally be achieved through a combination of technical measures, system management, and administrative procedures. It is generally preferable to incorporate the technical safeguards into the system application or program (i.e., the health record system) rather than relying on network infrastructure for security. Technical safeguards include personal identification and user verification techniques, access control software and audit controls, computer architecture, communications linkage of safeguards, and encryption.

Personal Identification and User Verification. Personal identification assists in ensuring that a user of a communication or computer system is authorized to do so and may be held accountable for his or her actions. The most common method of verifying the user's identity is through a secret password or code, which must be used to access a system or a particular part of a system. If password identification is used, the passwords should be at least five characters in length, and the system should require the users to change passwords frequently. Relying solely on passwords to identify users often fails to provide adequate security for computer systems. Users may share passwords, may leave passwords at their workstations or write them on desk blotters, or an unauthorized person attempting to gain access to the system may correctly guess one or more passwords if users use common words as passwords. User verification systems frequently involve a combination of identifiers, such as a key card in conjunction with a password or access code or some physical characteristic of the user (e.g., thumbprint). Biometric identification involves verifying the identity of the user, based on a unique physical feature of the user, such as fingerprint, written signature, voice print, typing pattern, retinal scan, or hand geometry. Biometric identification generally provides a high level of security, but may be cost-prohibitive for many health care providers.

Access Control Software and Audit Trails. Once a system has identified a user, it is still necessary to limit the user's access to the resources and data that he or she is authorized to access. Data access control software prevents a user from accessing or modifying a file unless the user has been given prior authorization. Through authorization checking, a system can determine whether a user's access request is valid, based on the permission assigned to the user, and then grant or deny the access request. Auditing access and attempted access by users helps to ensure user accountability. An examination of audit trails may also reveal suspicious patterns of access and lead to detection of improper conduct by authorized or unauthorized users.

Computer Architecture. The computer itself may be designed to enhance security by monitoring its own activities and preventing users from gaining access to data they are not authorized to see. It may also be designed to be secure from sophisticated tampering and sabotage.

Communications Linkage Safeguards. Because computer links to telecommunications lines may make the computers vulnerable to improper access through the lines or through taps on the lines, a security system should also include security features designed to limit such improper use or access. One means of limiting access via dial-up lines has been dial-back protection devices. New security modems combine features of a modem with network security features, such as passwords, dial-back, and encryption.

Encryption. Encryption is a method of protecting data vulnerable to unauthorized access or tampering. It is used to encode data for transmission or for storage in a computer. Encryption can provide an electronic signature to verify that a message has not been tampered with, and to protect against fraud or repudiation by a sender. Encryption can protect confidentiality by encoding a message so that its meaning is not obvious. An encrypted message is encoded in such a way as to permit interpretation of the message only with the appropriate key, to which only authorized parties have access. Encryption can also protect data integrity through message authentication. Message authentication allows a system to verify that a message arrived in exactly the same form that it was sent, without errors or alterations; that it came from the stated source; and that it was not falsified by an impostor or fraudulently altered by the recipient. Digital signatures can also be created through encryption. Like a handwritten signature, this digital signature can be used to verify that information has not been altered after it is signed, thereby ensuring message integrity.

Implementing System Security

With respect to inside users of a system, the security system should permit only authorized users to have access to health records. Access may be controlled and users may be identified in one or more of the ways discussed above, including passwords, key cards, access codes, and biometric identification. In addition, a system should allow access to the system through only one workstation at a time for each user identifier. It is wise to program a system to log off automatically when a workstation has not been used for a predefined period of time. A user's access to the system should be limited to that portion of the system or record that relates to the user's position and duties. A system can be programmed to lock out an individual who attempts to retrieve files that he or she is not authorized to access or who repeatedly attempts to gain access to the system using an improper access code. In such cases, the system can be programmed to sound an alarm at the workstation or at an operator's console. It is important to strictly limit access to sensitive records and portions of records containing highly sensitive health information for which the law provides a higher level of confidentiality protection. Such information includes HIV antibody test results, AIDS patient records, alcohol and drug abuse records, and records of celebrities. Because of the intense controversy over abortion, common sense dictates that abortion records be accorded the same level of protection as other highly sensitive health records, regardless of whether such protection is expressly required under applicable law.

The scope of a user's access should be periodically reviewed and modified as appropriate. It is vital that a user's access to the system be promptly terminated when the person's employment, medical staff membership, or other relationship justifying access to patient records is terminated. When a user's relationship with the provider is to be terminated involuntarily, it may be wise to terminate the user's access to the system just prior to notifying the user of the termination. Access to records by each authorized user should be periodically reviewed to discourage casual browsing through records. Such casual browsing increases the risk that confidentiality will be breached.

Provider policy should specifically prohibit revealing or sharing passwords and other user identifiers and should also prohibit attempting to access records beyond the scope of one's authorization. Hospitals and other institutional providers should require medical staff members to sign confidentiality statements, in which they acknowledge that passwords, access codes, and the like are for personal use only and assume responsibility for any entries made using the medical staff member's identifier. Policies against sharing passwords or other identifiers or permitting another person access to the system should be strictly enforced.

Implementing External Security

Improper access to computerized health records must also be prevented with respect to outside users of a health record system. Controlling access from multiple and sometimes remote locations is more difficult than controlling access from one centralized location. Dial-up access makes it possible for external parties to try repeatedly to gain access to a system without being visible if a system is unmonitored. There are several possible methods to combat external parties' attempts to gain unauthorized access to a health record system. Such methods include recording and monitoring attempts to gain access to the system; having the computer system call back users who request remote access; and requiring remote users to have physicians' "keys," such as encoded disks, in order to gain access.

Regardless of whether providers outsource their health records to a computer outsource vendor or acquire their own systems, third-party vendors and consultants will usually be involved in some way in developing, installing, operating, and maintaining the health record system. These third parties may have access to live patient data, either on site or from remote locations. Such third-party access to patient data may be occasional or ongoing. When a provider outsources its health records, the outsource vendor will have possession of the health records. Such vendors and consultants are generally not subject to the same legal or ethical obligations with respect to confidentiality as are providers. If such a third party improperly discloses confidential patient information, the provider permitting the third party access to patient information can expect to be held responsible for any harm resulting from the improper disclosure, unless the provider can demonstrate that all reasonable precautions to prevent such disclosure have been taken.

In many cases, the contract between the provider and the vendor or consultant will disclaim any liability for damages, such as those that would result from a disclosure in breach of a patient's confidentiality, or will limit the amount of damages for which the vendor or consultant may be liable. It is, therefore, advisable to include in all contracts with such third parties obligations for the third party

- to hold all patient information in strict confidence
- to use the information only to perform the third party's obligations under the contract
- to disclose only to the third party's employees who need access under the contract and who have signed a confidentiality agreement obligating them to hold all patient information in confidence
- to return the records in usable form upon request and upon termination of the contract
- to indemnify the provider for breaches of these obligations (It may not be possible to obtain such indemnification. However, the contract should not place any limits on the liability of the third party for breaches of its obligations.)

Some outside computer services or data organizations analyzing a provider's patient data may wish to obtain the provider's patient data for purposes not in keeping with the provider's duty to preserve patient confidentiality. It is not uncommon for an outside computer service or data organization to attempt to obtain a provider's patient data to create databases or other proprietary information products. Such third parties will seek to own and control the information products and will want the right to distribute them freely. Such distribution will generally not accord with the provider's confidentiality obligations, unless the information product cannot be used directly or indirectly to identify individual patients. All contracts with such outside computer and data services should address whether the service will be permitted to use patient information in its information products and establish the precautions the service will be required to observe concerning patient confidentiality if the contract permits the use of patient information in the organization's information products.

When patient information is transmitted over public channels of communication, including telephone lines, radio waves, microwaves, etc., as in the case of wide-area networks, protecting the information from outside access becomes more difficult and requires additional precautions. As communications protocols become more standard, the potential for unauthorized tapping of such communication channels will increase. One possible response to this confidentiality problem is to encrypt information communicated over such channels.

An additional threat to patient confidentiality results from the computer's capacity for mass storage and copying of records. One possible safeguard against the mass breach of confidentiality that would occur if numerous records are improperly accessed or disclosed is to restrict use of software functions that permit copying of multiple records at one time.

Computer Sabotage

Computerized health record systems make possible widescale alteration or destruction of patient data through computer sabotage. Viruses and other forms of sabotage, such as worms, bombs, and Trojan horses, can jeopardize the integrity and accessibility of information on the system by causing the system to slow or crash. Although both inside and outside users of the system potentially can commit sabotage, the biggest threat to computer security is often internal. Disgruntled employees may pose a substantial threat of sabotage.

The risk of sabotage by outside parties is present whenever there is any networking or electronic data sharing with outside parties, or disks or other storage media from outside sources are used on the system. It may be impractical to control this risk by eliminating networking and data sharing with outside computers and by not using any disk or other storage medium from an outside source, because connections with outside facilities and other databases may be essential for clinical, research, or other purposes. Joint Commission standards specifically address the need for hospital information systems to link up with external databases and bodies of clinical, administrative, and research knowledge. Antivirus software, which assists in detecting and/or blocking computer viruses, is a useful means of reducing this risk. It is advisable to check all disks and similar media from outside sources for viruses prior to using them on a health record system.

Hospitals should also be sensitive to the risk of sabotage from software vendors. In isolated cases, software vendors have sabotaged or threatened to sabotage a system after a provider withheld payment as permitted under the system contract, because the system fails to meet contractual standards. This form of sabotage involves the insertion of a virus or keylock into system software, which enables the vendor to lock or shut the system down in the event of a payment dispute. Contracts for the purchase, lease, license, or maintenance of a computer-based health record system should obligate the vendor and its agents to refrain from inserting viruses or keylocks into the system. Contracts should also provide that the vendor will indemnify the provider for any and all losses and damages resulting from insertion of viruses or keylocks by the vendor or its agents.

While no computer security technology or methods available to the provider can totally guarantee that breaches of system security will not occur, it is important to employ system security technology and techniques that are at least reasonable by current standards. Nevertheless, the need to preserve the confidentiality and ensure the integrity of health records will have to be balanced against the practical constraints on achieving perfect computer security.

Preserving Access to Computerized Records

Delivering quality patient care requires that health records be readily available. Federal reimbursement regulations, state hospital licensure requirements, and Joint Commission accreditation standards all require that health records for current hospital patients be readily accessible and stored so as to be promptly retrievable. Thus, a computer-based health record system must make records readily accessible and provide for prompt retrieval of the records. When a system crashes or experiences downtime, computerized records become inaccessible. It is, therefore, imperative that a system be designed and maintained to minimize downtime and that adequate backup mechanisms be available. Health record system downtime may hinder patient care and result in negligence liability. Excessive system downtime may also violate applicable licensure requirements and accreditation standards.

Several precautions can help preserve accessibility of computerized health records. First, it is important that system hardware be properly maintained and that system software be tested, debugged where necessary, and maintained appropriately. When considering acquisition of a particular system, it is wise to inquire about other users' experience with the system relative to downtime and the time required to bring the system back up quickly. Any agreement for acquisition of a computerized record system or any component thereof should contain performance standards, as well as warranties of reliability and covenants to provide ongoing maintenance and support. It is also important to take appropriate precautions against sabotage of the system to prevent a computer virus from locking up or crashing the system. It is also important that a provider conduct adequate backup procedures. A provider's disaster or emergency plan should include planning for emergency capabilities for the health record system.

Durability Concerns

Computerized health records must be durable to meet state licensure requirements, to be available as evidence in malpractice and other litigation involving the care received by a patient or the patient's medical condition, and to provide data for research. When health records are computerized, the problem of durability becomes more complex than is the case with paper records. There are two preconditions for durability of computerized records. The first is that the medium on which the information is stored must last for at least the minimum time a provider is required to retain medical records. The second is that the provider must be able to access old records created or maintained on older, and perhaps obsolete, technology.

Changes in technology can render a computer system obsolete before the need for records stored on the system has ended. Frequently old and new systems do not interact, making the older records inaccessible through the newer system. A provider may need to keep old equipment in good working order long after it is obsolete and another record system is in use. If an old and new system are able to interface, copying health records from one system to the other can be problematic. Prior to copying such records, providers should check with knowledgeable legal counsel to ascertain whether such copied records will be considered original records for evidentiary purposes and whether retention of the copies in lieu of the originals complies with state licensure requirements. When records are copied from one system to another, it is important to preserve evidence of the chain of copying. When copying records, it is also important to verify that both the medium onto which the record will be copied and the copying process comply with applicable state licensure requirements.

Before selecting a medium for creation and storage of computerized health records, the long-term durability of the medium should be investigated. Only media with proven durability should be used for health record storage. It is important to note that the durability of some storage media, such as certain types of optical disks, has yet to be proven.

Some state licensure regulations address health record storage and retention requirements in general terms, stating that hospitals must store records to provide easy retrieval and security. A few states have promulgated more elaborate requirements for record storage. Some states specify acceptable storage media for health records. A provider that adopts a method for storing computerized records should verify in advance that the method complies with state licensure requirements for record retention.

Accuracy Issues

Computerized health records, like paper records, must be completed in a timely and accurate fashion. Maintaining a complete and accurate record is essential not only for compliance with licensure and accreditation requirements but also to establish that appropriate care was provided to each patient.

Error in computerized health records can result from defective performance of either the hardware or the software or from human or machine input. In complex systems with open architecture, errors can result from unanticipated interactions among programs. To minimize the risk of error, a provider should have regular maintenance and performance checks conducted, and the results should be documented. The provider should also have a system to review human input for accuracy and should document that such review has occurred. Joint Commission standards require that an organization review the completeness, accuracy, and timeliness of health record entries at least quarterly. At a minimum, the review must be performed by the medical staff in cooperation with nursing, the health information or medical record department, management and administrative services, and representatives of other departments or services, as appropriate.

In addition, all laboratory and other types of equipment that generate input for a computerized records system should be well maintained and should be tested and calibrated periodically to minimize machine input errors.

The use of bar codes and other programmed codes can raise accuracy concerns. Optical scanning of bar codes is used to monitor services and supplies provided to patients and to enter clinical data, such as temperature, pulse, blood pressure, and respiration. Bar codes can also be applied to a patient's wristband and to packages of supplies. The use of such codes allows providers to create health records much faster than is possible if data are charted by hand or entered through a computer keyboard. Optical scanning equipment should be tested periodically and the test results recorded. There should be a mechanism for confirming input generated from bar codes or other programmed codes either visually or otherwise.

State Licensure Requirements

Many states impose specific requirements for health records in statutes and regulations governing qualification for licensure as a hospital or other health care facility. Many of these licensure requirements were formulated when paper records were the rule rather than the exception. Because state law is changing so rapidly in this area, this section will not include a detailed discussion of specific state requirements. It is important, nevertheless, for a provider automating its health records to check applicable state requirements to ensure that the record system and the records will meet applicable requirements with respect to the creation, authentication, and retention of health records, as well as requirements for record content.

Reimbursement Requirements and Accreditation Standards

It is important that a health care provider's records meet applicable governmental reimbursement standards and accreditation standards. Both the Health Care Financing Administration (HCFA) and the Joint Commission permit computerization of health records.

Medicare Conditions of Participation

To participate in the Medicare program, a provider must meet the applicable Medicare Conditions of Participation. The Conditions of Participation for hospitals include requirements for health records but do not include an express restriction on permissible media for creating and storing such records. Medicare Conditions of Participation for hospitals permit authentication of health records by signature, written initials, or computer entry.

Accreditation Standards

In theory, the Joint Commission is a voluntary organization administering a voluntary accreditation process. However, its accreditation standards are incorporated in some state hospital licensure requirements, at least in part, and a hospital is deemed to meet certain of the Medicare Conditions of Participation if it is accredited by the Joint Commission. The Joint Commission's accreditation requirements applicable to health records are primarily found in the standards concerning management of information. The Joint Commission clearly contemplates that hospitals may record a portion of or entire health records on computer. For example, the accreditation standards provide that authentication of health record entries may be by written signature or initials, rubber-stamp signature, or computer key. The Joint Commission also requires practitioners who use a computer key signature to sign a statement that the practitioner alone will use the code for the computer key.

Autoauthentication

Both the Joint Commission and the Medicare Conditions of Participation require that health records be authenticated by the responsible practitioner. Authentication involves signature or another approved means of identifying the practitioner responsible for a health record entry and assigning responsibility for the contents of the entry. Often, however, health professionals do not enter information directly into a computerized record system; rather, the information is dictated into a digital dictation system. Some hospitals have been using *autoauthentication*, which refers to a process whereby physicians sign on to a digital dictation system with a computer key and then dictate record entries. The dictated record entries are then transcribed and sent to the dictating physician, who is given a stated time period in which to make changes. If the physician fails to return corrections within this period, the physician is deemed to have approved the record entry for accuracy, completeness, etc.

Both HCFA and the Joint Commission have expressed concern that autoauthentication does not meet their respective standards. In particular, HCFA does not believe that autoauthentication complies with the Medicare Conditions of Participation, because physicians often do not authenticate the final record entry. The Joint Commission has also taken the position that an autoauthentication process does not conform with its accreditation standards for hospitals.

Automated Health Records as Evidence

In addition to enabling providers to respond properly to the medical needs of patients, health records serve as a diary of a provider's actions. It is, therefore, important that the information contained in a record be admissible as evidence in court when the care received by the patient or the patient's medical condition is an issue. Because of the widespread computerization of general business records, courts have developed standards for judging the trustworthiness of computerized records.

The Rule against Hearsay

One barrier to introduction of any health record as evidence in court is the rule against hearsay. Hearsay is generally defined as a statement made out of court by a declarant and proffered as evidence to prove the truth of the matter asserted in that out-of-court statement. Courts exclude hearsay from evidence, unless one of the exceptions to the hearsay rule applies. Because all health records, regardless of form, are written statements made outside the courtroom, they are classed as hearsay if offered as evidence to prove the truth of any matter asserted in the record.

One important exception to the hearsay rule is the business records exception. Although the statement of this rule may vary from jurisdiction to jurisdiction, generally, to come within the business records exception, records must be kept regularly in the ordinary course of business and must not have been prepared specifically for trial. The business records exception applies only to record entries made at or near the time of the event recorded. In addition, the identity of the person making or recording the entry must be captured in the record, and the record must have been prepared by a person with firsthand knowledge of the event recorded or from information transmitted by such a person. The person making the record or transmitting the information for the record must be acting in an ordinary business capacity at the time the record is made.

A computerized record made in the ordinary course of a provider's business should meet the requirement that the record be kept regularly and in the ordinary course of business. An automated record system should record the date and time of each entry and update to a health record, so that the time of the entry or update and its timeliness can be shown in court. The identity of the person who makes each entry or update should be captured by the system. If employees or health professionals share passwords or make entries under an identifier that is not their own, it will be impossible to ensure that the system's record of the identity of the person making the entry is accurate.

It is important that errors in computerized records be corrected appropriately. The system should preserve both the original entry and the correction, and it should record the identities of the persons making each original entry or correction so as not to create an appearance that the record has been altered or that records on the system are not reliable and trustworthy as evidence.

Write-once, read-many (WORM) or nonerasable compact disk, read-only memory (CD-ROM) technology may be attractive in this context, because records cannot be altered once information is recorded. Another method of preserving records in their original form is write-protecting the portions of computer disks on which patient information is stored so that the integrity of records is protected. Nevertheless, if a system uses reliable software and preserves erroneous entries, tracking the history of each entry and correction, the provider should be able to demonstrate the reliability of the record in court.

It is advisable for the provider to have an employee or technical consultant who can testify concerning the reliability of the system's identification and entry-dating features and the trustworthiness of the system as a whole, including system security features and procedures.

Records created and stored on a properly designed and maintained computer-based record system should fall under the business records exception (or a similar exception applicable to health records) to the hearsay rule if the procedures described above are followed. Under the business records exception to the hearsay rule, statements contained in such computerized records may be admissible if made by providers or staff acting in the ordinary course of business. Statements contained in such computerized records may also be admissible if made by the declarant for "purposes of medical diagnosis or treatment and describing medical history, or past or present symptoms, pain, or sensations, or the inception or general character of the cause or external source thereof insofar as reasonably pertinent to diagnosis or treatment." [Federal Rules of Evidence, Rule 803(4).]

Best-Evidence Rule

Another evidentiary rule relevant to the admissibility of computerized health records is the best-evidence rule. The best-evidence rule expresses a judicial preference for the original of a writing if the contents of a writing are in dispute. In the context of computerized records, a question arises as to whether a hard copy of the contents of the record is an "original" for purposes of the best-evidence rule. The Federal Rules of Evidence state the requirements for data stored on a computer or similar device. Rule 1001(3) states that "[i]f data are stored in a computer or similar device, any printout or other output readable by sight, shown to reflect the data accurately, is an 'original.' " The Federal Rules of Evidence also provide that duplicates are admissible to the same extent as originals, unless a genuine issue of authenticity of unfairness arises.

Some states' evidentiary rules also provide that computerized documents shall be accepted as originals. Other states permit admission of reproductions into evidence when the reproductions are made in the regular course of business and satisfy other criteria for trustworthiness. The trustworthiness of a record created on a computerized system refers to the reliability of system hardware and software, the use of proper procedures for creating and storing records, the assurance that entries are made by adequately trained personnel, and the prevention of unauthorized access to the records and of tampering with the system.

Facsimile Transmission of Health Records and Health Record Entries

The widespread use of facsimile (fax) machines to transmit information, including health records, from one location to another has created a new threat to confidentiality and may, in some circumstances, call into question the integrity or authenticity of orders and other health record entries transmitted by fax. Both paper and computerized records can be sent via fax machines; in addition, the use of a fax modem on a computer makes possible transmission of computerized records from one computer to another without generating any hard copy of the record as a necessary byproduct of the transmission. In either case, fax transmissions to external parties generally travel over telephone networks or other public channels of communication. Because there is a significant risk that fax transmissions will be misdirected, use of fax machines to transmit confidential health record information is risky and is extremely risky if highly sensitive patient information is involved.

These risks can be reduced, however, if proper maintenance and security techniques are used and if proper procedures are followed in transmitting health records by fax. Nevertheless, it is probably never prudent to send via fax highly sensitive health information, except in encrypted form or over nonpublic channels of communication that are highly secure (e.g., a local area network within a facility). The American Health Information Management Association recommends use of fax machines to transmit patient health information only when the original document or mail-delivered photocopies will not serve.

A provider sending confidential information by fax off-site should verify that the recipient is authorized to receive it. Some, but by no means total, protection against unauthorized access to a fax transmission can be obtained by calling the recipient before sending the transmission, alerting the recipient to stand by for the transmission, and verifying that the fax number to which the transmission will be directed is the correct number. The cover sheet on the document should also include a confidentiality legend, emphasizing the nature of the information contained in the transmission and requesting that the recipient contact the sender if the fax is received by someone other than the recipient shown on the cover sheet. Encrypting faxed information is another method of protecting its confidentiality. However, this process generally requires that the receiving fax machine or computer be equipped to decode the encrypted information, and this is often not the case. When sending faxes off-site, a provider should retain a record of each fax transmission (including the number of the receiving fax machine) and the contents of the fax.

When receiving orders or other health record information from outside the facility, a provider should also take special precautions. If caller identification is available, the receiving fax machine should be equipped with a mechanism for recording the number of the telephone from which the fax transmission originated. The personnel operating the fax machine should have a list of telephone numbers from which medical staff members transmit orders and should verify that the telephone number identified on the fax machine appears on that list. A hospital may also treat faxed orders like verbal orders and require authentication of the order by the appropriate medical staff member within the time period permitted for authentication of verbal orders. Nevertheless, the advent of computer fax boards, with their attendant opportunities for electronic manipulation, may make it difficult to establish the accuracy and authenticity of a faxed order in court, if either is disputed by the originating practitioner. In the context of computer fax boards and fax modems, use of cryptography for message authentication may be advisable.

Providers should refer to state rules of evidence to determine if, and under what circumstances, facsimile transmissions that become part of a health record are admissible in court. Fax machines used to transmit orders internally should be equipped to print the date, time, and address of the originating fax machine to help support the authenticity of internally faxed documents. The original of each such fax transmission should be retained.

Source: William H. Roach, Jr., and the Aspen Law Center, *Medical Records and the Law*, 2nd ed., Aspen Publishers, Inc., © 1994.

CURRENT TECHNOLOGY: CONFIDENTIALITY RISKS AND CONTROLS

Although health care information security involves three aspects of information protection—preserving the confidentiality of information, protecting its integrity, and ensuring its availability—the primary concern for most organizations at this point in the evolution of computer-based health records appears to be preserving patient confidentiality. As caregiver dependence on the information provided by computer-based health record systems grows, information integrity, ensuring the information is accurate and authentic, will become more important. The need to ensure that information is entered into the system by authorized persons and that no unauthorized modifications are made will become a higher priority.

But for now, polls and studies indicate that patients and health care professionals alike are concerned that the increased use of technology will lead to a greater loss of patient privacy. Anecdotal evidence indicates that many breaches of confidentiality in today's environment are primarily due to behavior, carelessness in using office equipment, or deliberate disclosure of the details of patient information. Even though some of the well-known incidents involve the use of technology, those incidents are mainly due to the failure to use available technological controls rather than inherent weaknesses in the technology. However, reminding staff members not to discuss patient information in elevators and cafeterias is not nearly as interesting or exciting as dealing with the actual and perceived exposures created by technology. Therefore, many health care organizations are touting encryption and similar high-tech mechanisms as the solution to information security problems while remaining vulnerable to the low-tech and behavior-related risks.

Enhanced technology, including encryption, will undoubtedly be a valuable component of successful information security programs in the future, but examining the risks and exposures related to the contemporary environment can lead to significantly improved information protection. Better protection of information in today's environment can be achieved by addressing some of the risks related to the ways in which health care professionals use current computer systems and office equipment.

The following list includes typical risks associated with current information-handling technology other than computer-based health record systems and controls that can be used to mitigate the risks. Even though these risks might seem mundane compared to sophisticated break-ins to computer-based health record systems, they can result in just as much harm to patients.

COPIERS

Risks

- Leaving confidential originals in the copier feeder or on the copier glass where they may be found by someone who should not see the information.
- Discarding imperfect copies in adjacent trash cans.
- Repair personnel discovering confidential information while clearing paper jams.

Controls

- Implement awareness training programs.
- Provide secure disposal containers near copiers.
- Insert confidentiality agreements in repair contracts.

FAX MACHINES

Risks

- Confidential faxes sent to the wrong location.
- Confidential information faxed to unauthorized persons.
- Fax machines shared by departments with differing information needs.
- Confidential faxes, both outgoing and incoming, left unattended in the fax machine trays or on adjacent tables.
- Extra copies of confidential faxes resulting from transmission failures discarded in open trash containers.
- Fax machines located in areas where confidential information can be seen by unauthorized persons.

Controls

- Create procedures for verifying fax numbers.
- Implement procedures for verifying recipients' authority to receive confidential information.
- Place secure disposal containers near fax machines.
- Place fax machines in secure locations.
- Provide separate fax machines for departments or units with differing needs.

TELEPHONES

Risks

- Persons overhearing conversations.
- Giving out confidential information to unauthorized callers.
- Unauthorized access to voice response systems.

Controls

- Implement awareness training programs.
- Create procedures for controlling access to voice response systems and limits on the type of information that may be distributed.

PRINTERS

Risks

- Printers shared by departments or units with differing information needs.
- Printers located where visitors can see information being printed.
- Extra or imperfect printouts discarded in open containers.
- Print jobs directed to the wrong location.

Controls

- Provide separate printers for units and departments based on need to print confidential information.

continues

Current Technology: Confidentiality Risks and Controls continued

- Locate printers in secure areas.
- Provide secure disposal containers near printers.
- Include confidentiality agreements in repair contracts.
- Ensure that staff members are aware of the locations of printers available on print menus.

CORDLESS AND CELLULAR PHONES

Risks

- Conversations overheard because phone is used in a public place.
- Conversations overheard via eavesdropping with scanning equipment.

Controls

- Implement awareness training programs.
- Use cordless telephones that encrypt the transmitted signal.
- Refrain from discussing patient-identifiable information on cordless and cellular phones.

VOICE PAGERS

Risks

- Confidential messages overheard when received on the pager.

Controls

- Implement awareness training programs.
- Establish policies prohibiting sending confidential messages to voice pagers.
- Notify staff members of voice mail capabilities that may include forwarding to voice pagers.

E-MAIL

Risks

- Confidential messages sent or forwarded to the wrong person.
- Confidential messages sent via Internet resulting in disclosure of patient information.
- Messages stored on backup tapes and subsequently seen by unauthorized persons.

Controls

- Establish policies for use of e-mail.
- Provide awareness training covering the policies and implications of using e-mail.

VOICE MAIL

Risks

- Confidential message left in the wrong voice mailbox or on the wrong answering machine.
- Confidential messages overheard during playback on answering machines or speaker phones.

Controls

- Implement awareness training programs.
- Develop policies for the use of voice mail for confidential information.

PC DISPLAYS

Risks

- Displays located in positions such that visitors and others can see confidential information.
- Computer displays left unattended with confidential information being displayed.

Controls

- Locate PC displays so that the screen cannot be seen by unauthorized people.
- Implement automatic time-out to blank screen when equipment is not in use.

TELEMEDICINE

Risks

- Patient privacy compromised because patient appears in the background of the video for another patient.
- Establishing video and image links to the incorrect location.
- Videotapes of sessions not properly protected.

Controls

- Provide private facilities for telemedicine and teleconferencing.
- Use appropriate systems controls to protect the system and files.

DICTATION AND TRANSCRIPTION SYSTEMS

Risks

- Physicians overheard while dictating.
- Poor password management results in disclosure of passwords and subsequent unauthorized access.
- Inadequate controls on transcription system and report files resulting in disclosure of confidential information.
- Transcription performed in insecure locations in offices or homes that permit unauthorized persons to discover confidential information.

Controls

- Implement information security controls on transcription systems.
- Include confidentiality provisions in contracts for transcription.
- Provide awareness training.

continues

Current Technology: Confidentiality Risks and Controls continued

HAND-HELD PC

Risks

- Computer stolen or lost.
- Information on the display viewed by unauthorized users.

Controls

- Provide awareness training for users on how to protect portable computers.
- Use encryption to protect information stored in portable devices.

PC MODEMS

Risks

- Modems installed in personal computers to be used for dial-out permitting unauthorized dial-in.

Controls

- Provide awareness training for users on how to protect portable computers.
- Use encryption to protect information stored in portable devices.

INTERNET

Risks

- Unencrypted patient information transmitted via Internet resulting in unauthorized disclosure.
- Unauthorized access to the organization's computer systems via Internet.

Controls

- Prohibit transmission of patient identifiable information via Internet.
- Implement encryption.
- Install appropriate firewalls between Internet and the organization's network and systems.

Because of the considerable amount of overlap in the risks and controls for the various types of technology, it is far more cost-effective to address confidentiality risks with an organization-wide information security program than to address the risks separately for each type of equipment and each department.

The information security program should include the policies, training, and controls to protect the information in all of its forms and all of its locations.

HEALTH INSURANCE PORTABILITY AND ACCOUNTABILITY ACT OF 1996

On Wednesday, August 21, 1996, President Clinton signed into law the Health Insurance Portability and Accountability Act that contains language regarding administrative simplification and privacy. Under the Act, the Secretary of Health and Human Services (HHS) is required to adopt standards for the following financial and administrative electronic transactions: health claims (including coordination of benefits), claims attachments, enrollment and disenrollment in a health plan, eligibility for a health plan, health care payment and remittance advice, first report of injury, health claim status, and referral certification and authorization.

In adopting standards, the Secretary of HHS is required to use those already developed by organizations accredited by the American National Standards Institute. If standards do not exist, the Secretary of HHS may adopt a standard after consultation with the National Uniform Billing Committee, the National Uniform Claim Committee, the Workgroup for Electronic Data Interchange, and the American Dental Association. The Secretary is also authorized to set implementation standards (guidelines) for each of the financial and administrative transactions.

The Secretary of HHS shall adopt standards providing for a standard unique health identifier for each individual, employer, health plan, and health care provider. Additionally, the Secretary of HHS, with the Secretary of Commerce, shall adopt standards for the electronic transmission and authentication of signatures for the financial and administrative transactions.

The Secretary of HHS shall adopt security standards to ensure that persons who maintain or transmit health information shall maintain reasonable and appropriate administrative, technical, and physical safeguards. The Secretary of HHS is required to adopt security standards that take into account

- the technical capabilities of record systems used to maintain health information
- the costs of security measures
- the need for training persons who have access to health information
- the value of audit trails in computerized record systems
- the needs and capabilities of small health care providers and rural health care providers.

The Act preempts any provision of state law that requires medical or health plan records (including billing information) to be maintained or transmitted in written rather than electronic form (state "quill pen" laws). Penalties for wrongful disclosure of individually identifiable health information include fines and imprisonment.

The Secretary of HHS is required to provide detailed recommendations to Congress within 12 months of enacting standards with respect to the privacy of individually identifiable health information. The recommendations shall address

- the rights that an individual should have regarding his or her identifiable health information
- the procedures that should be established for exercising such rights
- the uses and disclosures of such information that should be authorized or required

Congress is mandated to enact legislation addressing the privacy of individually identifiable health information within 36 months of enactment of the Act. If Congress fails to pass legislation, the Secretary of HHS is mandated to publish final regulations within 6 months of the deadline (42 months after enactment of the Act). In complying with these provisions, the Secretary of HHS is required to consult with the National Committee on Vital and Health Statistics and the U.S. Attorney General.

This article is reprinted in full with permission from the publisher, the American Health Information Management Association. It is reprinted from *In Confidence*, September/October 1996. For *In Confidence* subscription information, call 800-335-5535.

CONFIDENTIALITY AND SECURITY OF COMPUTER-BASED INFORMATION SYSTEMS—POLICY

	Issued By:	Policy #:
	Prepared By:	Revision #:
	Approved By:	Effective Date:
Subject: Confidentiality and Security of Computer-Based Information Systems		Page of

Mission: The hospital is dedicated to developing and providing the highest quality, compassionate health care to serve the needs of the community. Key to the delivery of quality health care is the design and implementation of programs that support and enhance appropriate access to health information.

Vision: All information regarding patients and employees is considered confidential. The hospital will develop consistent approaches to the handling of data across the system that will balance the patient's right to privacy and confidentiality with legitimate uses of data.

Scope: Computer-based information systems including information and data in any format (i.e., paper, electronic, or produced electronically) must be protected from unauthorized access, modification, destruction, or disclosure, whether accidental or intentional. Such protection will be consistent with the sensitivity and the value of the data. Protection can be provided through equipment, software, and procedures that address processing, transmission, and storage of data.

Policies:

1. Accountability/responsibility
   - *Accountability*: It is the responsibility of all employees to consider themselves accountable for the protection of the data, which begins with accessing the database and continues with the use of the information regardless of format. Policies and procedures support the confidentiality and integrity of the information systems within the corporation.
   - *Responsibility*: The information maintained in the computer-based information systems of the hospital is an asset of the corporation. Managers are responsible for the timeliness, security, and integrity of the data maintained within the scope of their position through the use of appropriate control measures and the support of hospital policies.

2. Access
   - ID/password
     - –Unique identification and password assignments will be made to staff members for access to information on a need-to-know basis, only upon written authority of the owner of the data. *Need-to-know* is determined by the individual's supervisor. Generally it can be categorized into these areas:
       a. access by care providers to individual patient data, for use in patient care or specific hospital operations
       b. access for research, planning, and quality improvement processes within the hospital
       c. access by those employees in the Health Record Department whose role includes health record processing and maintenance
     - –Individual IDs/passwords may not be shared with another user.
     - –Passwords are changed frequently, as designated by system design.
     - –Users are limited to one log-on at a time, as designated by individual platform design.
     - –An individual's multiple attempts to sign on with an improper access code will result in a lock-out status of the individual until access privileges are restored by Information Services.
     - –Access of all users is monitored by identification/password assignments. Warning notices are to be displayed on each screen to inform staff of the confidential nature of the information and that their access is being monitored.
     - –Maintenance of the access assignments will be completed with employee change in status (i.e., termination, change of position).

continues

Confidentiality and Security of Computer-Based Information Systems continued

	No:	Page of

- Employee's information
  - –Each system employee may choose whether his/her personal data will be accessible or restricted for view by medical staff only in the hospital system. The option of requesting restricted access on selected systems and not others will not be available.
  - –An employee's access to his/her own patient information must follow the process as defined in the release of information policies and procedures.
- Preemployment data will be retained only in the local employee health database.
- Sensitive information (psychiatry, substance abuse, VIP, protected patients) is defined in the release of information policies and procedures.
- Protected patients: Those patients with known risk of injury by others must be protected. Their identification will be protected by the assignment of an alias on the Admission/Discharge/Transfer (ADT) system. However, the health record number will remain unchanged and valid for the patient.

3. Integrity of database
   - A process must exist for each database by which information is validated within the system.
   - Integrity of data copied and transferred to another system is the responsibility of the receiving system. Responsibility for the correct transfer and validation of data lies with both systems and Information Services.

4. Security
   - Administration and maintenance
     - –Appropriate Information Services Departments will monitor and log access to the various systems within the hospital. A description of the methods used is available with each system's documentation.
     - –If misuse is suspected, the health information management specialist and/or department director should be notified. If appropriate, the director of security should be contacted for proper investigation.
   - Dissemination
     - –Secondary disclosure of individual patient information must be in keeping with the process, as defined in the release of information policies and procedures.
     - –Internal or external dissemination of data linking patient identifiers with clinical data should be evaluated against the recipient's need to know that information.

5. Compliance with confidentiality and data security policies
   - Failure to comply with confidentiality and data security policies, standards, and procedures will result in disciplinary action in accordance with human resources policies, which may include termination or suspension of employment. Compliance means conformity to data security policies and standards as well as the data security procedures developed to meet user needs.
   - Improper conduct includes, but is not limited to:
     - –lack of discretion or unauthorized disclosure of any information concerning patients, visitors, or employees
     - –attempting to obtain another person's password or security code
     - –using or attempting to use another person's password or security code or allowing the use of one's code by another
     - –unauthorized modification of information or database structure
     - –unauthorized access, whether internally or from a remote location
     - –unauthorized release of patient information
   - Monitoring compliance of security policies and procedures will be through collaboration between the systems administrator and appropriate management staff.

Recommendations:

1. *Accountability*: Statement on the main logo to the effect that, upon accessing the database, the individual bears an understanding of his/her responsibility for the confidentiality of the information.

continues

Confidentiality and Security of Computer-Based Information Systems continued

	No:	Page of

2. *Accessibility*: Further clarification needed regarding employee information on restriction of access to medical staff only. Need to address access for internal quality assurance/peer review activities/patient care (i.e., access to physician/provider identifiers).

3. Password
   - Need to define procedures for assignment of IDs/passwords.
   - Need to develop a single, facilitywide sign-on to support the integration of existing systems.

4. Documented medical staff/employee/student orientation and training should include:
   - maintaining data confidentiality and appropriate disclosure
   - use of individual systems to ensure accurate/efficient use of the software and data validation

5. Confidentiality statements reviewed and signed by all employees before ID/password assignments would include:
   - rules for use of information/data
   - disclosure of information

6. Confidentiality statements should be reviewed annually and signed as a reinforcement of this policy. It is recommended that this process be included as a departmental responsibility for orientation and continuing education. Employee acknowledgment of confidentiality statements should be automated.

7. Policy/procedure and accountability for system maintenance/audit/control/security/backup/logs/remote access should be developed.
   - maintenance of passwords (i.e., routine schedule of changing passwords, changes in employee status)
   - future consideration of the encryption of patient/physician identifying information when transmitted through wide-area networks
   - future contracts with third parties involving sharing of hospital information (should address redisclosure, retention, and destruction of information provided)

8. Appropriate resources will be available for administrating this process consistently and continuously.

Courtesy of Henry Ford Health System, Detroit, Michigan.

SECURITY AND SAFEGUARDING OF HEALTH AND HOSPITAL INFORMATION—ADMINISTRATIVE POLICY/PROCEDURE

PURPOSE

This policy provides direction and guidelines for the security and safeguarding of health and hospital information against loss, destruction, tampering, and unauthorized access and uses.

Loss, Tampering, and Unauthorized Access

The Health Records (HR) and Management Information Services (MIS) departments, as well as hospital leadership, will strive to ensure that health records and other information will be maintained in secure and restricted areas with access limited to those staff members who have a need for access based on either patient care needs and/or position responsibilities.

- All staff members are subject to the administrative policy on confidentiality and are aware of their responsibilities in protecting confidential patient information.
- Passwords for the hospital information system will be assigned on an individual basis for individual use only with appropriate access levels for positions. Passwords are not to be shared between staff members. In certain cases, generic passwords may be assigned to departments to locate basic information (i.e., identification of health record numbers for nursing staff members responsible for pulling health records after hours).
- Corrections or revisions to information in the hospital information system will be processed only by those staff members with appropriate access under the direction of the department manager.
- Health records will be removed from the Health Record Department for patient care purposes or with administrative authorization only.
  - All health records removed from assigned areas will be signed out through the computer system to maintain an accurate tracking mechanism.
  - Health records required in the patient care areas are maintained in a controlled setting with 24-hour staffing observation.
- Missing health records will be immediately reported to the health information management specialist, and a search of the last known locations will be undertaken. Staff members will be alerted of a missing record and requested to assist in locating it. The health information management specialist will maintain a listing of missing health records and will periodically (every three months) audit the list and verify whether or not the record has been returned to the file room.
- As the health record is considered a legal document, all entries will be considered final upon completion and may not be altered or removed. Appropriate corrections to health record documents are acceptable and should be made via these steps:
  1. Verification of the correct information (via computer, physician, etc.).
  2. Drawing of a single line through the incorrect information.
  3. Writing or typing in the corrected information neatly near the correction.
  4. Initialing and dating the correction

  If there is a question as to the accuracy of the record or if a patient disagrees with the information in the record, documentation is provided as an addendum to clarify the information; the original documented information is never altered or removed.

Destruction Due to Disaster

The hospital will make every attempt to safeguard health information records and other documents in structurally safe, fire-resistant, and water-resistant storage environments. Also, general safeguarding will ensure that combustible and/or hazardous chemicals and materials are maintained in a supervised environment with minimal risk for damage to hospital property. At all times, the hospital will meet building and fire codes and OSHA guidelines.

- Flooding/Water Damage

  Health records will be maintained in permanent storage in shelving units that are raised from the floor to prevent flooding and/or water damage. Should flooding or water damage occur, every attempt will be made to remove health records from the area with removal beginning on the lower shelves first, working upwards.

  If records cannot be removed prior to water damage, the health information management specialist and the administrative team will meet to determine what recovery mechanisms are feasible based on age and type of records, insurance coverage, costs, long-term damage, etc. If salvage operations are recommended, the health information management specialist will contact a reputable salvage vendor (based on American Health Information Management Association recommendation).
- Fire and Other Damage

  If records cannot be removed prior to fire or other damage, the health information management specialist and the administrative team will meet to determine what recovery mechanisms are feasible based on age and type of records, insurance coverage, costs, long-term damage, etc. If salvage operations are recommended, the health information management specialist will contact a reputable salvage vendor (based on American Health Information Management Association recommendation).

General Considerations

- An alternate site location for record storage will be considered if needed. Arrangements with local storage facilities may be initiated as determined by administration.

continues

Security and Safeguarding of Health and Hospital Information continued

- Confidentiality and security will be maintained along hospital guidelines if storage in alternate locations is necessary.
- A revised retention plan may be developed based on what records are recoverable. Legal opinions will be solicited from the hospital's legal counsel as needed.

Computerized Health Documents/Records

- Transcribed health information documents will be maintained in original paper format in the health record permanently. Backup copies of all transcribed documents will be maintained in the computerized transcription system for a period of six months. After six months, the documents will be downloaded and archived on magnetic media for a period of five years. The transcription system and archives are maintained in an area physically remote from the health record file room.
- If paper medical records are destroyed, it may be possible to provide copies of all transcribed documents as a basis for new health records.

Hospital Information System (HIS)

- On a weekly basis, the MIS Department will complete a full backup of the hospital information system on magnetic media. The backup will be maintained off-site (bank storage) with three weeks of backup maintained at all times.
- In the event of an HIS loss, the HIS vendor will provide assistance to the hospital in rebuilding the information system.

____

Administrator/CEO

Annual Review

____________________, ____________

____________________, ____________

____________________, ____________

Courtesy of Door County Memorial Hospital, Sturgeon Bay, Wisconsin.

PHYSICIAN ACCESS AND CONFIDENTIALITY AGREEMENT

Confidential information means information of the Medical Center that relates to the business of the Medical Center or the treatment of patients of the Medical Center or that is otherwise owned by the Medical Center and would be generally understood in the health care industry to be confidential information, and that is not available to the general public, including but not limited to information regarding:

- patients of the Medical Center, including but not limited to health records, charges and billings, conversations, admittance information, and patient financial information
- employees of the Medical Center, including but not limited to compensation, benefits, employment records, and disciplinary actions
- medical staff of the Medical Center
- the business and operations of the Medical Center, including but not limited to financial and statistical records, strategic plans, internal reports, memos, contracts, peer review information, communications, proprietary computer programs and technology and source code
- proprietary third-party information, including computer programs and technology, client or vendor information and source code

The Medical Center means the Medical Center and its affiliates.

I understand and agree as follows:

1. As a member of the medical staff of Bay Medical Center, I may learn of or have access to confidential information through the Medical Center's computer systems or otherwise.
2. I will access and use confidential information only as needed to perform my duties as a physician in the treatment of patients at the Medical Center and will not disclose confidential information to any other person except employees and members of the medical staff of the Medical Center who have a genuine need to know such confidential information to perform their duties or except as required by law.
3. I will safeguard and will not disclose my access code, password, or other authorization for access to confidential information to any other person, including an employee of the Medical Center.
4. I will immediately notify the Medical Center if I suspect or learn that my access code, password, or other authorization for access to confidential information or any confidential information has been misused or disclosed without proper authorization.
5. The Medical Center may, at any time and for any reason, revoke my access code or other authorization for access to confidential information.
6. I understand that violation of the foregoing agreements may constitute a violation of applicable criminal or civil laws and subject me to legal action.
7. This agreement shall be subject to and governed by the laws of this state.

____
Physician Signature   Date

____
Physician Name (Printed)

____
Witness   Date

Courtesy of Bay Medical Center, Bay City, Michigan.

EMPLOYEE CONFIDENTIALITY AGREEMENT

Execution of this agreement and continued compliance with all of the promises made and obligations imposed below are conditions of receiving authorization for access to any information maintained by ___________________________ Hospital.

I understand that, as part of my employment by ___________________________ Hospital, ("the Hospital"), I may be granted access to certain information maintained by the Hospital, including but not limited to health records information. As a condition of my employment by the Hospital, I agree that **all** information that I obtain during the course of my employment by the Hospital is strictly confidential ("Confidential Information"). I understand that Confidential Information includes, but is not limited to, all patient and health records information, quality assurance and utilization review information, strategic planning, computer password(s) issued to me, and proprietary information concerning any aspect of the Hospital's operations.

I also agree that any disclosures of, unauthorized use of, and/or unauthorized access to the Confidential Information will cause irreparable harm to the Hospital and may cause my immediate termination from employment. I undertake the following obligations with respect to Confidential Information:

1. to use Confidential Information for the sole purpose of performing the duties for which I have been hired
2. not to disclose any Confidential Information to any person whatsoever, except in direct connection with the performance of my job
3. not to copy or reproduce, or permit any other person to copy or reproduce, in whole or in part, any Confidential Information other than in the regular course of the services I am authorized and requested to perform for the hospital
4. to comply strictly with all Hospital policies regarding security of the Confidential Information
5. to report immediately to the Hospital any unauthorized use, duplication, disclosure, and/or dissemination of Confidential information by any person, including myself

I agree to indemnify the Hospital fully for any and all damages, including legal fees, the Hospital may incur as a result of my breach of this Agreement. I further agree that upon termination of my employment by the Hospital for any reason, I will immediately return any documents or other media containing any Confidential Information to the Hospital, and I will certify in writing that all such documents and other media have been returned to the Hospital. I understand that disclosure of any Confidential Information may cause the Hospital irreparable harm, for which monetary compensation may not be an adequate remedy, and I agree that the Hospital may seek injunctive relief if I breach, or attempt to breach, this Agreement.

I agree that all my obligations under this Confidentiality Agreement shall survive termination of my employment by the Hospital, regardless of the reason for such termination.

____________________	____________________	__________
Witness (Print)	Signature	Date
____________________	____________________	__________
Employee (Print)	Signature	Date

Courtesy of Shady Grove Adventist Hospital, Rockville, Maryland.

RELEASE OF INFORMATION AND ACCESS TO THE HEALTH RECORD

STATUTORY DUTY TO DISCLOSE MEDICAL INFORMATION

Reporting Laws

The law compels disclosure of medical information in many contexts other than discovery or testimony. Reporting laws have been enacted that require medical information to be reported to governmental agencies. The most common examples are vital statistics, communicable disease, child abuse, and wound reporting laws. Familiarity with these and other reporting laws is important to ensure compliance and to avoid reporting to the wrong agency. Reports to the wrong agency may not be legally protected, resulting in potential liability for breach of confidentiality.

Vital Statistics

All states require the reporting of births and deaths. These laws are a valid exercise of the state police power.

Public Health

Most states require reports of venereal disease and other communicable diseases. A California court observed that in addition to criminal penalties for not reporting, civil liability is possible in a suit by persons who contract diseases that might have been avoided by proper reports. Some states require reports of cancer and other selected noncontagious diseases. A few states require reports be submitted to state driver licensing agencies of conditions such as seizures that could lead to loss of license.

In 1994, a Missouri appellate court barred enforcement of a local court rule requiring correction facilities to disclose the infectious disease reports of inmates before court appearances.

Child Abuse

Most states require reports of suspected cases of child abuse or neglect. Some professionals, such as physicians and nurses, are mandatory reporters and thus are required to make reports. Anyone who is not a mandatory reporter may make a report as a permissive reporter. In some states any report arising out of diagnosis or treatment in an institution must be made through the institutional administration. Most child abuse reporting laws extend some degree of immunity from liability for reports made through proper channels. A mandatory reporter who fails to report child abuse is subject to both criminal penalties and civil liability for future injuries to the child that could have been avoided if a report had been made. There have been disputes in some states over when some activities, such as sexual activity of younger minors, must be reported as child abuse.

Adult Abuse/Domestic Violence

Some states have enacted laws that require reports of abuse of certain adults, especially older persons and the disabled, and reports of domestic violence.

Wounds

Many states require the reporting of certain wounds. Some states specify that all wounds of certain types must be reported. For example, New York requires the reporting of wounds inflicted by sharp instruments that may result in death and all gunshot wounds. Other states limit the reporting requirement to wounds caused under certain circumstances. For example, Iowa requires the reporting of wounds that apparently resulted from criminal acts. Thus, wounds that are clearly accidental or self-inflicted do not have to be reported in Iowa.

Other Reporting Laws

Some states require reports of other information, such as industrial accidents and radiation incidents. National reporting laws apply to hospitals that are involved in manufacturing, testing, or using certain substances and devices. For example, fatalities due to blood transfusions must be reported to the Food and Drug Administration (FDA). A sponsor of an investigational medical device must report to the FDA any unanticipated adverse effects from use of the device. Device manufacturers have a duty to report to the FDA when a death or serious injury has occurred in connection with the device.

Some states require that major adverse incidents be reported to a state agency. A director of nursing of a nursing home was personally fined in New York for failing to make such a report.

In 1977, the U.S. Supreme Court upheld a state law that required reports to a central state registry of all prescriptions of Schedule II controlled substances.

At least one state requires reports to private individuals. Florida requires hospitals to notify emergency transport personnel and other individuals who bring emergency patients to the hospital if the patient is diagnosed as having a contagious disease.

Access Laws

Some statutes do not mandate reporting, but authorize access to health records, without the patient's permission, on request of certain individuals or organizations or the general public.

Workers' Compensation

Some state statutes grant all parties to a workers' compensation claim access to all relevant medical information after a claim has been made. In some states, courts have ruled that filing a workers' compensation claim is a waiver of confidentiality of relevant medical information. However, in 1994, the West Virginia Supreme Court ruled that the physician-patient privilege applies in workers' compensation cases.

Federal Freedom of Information Act

The federal Freedom of Information Act (FOIA) applies only to federal agencies. A hospital does not become a federal agency by receiving federal funds, so the FOIA applies to few hospitals outside of the VA and Defense Department hospital systems. When the FOIA applies, medical information is exempted from disclosure only when the disclosure would "constitute a clearly unwarranted invasion of personal privacy." Thus, the Act provides only limited protection of confidentiality of medical information in the possession of federal agencies. However, the federal Privacy Act may provide some additional protection to such information.

State Public Records Laws

Many states have public records laws that apply to public hospitals. Some state statutes explicitly exempt hospital and health records from disclosure. In a 1974 case, Colorado's law was interpreted not to permit a publisher to obtain all birth and death reports routinely. In 1983, the Iowa Supreme Court addressed the effort of a leukemia patient to force the disclosure of an unrelated potential bone marrow donor whose name was in the records of a public hospital. The court ruled that names of patients could be withheld from disclosure and that although the potential donor had never sought treatment at the hospital, the potential donor was a patient for purposes of the exemption because the medical procedure of tissue typing had been performed. However, in a 1978 Ohio case, the state law was interpreted to require access to the names and the dates of admission and discharge of all persons admitted to a public hospital. In states that follow the Ohio rule it is especially important to resist discovery of nonparty records because removal of identifiers does not offer much protection when dates in the records may make it possible to identify the patient from the admission list.

Other Access Laws

Some federal and state statutes give governmental agencies access to health records on request or through administrative subpoena. For example, peer review organizations (PROs) have access to all health records pertinent to their federal review functions on request. A federal district court has ruled that Medicare surveyors have a right of access to records of non-Medicare patients as well as to those of Medicare patients. Hospital licensing laws often grant inspectors access without subpoena for audit and inspection purposes.

Source: Robert D. Miller, *Problems in Health Care Law*, 7th ed., Aspen Publishers, Inc., © 1996.

RESPONDING TO LEGAL PROCESS

Hospitals may be required to release health record information pursuant to legal process that they receive. The term *legal process* generally refers to all of the writs that are issued by a court during a legal action, or by an attorney in the name of the court but without court review. Hospitals generally are concerned with two types of legal process—the subpoena and the court order.

Subpoenas

Hospitals customarily receive two types of subpoenas: (1) a subpoena *ad testificandum*, which is a written order commanding a person to appear and to give testimony at a trial or other judicial or investigative proceeding, and (2) a subpoena *duces tecum*, which is a written order commanding a person to appear, give testimony, and bring all documents, papers, books, and records described in the subpoena. These devices are used to obtain documents during pretrial discovery and to obtain testimony during trial.

Those authorized to issue subpoenas vary from state to state. In most states, judges, clerks of the court, justices of the peace, and other officials are so authorized. In federal courts, only the clerks of the courts are so authorized. The form of the subpoena is prescribed by statute in certain states. A valid subpoena usually contains the following information:

- name of the court (or other official body in which the proceeding is being held)
- names of the plaintiff and the defendant
- docket number of the case
- date, time, and place of the requested appearance
- specific documents sought (if a subpoena *duces tecum*)
- name and telephone number of the attorney who caused the subpoena to be issued
- signature or stamp and seal of the official empowered to issue the subpoena

For federal courts, subpoenas generally are served in person by United States marshals; for state courts, generally by sheriffs. However, many state statutes provide that any competent person not less than 18 years of age may serve subpoenas. The manner of service varies from state to state: In some, the subpoena may be served by mail or delivery, and in others it must be physically handed to the person by the server. Usually, subpoenas must be served within a specified period of time in advance of the required appearance. In several states, statutes establish this period with specific reference to health records. An example of such a statute is that of Connecticut:

> A subpoena directing production of such hospital record shall be served not less than twenty-four hours before the time for production, provided such subpoena shall be valid if served less than twenty-four hours before the time of production if written notice of intent to serve such subpoena has been delivered to the person in charge of the record room of such hospital not less than twenty-four hours nor more than two weeks before such time for production.

Several cases have addressed the legitimacy of disclosing certain health records in response to a grand jury subpoena. For example, the Illinois Supreme Court has ruled that disclosure to a grand jury of the identities of abortion clinic patients does not violate the physician-patient privilege or the patients' constitutional right of privacy. Similarly, a grand jury may gain access to information that psychiatric patients have consented to release from their health records to insurers for reimbursement purposes, another court has ruled, because such consent constitutes a waiver of any physician or psychotherapist privilege that may exist, given the patients' "expectation that the confidential character of the records would necessarily be compromised pursuant to the reimbursement process."

Court Orders

Occasionally, a state or federal court, or a state commission, orders a hospital to release health records or other confidential patient information or to produce health records in court. Written court orders usually are served upon hospitals in a manner similar to that of subpoenas, but also may be issued verbally in court to the hospital's attorney. Provided the court order does not violate a statute or regulation, the hospital should make every effort to comply with it. A hospital can contest a court order and present its case to the court before any sanctions for failure to comply are imposed. Failure to comply with a final, valid court order subjects either the person ordered to act or hospital corporate officers, if the corporation has been ordered to act, to a contempt-of-court citation. Hospital corporate officers are liable if the institution declines to follow the order even if a hospital department head is the person who actually does not act.

A court order requiring the disclosure of health records will not violate the statutory physician-patient privilege if "sufficient steps" are taken to safeguard the identity of the patients involved, the Arizona Court of Appeals has ruled. Although the state supreme court had ruled previously that a trial court's order requiring physicians to disclose the names, addresses, and the means of contacting patients they had treated undermined the purpose and intent of the physician patient privilege, the question remained as to whether the removal of all information in health records that tended to identify the patients would render the records discoverable. In this case, the appeals court, noting that the Arizona Supreme Court had objected only to identification of the patients, ruled that the disclosure of anonymous records is permissible.

Compliance

A hospital should comply with valid legal process, properly served upon it, in the manner prescribed by its state's statutes. In recent years, many states have enacted statutes establishing compliance procedure with specific reference to subpoenas of health records. Other states have not enacted such statutes and thus treat subpoenas of health records like any other subpoenas. Hospital administrators should be aware of current developments in their own states in this rapidly changing area of the law. Failure to comply correctly with a subpoena, without reasonable justification, is punishable as contempt of court.

The time permitted for compliance with subpoenas of health records varies from state to state. For example, some states require that a hospital comply with the date specified on the subpoena. Others specify a time period by statute. Generally, the records must be sealed, then enclosed in an envelope, and may be opened only with the court's authorization. Most states expressly permit copies to be submitted in lieu of the original documents. A few states specify that the court may subpoena the originals if the copies are illegible or if their authenticity is in dispute.

In several states, records furnished in compliance with legal process must be accompanied by an affidavit from the hospital's record custodian to certify the records' genuineness. Mississippi requires that the affidavit state

- that the affiant is a duly authorized custodian of the records and has authority to certify said records
- that the copy is a true copy of all the records described in the subpoena
- that the records were prepared by personnel of the hospital, staff physicians, or persons acting under the control of either, in the ordinary course of hospital business at or near the time of the act, condition or event reported therein

- the amount of the reasonable charges of the hospital for furnishing such copies of the record

Other states have substantially similar provisions. These statutes provide, in addition, that if the hospital possesses none, or only part, of the records described in the subpoena, the custodian must so certify in the affidavit. The custodian also may be required to attend the proceeding if the subpoena orders that individual to do so.

In most cases, the health information management specialist is served with a subpoena because that staff member is deemed to have custody of the health records. However, very few states define the term *custodian*. Some states do specify that the custodian may be any person who prepares records, such as a physician, nurse, or therapist, or anyone entrusted with the care of the records.

A hospital is not expected to respond to requirements that would be considered unreasonable. If it receives a subpoena after the date upon which it is required by statute to be served, the hospital has no obligation to respond. Certainly, if the subpoena arrives the day after the designated response date that appears on the document, the hospital need not respond. The hospital cannot reasonably respond to a subpoena that commands presentation of records so voluminous or old that they cannot be reproduced by the return date given. Finally, a hospital is not expected to comply with a subpoena that commands production of records that are not in the hospital's possession.

For such cases, the administrator, with the advice of counsel, should develop responses for the hospital to subpoenas and court orders. If the attorney or official who initiated the subpoenas becomes unreasonable, the hospital should refer the matter to its legal counsel. If the subpoena was initiated by a plaintiff in an action against the hospital, the institution should not comply with the subpoena, but should require the plaintiff to file a motion to produce the records so that, if appropriate, the hospital will have an opportunity to argue against disclosure. If a subpoena is invalid or improper, the hospital may file a motion to quash it. The court or other issuing authority will determine after a hearing on the motion whether to enforce, modify, or quash the subpoena.

Hospital counsel can serve as important advisors to their clients in connection with the receipt of, and response to, legal process. The attorney not only should assist hospital administration and health records practitioners in designing a procedure for processing subpoenas and court orders but also should be available to advise the institution when it receives unusual subpoenas or those that demand records that may not be released in response to a subpoena. The hospital's counsel often is the best person to deal with other attorneys who have made unreasonable demands for records from the hospital.

The person assigned to process subpoenas of health records should respond in accordance with a procedure established by the hospital and approved by its attorney. The procedure should include at least the following steps:

- examination of the record subject to subpoena to make certain that it is complete, that signatures and initials are legible, and that each page identifies the patient and the patient's hospital number
- examination of the record to determine whether the case forms the basis for a possible negligence action against the hospital and, if so, to notify the appropriate administrator (in some hospitals, the health records department performs this function in coordination with the risk management or legal department)
- removal of any material that may not properly be obtained in the jurisdiction by subpoena, such as, in some states, notes referring to psychiatric care, or copies of records from other facilities, and correspondence
- enumeration of each page of the health record, and writing the total number of pages on the record jacket
- preparation of a list of the health record contents to be used as a receipt for the record if the record must be left with the court or an attorney (most health records departments use a standard form for this purpose)
- use of a photocopy of the record, whenever possible, rather than the original, in responding to legal process

Rather than send original health records to a court or an attorney through the mail, hospitals should designate a person to deliver them in person. Hospitals lose all control over their records once they are placed in the mail, and the loss of an original health record may be a serious problem for a hospital defendant in a negligence action for a patient who may require future hospitalization.

Source: William H. Roach, Jr., and Aspen Health Law Center, *Medical Records and the Law*, 2nd ed., Aspen Publishers, Inc., © 1994.

RELEASE OF INFORMATION: POLICIES AND PROCEDURES

General Principle

The facility undertakes a legal and ethical responsibility to foster and preserve the privacy and confidentiality of patient/client information in all its stages of development and use. Accordingly, there shall be strict adherence to this basic principle: prior consent of the patient/client is required before information is released or disclosed or made available for review except where a specific law or regulation or the internal administrative needs of the facility require or permit such access without patient/client consent.

Comprehensive and Centralized System

A comprehensive, centralized release of information unit shall be established under the jurisdiction and direct supervision of the health record department. All requests for release of information and/or access to patient/client care records of the facility shall be coordinated by the unit so that uniform, timely processing, consistent with the specific legal and regulatory constraints associated with each type of request, is achieved. This comprehensive system involves the following six functions:

1. coordinating intraorganizational units involved in release of information activities
2. coordinating intradepartmental functions
3. applying the detailed provisions of specific laws and regulations
4. honoring the patient's/client's right to authorize such release of information
5. applying routine administrative processes to all requests and accounting for exceptions to routine processing
6. safeguarding the process througthe application of quality controls

Intraorganizational Coordination

Responsibility for safeguarding patient/client privacy and confidentiality shall be shared by several organizational units that shall process release of information requests specific to their organizational jurisdiction. The practices set forth in these release of information policies shall be followed, regardless of the organizational unit releasing the information.

Organizational Unit	*Responsibility/Activity*
Legal counsel and/or risk management	Review all contract agreements with third-party payers regarding release of information requirements. Deal with unusual cases, referred by other organizational units.
Risk management	Respond to interrogatories. Review cases where interests of facility are potentially adversely affected.
Public relations	Make facility's guidelines on release of information available to media. Handle all such releases.
Patient/client billing/finance	Coordinate billing audits and release of information.
Patient/client care representatives	Process initial requests for patient/client access to records. Facilitate process for patient/client. Develop, with director of health records, an excerpt of release of information guidelines and patient/client access for patient/client handbook.
All direct patient/client care personnel	Process initial requests for patient/client access to records. Obtain release of information authorizations as appropriate. Initiate reporting of suspected child abuse and older patient abuse.
Laboratory personnel	Initiate reporting of communicable diseases as required by law.
Radiology personnel	Coordinate release of information when radiology films are requested.
Quality assurance/utilization review personnel	Coordinate release of information to private review organizations.

Intradepartmental Coordination

Within the health record department, release of information processes shall be shared among three key functions:

1. *Word processing/transcription.* Refer all requests for release of information made during process of dictation/transcription to central release of information unit.
2. *Coding/abstracting/statistics.* Process requests for statistical reports and impersonal data as set forth in policies for unit. Refer all other requests to central release of information unit.
3. *Storage and retrieval.* Process requests for access to records from internal sources (medical and other patient/client care staff and administrative staff) according to policies specific to unit. Refer all other requests to central release of information unit.

All other units of the health record department shall refer all inquiries and requests (in person, by telephone, or written) to the central release of information unit.

Compliance with Laws and Regulations

These policies and practices shall be consistent with state and federal laws and regulations that contain provisions relating to release of information from health records. Specifically, the following laws and regulations shall be reviewed regularly, and these policies shall be amended to comply with changed provisions:

- Uniform Business Records Act
- Uniform Photographic Copies of Business and Public Records rule
- Administrative Procedures Code
- Rules of Civil Procedure
- State Criminal Code
- Department of Health regulations (patient/client access)
- Mental Health Procedures Code
- Adoption and Surrogacy Proceedings Code
- Uniform Claims and Billing rule
- No-fault insurance provisions
- Health Care Cost Containment Act
- Workers' compensation regulations
- Occupational Safety and Health Act
- Child Protective Services Act
- Older Adult Protective Services Act
- Cancer Prevention, Control, and Research Act
- Communicable disease reporting requirements
- Vital statistics reporting requirements
- Coroner's jurisdiction
- Motor Vehicle Code regarding alcohol and drug testing
- Peer Review Protection Act
- Confidentiality of alcohol and drug abuse records

Administrative Processes

Requests for information from health records shall be processed in a timely, consistent manner as set forth in these policies.

Priorities and Time Frames

The following priorities and time frames shall apply to release of information requests processed by the health record department:

- *emergency requests involving immediate emergency care of patient/client:* immediate processing
- *priority requests pertaining to current care of patient/client:* within one workday
- *patient/client request for access to own record:* within three workdays of physician's approval
- *subpoenas and depositions:* as required
- *all other requests:* within five workdays

Courtesy Notification to Practitioners

The appropriate health care practitioners of the facility shall be notified when any of the following occurs:

- information is requested from the health record by the patient/client or representative
- patient/client or representative requests direct access to the complete health record
- legal action is initiated

Monitoring Process

A log shall be maintained to track the step-by-step process toward completion of each request for release of information. This log shall be reviewed and updated daily in order to give proper priority to requests and foster early intervention in problem situations. Information shall include the following:

- date request received
- name of patient/client
- name of person making request
- information released
- date released
- fee charged

Fee Schedule

A reasonable fee shall be charged to offset the costs associated with specific categories of requests. The fee shall be based on an assessment of such factors as cost of equipment and supplies, employee costs (wages and fringe benefits), and administrative overhead. Postage, including express mail costs when incurred at the request of the authorizing party, shall be included.

The fee is [_____] per record access and [_____] per record page copied for the following: private insurance companies, lawyers, workers' compensation review boards, patients/clients requesting access and/or copies for personal use, and private review organizations.

The fee for peer review organizations is that set by the Health Care Financing Administration.

When an abstract is provided, the fee is [_____].

Fees may be waived for good reason by the health information management specialist, who will note the reason for waiver in the release of information tracking log.

Vouchers for fees received shall be issued to the individual paying such fees; this shall be done at the time of receiving the fee. Only authorized employees in the release of information unit shall receive such fees. A copy of all vouchers, along with the fees received, shall be delivered daily to the cashier of the facility. No cash fees will be accepted; only checks or money orders for the exact amount will be accepted.

Preparation of Response

Unless the request specifies release of the complete medical record, only selected portions of the documents shall be released. An appropriate cover letter shall be prepared showing the items included. Where possible, an abstracted summary shall be completed instead of sending copies of portions of the health record.

No Redisclosure

Materials abstracted from the record for release shall be stamped as follows:

> INFORMATION IS CONFIDENTIAL. IT IS PROVIDED AS AUTHORIZED BY THE PATIENT/CLIENT. NOT FOR DISCLOSURE.

Retention of Request

The original request, authorization, and copy of the cover letter or abstract shall be retained in the health record for the appropriate record retention period for health and business-related records.

Use of Copying Service

To facilitate the timely processing of release of information requests, the services of a commercial copying service may be employed. Such contractual copying services shall meet the following conditions, which shall be specified in the appropriate contractual arrangement:

- Comply with federal and state laws and regulations concerning release of information.
- Adhere to the department's practices and procedures.
- Obtain a signed confidentiality statement for each service employee assigned to the facility.
- Provide field supervision on a timely and regular basis; at a minimum, continual availability by telephone and on-site supervision during initial orientation of service employee to the facility.
- Provide systematic quality control methods, including on-site visits at least once a month to review completed work and work in process.
- Carry out all work functions during the usual daytime hours of the department's operation.
- Perform all work on the facility's premises.
  - Copy the designated reports using the facility's equipment and supplies.
  - Reassemble the record and place it in the permanent file folder.
  - Prepare the original and copy of the transmittal form.
  - Complete the reporting form for work completed.
  - Prepare material for mailing, and deliver it to the facility's mail room.
- Maintain backup capability.
  - Maintain equipment for use in case of primary equipment breakdown.
  - Maintain alternate personnel in case of usual service personnel absence or illness.
- Carry an insurance policy for error/omission liability in the amount of [_____].
- Process all billing related to release of information.
- Copy all designated material for both nonbillable and billable requests.
  - Nonbillable requests are at no charge.
  - Billable requests are at [_____] per page.
- Refer all problem billing situations to the coordinator of the release of information unit of the facility.
- Compile a monthly statement of charges for services rendered, and present it no later than the close of the first workweek of the next month. The monthly statement of charges shall include a breakdown of costs as follows:
  - number of individual requests processed
  - number of pages per request
  - billable or nonbillable category of request
  - adjustments to be made (rebate to facility from billable requests at [_____] per request, reclaiming fees turned over to facility because check was made out to facility)

NOTE: The facility is supplying equipment, paper supplies, and postage; these costs will be excluded from the copying service's bill. Billing statements, as far as possible, shall not contain the name of the patient/client. The health record unit number shall be used to protect patient/client identity.

Facility Responsibilities

Release of information personnel at the facility shall carry out the following functions:

- Receive requests and determine their legitimacy.
- Review requests and determine that authorization requirements have been met.
- Initiate the necessary reply to those making requests if information will not be sent or if authorization is needed.
- Determine billable or nonbillable status of requests.
- Designate priority assignments to requests.
- Maintain the tracking log, and process inquiries concerning the status of requests.
- Select the material to be released.

Quality Control

A routine audit of release of information practices shall be carried out at least quarterly. The audit shall be carried out by the health information management specialist or designee. Particular attention shall be given to the following:

- validity of authorization
- appropriateness of material abstracted in response to the request
- retention of authorization, request, and cover letter for response
- procedures for telephone and in-person requests

- compliance with designated priorities and time frames
- proper processing of fees and prompt processing of fees received

Periodic inservice training shall be given to all employees involved in release of information processes.

At least annually, these policies and associated procedures shall be reviewed with risk management and legal counsel.

As noted in the general policies governing all department practices, an employee confidentiality statement shall be signed and reviewed and updated annually.

Capacity To Authorize

As a general principle, a written, current, valid authorization to release information shall be required as follows:

Patient/Client Category	*Required Signature*
Psychiatric, drug, or alcohol program patients/clients	See "Release of Information: Types of Authorization" for special considerations.
Adult patients/clients	The patient/client *or* a duly authorized representative (e.g., lawyer); proof of authorized representation required.
Minors who do not meet state's definition of emancipated minor	Parent *or* next of kin or legally appointed guardian; proof of relationship required.
Emancipated minors as defined by state law (e.g., is 18 years old, is a high school graduate, is/has been married, is/has been pregnant, or is/has been treated for reportable disease and information to be released relates to that episode of care)	Same as adult patient/client.
Deceased patient/client	Next of kin as stated on admission face sheet (relationship to be stated on authorization) *or* executor of estate.

Content and Format of Authorization

As far as possible, written authorization shall contain detailed, specific information directing the release of information. Authorizations shall specifically include the following:

- name and address of the facility
- name of the patient/client
- person or organization/company to whom the information is to be released
- purpose of the disclosure (e.g., support information for an insurance claim)
- signature of the patient/client or duly authorized representative
- date signed (date cannot precede the time period of the treatment dates for which information is to be released; date shall be reasonably current, e.g., signed within the last 90 days)
- information to be released (e.g., episode of care covered, treatment and/or procedure, specific test results, summary of most recent hospitalization, summary of all inpatient and outpatient care)

The signature of a witness to the patient's/client's signature is optional, but is encouraged.

To assist in obtaining the necessary information, an approved authorization form shall be used as far as possible. Letters, alternate forms, and blanket requests for any and all information shall be honored provided the required elements are included. The facility shall correspond with the person making the request to obtain a listing of the specific information desired.

Updating Authorizations

Updated authorizations shall be obtained from patients/clients who are continuing in treatment and for whom release of information is required for ongoing billing purposes. Admission office personnel for inpatient and ambulatory care units shall carry out this process of periodic update.

Revocation of Authorization

A patient/client may revoke an authorization by providing a written statement to the facility. This revocation shall become effective when it is received by the facility. If information associated with the billing process cannot be released to third-party payers as a result of the revocation, a letter shall be sent to the patient/client stating that he or she shall assume the responsibility of paying the bill directly.

Patient/Client Education

To facilitate timely and proper release of information, patients/clients of the facility shall be provided with a brief explanation of the release of information requirements. The excerpt shall be included in the patient/client handbook.

Refusal To Honor Authorization

Authorizations shall not be honored in situations where there is reasonable doubt or question as to the following:

- identity of the person presenting the authorization
- status of the individual as the duly appointed representative of a minor, deceased, or incompetent patient/client
- legal age or status as emancipated minor
- patient/client capacity to understand the meaning of the authorization
- authenticity of the patient/client signature
- current validity of authorization

In such situations, the unit employee shall refer the matter to the health information management specialist for review and direction.

Source: Joan Gratto Liebler, *Medical Records: Policies and Guidelines*, Aspen Publishers, Inc., © 1990.

RELEASE OF INFORMATION: TYPES OF AUTHORIZATION

Because there are differing circumstances associated with specific release of information requests, the users of these policies shall familiarize themselves with all the provisions stated. To assist the users in accessing the relevant section of the policies, the detailed provisions are grouped into five categories.

- Part A: No Authorization Required
- Part B: Telephone, In-Person, and Patient/Client Access Requests
- Part C: General Requests from Various Sources
- Part D: Requests Requiring Special Consideration
- Part E: Requests in Legal Proceedings

An alphabetical listing of common requests and references to the applicable part of these policies follows.

Request	*Part*
Access to own record	B
Accrediting agency	A
Adoptee	D
Adopting parents	D
AIDS	D
Alcohol abuse treatment	D
Alcohol blood testing	C
Armed services	C
Attending physician	
• on staff	A
• not on staff	A and C
Attorneys	C
Birth certificate	C
Blue Cross	A
Child abuse	D
Civil service	C
Clergy	C
Common good/public good	A
Communicable disease reporting	C
Communications media	C
Continuing care	A and C
Coroner	C
Courts	E
Death certificate	C
Deposition	E
Education	C
Emergency	A and B
Employees	D
Employers	C
Employment agencies	C
Extraordinary security, records requiring	D
Family and friends	C
FBI/Federal Bureau of Investigation	C
Government agencies	C
Guardians	C
Health care facilities	
• internal affairs	A
• external facilities	A and C
Health maintenance organizations	A
Immigration	C
In-person request	B
Insurance	C
Internal Revenue Service	C
Interrogatory	E
Labor union representative	C
Law enforcement	C
Licensing agency	A
Medicaid	A
Medicare	A
Occupational Safety and Health Administration	C
Older adult abuse reporting	D
Physicians	
• on staff/attending	A
• not on staff	C
Police	C
Press	C
Psychiatric treatment	D
Public Assistance, Department of	C
Railroad Retirement Board	C
Researchers	
• on staff	A
• not on staff	C
Residents and interns	C
Restricted access records	D
Sexual assault	D

Sheriff	C
Social Security Administration	C
Subpoena	E
Telephone request	B
Testimony, in court	E
Transfer of patient/client	
• direct	A
• subsequent care/continuing care	C
Welfare, Department of	C
Workers' compensation	C
Veterans Administration	C
Vocational rehabilitation	C

Part A: No Authorization Required

NOTE: Refer to parts B, C, and D for special situations.

No authorization is required to release routine information in the following circumstances:

- *True health care emergencies.* The need to know outweighs privacy and confidentiality considerations.
- *Unusual, rare circumstances where serving the common good outweighs privacy and confidentiality considerations.* These requests shall be referred to the chief administrative officer of the facility. Such requests will not be processed by health record personnel without the explicit, written directive of the chief executive officer or designee.
- *Release of nonconfidential information.* Such information includes name, date of admission and discharge, and verification of hospitalization *except* for psychiatric, drug, and alcohol program patients/clients and patients/clients who have requested that no information be released.
- *Conduct of facility's internal affairs.* Information shall be made available on a need-to-know basis for such activities as quality assurance review, risk management review, internal audit processes, and activities associated with compliance with requirements of regulatory and accrediting agencies.
- *Research studies conducted by members of the medical staff and associated nurse and allied health practitioners who are members of the ancillary staff.* The written approval of the appropriate professional staff committee or approval body shall be required.
- *Direct transfer of patient/client to another facility (such as hospital or skilled nursing facility) where information must be available at the time of transfer.* It is usually possible to obtain an updated consent as part of the transfer arrangement, and it is desirable to do so.
- *Direct transfer of patient/client to the care of the patient/client–designated amending physician.*
- *Third-party payers under specific circumstances.*
  - *Blue Cross, health maintenance organizations, and special employee benefit plans that contract with the facility to provide services for eligible members.* Plan members sign an agreement with the third-party payer for such release of supporting information. The facility's legal counsel shall provide the medical record department with specific listings of such contractual arrangements. The listing shall be attached to these policies and updated at least annually.
  - *Medicare, Medicaid, and Veterans Affairs.* Provision for payment and subsequent release of supporting information shall be included in the admission agreement/financial agreement.

Part B: Telephone, In-Person, and Patient/Client Access Requests

Telephone Inquiries

Information shall not be released. Else caller shall be instructed to make the request in writing and provide the necessary authorization with the written request. Assistance shall be given to callers to guide them in complying with the details of a proper authorization. *Exception:* Emergency situations will be processed as described below.

In-Person Inquiries

Oral requests made in person shall not be honored. Assistance in providing a written request and necessary authorization shall be given.

Emergency Requests

It is recognized that emergency situations arise that require the immediate exchange of information by telephone or facsimile transmission. As a safeguard, the employee shall take the following precautions:

- Obtain identifying information from the caller (e.g., health care provider name, address, telephone number).
- Indicate that a return call will be made after the information has been verified.
- Verify the identity of the caller by reviewing resource directories for hospitals, clinics, and medical practitioners.
- Review the health record for any prohibition of release of information; if present, refer the request to risk management.
- Return the call, providing limited information.
- Complete the appropriate form, noting the following information:

- date and time of request
- patient/client identification
- caller information/identification
- reason given by caller to classify situation as emergency
- information released verbally
- employee giving information
- employee receiving information

Patient/Client Access to Medical Records

As permitted and required by state and federal laws and regulations, patients/clients shall be permitted access to information in their health record, including the right to obtain a copy of a part or all of the record. *Exception:* The only exception to this provision is the specific contraindication by the attending physician. Such contraindication shall be noted in the health record, with supporting reasons. This statement shall specifically include that it is not in the best interest of the patient/client to have access.

Request for Access. The request for access form shall be completed by the patient/client.

Explanation to Patient/Client. The process for access shall be shared with the patient/client at the time of the request. This briefing shall include the necessity of physician approval and facility's process for obtaining it, and charges associated with making the record available and copying it.

Tracking Log. An entry shall be made in the release of information tracking log showing the name of the patient/client, date of request, date of physician approval, and date of actual review by patient/client.

Physician Approval/Disapproval. The approval of the attending physician shall be obtained. If the attending physician is no longer a member of the medical staff, the medical director's approval shall be sought. This approval shall be obtained by forwarding the patient request for access form to the appropriate physician.

- *Disapproval.* The physician shall complete, sign, and date the form showing the reason for disapproval, including the statement that it is not in the patient's/client's best interest to have access. This form shall be filed in the health record and retained according to record retention provisions. The patient/client shall be notified in writing by the physician, and a copy of this notification shall be made a part of the health record.
- *Approval.* The physician shall complete, sign, and date the form indicating approval. The form shall be returned to the release of information coordinator and shall be filed in the health record and retained according to record retention provisions. The release of information coordinator shall arrange an appointment with the patient/client.

Reasonable Access/Access by Appointment. To provide reasonable and timely access, patients/clients may review the record at a mutually agreeable time during normal workdays: Monday through Friday, 9 A.M. to 4 P.M. As far as possible, the appointment shall be made within three workdays of approval.

Record Preparation. The record shall be reviewed, and any material not specifically requested and approved for release shall be removed, including material received from other health care facilities. A copy of the record shall be made for review. Access to the original shall not be permitted in order to prevent tampering or inadvertent destruction or loss of any part of the record.

Review by Patient/Client. The review shall be conducted in the presence of the release of information coordinator unless the physician indicates that he or she will review the material with the patient/client. At no time shall a patient/client be permitted to review material on site without direct supervision by a facility employee. No interpretation of the meaning of an entry or of the care shall be given by an employee who is not a credentialed direct patient care provider. The patient/client shall be encouraged to discuss such questions with the attending physician.

Disagreement with Content. A patient/client who disagrees with an entry may make a separate entry, which shall be signed and dated by the patient/client and entered in the health record. The risk management coordinator and the attending physician shall be notified that the entry has been made.

Reasonable Fees. A bill for access and copying shall be prepared and presented to the patient/client, who shall make the necessary payment by check or money order made out to the facility. A patient/client may obtain a copy of part or all of the record. A reasonable charge may be made for providing this copy, as stated in the fee schedule for release of information.

PART C: GENERAL REQUESTS FROM VARIOUS SOURCES

A current, valid authorization shall be provided before information is released for the following categories of requests for access to or release of information from health records, except as noted.

Type of Request	*Comment/Special Notation*
Alcohol blood testing results	Authorization required except as stated. No authorization required to release results to authorities when individual consents to test and subsequent release of results.
Armed Services	See *Government agencies.*
Attorneys	See special provisions under psychiatric and mental retardation provisions.
Birth certificates	Not released by facility, even with authorization; refer person making request to state's division of vital statistics. Factual information relating to birth may be released but not a copy of birth certificate.
Civil Service	See *Government agencies.*
Clergy	Authorization always required.
Common good/public good	See part A.
Communicable disease reporting	See policies on statistics, abstracts, and required reporting.
Communications media	Refer to public relations department of facility.
Continuing care	
• direct transfer	See part A.
• subsequent acceptance for care	Authorization required in order to determine that facility is actually treating patient/client.
Coroner	
• pronounced dead at facility	No authorization required.
• expired elsewhere	Authorization of next of kin or executor of estate required.
Death certificate	Not released by facility, even with authorization; refer person making request to state's division of vital statistics. Factual information relating to death may be released but not a copy of death certificate.
Education	See *Research and education.*
Employers	Authorization required except as provided under workers' compensation.
Employment agencies	Authorization always required.
Family and friends	Refer to attending physician.
FBI/Federal Bureau of Investigation	See *Government agencies.* See *Law enforcement agencies.*
Government agencies	
• reports required by law or regulation	No authorization required.
• third-party payer	No authorization required for verification of treatment, assessment of continuing eligibility, or data to support claim.
• all other requests	Authorization required.
Guardians	Duly appointed guardians act on behalf of/in place of patient/client because of incapacity to authorize.
Health care facilities	See *Continuing care.*
Immigration	See *Government agencies.*
Insurance	
• no-fault	No authorization required if permitted by/required by state no fault insurance regulations.
• private/payer	Authorization required.
Internal Revenue Service	See *Government agencies.*
Labor union representative	Authorization required.
Law enforcement agencies	Court order of authorization required except as provided under special circumstances; see also *Alcohol blood testing results.*
Occupational Safety and Health Administration	No authorization required to review exposure records and related health records as provided by regulations; *exception:* alcohol and drug abuse and counseling/treatment records are excluded.
Physicians	
• on staff/attending	No authorization required for access/release of information for patients/clients under care.
• not on staff	Authorization required to determine that physician is attending physician at time of request.
Police	See *Law enforcement agencies.*
Press	See *Communications media.*
Public Assistance, Department of	See *Government agencies.*

continues

Part C: General Requests from Various Sources continued

Type of Request	*Comment/Special Notation*
Railroad Retirement Board	See *Government agencies.*
Research and education	See part D for psychiatric, drug, and alcohol abuse records.
• medical/professional staff	Approval of appropriate medical staff committee required; identity of patient/client must be safeguarded.
• nonmembers	Approval of appropriate medical staff committee and patient/client authorization required.
• residents and interns	No patient/client authorization required unless record is that of family member. Attending physician's authorization required for access to psychiatric, drug, and alcohol abuse treatment records.
• students in approved training programs at facility	No patient/client authorization required unless record is that of family member. Authorization/approval of access required from director of training program in which student is enrolled. Authorization/approval for access required from facility's director of specific training program.
Sheriff	See *Law enforcement agencies.*
Social Security Administration	See *Government agencies.*
Veterans Affairs	See *Government agencies.*
Vocational Rehabilitation, Bureau of	Authorization required.
Welfare, Department of	See *Government agencies.*
Workers' compensation	
• to employee	See patient access provisions (part B).
• to employer	Only as specifically permitted by state's workers' compensation act.

Part D: Requests Requiring Special Consideration

Part D covers special considerations associated with the following categories of requests:

- employee patients/clients
- adoptees and adopting parents
- records requiring extraordinary security
- child abuse cases
- older adults abuse cases
- AIDS-related cases
- mental handicap/mental retardation cases
- psychiatric cases
- sexual assault cases

Employee Patients/Clients

Requests for access to or information from records of employees who are or have been treated in the facility shall be treated in the same manner as any other request. If information must be processed from the health record of an employee holding a full-time or part-time position in the health record department, the processing shall be carried out by a member of the management team of the department.

Adoptees and Adopting Parents

Requests by adoptees for records relating to the identity of biological parents shall be referred to the state's division of vital statistics.

The medical history and other material relevant to the adoptee's health care may be provided to the adopting parents. This type of request shall have the specific authorization of the attending physician, who shall be requested to share the information with the adopting parents. All data that could identify the adoptee's natural family shall be deleted. The information to be released shall be prepared by health record personnel and checked by the attending physician as a safeguard of the protection of this potentially identifiable information.

Records Requiring Extraordinary Security

Requests for information from or access to such records shall be handled by the health information management specialist. Access to these records for release of information shall be permitted only with the specific permission of the facility's legal counsel.

Child Abuse Cases

In cases where the parents request access to or information from a minor's record and the case involves known or suspected child abuse, health record personnel shall refer the matter to the risk manager. The risk manager shall make a determination about access and/or release of information.

Older Adults Abuse Cases

In cases where the adult children or guardians request access to or information from a record and the case involves known or suspected older adult abuse, health record personnel shall refer the matter to the risk manager. The risk manager shall make a determination about access and/or release of information.

AIDS-Related Cases

Particular care shall be taken to protect the privacy of patients/clients with known or suspected conditions relating to AIDS or ARC. The written authorization of the patient/client is required for release of information relating to test results or diagnostic statements except as provided for in state laws (such as required reporting to state agencies).

Mental Handicap/Mental Retardation Cases

The parent or legally appointed guardian shall give the consent if a patient/client is unable to understand and/or sign an authorization because of a condition relating to mental handicap/mental retardation. All other provisions as for general release of information apply.

Psychiatric Cases

NOTE: See also "Department of Health and Human Services, Public Health Service, Confidentiality of Alcohol and Drug Abuse Records: Final Rule—Summary" and specific provisions of the state's mental health act.

The provisions of this policy shall be reviewed in detail with the legal counsel of the facility with particular attention given to state laws and regulations concerning

- mental health procedures act
- drug and alcohol abuse and dependence
- cost containment council
- peer review organizations
- motor vehicle code
- access to identifiable data by researchers
- capacity of minors to receive treatment and consent to release of information without parental consent

Patient Notification and Education. Patients shall be notified of the provisions for release of information in two ways:

1. general statement in the patient/client handbook
2. specific orientation through discussion initiated by the designated health care practitioner directly caring for the patient/client

No Redisclosure. When material is released from the health record, the following statement shall be attached to the information:

> THIS INFORMATION HAS BEEN DISCLOSED TO YOU FROM RECORDS WHOSE CONFIDENTIALITY IS PROTECTED BY STATE STATUTE. STATE REGULATIONS LIMIT YOUR RIGHT TO MAKE ANY FURTHER DISCLOSURES OF THIS INFORMATION WITHOUT THE PRIOR WRITTEN CONSENT OF THE PATIENT/CLIENT TO WHOM IT PERTAINS.

Patient/Client Access to Own Records. The same provisions and procedures apply to patient client access to psychiatric records as for general health records, with these additional provisions:

- Access may be limited if disclosure would reveal the identity of another person or breach the trust of a person providing information on the condition of a guarantee of anonymity.
- Access to presentencing material incorporated into the health record shall be permitted only with the consent of the sentencing judge.
- Access to parole or probation material shall be permitted only with the permission of the office/board of parole and probation.
- Minors who are at least 14 years of age shall be permitted access to their own records and may restrict access to such records in the same manner as an adult patient as provided by the state's mental health act.

The health record shall be reviewed by a designated member of the professional treatment team who shall be present at the time the patient/client reviews the record.

Content of Authorization. The authorization form for release of information shall contain the following:

- name of patient/client
- name of this facility
- kind and amount of information to be released, including, as far as possible, dates or period of treatment
- name or title of the person or organization to which information is to be sent
- purpose of the disclosure (e.g., reimbursement, continuing care)
- date of signing the consent
- signature of the patient/client or guardian where required
- signature of the individual authorized to sign for the patient/client in lieu of the patient/client, when required
- revocation statement that the consent may be revoked at any time but not retroactive to the time material has already been processed by the facility on the basis of the consent and that the consent will expire on the specific date or under specific named conditions

Capacity To Authorize. As a general principle, a written, current, valid authorization specific to psychiatric information processing shall be required. The signed authorization requirements are as follows:

- *Adult patient/client:* Signature of the patient/client *or* duly authorized representative; proof of authorized representation shall be required.
- *Minors over the age of 14:* Same as for adult, as provided by state statute.
- *Minors under the age of 14:* Signature of parent *or* next of kin *or* legally appointed guardian; proof of relationship shall be required.

Release of Information without Authorization. No authorization shall be required to release routine information in the following circumstances:

- True health care emergencies where the need to know outweighs privacy and confidentiality considerations (information shall be limited to that strictly needed for the emergency).
- Unusual, rare circumstances where serving the common good outweighs privacy and confidentiality considerations (shall be referred to the chief administrative officer of the facility; such requests shall not be processed by health record personnel; these situations shall always be handled by the chief administrative officer or designee).
- Third-party payers requesting limited information such as the name of the treating professional, types and cost of treatment or a short description of the general purpose of treatment (as far as possible, patient/client authorization shall be obtained at time of admission).
- Referrals made for continuity of care purposes to private practitioners or private or government treatment facilities (as far as possible, patient/client consent shall be obtained during the discharge planning process).
- Court or mental health review officer in the course of legal proceedings relating to voluntary or involuntary commitment.
- Attorney assigned to represent the patient/client at such proceedings.
- County mental health administrator as specified in the state's mental health act.
- Health care cost containment council as stipulated in related statute.
- Professional treatment staff of state or county correctional institutions as specified in appropriate statutes.
- Mandated reports to state agencies for child abuse or older adult or patient/client abuse.
- State licensure and accrediting agencies and peer review organizations.
- Non–patient-identifiable clinical or statistical data collected by the facility.
- Research within the facility, except where state statute requires specific patient/client consent to access of records.

Sexual Assault Cases

- *Evidentiary report.* The appropriate release of information for processing this form shall be obtained from the patient/client at the time of treatment.
- *Report to police.* As required by state law, the applicable reporting form shall be completed. No authorization shall be required as this is a required report.
- *Notification of child protective services.* As required by state law, the applicable reporting form shall be completed. No authorization shall be required as this is a mandated report.

Part E: Requests in Legal Proceedings

The release of information unit shall coordinate the various processes associated with responding to subpoenas and court orders associated with legal proceedings.

Interrogatories

Interrogatories shall be referred to the risk manager, who shall request the record, review it, and provide the oral or written answers as required by the legal instrument.

Subpoenas

These shall be processed in a timely manner. Detailed procedures shall be developed and implemented to reflect the specific process for determining validity, complying within the mandated time frame, and assessing fees, including prepayment provisions.

The record shall be reviewed to determine the relevant portions that are subject to subpoena. Material of an administrative nature (e.g., correspondence, admissions agreement) and material of a nonmedical nature shall be removed unless the subpoena is specific as to these materials.

Availability of Documents for Patient/Client Care. Documentation is needed for ongoing patient/client care and associated uses. Therefore, a copy of the health record shall be made and retained in the permanent storage and retrieval area (or legal action file) while the health record is held at court. In situations where a copy of the record is an acceptable alternative, a copy shall be supplied and a notarized statement attached indicating that the copy is an exact duplicate of the original record. The health information management specialist or designee shall sign the notarized statement.

Notification of Interested Parties. The attending physician shall be notified when legal proceedings are undertaken. The patient/client shall be notified as required by state laws or regulations.

Inability To Comply. Under certain circumstances, the facility may be unable to comply with a subpoena.

- *Inability to comply because of legal restrictions.* Certain records, such as drug and alcohol abuse treatment and psychiatric treatment records, are given privileged status under applicable federal, state, and/or local laws and regulations. A court order is required for their release. The usual practice shall be this: The employee shall appear in court at the designated time and indicate that the records are subject to these provisions, noting that they will not be produced for inspection without a court order. Upon receipt of a court order, the records shall then be produced and entered as evidence.
- *Inability to comply because of loss of records.* When a record has been lost or destroyed, a formal statement shall be prepared and signed by the health information management specialist. This statement shall include specific reasons for the inability to produce records as directed. The risk manager shall be contacted before this statement is filed in response to the legal instrument.
- *Inability to comply because of method of record retention.* When the hard copy/original record is not available because it has been destroyed after microfilming or placing on optical disk, the court officer or attorney shall be notified that a copy of the material may be made available. A printout of the material may be made, with a signed statement as to its status as an exact copy/printout attached. This certification shall be signed by the health information management specialist. Acceptance of and arrangements for this copy shall be made, as far as possible, prior to presenting the material in court. The microfilm or disk shall be made available for inspection and comparison. Care shall be taken that only the record of the specific patient/client is accessed.

Tracking Log Information. The appropriate entries shall be made in the tracking log to show receipt, notifications, and all related actions associated with each court order or subpoena.

Legal Action File. Records involving litigation against the facility or a member of the medical staff shall be retained in a separate legal action file. Access and removal shall be made only with the explicit approval of the health information management specialist or designee.

Retention of Subpoena. Subpoenas and court orders shall be filed in the patient/client record and retained under the usual record retention practices.

Fees. The following fees shall apply:

- *Copying fees.* These shall be assessed and a bill prepared according to the fee schedule for release of information.
- *Witness fees.* The employee of the facility shall receive the usual salary/wages from the facility; therefore, witness fees shall be turned in to the appropriate financial unit of the facility. Reimbursement for mileage and related (prior approved) costs, such as meals, shall be made to the employee in accordance with the usual travel reimbursement vouchers and procedures.

Source: Joan Gratto Liebler, *Medical Records: Policies and Guidelines*, Aspen Publishers, Inc., © 1990.

DEPARTMENT OF HEALTH AND HUMAN SERVICES, PUBLIC HEALTH SERVICE, CONFIDENTIALITY OF ALCOHOL AND DRUG ABUSE RECORDS: FINAL RULE—SUMMARY

STATUTORY AUTHORIZATION:	Section 527—Public Health Service Act
REGULATIONS:	42 CFR Part 2
DATE EFFECTIVE:	August 10, 1987

APPLICABILITY

Any program that is specialized to the extent that it holds itself out as providing or provides alcohol or drug abuse diagnosis, treatment, or referral for treatment and that is federally assisted, either directly or indirectly.

PURPOSE

Protects information about alcohol and/or drug abuse records by requiring specific patient authorization for release of such information.

AUTHORIZATION REQUIREMENTS

The authorization to disclose must meet these requirements:

- be in written form
- contain the following:
  - specific name or general designation of the program or person permitted to make the disclosure
  - name or title of the individual or name of the organization to which disclosure is to be made
  - name of the patient
  - purpose of the disclosure
  - how much and what kind of information is to be disclosed
  - signature of the patient and, when required for a patient who is a minor, the signature of a person who is authorized to sign in lieu of the patient
  - the date on which the consent is signed
  - a statement that the consent is subject to revocation at any time except to the extent that the program or person that is to make the disclosure has already acted in reliance on it
  - the date, event, or condition upon which the consent will expire if not revoked before

NO REDISCLOSURE WITHOUT SPECIFIC CONSENT TO REDISCLOSE

Each disclosure made with patient's written consent must be accompanied by the following statement:

> The federal rules prohibit you from making any further disclosure of the information unless further disclosure is expressly permitted by the written consent of the person to whom it pertains or is otherwise permitted by 42 CFR Part 2.

MEDICAL EMERGENCIES

Information may be released to medical personnel who have a need to know information about a patient for the purpose of treating a condition that poses an immediate threat to the health of any individual and that requires immediate medical intervention.

RESPONSE TO SUBPOENAS

A response to a subpoena is not permitted unless an authorizing court order is entered.

For further details, consult the complete regulations covering this topic.

Source: Joan Gratto Liebler, *Medical Records: Policies and Guidelines*, Aspen Publishers, Inc., © 1990.

CASE MIX INFORMATION CONFIDENTIALITY—POLICY/PROCEDURE

PURPOSE

The purpose of this policy/procedure is to ensure a consistent process for accessing case mix information (combined financial and clinical patient data), to set forth confidentiality standards that shall be maintained for all information sharing, and to regulate the distribution of data for internal and external functions.

In developing these policies and procedures, several issues were considered

- the right of patient confidentiality
- the standards of the Joint Commission on Accreditation of Healthcare Organizations and state statutes pertaining to hospital information systems
- hospital policies and procedures pertaining to individual information systems within departments or divisions
- the right of medical staff confidentiality

POLICY EXCLUSIONS

This policy/procedure does not apply to

- use of patient-specific information for the purposes of patient care during an individual's episode of hospital care
- information generated from the health record database for the sole purpose of creating Joint Commission–required disease, operation, and physician indices (covered under department-specific confidentiality policies)
- information generated for the purposes of medical staff credentialing and peer review (covered under department-specific policies)
- information included in the human resources module of the hospitalwide system

POLICY

Underlying this policy/procedure is the need to treat case mix information in a confidential manner while still allowing sufficient access to those who need to know for purposes of planning, marketing, and financial and clinical analysis. When accessing and using case mix information, all reasonable steps shall be taken to ensure the confidentiality of sensitive information is protected from unauthorized disclosure or use.

DEFINITIONS

Case Mix Information

All data included in the hospitalwide information system that may or may not reside wholly within the module entitled "case mix." This includes clinical and financial information that originates in the health record and/or accounts receivable module. The only module not covered by this policy/procedure is the human resources module. A separate confidentiality policy/procedure is designed for this data system.

Case Mix Manager

An individual or his designee who receives and processes information requests and produces reports using case mix data or data available in other modules of the hospitalwide information system.

Individuals Allowed To Request Information

All information requests must originate from a hospital department manager or nurse manager regardless of the individual who will perform analysis of the desired information. Salaried physician directors and medical staff members may request information subject to the necessary approvals for sensitive information.

Individuals Authorized To Approve Data Release

For sensitive information: hospital president or his or her designee. *For nonrestricted information:* hospital president and vice presidents of hospital divisions.

Nonrestricted Information

Any information that does not fall into the definition of sensitive shall be considered nonrestricted information.

Request Form

Standard form for documenting an information request for case mix information.

Sensitive Information

The following information shall be considered sensitive: patient name, address (excluding ZIP code), and phone number and physician name and number. In addition, any information requested by physician directors or medical staff members or data to be used for dissemination to external groups, including corporate affiliates, shall be considered sensitive and shall be subject to the same release policies as sensitive information.

PROCEDURES

1. All case mix information requests shall be processed by the hospital case manager. A completed information request form will be submitted at least two weeks prior to the desired date of the report run. The requestor is responsible for obtaining all necessary authorizing signature(s) prior to submission of the request to the case mix manager (see definitions above).
2. New information request forms must be submitted for each request except in the case of standard reports for periodic generation, for which only one initial request form must be submitted. In the event the data to be included in standard reports are changed, a new request form and authorizing

continues

Case Mix Information Confidentiality continued

signatures must be submitted.

3. In the event that the request form is not complete (including authorizing signatures) when received by the case manager, the data request may be denied and the form returned to the originator for completion prior to proceeding with the report generation.
4. The case mix manager may contact the requestor to obtain additional facts pertaining to the data request in order to ensure that the most useful report will be generated.
5. All individuals receiving case mix information agree to respect the confidentiality and propriety of this information. Any person who breaches confidentiality shall be subject to disciplinary action in accordance with designed hospital policies/procedures. Where information is divulged to external groups, adequate steps shall be taken to ensure that such information is treated as confidential and proprietary, including the requirement that a written agreement be executed that such information will not be redisclosed without authorization from the initial authorized signer.
6. The case mix manager shall maintain a supply of information request forms and shall have access to case mix information as necessary to perform the duties assigned to this position.

REQUEST PROCESS

1. Obtain request form from case mix manager.
2. Complete request form.
3. Send form to authorized signer for approval.
4. Receive request form back from signer and forward to case mix manager.
5. Case mix manager: Review request form and
   a. Determine if sensitive information is included in the request and verify authorizing signature; if only nonrestricted information is being requested, verify authorizing signature.
   b. Return to originator if incomplete or if additional information is required.
   c. Process request if all necessary elements are included and the data elements necessary for report generation are clear.
   d. Forward report to requestor and other identified recipients (if any).
   e. Maintain copies of information request forms for at least two years.
   f. Maintain standard report log for data requests; this will be periodically generated.

Courtesy of Patrice L. Spath, Brown-Spath & Associates, Forest Grove, Oregon.

CASE MIX INFORMATION REQUEST FORM

REQUESTED BY: ______________________________ DATE: ______________

DEPARTMENT: ______________________________ PHONE: ______________

DATE REPORT NEEDED: ______________________________

WHAT DO YOU HOPE TO LEARN FROM THIS REPORT?

____

____

____

____

WHAT INFORMATION DO YOU WANT INCLUDED IN THIS REPORT? (Optional: Attach layout)

____

____

____

____

OVER WHAT TIME PERIOD DO YOU WANT INFORMATION?

____

HOW DO YOU WANT THE INFORMATION SORTED? (You may choose primary and secondary data sorts.)

____

____

WHO ELSE DO YOU WANT TO RECEIVE THIS REPORT?

NAME: ______________________________ DEPT: ______________

NAME: ______________________________ DEPT: ______________

NAME: ______________________________ DEPT: ______________

NAME: ______________________________ DEPT: ______________

HOW OFTEN DO YOU WANT THIS REPORT GENERATED?

___ As requested ___ Monthly ___ Quarterly ___ Semiannually

___ Annually ___ Other (Specify) ______________________________

REPORT FORMAT: ___ Hard copy ___ Graph ___ PC file (5 1/4" disk) ___ PC file (3 1/2" disk)

AUTHORIZING SIGNATURES:

______________________________ ______________

Requestor Date

______________________________ ______________

Division Vice President Date

______________________________ ______________

Hospital President Date

Nonrestricted Information: Division Vice President signature required

Sensitive Information: Hospital President signature required

FOR INTERNAL USE:

Report name: ______________________________ Preparation time: ______________

Date Report sent: ______________________________ Prepared by: ______________

Courtesy of Patrice L. Spath, Brown-Spath & Associates, Forest Grove, Oregon.

HEALTH RECORD ACCESS—POLICY AND PROCEDURE

	Issued By:	Policy #:
	Prepared By:	Revision #:
	Approved By:	Effective Date:
Subject: Health Record Access		Page of

PURPOSE

This policy establishes the parameters for access to the health record by authorized personnel.

AUDIENCE

This policy is for use by patient care providers, authorized health record requestors, and custodians of health records.

POLICY

The health record should be readily available to all practitioners who encounter the patient on either a scheduled or a nonscheduled (Emergency Department) basis.

It is the legal responsibility of all hospital employees (including physicians) and students to use the records in the normal course of business and to protect the confidentiality of the information within the record. Access to the health record is to be restricted to only those individuals who have a *need to know* and who provide a valid ID badge and/or appropriate documentation to access the information. Appropriate procedures must be provided for making records accessible to legitimate requestors.

Federal Medicare guidelines and Joint Commission on Accreditation of Healthcare Organizations guidelines require that original health records not be removed from the hospital campus except in accordance with a court order or subpoena. The exception to this rule is that records will be released to an attending clinical faculty physician who has a joint appointment with the hospital or who is otherwise jointly approved by the Health Information Management Department and hospital administration.

Records shall not be sequestered in places such as lockers or desks or in any other way made unavailable for immediate access. Individuals who violate this policy are subject to appropriate disciplinary action up to and including termination.

PROCEDURES

Any release of information from the health record to an outside requestor must be processed through the Health Information Management Department in accordance with federal and state laws and hospital policies. Release of confidential information must ensure that the patient's right to privacy is upheld. Information will be released only if proper patient authorization is received, upon receipt of a valid subpoena or court order, or in accordance with applicable laws and contractual agreements.

Checking Out Health Records

Health records will be issued only to legitimate requestors after initial approval by their department chairman, director, or executive director (if appropriate) and the Health Information Management Department.

The following requestors may check out health records for patient purposes:

- patient treatment areas located within the hospital campus
- faculty physicians' offices located within the hospital campus
- any approved off-site locations (not to exceed 24 hours)
- other approved requestors located within the hospital campus

The following requestors check out records (not to exceed 10 per requestor) for administrative or research purposes:

- hospital billing offices
- hospital resource utilization
- medical staff committees

continues

Health Record Access continued

	No:	Page of

- sponsored research for approved studies
- any other legitimate requestors authorized according to above

Only complete health records (according to medical staff documentation guidelines) may be checked out to the requestors listed above.

Incomplete health records will not be checked out but are available for review in the Record Processing Section of the Health Information Management Department.

The following requestors may check out records for quality assurance:

- quality assurance committees (hospital, medical staff, and joint)
- individual clinical departments' quality assurance committees
- authorized personnel from the quality management department
- risk management personnel

Retentions and Returns

Retentions and responsibility for unit health records are as follows:

- Inpatient nursing units shall keep records until 8:00 A.M. of the day following patient discharge. They are transferred to the health record technician area within the nursing unit from four to nine working days following discharge. Records are then transferred to the Record Processing Section of the Health Information Management Department.
- Outpatient treatment areas must return records the same day as the patient's visit. For records going to the hospital clinics, as many records as possible should be returned to the Health Information Management Department throughout the day via the conveyor system.
- Pediatric records in use at 4:00 P.M. are to be placed in a central clinic location accessible to the Health Information Management Department and returned to the Health Information Management Department clerk by 9:00 A.M. the following day.

All records covering autopsies except Medicare and Medicaid records must be returned to the Record Processing Section within four working days of the autopsy.

- Medicare and Medicaid records are to be returned to the Records Processing Section of the Health Information Management Department within 36 hours if the autopsy was performed during the weekend.
- Medicare and Medicaid records are to be returned to the Record Processing Section by 12:00 noon on Tuesday if the autopsy was performed during the workweek.
- All other authorized requestors may keep the record until 5:00 P.M. the same day as received, then must return records to the Health Information Management Department.
- Failure to comply with these rules on retention and return of health records could result in loss of record checkout privileges. If a health record is needed for an extended period of time, special request must be approved by the health information management specialist or his/her designee.

Responsibility

- If an approved health record requestor transfers a record to another location, it is his/her responsibility to complete a transfer slip or send a message to the Health Information Management Department to give notice of the record location change.
- The requestor will continue to be charged with having possession of the record until the Health Information Management Department receives this notice.
- When a record is signed out of the Health Information Management Department and needed for direct patient care from 5:00 P.M. to 8:00 A.M., Monday through Friday, and on weekends or holidays, it is the responsibility of the area or person in possession of the health record to provide it to the current requestor.
- If a requesting party does not return all records to the Health Information Management Department by the end of the day received, no additional records will be released to that party until all overdue records are returned.
- Prior to retrieving health records from the Health Information Management Department, the requestor must show proper identification.

Courtesy of Department of Health Information Management, University of Texas Medical Branch at Galveston, Galveston, Texas.

DUPLICATION, TRANSFER, AND LOAN OF RECORDS—POLICY AND PROCEDURE

Health and administrative records may be copied, loaned, or transferred to other employees of system facilities who have a need for the records in the performance of their duties (treatment, examination, research, adjudication, and other related purposes). Loaning or mailing original health records is strongly discouraged. Facilities are encouraged to utilize available electronic means of copying for record transfer.

For most cases where a patient is treated or seen at another system facility, the Patient Data Exchange (PDX) software package will be used to expedite the transfer of needed medical and administrative information between facilities. Facilities should use the PDX encryption feature when transmitting data to other system facilities. It is strongly urged that facilities utilize encryption when transmitting patient-identifiable data over networks that are not organized or controlled by the system. Additional needed information may be copied and sent via overnight mail or fax.

- Procedures relating to the duplication of medical, administrative, and perpetual records will be established and controlled by the health information management specialist. To ensure continuity of care, the health information management specialist will, when necessary, coordinate the prompt duplication of all medical data required—for example, records, slides, pacemaker records, prosthetic records, and X-rays.
- Records will be reviewed before transmittal to ensure all required documentation is present and securely filed.
- Records to be sent through the mail will be packaged carefully to guard against damage to the record or improper routing of the record.
- Local policy will document the intrahospital loan of health records for research purposes Intrahospital researchers will review the records in an area designated by the health information management specialist that provides for record security and promotes prompt retrieval of the record for treatment purposes.

Copies or extracted copies of health records may be loaned to nonsystem hospitals for use in connection with the treatment of system patients at system expense. Consent of the patient is not required for the loan of the health record for such purposes.

Procedures relating to the transfer and loan of health, administrative, and perpetual records will be established and controlled by the health information management specialist.

Source: Department of Veterans Affairs, Washington, D.C.

RELEASE OF DATA TO THIRD PARTIES

Providers should contractually define the use of personal medical data released to third-party payers. The general rule is that patients or their authorized representatives can authorize disclosure of confidential patient information. A patient's consent to disclosure must be an informed consent, however, which requires genuine disclosure of the intended uses of the information. It is incumbent upon the health care provider to ensure that the release of medical information is within the intended scope of the patient's consent. Before permitting access by third parties to patient-identifiable data, the provider should define its ownership rights in the data and the scope of the use of the data by the third party to minimize the risk of improper disclosure. Blanket consents obtained by insurance companies through the original enrollment process have led to broad consents that have been used to justify secondary use of medical data by pharmaceutical companies, employers, workers, direct market mailers, and others. One secondary use of medical data for purposes not disclosed at the time consent was obtained is for the compilation and sale of lists of persons with specific conditions or diseases.

To guard against being held liable for improper disclosure of confidential medical information that may be released to third parties, providers should consider the following actions:

- Obtain written patient consent that discloses the intended use of the data.
- Refrain from releasing information for purposes that are not disclosed to the patient at the time patient consent was obtained.
- Establish the provider's ownership rights in the data.
- Define and limit the purpose for which the third party is being given access to the data.
- Limit the scope by which the third party may use, disclose, or distribute the data, or prohibit third-party disclosure and/or distribution altogether.
- Restrict access to patient-identifying information. Where there is a need for third-party access to patient identifiers, limit access to specified personnel of the third party.
- Require third-party written confidentiality agreements that include separate agreements by employees, agents, and subcontractors of the third party.
- Require indemnification by third parties for harm the provider suffers as a result of a breach of confidentiality.
- Control data content and format, eliminating patient-identifying information where it is unnecessary to accomplish the purpose for which access is being given.
- Establish security policies and require third parties to agree contractually to comply with all applicable security policies and procedures of the provider.

Mass storage of patient-identifiable health data raises questions of adequate security to limit access and use of this information. Physicians and hospitals should establish their ownership rights in their data when agreeing to release certain data to third parties. Providers can sell their aggregate data subject to removal of patient-identifiable information or receipt of adequate informed consent. Patients in general have a right of access to the information in their health records and can request copies of same. In most cases, however, the patient has been found not to have an ownership interest in the record. Hospitals should treat the compilation of medical data as proprietary information of the hospital and should assert their rights to maintain the proprietary status of this information when contracting with third parties that may have access to and limited use of the information.

Source: Jonell B. Williamson, "Preserving Confidentiality and Security of Patient Health Information," *Topics in Health Information Management*, Vol. 16, No. 4, Aspen Publishers, Inc., © May 1996.

HEALTH RECORD STORAGE AND RETENTION

STORAGE AND RETRIEVAL SYSTEMS: POLICIES AND PROCEDURES

Comprehensive and Centralized System

A comprehensive, centralized system for the storage and retrieval of health records, from creation through destruction, shall be established and maintained as a major function of the health record department. The processes and procedures of the centralized system and related subsystems shall be developed to achieve the following:

- foster continuity of care through ready accessibility and prompt retrieval of health record information
- support the uses of the health record as set forth in the policies of the department
- comply with all related legal, regulatory, and accrediting agency considerations summarized in the record retention schedule included in these policies
- safeguard records and documents from tampering, loss, and inadvertent destruction
- restrict access to records by unauthorized individuals

The storage and retrieval filing system shall be the unit filing system whereby all documents relating to one patient/client are filed together and accessed through a unit numbering system.

These systems shall be adapted to take into account particular considerations relating to the following:

- records of employees who are treated as patients/clients in the facility
- records of cases of an unusually sensitive nature
- records of individuals of unusual fame or notoriety
- records relating to cases under active litigation

Records shall be filed and maintained in the health record department under the direction of the health information management specialist or designee. Records shall be processed and filed separately and held in a restricted, locked file. Access shall be permitted only by direct authorization of the health information management specialist or designee.

If a patient/client is readmitted, the attending physician shall review the record and select the materials that are needed for the care of the patient/client. The material shall be copied for the attending physician, who shall return it after the patient/client is discharged.

Legal, Regulatory, and Accrediting Requirements

These policies and practices shall be consistent with the relevant state and federal laws and regulations that contain provisions relating to retention of health record data in original and alternate storage medium (microform, magnetic tape, etc.). The requirements of accrediting agencies shall be met, and the guidelines of professional associations shall be followed where practicable and permitted by law or regulation.

Specifically, the following shall be reviewed regularly, and these policies shall be amended to comply with any changed provision:

- state laws or regulations
  - uniform preservation of private business and public records
  - uniform photographic copies of business and public records
  - Medicaid and medical assistance
  - workers' compensation
  - department of health regulations for general and special hospitals
  - state codes regarding definition of minority/majority status and statute of limitations
- federal laws and regulations
  - Conditions of Participation (Medicare)
  - Occupational Safety and Health Administration (OSHA) if applicable
  - regulations for specialty programs
- contractual and advisory provisions of facility's liability insurance carrier
- accrediting agency standards (Joint Commission on Accreditation of Healthcare Organizations *or* American Osteopathic Association)
- guidelines of professional associations
  - American Medical Record Association
  - American Hospital Association
  - National Micrographics Association
  - American College of Obstetrics and Gynecology
  - American Electroencephalographic Society
  - College of American Pathologists

Retention Schedule

General Principles. The most stringent requirements shall be met, and the following special considerations shall be noted:

Category	*Retention*
Minors	Retain data until patient reaches majority plus [number of] years.

Patients who have a mental disability	Retain data until impairment clears plus [number of] years.
Unusual or innovative treatment	Deferred destruction.
Formal interest expressed by legal counsel for patient or individual affected by data in record	Deferred destruction.
Patients/clients treated under specific contract with an employer	Determine, with legal counsel, whether OSHA 30-year retention requirement applies.
Date of last activity	Determine through use of activity codes.
Specific form of retention	See next section of this policy.

Applicability. The record retention schedule shall apply to all primary and secondary records under the direct jurisdiction of the health record department.

Intraorganizational Coordination. The schedule shall be coordinated with the overall facility policies on record retention. Particular coordination shall be undertaken concerning the following:

- billing data with diagnostic and/or code information
- employee records
- X-rays, EEGs, and EKGs
- quality assurance and utilization review

Specific Retention Schedule.

Record/Data	*Form*	*Retention*
Patient/client master index		
Birth register		
Death register		
Diagnostic index		
Operations and procedures index		
Health record data abstracts		
Statistical reports		
Physician index		
Utilization review reports and minutes		
Quality assurance reports and minutes		
Trauma registry		
Cancer registry		

Form of Record Retention

The records/documents shall be retained as hard copy or a combination of hard copy and microfilm, optical disc, magnetic tape, or a computerized form, as best meets the following:

- legal, regulatory, and accrediting provisions,
- ease of use for patient/client care purposes
- level of activity (patient/client care use, research use, administrative use)
- compatibility with existing systems
- availability of cost-effective alternatives, such as commercial storage, on-site remote storage, or microfilming (on-site or commercial vendor)

The usual retention form for each class of patient/client record is indicated in the record retention schedule.

Selection of Storage Form

The health information management specialist, in cooperation with the medical staff committee charged with making recommendations concerning health record systems, shall determine the most effective form for the retention of records and all related data. The factors to be considered include the following:

- personnel
  - labor costs
  - properly trained
- equipment and supplies
  - camera
  - processing equipment
  - supplies
- physical space
  - for equipment
  - for processing
  - for temporary holding
  - for permanent holding
- availability of data/records
  - during processing
  - after processing
  - access time (STAT/emergency, readmission, administrative use)
  - additional cost for special access
- custom features
  - not allowed
  - done at additional cost
- project completion time
- confidentiality
  - during processing
  - after processing
- bonded/insured
- authentication certificate provided
- certificate of destruction
- quality controls
- volume discounts
- total cost per year of retention

Applicability of Policies and Practices

When data are stored in microform or on magnetic tape, the same policies and practices concerning access, use, tracking, and return as for hard-copy original records shall apply. Additional refinements of these policies and practices may be made to accommodate specific aspects as needed by the specific retention form.

Method of Filing

Records/documents shall be filed according to the standardized method of terminal digit filing to increase the accuracy of filing and to permit ease of retrieval.

Storage Space Specifications

Storage space shall be selected and maintained to protect records from unauthorized access, loss, and inadvertent destruction. Therefore, storage space shall be selected to meet the following specifications:

- adequate lighting
- controlled environment (60 to 80° F, 50 percent humidity)
- freedom from dust
- protection against fire, including sprinkler system
- freedom from potential hazards, such as flooding or damage from broken water pipes

The selection and layout of shelving shall permit the following:

- ease of access to records
- adequate spacing of records to prevent overcrowding
- safety for employees

Appropriate safety practices shall be adopted and posted in the storage area to foster a hazard-free work environment. Support equipment, such as ladders and step stools, shall be selected and maintained in keeping with accepted safety practices.

Access to Storage and Retrieval Areas

Only authorized personnel shall be permitted direct access to the storage and retrieval areas so that the following are achieved:

- proper safeguards against unauthorized use are maintained
- fixed responsibility for file integrity and accuracy is assigned

In the rare circumstance that no health record department manager or storage and retrieval clerk is available, the administrator on call may have access to the department for the purpose of obtaining a record to meet an emergency need.

Intradepartmental Coordination

The activities associated with the storage and retrieval function shall be coordinated with other departmental units, specifically:

- *Patient/client identification/numbering system.* In keeping with the facility's commitment to the unit record, all health record documents shall be filed in one central record for each patient/client. This record and all documents shall be identified with the patient's/client's unit number. If errors are noted in the unit number, storage and retrieval personnel shall notify the master numbering unit so that corrections may be made.
- *Incomplete record processing.* Material to be filed in incomplete records shall be processed by personnel in the discharge processing unit. Storage and retrieval personnel shall take such material to the unit without delay. Storage and retrieval personnel shall obtain the completed records from the unit on a regular basis during the workday. The record sign-out/tracking system shall be identical for the two units. Requests for records held in the discharge processing unit shall be directed to that unit for handling. Delivery and retrieval of both complete and incomplete records shall be done by storage and retrieval personnel.

Requests for Records

An effective process for requesting health records shall be developed consistent with the stated uses of the health record. Priority shall be given to direct patient/client care uses, with due consideration given for other uses. The record retrieval system shall accommodate both scheduled and demand-basis requests. The needs of the various users shall be balanced to permit adequate access for all approved users. The following considerations are associated with categories of requests:

- authorized users
- location during use
- retrieval priority
- time period for use
- fees
- special considerations

Reasonable requests for an extension of the charge-out period shall be accommodated as far as possible. The appropriate request for extension form shall be completed and sent to the health record department before the time period has expired. This designated form shall include a signed statement that the user has the record in possession at that time.

Adjunct Functions and Services

Forwarding Records: Readmission/Continuing Care

The complete health record shall be forwarded to the appropriate inpatient service when a patient/client is

- readmitted
- admitted from the emergency department of the facility
- admitted from an outpatient unit of the facility
- admitted from a facility-sponsored hospice or home care program

The health record shall be held in the designated area in the inpatient service and coordinated with records/data reflecting the current admission. The record shall be retained in that location until patient/client discharge, when it shall be returned to the health record department along with the current record.

The complete health record shall be forwarded to the specific outpatient clinic when a patient/client is referred to the clinic after discharge or is a continuing patient with previous outpatient or emergency care from the facility. The record shall be delivered and returned each clinic day, as requested (see exceptions noted under subsidiary health record units).

The complete health record shall be forwarded to the facility-sponsored home care or hospice care (on-premises location) when a patient/client is

- referred to the program after inpatient discharge
- referred to the program from outpatient services
- readmitted to the program

The record shall be delivered and returned in accordance with the system of record request (see exceptions noted under subsidiary health record units).

Delivery and Return of Records

Health record personnel from the storage and retrieval unit shall deliver and pick up all health records. Routine, scheduled pickup and delivery schedules shall be developed for the various inpatient, outpatient, and emergency care services.

Processing Continuing Care and Late Reports

There shall be a system for the prompt, accurate filing in the appropriate record section (e.g., outpatient or specific admission) for reports generated in the course of ongoing care or reports received after the health record has been assembled. The usual time frames for processing are as follows:

- *inpatient record:* twice daily processing
- *outpatient visit scheduled:* same day filing
- *closed records:* two workdays
- *hospice or home care active patient:* daily processing

If the patient/client identification on reports is missing or incomplete, the report shall be returned to the originating service.

Subsidiary Health Record Units

In order to balance the needs of preserving the unit record and the integrity of the health record system with the patient/client care staff's need for readily available health record data, the centralized health record system shall be augmented with subsidiary health record units. These units shall be set up in designated outpatient care areas. They shall remain under the direct jurisdiction of the health information management specialist. All health record service policies, procedures, and practices shall apply to these units. All health record functions shall be carried out by health record department staff.

The criteria for the establishment of a subsidiary health record unit shall be developed by the health information management specialist with the approval of the chief executive officer and the medical director of the facility.

The request for designation of a subsidiary health record unit shall be initiated by the medical director of the clinic or program and reviewed for approval by the health information management specialist.

The establishment of these subsidiary units is intended for clinics and programs in which patients/clients are expected to participate in active assessment, monitoring, or treatment processes that require frequent repeat visits (e.g., weekly visits for two or three consecutive months). The following clinics and programs shall be actively considered for subsidiary units:

- prenatal care
- radiation oncology
- pain management
- allergy and dermatitis
- methadone
- physical medicine and rehabilitation
- home care
- hospice care

Criteria for housing an individual health record in the subsidiary unit are as follows:

- care plan indicates that the patient/client is to be scheduled for frequent visits
- care plan indicates that the clinic/program is the primary focus of care

Health records so designated shall be charged out to the subsidiary unit for the duration of the period of active care.

Coordination with Appointment System

To promote continuity of care and minimize delay because of record unavailability, the health information management specialist shall develop appropriate procedures to coordinate activities with the appointment system for the various clinics and programs. These coordinated activities shall include at a minimum the following:

- design of a health record requisition form for clinic/program appointments
- inclusion of complete and accurate patient/client identification on requests
- timely transmittal of requests to the health record department

Activity Monitoring

The last date of activity shall be noted on the permanent folder to facilitate record retention/planned destruction processes. The first time the record is accessed in a given year, the yearly activity code shall be checked.

Maintaining File Integrity

A series of practices shall be adopted to foster the integrity of the files during all stages of use. At a minimum, these processes shall include the following practices:

- selection of adequate support equipment and materials
- record tracking system
- quality assurance/audit for accuracy
- periodic removal of inactive material

Support Equipment and Materials

Support equipment and materials shall be selected to foster accuracy in filing and ease of accessibility in retrieval functions. Shelving equipment shall be durable to withstand sustained use. File guides shall be placed at a ratio of [number of] guides to [number of] records. The health record folders shall be color coded to the terminal digit system, prenumbered, preprinted, and marked with the appropriate bar code for tracking purposes.

Record Tracking/Charge-Out System

A comprehensive record location control system shall be implemented for both complete/permanent files and incomplete records. Each time a record is removed from its designated location, it shall be logged into the tracking system. The process of tracking shall be initiated at the time of patient admission so that the record's location from inception through authorized destruction is known. The basic charge-out information shall consist of the following:

- patient/client name and unit number
- user name and department
- date charged out

As far as possible, this tracking system shall be computerized using bar coding. The specific bar code system selected shall be compatible with the hardware of the facility's computer system and shall conform to the standards of the Health Industry Bar Code Council. The computerized system shall have the capacity to provide the following:

- record tracking
- retrieval listing (placing record requests into numeric sequence according to the terminal digit filing system)
- reserve listing (showing pending requests)
- overdue listing (records due for return)

The system shall be coordinated with the discharge processing unit for tracking records during the completion process.

Quality Assurance/Audit for Accuracy

A series of ongoing controls, supplemented with specific inspections and reviews, shall be carried out to foster the accuracy, integrity, and availability of stored data. These measures shall include

- continuous practices
  - limited access
  - assigned personnel responsibilities for each section of the files
- weekly review
  - inspection of physical space for evidence of overcrowding, damage by pests, and problems with temperature and humidity
  - color code errors in terminal digit sections
  - unfiled records
  - placement of records in numeric order

- review of record tracking/charge out system (timely return, correct placement of outguide, proper updating to show current location)
- check of internal filing (placement of documents in correct health record)
- monthly review (availability rate, i.e., comparison of number of records requested with number of records available)

The weekly reviews may be carried out using a sampling method with a 95 percent confidence level established for the sample. The reviews shall be carried out by supervisory or management-level employees of the department.

Periodic Check for Inactive Records

On a periodic basis, at least annually, the files shall be reviewed to determine activity level. Inactive material shall be processed according to the record retention schedule.

Inactive Storage

Records that exceed the record retention requirements for hard copy retention shall be removed from active storage and processed according to the record retention schedule in these policies.

Remote Storage Considerations

When on-site, remote storage is selected as the approved retention location, the physical/environmental specifications for the storage space shall be met. Appropriate means of preventing unauthorized access shall be implemented. Particular consideration shall be given to employee safety and security during travel to and from the site and during work assignments at the site.

Contract Specifications: Microfilming Service Bureaus

Contractual provisions with microfilming service bureaus shall contain the following provisions as a minimum:

- provision for proof of bonding and signed security agreements
- provision for data security and patient data confidentiality (all employees of the microfilming service bureau who handle health records shall sign the standard confidentiality statement)
  - during pickup, delivery, and processing
  - during transport to and from service bureau
- provision for adequate protection of records during processing (must meet same standards as facility concerning physical space and environmental standards, including fire and theft systems)
- provision for comprehensive service
  - removal of records from shelves
  - packing into cartons
  - premicrofilming preparation, including repairing torn documents, placing laboratory work into a fully visible display format, checking for misfiles, checking for patient identification, and placing target sheets between admissions
- provision for availability during processing
  - on-site workroom access
  - photocopy preparation
  - scheduled access and delivery
  - rush/STAT access and delivery
  - regular return of processed material (at least weekly return by batch)
- provision for meeting microfilming standards of the National Bureau of Standards for permanent micrographic copy
- provision for using reduction ratio compatible with facility's reader and reader-printer equipment and/or computer equipment
- provision for a certificate of authenticity that the microfilm is a complete and accurate copy of the record as given to the company by the facility for processing
- provision for review/verification check/quality check by facility personnel to determine acceptability of microimaging (replacement at no cost for work found unsatisfactory)
- provision for destruction of original when authorized
  - use of a method approved by the facility
  - preparation of certificate of destruction
- provision for work completion time
- provision for statement of cost and billing
  - detailed statement of cost
  - guaranteed rate for contract period
  - detailed monthly billing
- provision for discontinuance of contractual agreement (advance notification of at least six months in order to terminate agreement; all outstanding work to be completed before contract terminated)

Contract Specifications: Commercial Storage

Contractual provisions with incorporated commercial storage companies shall contain the following provisions as a minimum:

- provision for data security and patient data confidentiality (all employees of company shall sign the standard confidentiality statement)
  - during pickup, delivery, and processing
  - during transport to and from storage

- provision for proof of bonding and signed security agreements
- provision for adequate protection of records (must meet same standards as facility regarding physical space and environmental standards, including fire and theft alarm system)
- provision for comprehensive service
  - removing from shelves
  - packing into containers
  - preparing transmittal list
  - cataloging/indexing
  - accessing (at storage center in designated work area and during delivery)
- provision for refiling
- provision for destruction when authorized
  - use of a method approved by the facility
  - preparation of certificate of destruction
- provision for billing and cost statements
  - detailed billing on monthly basis
  - guaranteed rates per contract period
  - detailed statement of services (cost breakdown)
- provision for discontinuing contractual agreement (advance notification of at least one full year)

Destruction of Records

Planned Destruction

Planned destruction of records/data shall be carried out according to the approved record retention schedule as part of the normal business routine of the facility. This process shall be carried out under the direct supervision of the health information management specialist or designee. No further approval for the destruction of records/data shall be required when such destruction is in accordance with the approved record retention schedule.

Inadvertent Destruction

When records/data are destroyed inadvertently (such as with fire or flood) notification shall be made as follows:

- *Internal notification of chief executive officer.* For records that meet minimum regulatory requirements but not organizational requirements, the certificate of destruction shall carry the information relating to the inadvertent destruction.
- *External notification of licensure/regulatory and accrediting agencies.* For records that do not meet minimum regulatory or accrediting agency time frames, notification shall be made by the chief executive officer. The notice to the chief executive officer shall carry the information relating to the cause of the inadvertent destruction.

Method of Destruction

Health record data shall be destroyed in such a way that there is no possibility of reconstructing any of the information. One of the following methods shall be used: shredding, incineration, pulping. The health information management specialist shall determine the specific method annually, based on the availability of timely, cost-effective record destruction services. The use of contractual arrangements with a commercial record destruction company shall be permitted provided that appropriate guarantees of the confidentiality of the data are included in the contractual agreement. The confidentiality of the data shall be maintained throughout all stages of the destruction process.

Documentation of Destruction

The health information management specialist or designee shall complete the certificate of destruction for both planned and inadvertent record destruction. This certificate of destruction shall include the following:

- date of destruction
- method
- patient/client names and unit numbers
- appropriate statement
  - destroyed in normal course of business
  - inadvertently destroyed but met basic regulatory/accrediting agency retention requirements
  - inadvertently destroyed but did not meet basic regulatory/accrediting agency retention requirements
- signature of individual supervising the destruction
- signature of witness

When a commercial record destruction company carries out the destruction process, the designated official of the company shall complete the record destruction certificate and provide it to the facility. All certificates of destruction shall be maintained indefinitely in a central file in the health records department.

Excerpt of Record

The following information shall be excerpted and retained indefinitely for each record scheduled for destruction:

- patient/client name
- unit number
- admission and discharge date
- name of attending physician
- diagnoses

- operations, operative report, pathology report, and name of surgeon
- discharge summary

This information may be kept in hard copy or in microimage.

Discontinued Operations

The facility shall follow licensure regulations concerning

- required retention period
- provision of secure retention in an approved location (such as a commercial record retention company)
- notification to patients/clients or their representatives to allow them to claim their own records

Policy Approval and Distribution

The policies relating to the use, retention, and destruction of records shall be reviewed and approved by the chief executive officer, legal counsel, and the medical staff committee (health records).

The approved policies shall be distributed to all patient/client care services, research units, outpatient and emergency services, facility-sponsored hospice and home care units, the social service unit, risk management, the financial officer, and the chief executive officer.

Source: Joan Gratto Liebler, *Medical Records: Policies and Guidelines*, Aspen Publishers, Inc., © 1990.

WORKSHEET FOR COMPARISON OF STORAGE OPTIONS

FACTORS	IN-HOUSE HARD COPY	COMMERCIAL STORAGE HARD COPY	IN-HOUSE MICROFILM	SERVICE BUREAU MICROFILM
Personnel				
• labor costs				
• training				
Equipment and supplies				
• camera				
• processing equipment				
• supplies				
Physical space				
• for equipment				
• for processing				
• for temporary holding				
• for permanent holding				
Availability of data/records				
• during processing				
• after processing				
• access time				
– STAT/emergency				
– readmission				
– administrative use				
• additional cost for special access				
Custom features				
• not allowed				
• done at additional cost				
Project completion time				
Confidentiality				
• during processing				
• after processing				
Bonded/insured				
Authentication certificate provided				
Certificate of destruction				
Quality controls				
Volume discounts				
Total cost per year of retention				

Source: Joan Gratto Liebler, *Medical Records: Policies and Procedures,* Aspen Publishers, Inc., © 1990.

HEALTH RECORD REQUIREMENTS

Records That Must Be Kept

A hospital must maintain a record for each of its patients. This requirement is imposed by state licensure laws, Joint Commission on Accreditation of Healthcare Organizations (Joint Commission) standards, and conditions of participation in federal reimbursement programs. In addition, a small number of judicial opinions have held that, under certain circumstances, a hospital is liable to a patient for failure to maintain a proper record. To avoid civil liability and maintain its license, certification, and accreditation, therefore, a hospital must develop and enforce appropriate recordkeeping policies. These policies should set forth clearly the types of information to be included in each record, how long each record must be kept, and proper methods for final destruction of a record.

The health record consists of four types of data concerning an individual patient: (1) personal, (2) financial, (3) social, and (4) medical. Personal information usually is obtained on admission and includes name, birth date, sex, marital status, next of kin, occupation, identification of physicians, and other items needed for specific patient identification. Financial data include the name of the patient's employer, health insurance company, types of insurance and policy numbers, Medicare and Medicaid numbers, if any, and other information that will enable the hospital to bill for its services. Social data include the patient's race and ethnic background, family relationships, community activities, and life style. It also includes any court orders or other directions concerning the patient and other information related to the patient's position in society that may indicate a need for special confidentiality protection.

Medical data form the patient's clinical record, a continuously maintained history of the treatment provided in the hospital. These data include the patient's chief complaint, medical and family histories, results of physical examinations, planned course of treatment, physicians' diagnosis and therapeutic orders, evidence of informed consent, clinical observations, progress notes made by the medical staff, consultation reports, nursing notes, reports and results of all procedures and tests including pathology and clinical laboratory tests and examinations, operative record, radiology and nuclear medicine examinations and treatment, anesthesia records, other reports generated during the patient's treatment, and conclusions made at the termination of hospitalization. Medical data also may include information obtained from outside sources, including diagnostic tests performed at another facility before the patient's admission to the hospital where reliance on the outside reports by hospital medical staff is reasonable medical practice and consistent with hospital policy.

The health record may be written, typed, or computer generated. Regardless of its form, the health record should be a complete, accurate, and current account of the history, condition, and treatment of the patient and the results of the individual's hospitalization or outpatient treatment. The computerized record can expand the information network on a patient, enhancing completeness and accuracy as well as immediate availability of the record to authorized personnel. However, computerized health records present special concerns.

The health record is used not only to document chronologically the care rendered to the patient but also to plan and evaluate the treatment and to enhance communication among the patient's physician and other health care professionals treating the individual. The record provides clinical data for medical, nursing, and scientific research. Individuals who conduct medical and nursing audits and peer review evaluations rely heavily on documentation in health records.

Hospital health records are important legal documents for the hospital and the patient. For example, where hospital bylaws direct individual departments to develop standards of care, examination of health records can provide verification that the standards are being maintained. Administrative and clinical assessment programs may be targets of legal scrutiny, and health records can aid in the evaluation and justification of such programs.

The most important legal function of health records is to provide essential evidence in the defense of professional negligence actions. Because such actions often are litigated two to five years after the plaintiff received the treatment in question, the health record frequently is the only detailed record of what actually occurred during the hospitalization. Persons who participated in the plaintiff's treatment may not be available to testify on behalf of the defendants or may not remember important details of the case. A properly created record enables the hospital to reconstruct the patient's course of treatment and to show whether the care provided was acceptable under the circumstances. The contents of the hospital record usually are admissible in evidence for or against the hospital and physicians. It is essential, therefore, that everyone involved in health record documentation and management understand the legal implications of the record so that they will create and maintain a record that will be useful to them in any future litigation.

Legal Requirements for Content of a Health Record

The requirement that hospitals maintain health records is found in state and federal statutes and regulations, municipal codes, and hospital accreditation standards. In some state statutes, a general definition of *health records* provides guidance on what the records should contain.

For all hospitals seeking to participate in federal reimbursement programs, the federal law and regulations setting forth conditions of participation also impose record retention requirements. The law and regulations setting forth the Medicare program provide that a hospital must maintain clinical records on all patients. Regulations issued by the Health Care Financing Administration (HCFA) require each hospital to maintain a health record for every inpatient and outpatient that is accurately written, promptly completed and properly filed and retained, and accessible. Moreover, the HCFA regulations on the conditions of participation for hospitals provide that all records must contain the following information as appropriate:

- evidence of a physician examination, including a health history, performed no more than 7 days before admission or within 48 hours after admission
- admitting diagnosis
- results of all consultative evaluations of the patient and appropriate findings by clinical and other staff involved in the care of the patient
- documentation of complications, hospital-acquired infections, and unfavorable reactions to drugs and anesthesia
- properly executed informed consent forms for procedures and treatments specified by the medical staff, or by federal or state law if applicable, to require written patient consent
- all practitioners' orders, nursing notes, reports of a treatment, medication records, radiology and laboratory reports, vital signs, and other information necessary to monitor the patient's condition
- discharge summary with outcome of hospitalization, disposition of case, and provisions for follow-up care
- final diagnosis with completion of health records within 30 days following discharge

In some cities, local or municipal codes require hospitals to record certain information not otherwise required by state law or regulation. Various state hospital associations also may have established guidelines for the contents of health records. Finally, the Joint Commission requires hospitals to maintain patient care records, mandating that a health record be "initiated and maintained for every individual assessed or treated." Its standards of accreditation also impose content requirements.

Whether or not specific statutory or regulatory guidelines apply, hospitals should adopt institutional policies concerning the content of health records. The policy may be a detailed list of data required or may reference other guidelines, such as state statutes, regulations, or Joint Commission standards. In general, detailed policies require closer periodic review to keep them current, while broad policies remain applicable as circumstance and practice change. Hospitals should balance the need for providing enough specificity to guide health records practitioners and hospital staff against the desire to avoid continual policy revisions. Most accredited hospitals in states with no statutory or regulatory direction on patient record content rely on the Joint Commission accreditation standards as a guide to record content policy.

To maintain the currency of their health record policies, hospitals should keep abreast of state, federal, and Joint Commission health records requirements. State and local associations of health record practitioners often publish changes in the applicable law and accreditation standards. Hospitals also receive notice of these changes from state and national hospital associations and from hospital legal counsel. All health care institutions should develop reliable ways of monitoring new laws and regulations and communicating any changes to the individuals responsible for making policy recommendations concerning health record content, particularly health record practitioners and the medical staff.

These individuals should understand the various functions of the health record and their interrelationships, as well as how those functions are affected by the nature of the specific institution and current legislative, regulatory, and licensing requirements. Creating an effective record content policy requires the involvement of a variety of disciplines within the institution. Policy makers must be willing to find ways to make practical adjustments to medical record content. In doing so, they should strike a balance between the administrative, financial, and other demands placed on the health record and the record's basic patient care function.

Record Retention Requirements

In determining how long to retain health records, a hospital should consider federal or state laws and regulations, sound hospital administrative policy, and sound medical practice. The nature of the institution and the resources available to maintain documents for an extended period also will influence the hospital's retention policy. Achieving a practical and workable health record retention policy becomes more difficult in an era of reduced financial resources.

The hospital should consider eight factors in establishing a retention policy: (1) statutory and regulatory requirements, (2) statutes of limitations and potential future litigation, (3) requirements of the hospital's malpractice insurer, (4) the need for records information in medical research and teaching, (5) storage capabilities, (6) cost of microfilming, (7) computerization and other long-term storage methods, and (8) recommendations of hospital associations. Clearly, the hospital first must comply with all applicable statutory and regulatory retention requirements. When the hospital considers it prudent to have a retention period longer than statutory or regulatory requirements, however, it may establish one.

Statutory and Regulatory Concerns

Medicare conditions of participation require hospitals to retain the original record or a legally reproduced form for a period of at least five years. A few states also impose record retention requirements on general hospital health records by statute. In most jurisdictions, record retention requirements, like content requirements, appear in regulations issued by the state hospital licensing agency. While laws vary, there generally are four categories: (1) those requiring hospitals to preserve the entire health record for very long periods, (2) those requiring the records to be maintained for 10 years, (3) those requiring fewer than 10 years, and (4) references to other sources of law and guidance constituting the retention requirement of the state. Many jurisdictions also have special retention provisions for certain portions of a patient's record (such as X-rays, graphic data, and discharge summaries), special procedures for records of patients who are minors, and other provisions for records pertaining to deceased persons.

In addition to the general retention requirements described above, Medicare conditions of participation and several states have special statutory or regulatory provisions governing how long a hospital should maintain specific portions of a patient's record, such as X-rays, scans, and clinical laboratory reports. Hospitals also must comply with retention laws on vital statistics, including records of births and deaths.

Many states prescribe special retention requirements for records of patients who were minors at the time of treatment. These requirements usually indicate that hospitals must keep records until the patient reaches majority plus some additional time, or until the expiration of the general retention requirement, whichever is longer. The prescribed extension ranges from 1 to 10 years beyond the age of majority.

A few states also address the issue of deceased patients' records. These regulations allow the facility to destroy records of a deceased patient before the expiration of the general retention requirement. Oklahoma, for example, requires a hospital to maintain a patient's records for a minimum of five years after the patient was last seen, or at least three years beyond the patient's death.

In states that have adopted the Uniform Preservation of Private Business Records Act, the three-year records preservation requirement may apply to the health records of private hospitals if there is no statutory retention specifically governing health records. So far only four states have adopted the Act, and three of those legislatively have established longer retention periods for health records. However, in Illinois, where there is no statutory retention period for health records, the Act may govern although it does not refer specifically to health records.

Statutes of Limitations

Another key factor in establishing a record retention policy is the statute of limitations on contract and tort actions. A statute of limitations is a period established by statute, measured in years, within which a party may bring a lawsuit. The time periods vary with the cause of action, e.g., contract, tort, or real estate.

Except in the case of minors' records, retaining the record for the limitations period would not impose a burden on the hospital health records department because limitation periods generally are shorter than the period the record would be retained for medical reasons. If the statute of limitations were used as a guide, the health record of a minor would be kept until the patient reaches the age of majority plus the period of the statute. For example, in a state where the age of majority is 21 and the statute of limitations for torts is two years, the retention period for a newborn's record would be 23 years; in states in which the age of majority is 18 and the statute of limitations for torts is two years, the retention period for a newborn's record would be 20 years. While the possibility of an infant's waiting until majority to bring suit is slight, it can happen. Although most suits by minors are brought soon after the accident causing the injury, a hospital is protected best if it retains records until the minor reaches majority and for an additional time equal to the applicable state statute of limitations on tort actions.

Association Guidelines

The American Hospital Association (AHA) and the American Health Information Management Association (AHIMA), formerly the American Medical Record Association (AMRA), have adopted a policy that recommends retaining complete records in original or reproduced form for 10 years after the most recent patient care entry and retaining certain parts of the record permanently. The guidelines recommend that after 10 years, the complete record may be destroyed, unless destruction is prohibited by statute, ordinance, regulation, or law if the institution

- Retains basic information such as dates of admission and discharge, names of responsible physicians, records of diagnoses and operations, operative reports, pathology reports, and discharge résumés for all records so destroyed.
- Retains complete health records of minors for the period of minority plus the applicable period of statute of limitations in the state in which the health care institution is located.
- Retains complete health records of patients under mental disability in like manner as those of patients under disability or minority.
- Retains complete health records for longer periods when requested in writing by one of the following:
  - an attending or consultant physician of the patient
  - the patient or someone acting legally in his or her behalf
  - legal counsel for a party having interest affected by the health records

In addition, some state hospital associations have issued record retention guidelines that may be useful in developing a hospital record retention policy.

Destruction of the Record

On expiration of the health records retention period or after the record has been copied onto microfilm or computer or converted to other machine-readable form, the record usually may be destroyed. In some states, the method of health record destruction is controlled by statute and regulation. The Tennessee statute states

> Upon retirement of the record as provided in . . . this section, the record or any part thereof retired shall be destroyed by burning, shredding, or other effective method in keeping with the confidential nature of its contents. Destruction of such records must be made in the ordinary course of business and no record shall be destroyed on an individual basis.

Other states require hospitals to create, in accordance with applicable regulations, an abstract of any pertinent data in the health record before destroying the record. Although the states that have specified the method of record destruction generally permit destruction by shredding or burning, the Environmental Protection Agency recommends shredding and recycling. Hospitals that deliver their health records to a commercial enterprise for destruction should do so pursuant to a written agreement that sets forth safeguards similar to those discussed for microfilming agreements, including the method of destruction, safeguards against breach of confidentiality, indemnification provisions, and certification that the records have been destroyed properly.

Hospitals that destroy their own records also must establish procedures to protect the confidentiality of record information and ensure that records are destroyed completely. The hospital employee responsible for record destruction should certify that the records have been destroyed properly. Whether its records are destroyed commercially or by the hospital, the hospital should retain certificates of destruction permanently as evidence of its record disposal.

The hospital's health records policies should include provisions governing destruction of records, and these provisions should be applied uniformly. Where it can be shown that a hospital failed to apply such a policy uniformly or where destruction was contrary to hospital policy, courts may allow the jury in a negligence suit to infer that if the records were available, they would show the hospital had acted improperly in treating the plaintiff.

Source: William H. Roach, Jr., and the Aspen Health Law Center, *Medical Records and the Law*, 2nd ed., Aspen Publishers, Inc., © 1994.

RECOMMENDED RETENTION PERIODS FOR HOSPITAL RECORDS

Use as a guide when your state or the federal government does not specify a retention period.

Record	Retention period
Annual reports to government agencies	Permanent
Birth registration copy	Permanent
Death registration copy	Permanent
Delivery room log	Permanent
Disease index	10 years to permanent
Emergency department reports	10 years
Fetal heart rate monitoring	10 years
Indexes to patients' health records	Permanent
Operation index	10 years to permanent
Patient index	Permanent
Patients' health records	10 years after most recent care usage
Physician index	10 years
Surgery log	Permanent
Tumor registry files	Permanent

Reprinted with permission from *Healthcare Records: A Practical Legal Guide*. Copyright 1990, Healthcare Financial Management Association.

CERTIFICATE OF DESTRUCTION: RECORDS DESTROYED IN NORMAL COURSE OF BUSINESS

CERTIFICATE OF DESTRUCTION

DATE OF DESTRUCTION: ______________________________

METHOD: ______________________________

RECORDS DESTROYED:

PATIENT/CLIENT NAME	UNIT NUMBER

These records were destroyed in the normal course of business according to this facility's approved record retention schedule.

______________________________ Witness

______________________________ Director of Medical Records

Source: Joan Gratto Liebler, *Medical Records: Policies and Guidelines*, Aspen Publishers, Inc., © 1990.

RISK MANAGEMENT

REDUCING LOSS OF DATA IN A DISASTER

If you are a clinical data manager, floods, hurricanes, fires, and earthquakes are not the worst things that can happen to your valuable and proprietary data—not being prepared for those disasters is.

And while $75,000 diesel-powered backup systems and pricey chemical fire suppressant installations may not be viable or practical disaster preparedness strategies for many clinical data departments, many relatively inexpensive steps can be taken to help safeguard and prevent the total loss of data, beginning with the selection of the site that will house the practice and its data.

One certified disaster recovery planner says that having a comprehensive disaster plan in hand well before the unthinkable happens is a data manager's best defense, as panic and chaos often abound immediately before and after a disaster situation. In today's data-driven world, the loss of proprietary clinical data could be potentially more devastating than the loss of the structure that houses the practice.

The postdisaster environment is chaotic; it is extremely important to have a written plan in place and communicated throughout the organization before the disaster strikes. The written plan must be specific and detailed, yet be flexible enough to respond to a multitude of contingencies.

So how does a small medical practice or satellite facility prepare for what it hopes will never happen? Here are steps to developing a disaster plan to safeguard your data.

IDENTIFY AND PRIORITIZE RISKS

Before beginning to write the plan, it is important to identify and prioritize the disaster risks—flood, hurricane, earthquake tornado, and fire. It is important to have well-designed plans for disasters that could potentially strike your geographic area. For example, a practice in Florida would not rank earthquakes very high on the list of potential risks, but data managers in Southern California would.

Risk identification will help expand the disaster plan to respond to other disasters. It is also vital to identify the crucial areas of your business that must be operational for your business to survive.

Obviously, protection of the physical facility in which the practice is located is of utmost importance to securing and safeguarding the data. For flood protection, the most important factor is elevation, which is determined by the practice's site selection. For wind protection, the protection of the outside building envelope is crucial. Once wind punctures the outside structure of a building, the damage is rapidly spread through each floor that has been penetrated.

Small medical practices and satellite facilities of larger organizations typically are not located in stand-alone buildings. For that reason, it is important to coordinate a disaster plan with other building tenants.

IDENTIFY AND PRIORITIZE DATA

Because disasters usually do not come with fair warning, before developing an actual plan for backups, data storage, and possible file salvage, it is important to classify data into three categories:

1. *Vital.* Those records that, if destroyed, will result in a direct material financial loss or are absolutely essential to the continued life of the practice. These are generally irreplaceable, and in the clinical data sense include patient charts, electronic health records, and proprietary data that cannot be duplicated. Billing and accounts receivable records should also be included in this category.
2. *Important.* Those records that, if destroyed, will cause serious inconvenience or be expensive to replace. Important records are generally replaceable, although their replacement will result in a significant cost of time and money. Computer equipment serial numbers, insurance policy numbers, and agent's phone numbers are important because data gathering equipment may need to be replaced after a disaster. Fire can destroy the serial numbers on equipment.
3. *Useful.* Those records that, if destroyed, will cause a temporary inconvenience or minor expense to the business, such as reports or studies.

DEFINE DATA BACKUP AND STORAGE PROCEDURES

The procedures for and extent of storage—either off-site in a secured storage facility or in the office on a floppy disk—depend on the classification assigned to the data. Storage and backup procedures are also different for paper records than for electronic records.

Networking all the computers in an organization allows a central operation to save the information in one place for regular transfer to tape or a disk for off-site storage. Just five years ago, many large companies did not have a networked system and relied on each person with a PC to back up data regularly. Failure to do so regularly and correctly led to the complete loss of all clinical data files for many Florida practices in Hurricane Andrew.

As a result, many companies have invested in networked systems and a health information management specialist to properly safeguard the information. Simply backing up data files is not enough. They should be saved at the site, duplicated, and

continues

Reducing Loss of Data in a Disaster continued

geographically dispersed to a secure storage facility. There should be one person responsible for the backup, sending it in a batch file or on tape to a storage facility. This person should also be a key player in the disaster plan development.

There is no substitute for duplication and geographic dispersal of information. That is probably the single most important safeguard for your data.

But while electronic data can be backed up weekly, daily, or virtually instantaneously, vital clinical data that resides only in paper form requires another set of disaster planning procedures.

While it is not feasible or practical to duplicate paper records on a weekly or even a monthly basis, it is still important to have master copies stored in an off-site facility. Although these files may only be backed up one time each year, the potential data loss will be limited, as opposed to losing many years of clinical patient data.

Whether in electronic form or on paper, all duplicate data files should be stored in an off-site facility that specializes in safeguarding data. It is critical to have backups in a hardened container with safeguards against water, fire, wind, and power loss.

Following the 35-mile rule for geographic dispersal can help avert the destruction of both copies of the data. While it doesn't make sense to store backup information 35 miles upstream on the same river that tends to flood every few years, in general if backups are separated by about 35 miles, a major disaster will not completely destroy both sites.

FORM A DISASTER RECOVERY TEAM

With data prioritized and backup and storage procedures set, it is now time to establish a disaster management team. This team is composed of senior management personnel representing all of the important areas of the practice—clinical data records, billing, accounts receivable, and so forth.

In smaller practices, it is possible for one person to develop and update the plan; however, it is important to have one or two other employees completely familiar with it. The disaster management team is responsible for the development, rehearsal, and continual update of the plan. Several key team members should have master copies of the plan, and one should be stored at the hardened storage facility.

The team should also have preinterviewed and selected salvage vendors for paper records, electronic files, and equipment.

Contrary to popular belief, a flood may not completely destroy paper records. Specialized salvage vendors can use a process in which wet files are taken off-site, frozen, and thawed in temperature- and humidity-controlled locations. Water damage to computer equipment and disks can also be dealt with by specialized salvage vendors who dry, clean, and repair wet equipment.

But fire is by far the most devastating disaster, destroying paper files and melting and burning data gathering equipment and files. Smoke can severely damage computer equipment because it is highly corrosive.

While salvage vendors can be located in the phone book, it is important to have a list of several different types of recovery vendors on hand before a disaster strikes. The list should include salvage vendors in your immediate area and ones who are located further away. In a communitywide disaster, local salvage vendors are going to be in great demand.

WHAT TO LOOK FOR IN AN OFF-SITE STORAGE FACILITY

- *Structural integrity.* Make a site visit. Some places are built like fortresses and some are simply warehouses. The more solid the facility, the safer your data is going to be.
- *Retrieval procedures.* Ask the operator how files are retrieved. Is the system computerized? How long does it take to find and deliver files? What are the delivery services?
- *Paper record safeguards.* What types of water and flood protection does the facility have? How many square feet will your files require, and how will you be charged?
- *Electronic record safeguards.* Does the facility have a special vault for computerized equipment and records? Does the area have chemical fire suppressants, backup power, and temperature control? Are the staff capable of pulling and shipping backups to offsite emergency computer workstations in a satisfactory amount of time?

WHAT TO INCLUDE IN THE DISASTER PLAN

The disaster management plan should address the following areas:

- telephone lists of clients, patients, suppliers, employees, salvage vendors
- supplies to secure and protect the facility and data-gathering equipment
- fire safety and prevention
- review and rehearsal procedures
- postdisaster communications

Because disasters affect everyone at a facility, procedures should include input from all departments.

It is important to rehearse and practice the disaster plan. Make sure it works for everyone involved, make sure backup files are actually readable, and have drills in which all aspects of the disaster are simulated.

Source: "Planning and Preparedness Can Help Reduce the Loss of Data in a Disaster," *Clinical Data Management*, Vol. 3:7, Aspen Publishers, Inc., © 1996.

COMPANY XYZ LARGE AMBULATORY CARE CLINIC HEALTH INFORMATION DISASTER PLAN

Sample Outline for Flood within Facility during Operating Hours

ASSUMPTIONS

- During work hours
- No need to evacuate
- Emergency power available
- Flood restricted to basement in which health information management department located
- Clinic operational

PREVENTIVE MEASURES

- Retain dictation on disk for three months.
- Back up computerized files every evening.
- Turn off and unplug electrical equipment when contact with water is imminent.
- Seal room(s) to contain waters or employ strategies to protect information and equipment from water falling from above as appropriate.

HIGH-PRIORITY TASKS DURING EMERGENCY/ CONTAINMENT MEASURES

- Obtain portable phone.
- Notify other departments of situation and emergency protocols.
- Move records/equipment/storage media away from area being flooded; organize health information logically and label clearly for continued access.
- Respond to requests for records via portable phone rather than computer.
- Continue to provide patient charts as requested by units.

HIGH-PRIORITY DISASTER RECOVERY TASKS

- Contact fire, water, storm damage restoration company; contract for services as needed.
- Reconstruct/reacquire documents from
  - dictation system
  - word processing system
  - computer system
  - holders of document copies
- Move records and equipment back to home location.
- Catch up on filing.
- Document data that cannot be recovered in patient record.
- Meet with staff to identify opportunities for improvement.

Repeat process for other plausible disasters and hours when the department is not staffed.

Source: Nancy A. Davis, "Security and Safeguarding of Health and Hospital Information," *Journal of AHIMA*, Vol. 67:4, American Health Information Management Association, © 1996.

COMPANY XYZ LARGE AMBULATORY CARE CLINIC HEALTH INFORMATION DISASTER PLAN STAFF COMPETENCE CHECKLIST

STAFF COMPETENCY CHECKLIST

	Yes	No
1. Staff member demonstrates familiarity with the disaster manual by quickly locating various disaster protocols and emergency phone numbers.	____	____
2. Staff member can articulate methods of protecting health information and equipment from rising and falling water.	____	____
3. Staff member accurately demonstrates retrieval and use of portable phone.	____	____
4. Staff member correctly identifies those individuals who must be notified in case of disaster.	____	____
5. Staff member accurately verbalizes transportation and storage options for relocating equipment and health information.	____	____
6. Staff member accurately verbalizes the emergency protocols to be communicated to units.	____	____
7. Staff member accurately identifies responsibilities in case of disaster.	____	____

Add additional criteria as indicated for other plausible disasters.

Source: Nancy A. Davis, "Security and Safeguarding of Health and Hospital Information," *Journal of AHIMA*, Vol. 67:4, American Health Information Management Association, © 1996.

6
Quality Improvement

Chapter 6

Quality Improvement

QUALITY IMPROVEMENT AND BENCHMARKING ISSUES

BUILDING A QUALITY IMPROVEMENT PROGRAM AROUND PATIENT CARE

Changes occurring in the health care industry are substantive and constitute a paradigm shift in thinking and behaving. Moving from vertically organized hospitals and concern for *a* department or unit to horizontally organized, integrated health care systems with accountability for cost-effective patient care outcomes across the continuum of health care requires commitment, flexibility, speed, and a thorough understanding of the momentum that is driving the industry. This new way of thinking and behaving requires a learning organization—that is, leaders with a vision of the continual development of the organization, its people, its capabilities, and its capacity to enhance or to create its own future.

Learning Organizations

A learning organization is on a continual mission with

- a strong sense of shared vision (coauthored by people at the top and on the front lines who are able to articulate their actual work contribution toward the same goal)
- people who are open to new ideas and perspectives and valued for their opinions (legitimate disagreements can be shared)
- a genuine sense of curiosity that is congruent and diffused throughout the organization
- an ability to produce extraordinary results (a natural byproduct of learning)

Learning organizations delve into the hard work of surfacing the deep-rooted assumptions about how they organize and how the work gets done, hence challenging the existing culture.

Two complementary methods of advancing learning in an organization are total quality management (TQM) and systems thinking. The value of TQM, a philosophical approach to participatory management, is in operational learning—the methods, tools, and processes that can be used to examine the complexity of a problem or issue needing improvement. Systems thinking promotes a larger, whole-system perspective of the interconnectedness of an issue with other parts of a system. These two methods are required if an organization intends to make the transformation from the traditional quality assurance (QA) driven by accreditation and regulatory requirements to reorganizing quality management around patient care, resulting in cross-functional, clinical, and operational processes that are integrated and work seamlessly across the system.

A successful quality improvement (QI) program is flexible, effective, and efficient in monitoring and improving patient care and professional practice. The design of such a program demands fundamental and sweeping changes in existing philosophies and work processes. It requires a well-conceived vision of an organization's expected future before the organization systematically plans well-defined goals and objectives, assesses existing activities, and develops an integrated quality process that will successfully improve operations and performance consistent with the needs and expectations of consumers, professionals, and regulatory, accrediting, and reimbursement bodies. The QI program recognizes that quality, cost, and access are interrelated and are included in the strategic planning process.

Strategic Planning: Building a QI Program around Patient Care

Although strategic planning and a QI program are not synonymous, they are intimately linked. Leaders in an organization who are developing a strategic plan must also be involved with the quality improvement council. These leaders are responsible for changing an organization's strategic and operational systems to match the new QI structure. Quality must be incorporated into the organization's overall vision and mission statements; a separate statement regarding quality is perceived as an add-on program and not part of daily work.

Planning a QI program requires knowledge of what constitutes quality and time to process the implications so that organizational and professional prerogatives can be balanced. As consumers both internal and external to the organization place added value and emphasis on quality issues, an effective strategic vision must go beyond just understanding quality concepts to believing in the absolute necessity for continually improving. Dual directionality must be evident in a QI program; governing boards and top management must live the philosophy of TQM from the top down; every other member of the organization must believe and participate from the bottom up. TQM requires a continuous quality improvement (CQI) mentality in the total process of providing patient care.

In building the concept of quality into every aspect of an organization's business, day-to-day work meshes with strategic planning; strategic quality planning takes traditional QA and the need for measurement and integrates QA with CQI. Although QA and QI are not synonymous, their relationship is symbiotic. The measurement of quality is one step in the QI process; monitoring quality of care and performance indicators that suggest potential problems may exist should result in recommendations for improving care and performance. QA programs should be incorporated into the structure of the organization's QI program. QI supports and enhances the measurement of key clinical processes and outcomes (QA); it also includes financial and other operational data and works in concert with strategic planning and other sources to improve the overall quality of patient care. "Comparing QA and QI" compares and contrasts some of the similarities and differences between the two.

Assessing an Existing Quality Program: Readiness for Change

To survive the rapid global changes, organizations must constantly rethink their assumptions about society, the community of customers, their values and mission, their core competencies, their competitors, their markets, technology, and their strengths and weaknesses. Their theory of business must mirror current reality. Acknowledging the many approaches to CQI, all organizations share the premise that producing high quality requires leaders who are committed to and involved in improvement efforts, front-line employees who are empowered to identify and solve quality problems, and caregivers who are trained in CQI methods.

The challenges of CQI activities arise from the interplay of dynamic processes that can be framed in relation to four dimensions: technical, cultural, strategic, and structural. The *technical dimensions* include training in CQI techniques and tools, data collection and analysis, decision making, and a comprehensive understanding of how daily work is produced and delivered. The *cultural dimension* involves the beliefs, values, norms, and behaviors exhibited in everyday work that demonstrate a commitment to a shared purpose—patient care, teamwork, and cooperation in formal and informal social interactions and in the systems used to reward performance. The *strategic dimension* links the organization's key strategic priorities—core clinical and administrative processes, competencies, and capabilities—and its CQI efforts. The *structural dimension* encompasses specific organizational structures and systems such as committee structures, information systems for data gathering and analysis, and mechanisms for promoting continuous learning.

Quality activities exist in every organization, department, or service. However, the comprehensiveness of a program, its effectiveness, and its efficiency need to be periodically reviewed and evaluated. The availability, acceptability, and appropriateness of staff, facilities, and support need analysis. The concept of quality assessment/assurance (QAA)—that is, the measurement of the level of care provided and the mechanisms to improve it—must be clearly and personally defined, implemented, and evaluated. Assessing the QI program will help prevent organizations from becoming complacent with the status quo, from not fostering opportunities for innovation and misappropriating human resources.

Although the assessment analysis of a program may take many forms, several questions must be answered when examining the program's purpose, scope, and effectiveness in fostering the approach to continually improving quality.

- Are the leaders in the organization intimately involved in the quality program (i.e., are leaders members of the QI council or cross-functional teams)?
- Is there a clearly written QI plan beginning with a succinctly articulated vision statement?
- Based on the vision statement, does the stated philosophy or mission drive comprehensive, realistic, measurable, and achievable goals and objectives within available resources?
- Do the philosophy and mission statements meet all of the requirements of various internal and external review bodies (i.e., consumers, professional organizations, accrediting agencies, and state and national governments)?
- Does the program articulate systems thinking, a complete cycle that begins with problem identification and promotes sustained problem resolution with continuous improvement?
- Are all resources and support systems appropriately coordinated and used?
- Are roles and responsibilities defined in terms of integrated strategies and quality-related goals (i.e., are authority, accountability, and confidentiality clearly designated)?
- Does the patient care or support system of concern need to be reengineered from scratch, or can it be redesigned and improved through incremental change (CQI)?
- What program strengths can be enhanced?
- What program weaknesses require improvement?

Human attitudes and perceptions make or break an organization's efforts to improve quality. Although a program may include all the technical elements, its effectiveness and efficiency can be limited by misunderstanding and lack of true involvement and commitment. When conducted anonymously, an assessment tool may more honestly reveal hidden rejection or minimal or full support regarding CQI. (*See* "QI Program Assessment" form.) A tool, designed to elicit a yes/no response with an expectation for comments, should be distributed to all people in the organization and to critical and involved external consumers for education regarding the intent of the QI program as well as for assessment purposes.

Everyone owns the organization's QI program. By challenging the current processes, everyone becomes involved, not just as part of the problem, but as part of the solution. Understanding the intent of the QI program is essential to setting priorities consistent with the strategic plan and the organization's core functions and processes.

The aggregate data will identify perceptions of purpose and scope of program, activities that are performed effectively, and those requiring strengthening. Perceptions of overlap in authority and responsibility, duplication in efforts, and approaches for enhancing integration and coordination of activities can provide valuable opportunities for clarification and education. An assessment of what exists will provide the basis for designing a well-defined, comprehensively organized QI plan to objectively measure and improve patient care and professional practice.

Designing a QI Program

When key leaders in an organization are educated in the principles of TQM and CQI, and managers and all employees become comfortable with the team approach to studying opportunities for improvement, quality becomes an integrated way of managing. The acceptance that the goal of quality programs is to continually improve processes, products, and services is critical; avoid finger-pointing and the bad apple syndrome. Avoid useless and meaningless jargon! The language used to reflect that commitment is important only to the degree that it has meaning for everyone involved. Whether TQM, CQI, QI, QA, QAA, quality resource management (QRM), or some other term or acronym is used to reflect an organization's commitment to its internal customers (i.e., all employees) and external customers (e.g., patients, physicians, members of the business community, accrediting and other review bodies, third-party payers) to continually examine processes for the purpose of improving is of less importance than achieving consensus so that all individuals are committed and willing to expend the time, energy, and resources necessary to provide a system of accountability.

Assuming that every process can be improved, there is a shared responsibility by all employees to build quality into every service; no one person, department, or discipline alone is responsible. Although traditional quality activities have been perceived primarily as an oversight concept designed to enhance public accountability, a comprehensive, integrated QI program will always require *professional clinical judgment* as well as the *consumer's perception* of care or a service to successfully improve operations and performance by removing waste and unpredictability, and to comply with regulatory, accrediting, and payer entities.

Adopting CQI methods as the foundation of a solid, ongoing quality program requires a long-term commitment; the process is evolutionary and requires significant resources and time. A passion for improving quality and a change in culture may not really occur for 1, 3, 5 or even 10 years. Information alone, knowing the jargon, and a desire to "do good" will not automatically bring about immediate change. A learning culture in which risk and pilot projects are expected and supported takes time to evolve. A cultural change within the organization requires a philosophy and policy change that communicates commitment and direction to employees and external customers.

Vision

The Joint Commission on Accreditation of Healthcare Organizations (Joint Commission) has emphasized that the role of leader involves clinical leaders and staff managers as well as the governing body, chief executive officer, and other senior managers. Together, this body must develop a vision that

- is based on an organization's core business—why it exists
- is brief, succinct, tied to individual motivation, challenging but achievable, and explicit in the mission statement
- drives the organization's mission and goals—where the company is, and where it should go
- addresses internal and external consumers' needs and expectations
- respects everyone's knowledge and contribution to the CQI process
- eliminates barriers between services and disciplines to enhance team building and promote communication and uses a scientific approach to problem solving
- requires ongoing education and training
- expects performance measures consistent with organizational and professional goals
- requires quality to be built into the process, which reduces process variation and emphasizes prevention rather than inspection

The organization's culture as reflected in its mission statement encourages employees to be proactive and outcome oriented, identifying the outcome and working backward through structure and processes that increase efficiency, productivity, and profitability. The mission statement of a fully integrated system guides the organization's activities relating to

- *people:* the creation of an environment that attracts, retains, and supports the development of people who share the organization's values and culture
- *customers:* clear evidence that service is of demonstrated value for patients, families, physicians, payers, and purchasers
- *community:* improvement of the health status of the communities the organization serves
- *system integration:* positioning the organization to be successful in the changing health care industry
- *finances:* increasing the organization's financial strength

Goals/Objectives

All quality activities support the accomplishment of goals, which are stated in relatively broad but measurable terms, address rights of patients to maximum health care, reduce liability, and expect proper use of resources by competent practitioners. The statement of purpose in the QI plan may incorporate these goals.

Objectives, derived from the program's goals and written in specific, measurable terms, are related to the eventual achievement of the goals. Objectives may address the achievement of an optimum level of care in a cost-effective and safe manner, compliance with specific standards governing practice, methodologies used, and integration with other processes and programs. Goals and objectives may periodically change. New ones are set as old ones are achieved or become inappropriate as the organization assumes new directions.

Once goals and objectives are established for the organization's QI program, each discipline, service, or product can determine its unique methods and approaches to achieving the overall goals and objectives, recognizing the needed interrelatedness with others to serve and improve the outcomes for their populations. Program goals and objectives provide the concrete basis for evaluating the status of all existing quality activities as well as providing a foundation for future quality initiatives. Such initiatives will be implemented through strategic quality planning, quality assurance/quality control, and other QI improvements, using a consistent methodology such as Shewhart-Deming's Plan-Do-Check-Act (PDCA); the Hospital Corporation of America's FOCUS-PDCA, which added to the Shewhart-Deming cycle; Juran's Trilogy: quality planning, quality control/quality assurance, and QI; Donabedian's structure, process, outcome model; or another methodology that provides a useful QI framework.

Standards

Because each health care organization is different in purpose, size, and resources, its QI program should reflect its uniqueness. It should use the data gathered from an extensive assessment, as well as the appropriate standards and suggested formats established by various review bodies, including the Joint Commission; the National Committee for Quality Assurance (NCQA); professional organizations such as the National League for Nursing Community Health Accreditation Program and Benchmarks for Excellence in Home Care; governmental groups such as Medicare (OASIS) and Medicaid (the NCQA Health Plan Employer Data and Information Set [HEDIS 3.0]); and other applicable standards. The National Library of Healthcare Indicators (NLHI) has been developed by the Joint Commission to complement the measures developed by the Agency for Health Care Policy and Research (AHCPR) and its recently established indicator typology initiative known as CONQUEST (a computerized needs-oriented quality measurement evaluation system); NLHI is focused on supporting QI activities in relation to the accreditation process.

In addition to the preceding standards, the Malcolm Baldrige National Quality Award, which is given to organizations that best exemplify QI, has had a sustained impact. The International Standards Organization (ISO) has produced the ISO 9000 and ISO 14001 series of quality management and quality assurance standards. These standards apply to any organization doing business in the international market. Business and industry are examining organization performance in the areas of customer satisfaction, market share and profitability, quality and cost, and employee relations. Thus, these organizations are expecting the same scrutiny of health care organizations.

Source: Claire Gavin Meisenheimer, *Improving Quality: A Guide to Effective Programs*, 2nd ed., Aspen Publishers, Inc., © 1997.

COMPARING QA AND QI

QUALITY ASSURANCE	QUALITY IMPROVEMENT
Is coordinator/committee driven	Has prepared leaders; is management/team driven; has QI council support; everyone is accountable
Is problem and people focused	Is processes and systems focused
Is reactive; inspects for quality; quality costs not emphasized	Is proactive; builds in quality up front; quality costs are emphasized
Has limited customer input; has regulatory compliance	Is customer driven: internal, external
Is monitoring and measurement driven; has unit-based and multidisciplinary QA committees	Has involved/knowledgeable teams; has cross-functional teams
Identifies scope and aspects of care	Has defined QI initiative (precedes organizing a team)
Establishes indicators and thresholds	Establishes indicators; clarifies current knowledge of QI initiative and process
Focuses on outliers, special causes	Theorizes reasons for defects in the system; strives for improvement by reducing common causes
Monitors care by collecting and organizing data for each indicator; rudimentarily uses statistical methods	Goes beyond collecting data for each indicator; uncovers root causes of variation; considers/implements solutions; collects data; uses analytical and statistical process control (SPC) tools
Evaluates care against thresholds; identifies areas to improve	Compares data with theory; benchmarks/identifies best practices; addresses resistance to change
Takes action to improve care	Implements solutions to improve care/systems
Assesses effectiveness of actions; documents improvement	Assesses effectiveness of system; checks performance and lessons learned
Communicates results	Communicates results; monitors control system (acts to hold gain); continues to improve system

Source: Claire Gavin Meisenheimer, *Improving Quality: A Guide to Effective Programs*, 2nd ed., Aspen Publishers, Inc., © 1997.

QI PROGRAM ASSESSMENT

Dear Members of the ______________________________ Organization/Agency:

Your input is critical in assessing our *current* quality improvement plan. As you know, quality improvement—the ongoing measurement of key processes and outcomes, in conjunction with strategic planning and other sources to improve clinical and administrative performance—is only as effective as we make it.

Please place an X in the Yes/No columns *with* explanations or suggestions of **who, what, where, how,** and/or **when** in the Comments column.

	Yes	No	Comments
• Does our organization's culture: 1. demonstrate commitment from leaders and foster our vision?			
2. exhibit transformational leadership by using systems thinking and processes and shared governance behaviors throughout the organization?			
3. promote total quality management (TQM) in our customer-driven strategic planning?			
4. emphasize continuous quality improvement (CQI) as a key value in our philosophy/mission, goals, and objectives?			
5. create a constancy of purpose in aligning our philosophy/mission statement, goals, and objectives with services and programs?			
6. link all quality initiatives with the strategic plan, budget, policies, and procedures? (Are quality efforts integral or parallel to the daily workings of the organization?)			
7. value the uniqueness and contributions of all individuals in the organization; all are treated equally?			
8. support an integrated network with a cross-functional team approach; go beyond the traditional boundaries in learning to build patient-centered integrated models of care versus professional-centered models of care?			
9. provide a human resources program that supports interdependent teamwork and a customer focus on the basis of the performance evaluation and compensation system?			
10. value learning and risk taking with adequate resources?			
11. provide adequate human and technical resources to define, capture, statistically analyze, and report useful, understandable data?			
12. communicate how best practice strategies and benchmarking significantly impact our competitive strategies?			
13. encourage replicating internal and external successful practices across the organization to accelerate the rate of improvement?			

continues

QI Program Assessment continued

	Yes	No	Comments
14. understand the culture of our competitors; suppliers?			
• Does our quality improvement (QI) plan 15. use an understandable framework?			
16. state our quality vision?			
17. clearly define our goals that stretch us, with achievable objectives?			
18. outline our program's scope of care and services?			
19. identify person(s) or position(s) responsible for coordinating/facilitating the program?			
20. describe our QI council: purpose, functions, membership, roles?			
21. address the issue of responsibility and authority?			
22. delineate lines of communication including reporting mechanisms?			
23. address confidentiality?			
24. delineate the approach to measuring dimensions of performance related to functions, processes, and outcomes?			
25. include a plan for periodic evaluation?			
• As a result of *our* QI efforts, do *you* think: 26. *all* employees support and can articulate our organization's core values and culture?			
27. *all* employees can describe the CQI process and how it is working?			
28. we use QI language appropriately (no meaningless jargon/buzzwords)?			
29. we appropriately use standards established by: –professional organizations?			
–Joint Commission on Accreditation of Healthcare Organizations, National Committee for Quality Assurance, National League for Nursing Community Health Accreditation Program, and other voluntary accrediting bodies?			
–state and/or federal government (i.e., Medicare, Medicaid, Agency for Health Care Policy and Research, etc.)?			
30. care plans, clinical guidelines, and caremaps are written and used well across the continuum of services?			
31. critical processes are known and continuously improved?			
32. *you* have assumed greater ownership of the work structures and the CQI processes (more self-motivated, self-managed, patient-focused versus professionally self-focused); (feeling empowered)?			
33. *your* practice has improved, including patient outcomes?			

continues

QI Program Assessment continued

	Yes	No	Comments
34. ways to document patient care, including patient/family involvement, have improved?			
35. we have eliminated professional and service organizational barriers/boundaries to achieve the necessary integrated work processes?			
36. staff performance appraisals are linked to job descriptions, expected competencies, and realistic performance outcomes?			
37. we competently ensure patient and staff safety including reducing the risk of infection?			
38. patient and family education has been enhanced, fostering relevant and improved outcomes?			
39. internal and external customer satisfaction has increased; needs and expectations are met?			
40. we use our QI program to improve clinical and administrative performance and to minimize costs and other resource consumption?			
41. risks of litigation for our organization have decreased?			
42. we value learning and self-development: orientation, continuing education, and competency systems work well?			
43. we use our QI data as a marketing strategy?			
44. your involvement with state, federal, and voluntary surveyors/accreditors has been helpful to our QI efforts?			
45. we evaluate our performance improvement requirements, successes, and lessons learned on (at least) an annual basis?			
• Additional Comments:			
Name and Service (Optional)			

Source: Claire Gavin Meisenheimer, *Improving Quality: A Guide to Effective Programs*, 2nd ed., Aspen Publishers, Inc., © 1997.

BENCHMARKING

What Is Benchmarking?

Benchmarking is the sharing of performance information to identify the operational and clinical practices that lead to the best outcomes. Health care groups begin by measuring each other's operating data, identifying the best performer out of a group, then adapting the practices that make that performer the best. Benchmarking provides the participants with the guidance they need to make informed decisions among a group of clinical and administrative options.

Benchmarking is both a project and a process. As a project it is a one-time event; as a process it is continual and integrated into the culture and daily operations of the institution. Team members get most of the value out of benchmarking by understanding day-to-day operations. As we will see, leading organizations involve front-line management and physicians in the process. This involvement is more than a passive review; they gain understanding of the factors that will create excellence in their own organizations.

Benchmarking is a comparison process that becomes a hunt for new opportunities for improvement within health care organizations. If we recognize that each health care institution is a mosaic of clinical, operational, and administrative processes, we will understand that the term *best* can only be applied on a piecemeal basis. We can be very good at one piece and very bad at another. Each organization, even the best, will always have some activities that fall short of highest performance. This raises the first barrier to effective benchmarking—it points out poor performance. In today's litigious environment, identifying a gap can raise questions about the competence of physicians, the effectiveness of the hospitals, and the motivation of the managed care provider.

The Joint Commission on Accreditation of Healthcare Organizations (Joint Commission) is currently working on this issue. It is adding a focus on comparative analysis and an understanding of performance gaps to its requirements for hospital accreditation. The obvious risk is that process improvement can actually become punitive in nature. If so, the great advantages of improvement may be lost by creating the very information that it requires to improve. The Joint Commission therefore does not consider poor outcomes in themselves to *disqualify* an organization from accreditation. Instead it looks for internal processes that seek to identify poor performance and to find processes that raise the performance levels of each institution.

Report carding is currently a hot topic in the medical profession. There are increasing concerns related to the economic credentialing of physicians and the impact that the focus on money will have on the quality of health care in this country. The argument presumes that cost and quality are always correlated. While benchmarking we will seek solutions that push the envelope to improve both cost and quality. We will see findings that cost nothing to implement while improving overall performance significantly.

Measuring performance becomes the first step in the analysis we call benchmarking. By identifying the gap between your performance and others, you can then peel back the layers of an organization to understand the processes that drive excellence.

Why Benchmark?

The changing environment dictates changes in ourselves. Change should be a normal part of the process of running a hospital or a medical practice. While the apprenticeship system in the medical profession propagates procedures from preceding generations, we should be aware that change is ongoing, whether or not we individually choose to participate. Therefore, when debating whether we want to benchmark, we need to be aware of philosophies and concerns that drive improvement

- *We should want to improve.* A basic premise of competition is that the providers of the highest quality and lowest cost services will win. The Japanese have been demonstrating the impact of improved products and services for a number of years. The health care community is rapidly feeling the impact of competition on a regional level.
- *We should understand our own performance levels.* A second premise guides peer review efforts in health care—we need to understand where we have performance shortfalls. Without an understand of our own performance gaps, we cannot work to improve our efforts at delivering the quality and cost demanded by the environment.
- *Regulators focus on hospitals.* Federal and state regulators are increasing their efforts to stem the growth of health care costs. As a result, efforts like the state health care cost-containment initiatives are forcing individual hospitals to provide information to a central database of clinically oriented cost and outcomes statistics. These data will eventually be used to select providers as well as to drive improvement.
- *Competition continues to increase.* The rapid growth of the health care infrastructure and excess capacity in the United States has led to increased marketing efforts for many health care products and services. Almost on a weekly basis we see mergers among health care institutions.
- *The environment is conducive to exchanging information.* The growth and successes of benchmarking in industrial settings have led to a greater acceptance of the concept. Since organizations have been willing to ex-

change information and the results have been well documented, the health care community is more prepared to follow the same steps for self-improvement.
- *Managed care organizations are evaluating the effectiveness of health care providers.*

Managed care organizations also require that physicians and other health care providers work together to provide patients with high-quality and cost-effective care. The traditional orientation and training of physicians and the goals and functioning of managed care organizations are frequently in conflict. Managing and resolving this clash of cultures is a unique opportunity and challenge for the physician-manager in managed care. The physician's need for autonomy must be reconciled with the organization's need for structure, control, and accountability. The physician's need to use skills to improve patients' health must be reconciled with the organization's need to use expensive services only when they are of proven added value. Lastly, physicians must alter their orientation to practice autonomously so that they can be part of an efficient and effective team that collaboratively delivers care to patients.

As an example of how physicians must change their orientation from autonomous practice to being part of a team, consider an internist working in a traditional multispecialty group who refers a newly diagnosed diabetic patient with an infected toe to an emergency room (ER). The patient is admitted to the hospital for intravenous antibiotics. After discharge, the internist sends the patient to an endocrinologist to receive more instruction on maintaining adequate glucose control and to a podiatrist to receive instruction on foot care.

In an efficient managed care plan, the internist evaluates the patient in the office and arranges for a physician's assistant to start an intravenous line to administer antibiotics. An office supervisor arranges home intravenous antibiotic therapy. The internist starts the patient on insulin and then refers the patient to a diabetes class to learn about the disease and the specifics of diet, insulin use, and the importance of proper foot care. Finally, the internist might arrange for a colleague to reevaluate the patient in the office the next day if the internist is unavailable.

To be successful, then, physician-managers must effectively span the two cultures and reconcile the conflicts. They do this by empowering physicians and other health care professionals to maintain control over their professional lives despite the need for accountability and structure. Physician-managers do this in several ways. They encourage clinicians and their staff to innovate and create new methods of organizing their clinical practices; these methods further the mission of their organizations while simultaneously meeting their individual needs. They work collaboratively with physicians and managers to build efficient systems that support the delivery of high-quality and cost-effective care. Finally, they foster teamwork among health care providers, staff, and nonclinical managers.

Source: Mark T. Czarnecki, *Benchmarking Strategies for Health Care Management*, Aspen Publishers, Inc., 1995. Copyright © The Benchmarking Network, Inc., Houston, Texas.

PROFESSIONAL PRACTICE STANDARDS OF THE AMERICAN HEALTH INFORMATION MANAGEMENT ASSOCIATION—QUALITY ASSURANCE FUNCTION

EXTERNAL REQUIREMENTS AND STANDARDS			
Monitor External Regulations	**Yes**	**No**	**Comments**
Are copies of the most current regulations and requirements available to the health record staff? Does a process exist to identify proposed changes in current regulations from: • Joint Commission on Accreditation of Healthcare Organizations? • HCFA (Medicaid/Medicare)? • State? • Local Board of Health?			
Is the procedure for commenting on proposed regulations understood?			
When there is a comment period for revision of regulations, does the health information management specialist participate?			
Does the health record management staff read journals that cover changes in external regulations related to health care?			
Interpret Regulations	**Yes**	**No**	**Comments**
Does the health management information specialist have a direct relationship with administration, medical staff, and others involved in regulation interpretation for the institution?			
Is a mechanism available to update hospital and medical staff policies to reflect changes in external regulations and standards?			
Implement Regulations	**Yes**	**No**	**Comments**
Is there a mechanism to revise institutional policies and procedures when regulations and standards change?			
Has implementation of revised procedures been scheduled to coincide with the time when regulations become effective?			
Are policies and procedures sufficiently detailed to ensure regulatory compliance?			
Are employees and other members of the health care team sufficiently trained to comply?			
Is there a mechanism to evaluate effectiveness of the policy or procedure?			
Personnel Training	**Yes**	**No**	**Comments**
Have inservice programs related to changes in external requirements and standards been presented?			
Have appropriate staff members attended workshops dealing with recently enacted external regulations that affect the facility and/or the department?			
Are external opportunities for training with reference to external regulations publicized in the department?			
Is the opportunity to attend outside educational programs provided for technical personnel?			

continues

Professional Practice Standards of the AHIMA—Quality Assurance Function continued

QUALITY ASSURANCE SYSTEMS			
Policies and Procedures	**Yes**	**No**	**Comments**
Does the health information management specialist strengthen and update knowledge of quality assurance issues by: • reading appropriate publications? • attending seminars?			
Does the health information management specialist participate in the facilitywide quality assurance program?			
When documentation in health records reveals a potential problem in health care delivery, is the proper course of action followed to notify appropriate parties?			
Are the medical staff and ancillary departments encouraged to contribute to problem identification and quality assurance activities?			
Does the health information management specialist suggest changes to improve and update institutional policies and medical staff bylaws rules and regulations?			
Health Information Management Specialist's Role	**Yes**	**No**	**Comments**
Is the health information management specialist willing to assume responsibility for managing the quality assurance program?			
Does the health information management specialist offer expertise in various areas of benefit to the quality assurance program? • data collection/analysis? • evaluation techniques? • utilization review? • communications? • organization and administration? • health care legislation?			
Does a representative of the health record management staff actively participate on the quality assurance committee?			
Quality Assurance Data	**Yes**	**No**	**Comments**
Is the health record department involved in data gathering and control, screening health records, establishing criteria, and other activities related to the overall hospital quality assurance program?			
Is a schedule established so departmental quality assurance-related activities are completed in a timely manner?			
Are verification checks performed to ensure the accuracy of reports documenting quality assurance activities?			
Are written policies regarding release of quality assurance data available?			
Are quality assurance data stored securely?			
Data Collection	**Yes**	**No**	**Comments**
Do present data collection activities promote data reliability?			

continues

Professional Practice Standards of the AHIMA—Quality Assurance Function continued

QUALITY ASSURANCE SYSTEMS			
Is the reliability of data collected for utilization review and quality assurance purposes continually reviewed?			
Are the most efficient sources identified and used for quality assurance data collection?			
Do the present data collection activities reduce duplication of effort?			
Are quality assurance data collected in a manner that reduces data redundancy?			
Are quality assurance data collected in a cost-effective manner?			
Quality Assurance of Health Record Documentation	**Yes**	**No**	**Comments**
Does a mechanism exist whereby those responsible for the quality assurance program are notified of problems with health record documentation and/or content?			
Is appropriate follow-up conducted when problems related to the content and/or documentation in health records are brought to the attention of those responsible for the quality assurance program?			
When the health record service takes action to correct content and documentation problems, does the quality assurance program give support?			
Personnel Training	**Yes**	**No**	**Comments**
Does staff orientation stress the importance of quality assurance?			
Are employees encouraged to suggest areas for quality controls?			
Are external opportunities for programs on quality assurance publicized in the department?			
Are quality assurance efforts discussed in departmental meetings?			
Do inservice programs include results of quality assurance activities?			
Cost/Benefit Analysis	**Yes**	**No**	**Comments**
Is the quality assurance program sufficiently staffed to meet the needs of the institution?			
Is the cost of providing quality assurance services identified and evaluated as reasonable and appropriate?			
Are the consequences of maintaining a poor quality assurance program identified and an action plan for improvement developed?			
Is quality assurance documentation adequate to fulfill Joint Commission requirements?			

Source: *Professional Practice Standards*, American Health Information Management Association, Chicago, Illinois, © 1984.

OPPORTUNITY FOR IMPROVEMENT FORM

☐ Patient care improvement opportunity
☐ Business/administrative process improvement opportunity (nonclinical areas)
☐ Risk management/safety/equipment improvement opportunity

Describe Situation:

____
____
____
____
____
____

Suspected Cause of This Situation:

____
____
____

Correcting This Situation Will Result in Improvements in the Major Function of:
(Check all that apply.)

☐ Rights of patients
☐ Assessment of patients
☐ Entry to setting or service
☐ Nutritional care of patients
☐ Treatment of patients
☐ Use of medications
☐ Use of blood/blood products
☐ Operative and other invasive procedures
☐ Education of patients and family
☐ Coordination of care
☐ Information management
☐ Human resources management
☐ Managing the patient care environment
☐ Prevention and control of infections

Person Preparing Report ________________ Date _______ Dept ________

Disposition by Quality Council:

☐ Return to originator for more information.
☐ File for later consideration; situation not reflective of current quality improvement priorities.
☐ Intradepartmental improvement opportunity; referred to __________ Department.
☐ Interdepartmental improvement opportunity; referred to __________ Team/Committee.
☐ Other: ____________________

Date of disposition: ________________

Source: Patrice Spath, *AIMing for Quality Results: An Improvement Primer for Healthcare Organizations*, Forest Grove, OR, © Brown-Spath & Associates, 1994.

QUALITY MONITORING REPORT

HEALTH RECORDS QUALITY MONITORING REPORT
(or Department Performance Indicators)

	Comparison figure *or* benchmark	month 1	month 2	month 3
Coding/Abstracting (total # records)				
% of coding errors (acceptable range ____% to ____%)				
% of abstracting errors (acceptable range ____% to ____%)				
% of records requiring re-abstracting/recoding (acceptable range_____% to _____%)				
% of records not coded or abstracted within ______ days of discharge				
Filing/Retrieving (total # records)				
% of records not pulled within				
_____ minutes of a clinical request				
_____ hours of a reimbursement request				
_____ days of a legal request				
_____ hours of a patient's request				
# records misplaced for > 30 days				
# orphaned (loose) documents that require filing				
Transcription #/% histories and physicals, operative reports transcribed within 24 hours				
#/% STAT reports transcribed within 24 hours				
#/% errors in transcribed reports				
#/% blanks left in transcribed reports				
Release of Information (total # requests)				
#/% requests not responded to within: 24 or 48 hours, 1 week, 2 weeks, etc.				
#/% second requests				
#/% complaints regarding release of information				
#/% of compliments				
Customer Service #/% complaints from: • patients				
• physicians				
• third parties				
#/% compliments from • patients				
• physicians				
• third parties				
Customer satisfaction index (based on formal or informal surveys) (acceptable range _____% to _____%)				

continues

Quality Monitoring Report continued

Management	**Comparison figure *or* benchmark**	**month 1**	**month 2**	**month 3**
Average # sick days for all employees (acceptable range ____% to ____%)				
% overtime/regular hours (acceptable range _____% to _____%) (standard is < 2%)				
Employee turnover				
% resigned				
% fired				
% hired				
% performance appraisals done on time (acceptable range ____% to ____%)				

Other Department Indicators

What indicators in your department provide meaningful information on the quality level of the services provided?

____

____

____

Source: Jennifer I. Cofer, *Continuous Quality Improvement for Health Information Management*, Opus Communications, Inc., Marblehead, MA, © 1998.

7
Department Management

Chapter 7

Department Management

THE MANAGEMENT PROCESS

THE PLANNING PROCESS

Introduction

The most critical step in the planning process is the actual implementation once a decision on the direction to take has been made. All too often an excellent plan will be developed through use of a comprehensive structured process only to fail miserably because of a lack of commitment to implementation.

Daily Informal Planning

Managers perform a level of informal planning daily. They plan work schedules for themselves and their subordinates. They set goals and objectives, identify alternative strategies to achieve these, and then select from among the available alternatives. The key is that most management-level employees perform some level of planning daily and these microplanning activities, when aggregated with all other activities, help determine the long-term success or failure of any organization.

With this as a background, it is easy to understand why many organizations never come close to achieving their full potential. Employees at all levels in an organization often do not recognize their importance to the overall success of an enterprise, and management frequently does a poor job of communicating and reinforcing this concept. The result is a general lack of attention to detail. What is needed is for each employee to take pride in his or her work and act and make decisions as if it were his or her own organization.

Managers fail to recognize that operating a successful organization requires attention to countless details, all of which are important and all of which must be addressed. A manager will identify a strategic project and undertake the work necessary to evaluate the alternatives available, eventually choosing the most appropriate one. Over time, however, new projects arise and are granted a higher priority than existing projects. Additionally, daily operational "emergencies" prevent managers from following through on special projects.

The manager must assume the responsibility of implementing the project (plan) initiated. He or she should be rewarded for successful completion of the project. Lack of success should be dealt with in a manner consistent with the guiding principles and philosophies of the employer.

Ensuring Successful Implementation

To ensure successful implementation of a project, certain questions should be answered before implementation begins. These questions include the following:

- What is to be accomplished and why?
- What specific (sequential) steps need to be completed and by whom?

- When will steps be started and completed?
- What resources (dollars, people, etc.) are needed?

The manager should identify in writing the task to be accomplished and its importance. This will provide him or her with the ability to refer to the underlying reasons for initially undertaking the project. Additionally, documenting the reasoning behind the project will enable others to understand the rationale behind making the decision in the first place.

In addition, the manager should evaluate and document the specific steps needed to complete the task and how these are to be accomplished. If possible, the sequence of steps should be considered. Certain steps can be completed simultaneously, whereas others may need to be addressed sequentially. By evaluating these requirements first, the manager will identify who will be responsible for completing certain steps, when they will be completed, and what resources will be required.

In establishing time frames, both start and completion dates should be estimated. The time provided between these target dates should be an appropriate period based on available facts. It should not be so short as to be unreasonable, nor should it be too long.

Finally, the manager should identify the resources needed to complete the project and obtain appropriate approval for those resources. Otherwise, a substantial amount of work could be undertaken for no reason.

Answering questions will require the manager to evaluate implementation parameters fully in advance, thus eliminating many future surprises. Additionally, establishing a checklist of questions and steps to be performed will provide the manager and others with a method to measure the progress of the implementation process.

Simply stated, implementation ensures that the tasks outlined in the planning process are accomplished. Because of the varied requirements that could be included in a plan, a more specific definition is not practical.

Monitoring the Implementation Process

Once the initial plan is developed and implementation commences, the manager should establish a methodology for monitoring both the implementation process and the results. Monitoring of the implementation process should occur frequently, perhaps daily or weekly, and should take the form of comparing achieved results or activities with those outlined in the plan. For example, a plan might be to convert manual storage of historical data to computer storage. By the end of the third week of implementation, the plan might call for a written comparison of five database software packages to have been performed. How do the results achieved compare to the plan? Is the manager ready to choose from the alternatives available? The frequency and form of the monitoring will vary, depending on the complexity of the plan, the number of people involved in it, and so forth. Generally, the more variables, the more carefully the implementation process should be monitored.

The success of the plan should be reviewed monthly to begin with, and then review should be extended to a longer period of time, such as quarterly or semiannually. Of course, the actual time periods will vary, depending on specific facts and circumstances.

In reviewing the success of the plan, the manager should determine whether the achieved results are consistent with those anticipated during plan development. Significant variations should be documented, as these will be useful tools for subsequent planning projects.

Source: Kevin McManus, "Planning Is the Key to Success," *Topics in Health Record Management*, Vol. 9:4, Aspen Publishers, Inc., © 1989.

HEALTH INFORMATION MANAGEMENT DEPARTMENT: REENGINEERING ACCOUNTS RECEIVABLE AND DOCUMENTATION

The national health care delivery system is awash in a sea of change. This is evidenced by the numerous mergers, acquisitions, alliances, and partnerships taking hold throughout the country. The forces behind these changes are managed care and capitation. The financial underpinnings of who pays for health care and how have altered the way the delivery of this care is organized. They have, in fact, fundamentally altered the traditional roles of providers, payers, and vendors. Reengineering and partnerships have become central to the success of these participants. Pharmaceutical companies have begun aligning themselves with providers by offering disease management; providers are aggressively marketing their health care product lines to compete for managed care market share, and payers are generating report cards on health care systems' costs and outcomes. In the midst of all this change, one notion rings true: If you change the mechanisms through which health care is paid, you alter the entire landscape of the health care delivery system. This is evidenced by historical examples such as Medicare/Medicaid and the evolution of the prospective payment system.

The advent of diagnosis-related groups (DRGs) in the health care industry spirited the health record/health information management (HIM) departments from the basement to the boardroom. Those who are responsible for the management of coding and DRG reimbursement for their health care organizations have responsibilities that have continued to escalate in size of impact upon the fiscal viability of these organizations. Although capitation will alter this impact, it will not diminish its ongoing significance. As capitation and managed care market penetration increase throughout the country, HIM departments will continue to manage the data-driven reimbursement systems through reengineering the processes that support efficient, accurate, timely, and optimum coding of the clinical documentation that resides in health record systems. The successful HIM organizations will assert themselves in supporting the effective transition to new reimbursement methodologies with redesigned processes/systems that increasingly optimize reimbursement throughout the transition to capitation. They will seize the opportunity to manage the changes in reimbursement methodologies through aggressive, team-based work redesign initiatives that simplify the task of providing essential clinical documentation and the processes that support processing, coding, and transmission.

It is within the midst of all this change that opportunities abound to build a foundation for efficient accounts receivable (A/R) management and documentation processes. How does one build this successful foundation, particularly in a complex academic medical center? The University of Texas Medical Branch at Galveston (UTMB) is one place where the successful building of this foundation is taking place. UTMB is an integrated health care delivery system comprising a 904-bed major teaching hospital and more than 140 clinics offering a full range of services to the residents of the state of Texas along with patients worldwide. These facilities provide health care for 38,000 discharges a year and 510,000 outpatient visits annually. UTMB also provides care under a capitated health plan for more than 112,000 covered lives within the Texas Department of Criminal Justice. Its research programs receive funding of more than \$60 million annually and support an extensive academic program comprising four schools.

The HIM Department comprises 137 full-time equivalents (FTEs) providing a wide range of services 24 hours a day, 7 days a week. The Data Management Division (DMD) has the responsibility for inpatient and outpatient coding, clinical data abstracting, and record processing (assembly, analysis, and completion). The staff comprised approximately 55 FTEs historically organized along traditional sections of the division. These sections were managed by several layers of managerial/supervisory staff. Communication and collaboration within and among these sections were fragmented, resulting in a compromised understanding of the goals and objectives of HIM. As a result, the division lacked a focused strategy for improving the processes within and across functional sections of the department. There was also no effective strategy for analyzing the source documentation in the record with a focus on providing education regarding improvements in efficient and effective documentation.

During 1994, the scope and depth of the challenge were clear. The time between discharge and billing was longer than eight days. The revenue in A/R for inpatient cases was approaching \$14 million. Although the health record was rapidly growing in size, with more documentation, it was increasingly clear that more was not better. Medical staff and patient care teams were claiming that patients were, for the most part, sicker than the average population, as was reflected in resource consumption and cost per case, yet there was a wide gap between these costs and reimbursement. A sampling of Medicare and Medicaid records was done that indicated a significant opportunity to improve clinical documentation and enhance DRG coding. This confirmed the belief that case mix intensity (CMI) was incongruent with other data.

Seizing the Opportunity

The existing processes within the DMD had evolved over many years and had been built on old paradigms. The changes to these processes would need to be fundamental in nature and based on new paradigms. UTMB was beginning to embrace a continuous process improvement (CPI) culture, and the HIM Department had jumped to the forefront in using CPI tools to redesign its processes. HIM had begun a reorganization to a flatter and more streamlined organizational structure based upon a self-empowered team model. The Record Management Division of HIM was in the midst of dramatic change in organization and process redesign, and preliminary outcomes were extremely encouraging. The opportunity for the DMD was clear, and the time was right for real change.

The management structure of the DMD was reduced from five layers to one between the director and staff. After extensive discussion with staff, the DMD was reorganized into seven teams defined along functional product lines. These teams were led by team leaders who had no hire/ fire responsibility yet were charged to support, coordinate, and facilitate their teams. The teams were provided some basic parameters and ground rules within which to operate and were told of the outcomes that needed to be achieved. They were supported by the management team in being provided ongoing direction in CPI techniques/tools. The teams were encouraged to take thoughtful risks in their work redesign. The new paradigm was to reward thoughtful changes even if those changes were not successful. The focus was on the notion "If you see a snake, kill it," and then communicate it.

Concurrently, HIM was proceeding with another of its fiscal year 1994–95 business plan initiatives. This initiative was to secure a contractual relationship with a consulting firm to analyze health record documentation, coding operations, CMI outcomes, reimbursement, and education of clinicians. A request for proposal was written that outlined the need for a three-phase program. The program would start with documentation/data analysis using UTMB health record information along with benchmark CMI and comorbid complication (CC) capture data. The second phase would consist of a comprehensive and focused education program targeting practically any clinician who documented or coded from the health record. The third phase would consist of an analysis of outcomes achieved a few months after implementation and would target correction of any subsequent deficiencies/variances that were DRG specific and needed correction to achieve the desired objectives/outcomes.

After a review of various proposals, a contract was awarded to Hyatt, Imler, Ott, and Blount (HIOB) to implement the DRG options program. The director of HIM, accompanied by this consulting firm, met with the Medical Staff Department chairs and senior faculty to communicate the plan and desired outcomes and to seek their support. Through the ensuing conversations, they learned that the approach to this initiative to streamline/reduce the burdensome task of documentation was to target the essential documentation that would accurately reflect the acuity of the cases while resulting in accurate CMI/ CC capture and reimbursement. The medical staff leadership embraced the program and strongly encouraged full participation of the faculty and residents. The balance of clinicians were provided similar information and committed their support as well. In the fall of 1994, the DMD of HIM began implementing a series of data management initiatives, among these being the A/R management redesign and DRG options programs.

Partnerships in Reengineering

The HIM director and the director of hospital patient financial services (HPFS) partnered to support and facilitate the redesign of the A/R management processes. They began by leading the DMD teams through a work flow analysis of the existing processes. Through continuous quality improvement tools and techniques (e.g., brainstorming, flowcharting, etc.) supported by work inflow/outflow data, the teams identified new work designs that would support the rapid processing of health records through the coding and billing operations. They developed measurable targets that would assist in organizing the systematic processing of these accounts. They revised staffing patterns to smooth out the peaks and valleys in work flow. They identified and implemented opportunities to organize and facilitate communication among the DMD teams through the use of departmentwide e-mail and beepers. They partnered with their colleagues in the HIM Record Management Division to improve their access to unprocessed/uncoded records routed to clinics for follow-up care. Teams of health record technicians (HRTs) in the DMD were organized to retrieve records from the floors after discharge and to process records before coding. The HRTs were stationed on the patient floors and performed assembly and analysis functions while on the floor.

To get records coded more quickly, coders were sent to the HRT stations with laptop computers and coded records before assembly and analysis. Large accounts were the priority. Benchmarking data from other hospitals showed that most patients are discharged and then seen in clinic between zero and five days after discharge. The speed with which the patient population moved between care settings was faster than the process for getting records completed and coded for billing. Because patients go back to clinic so quickly after discharge, records get pulled from coding for patient care before coding is completed. Getting the records back to coding as soon as possible after the clinic appointment was critical.

The Record Management Division played a critical role in helping coding capture the uncoded records that were pulled for patient care. Two people were assigned as trackers for large accounts and for records still in clinic. Communication between the trackers and the coders was facilitated with the use of e-mail and beepers. The same communication tools were used between the trackers and the HRT stations on the floors. This would let the HRTs know that they had a big bill on their floor and needed to process it immediately. Beepers assisted with communication while staff were en route to record locations.

DMD staff partnered with health care information systems (HIS) staff to acquire electronic access to reports that would improve the management of coding and other patient data flowing from the HIM local area network through the interface to the mainframe patient accounting/billing systems. Although many of the redesign ideas were implemented immediately, the teams developed a parking lot list to ensure that other important, but not necessarily urgent, issues were not forgotten.

Once the extensive analysis of internal and external/benchmark data was complete, the DMD coding team, supported by the HIOB team, attacked the second phase of the DRG options program: medical staff education. The HIM director, HPFS director, and admitting director partnered to maximize the probability of a successful outcome of this phase of the program. The resource utilization (RU) staff and HIM coding staff were seen as the team to participate jointly in the massive education program that was about to roll out to the UTMB clinical staff. HIOB provided much of the curriculum and material for this educational effort. The outcome of this effort was threefold:

1. Target the clinical information that is essential for accurate documentation of care by clinical subspecialty.
2. Provide the operational mechanisms to assist the staff in choosing the appropriate verbiage to document the CCs associated with the care they were providing.
3. Instruct the physicians regarding the link between accurate and concise documentation and optimum DRG reimbursement.

Once this team was formed, preparation for this education began with arrangement of more than 200 inservices for the clinical staff, spanning 10 clinical areas, several residency programs, clinical faculty and chairs, and the Medical Executive Committee. Arrangements were also made to videotape many of the educational sessions for future orientation and continuing education. Educational forums of 30 minutes each were provided practically around the clock over a period of seven weeks. The HIM coding staff and the RU staff initiated ongoing team meetings to identify challenges and opportunities to fine-tune the implementation of this program. They worked through the formative stages of their new team relationship and began to mature into a highly functional team, developing effective management reporting tools to monitor outcomes and make quick adjustments.

Approximately three months after implementation of the DRG options program, HIOB analyzed the outcomes by DRG and clinical subspecialty. Through this analysis, additional clinical staff were targeted for education and/or remedial training. The HIM coding staff and the RU staff were supported with assistance in further fine-tuning of their new joint partnership, and tools were refined to become more efficient and effective. An exit conference was convened with senior administrative clinical staff along with key members of the HIM/RU teams supported by the consulting staff. Based on the outcomes/results summarized by HIOB and UTMB staff, it was clear that a successful program positioned to provide significant return on the investment had been achieved.

Outcomes of the Reengineering Partnerships

The A/R management outcomes produced by the DMD teams within HIM in partnership with HPFS and HIS exceeded expectations. As production statistics were e-mailed throughout the departments and graphics depicting the drop in inpatient A/R were posted, one could feel the building excitement and pride of the staff. The day's revenue in uncoded health records decreased from approximately 14 days to less than 4 days and has begun a steady but slower decrease that is expected to stabilize at less than 3 days.

The DRG options program has evolved into an incredible success that exceeded expectations severalfold. CMI, CC capture, and corresponding reimbursement now more accurately reflect the acuity of cases. Overall CMI increased an average of 25 percent. CC capture rates have also increased for fiscal years 1993 through 1995.

In the meantime, the program has actually simplified/reduced some of the documentation for clinicians. The data afforded by this program are routinely used by the HIM/RU team to continue to target DRG-specific subspecialties for ongoing education and support. Several medical staff departments have requested and been provided focused educational forums in which information/insights are shared. The byproduct of this continuing education is reflected in continuous improvement of documentation and financial outcomes.

The DMD within HIM has regularly celebrated its successes over the past eight months as the results of its initiatives have been recognized within UTMB. These celebrations often include the chief financial officer and the department directors of HIM, HPFS, and admitting along with the physician cochair of the Health Information Committee. Although these celebrations began with the early/small successes of these teams, they now focus on the lofty accomplishments of teams partnering in reengineering processes.

Source: James H. Braden, Doreen Swadley, and Suzanne Sims, "Health Information Management Department: Reengineering Accounts Receivable and Documentation," *Topics in Health Information Management*, Vol. 16:3, Aspen Publishers, Inc., © 1996.

JOB DESCRIPTIONS

CODER JOB DESCRIPTION

JOB TITLE: Coder

RESPONSIBLE TO: [as designated on department organizational chart]

Responsibilities

Under the general direction of the director (or designated assistant), health information department, this specialist is responsible for accurate coding of all inpatient, outpatient, and emergency service diagnoses and conditions, working from the appropriate documentation in the health record of the patient. Classification systems include ICD-9-CM and CPT-4 as well as other specialty systems as required by diagnostic category. All work is carried out in accordance with the department's approved policies and procedures.

Job Setting and Conditions

This position is an advanced level technical position in the health information department of this [*n*]-bed facility. The position is full time, day shift. Normal working days and hours are Monday through Friday, [specify hours], with a paid 45-minute lunch period. Adjustments to the normal schedule are required rarely, and usually only under emergency circumstances.

Job Duties

In accordance with department policies and procedures, this worker carries out these six major and closely related duties and responsibilities:

1. Codes all diagnoses, treatments, and procedures according to the appropriate classification system for the category of patient encounter.
2. Completes the coding with an error rate of no less than [*n*%] within the work standard for the unit.
3. Assists physicians and other direct patient care professionals in questions regarding level of detail for diagnostic entries, according to the organization's guidelines.
4. Prepares workload reports and participates in department's total quality management studies.
5. Promotes public relations through prompt and courteous service.
6. Fosters respect for patient privacy by maintaining confidentiality in all phases of the work.

Education and Experience

- The specialist must have a high school diploma or the equivalent.
- The specialist must be an accredited record technician, registered record administrator, and/or coder specialist, or possess equivalent training in coding systems, advanced medical and anatomical terminology, clinical medicine theory, and reimbursement principles.
- The specialist should possess in-depth knowledge of health record content and sequence.
- The specialist should possess in-depth knowledge of coding/classification systems appropriate for inpatient, outpatient, and emergency care, specifically [give detailed listing here].
- The specialist should be knowledgable of use of coding software.
- A trainee is not acceptable for this position due to the specialty knowledge base associated with coding requirements.

Skills

- fluent in English
- able to process work, error free, within presented deadlines and time frames

Physical and Mental Demands

- ability to withstand the pressure of continual deadlines and receipt of work with variable requirements
- ability to concentrate and maintain accuracy in spite of frequent interruptions
- ability to be courteous, tactful, and cooperative throughout the working day
- ability to use judgment in carrying out all phases of the work
- ability to maintain confidentiality with regard to all phases of the work
- visual acuity of 20/60 in at least one eye (with/without corrections)
- hearing sensitivity bilaterally within normal limits (0–24, db HL) aided/nonaided or speech discrimination within functional limits for telephone and personal communication
- ability to communicate verbally
- manual dexterity
- moderate physical effort: lift/carry up to 30 pounds occasionally during workday
- ability to lift supplies/equipment occasionally
- occasional bending, stooping, kneeling, crouching, reaching

- ability to use standard office equipment including computers, photocopy and facsimile machines, and readers/printers

Special Requirements

- none

Working Conditions

- exposed to hazards from electrical/mechanical/power equipment
- subject to irregular hours occasionally
- uses computer equipment extensively

Bloodborne Pathogen Risk

There is no direct patient care contact. Tasks involve no exposure to blood.

NOTE: Modify this statement if the worker will do in-house, concurrent coding and will carry out this work at nurses' stations in direct patient care areas.

DATE:

APPROVED BY:

Checklist for Compliance with Occupational Safety and Health Administration Ergonomics Regulations—Coder

Indicator	Yes	No
Performance of same motion or motion pattern every few seconds for more than two to four hours at a time		✓
Fixed or awkward postures for more than two to four hours	✓	
Use of vibrating or impact tools or equipment for more than three to four hours during a shift		✓
Forceful hand exertions for more than two to four hours at a time		✓
Unassisted frequent or heavy lifting for more than one or two hours		✓
Job duties with potential for causing or aggravating musculoskeletal and nervous systems—for example:		
• lower back injuries	✓	
• tendon disorders		✓
• carpal tunnel syndrome		✓
• eye strain	✓	
• noise		✓
Ergonomically correct workstation, including		
• desk height	✓	
• chair height	✓	
• video display terminal and screen positioning	✓	

Equipment and Space Allocation and Layout Grid—Coder

Number of Employees

Day__________ Evening__________ Night__________

Key Activities

Coding of all conditions, diagnoses, and treatments: all patient groups.

Contact with Clients and Patients

None.

Contact with Professional Staff

Professional staff contact occurs, but usually accomplished by telephone.

Intradepartmental Relationships

Incomplete health record processing.

Extradepartmental Relationships

Billings/finance unit.

Other Contacts

None.

Privacy and Security Considerations

- All material processed is confidential patient care documentation.
- Night shift personnel work alone in this area of the facility.
- Computers and related equipment are attractive items for theft.
- Display screen of computer needs to be placed so that material cannot be read by others.
- There is limited access to work area.
- There are special security alarms for night shift personnel.
- There are equipment locks/antitheft devices on all equipment.

Noise Control

Acoustical ceiling.

Lighting and Electrical Needs

- close work; detailed clerical work processing throughout the working hours
- convenience lighting at workstation
- overhead ambient lighting: 100 foot candles
- direct lighting at workstation: 100 foot candles
- grounded outlets
- power surge protection
- sufficient outlets to eliminate the need for extension cords

Telephone and Other Communication Devices

Telephone:
- internal access lines
- external line
- equipment secured from unauthorized access

Temperature and Humidity

- standard specifications for worker comfort to enhance productivity: heating, air conditioning
- standard specifications for equipment care, with special regard for computer equipment requirements
- humidity control: 40–50 percent

Special Architectural Support or Weight-Bearing Considerations

Standard office equipment: 150 pounds per square foot.

Work Surface Requirements

- range of motion availability: work done while sitting at desk
- range of motion availability: work done while standing
- sorting space
- distribution of completed work
- table height: adjustable up, down, and tiltable; lock-in position for height adjustment feature
- no sharp edges
- allowance for adequate leg room
- allowance for easy movement from one task to another
- easy-to-reach shelving/storage space for an average of [*n*] health records per day and for coding reference materials; accessible from sitting position

Flooring

- resilient
- no carpeting (static reduction)

Equipment and Ergonomic Considerations

- chairs
  –height adjustable
  –high backrest
  –adequate lumbar support
  –lock-in position: backrest
  –backrest adjustable: forward tilt; up or down
  –stable (five-leg brace}
- video display terminal (VDT) space
  –VDT tiltable
  –VDT movable to desired distance for ease of viewing
  –VDT with glare-free features
  –keyboard: adjustable height to maintain straight wrists

Square Footage

- standard allowance in net allowable square feet (NASF)
  – per employee: minimum of 120 NASF
  – per supervisor: minimum of 150 NASF
- aisle space: five-foot minimum

Source: Joan Gratto Liebler, *Medical Records: Policies and Guidelines*, Aspen Publishers, Inc., © 1996.

DATABASE ANALYST JOB DESCRIPTION

Revised Date
Department
FLSA Code
Pay Grade

POSITION SUMMARY

Ensures accuracy, integrity, and security of all databases. Conducts database searches, designs and conducts user training courses, and maintains a library for all computer documentation.

POSITION ACCOUNTABILITIES AND PERFORMANCE STANDARDS

1. Selects, trains/orients, assigns department staff, evaluates performance, and makes recommendations for personnel actions.
2. Maintains established hospital and departmental policies and procedures, participates in quality assessment and improvement processes, and maintains safety, environmental, and infection control standards.

   Application of Knowledge Performance Standards

   - Maintains documented hospital and unit-specific annual competency requirements.

3. Maintains departmental reports and records and collects statistical data for administrative and regulatory purposes.
4. Assumes responsibility for data entry and integrity of information, production of special project reports, database searches, dictionary maintenance, user education, documentation generation, and monitoring production of data for government agencies.

   Application of Knowledge Performance Standards

   - Establishes individual databases. Sets up dictionaries, educates users in data entry and searches, and assists in defining user needs and organizing to create appropriate databases.

   Recordkeeping Performance Standards

   - Conducts special projects and prepares reports as requested.

5. Plans and supervises the work of the transcription and tumor registry areas.
6. Develops and implements procedures to respond to subpoenas and insurance company requirements for information to ensure that released information meets legal requirements.

   Recordkeeping Performance Standards

   - Signs certification documents for court records.

7. Cooperates with other personnel and stakeholders to achieve organizational mission and strategic objectives, and maintains positive relations throughout the facility.

   Application of Knowledge Performance Standards

   - Demonstrates knowledge of organizational mission through role model behavior.

   Communications Performance Standards

   - Interacts with coworkers on a regular basis for planning and cooperation.
   - Maintains positive interpersonal skills by listening to issues, giving direct feedback, and facilitating open communication with staff and leadership regarding concerns, issues, and compliments.

   Collaboration Performance Standards

   - Demonstrates attitude of cooperation and professionalism.
   - Facilitates harmonious relationships intradepartmentally and with coworkers, providing support and assistance to staff to ensure quality patient care.
   - Maintains effective relationships with all customers, providing support and assistance to coworkers to ensure quality patient care and to promote learning congruent with the organizational culture.

8. Performs other related duties as assigned or requested.

POSITION QUALIFICATIONS

- Minimum education: bachelor's degree
- Minimum experience: sufficient experience in computer technology and in the field of computer services
- Preferred field of expertise: Registered Record Administrator
- Working conditions: OSHA Exposure Category III
- Skills: Other
  –Communications
  –Medical Terminology
  –Word Perfect 5.1
  –Windows 3.1
  –Diagnosis/Procedural Coding System

Courtesy of St. Mary's Hospital and Medical Center, Grand Junction, Colorado.

STORAGE AND RETRIEVAL CLERK JOB DESCRIPTION

JOB TITLE: Storage and Retrieval Clerk

RESPONSIBLE TO: [as indicated on department organizational chart]

Responsibilities

Under the general direction of the director (or designated assistant), health information department, this specialist is responsible for processing all requests for health record retrieval from permanent storage area for patient records; filing new records and refiling continuing records; processing all incoming reports needing filing in these records. No supervisory or management functions are carried out by this employee; employee works under continual, regular supervision. All work is carried out in accordance with the department's approved policies and procedures.

Job Setting and Conditions

This position is a basic, entry-level clerical position in the health information department of this [*n*]-bed facility. The position is full time, day shift. Normal working days and hours are Monday through Friday, [specify hours], with a paid 45-minute lunch period. Adjustments to the normal schedule are required rarely and only under emergency conditions.

Job Duties

In accordance with department policies and procedures, this worker carries out these 12 major and closely related duties and responsibilities for all inpatient, outpatient, and emergency service records held in the central files:

1. Maintains file area in permanent, archived file unit of the department and both immediate, active files and files held in remote storage on site.
2. Receives and processes all requests for health records from file area.
3. Coordinates delivery of health records with messenger and acts as messenger to deliver priority records in absence of immediately available messenger.
4. Processes all incoming (continuous care and late receipt) reports needing filing in the permanent records and immediately forwards to incomplete health record processing those reports for records held in that area.
5. Coordinates verification and correction of patient numbers by referring duplicate numbers, incomplete identification, or similar items to master parent index unit.
6. Maintains health record tracking system for all records distributed from and received by the unit.
7. Prepares workload reports and managerial support data.
8. Maintains basic equipment and workstation.
9. Pulls health records for sending to outsourced commercial storage/microimaging, according to designated record retention schedule; prepares related cover documents.
10. Carries out regular review of files to prevent, identify, and correct misfiles.
11. Promotes public relations through prompt and courteous service.
12. Fosters respect for patient privacy by maintaining confidentiality in all phases of the work.

Education and Experience

- This worker must have a high school diploma or the equivalent.
- This worker must possess basic clerical training, which includes computer skills, basic filing skills, and fundamental knowledge of office procedures.
- This worker should have a basic knowledge of health record content and sequence.
- This worker must possess relevant experience in clerical duties sufficient for individual development to the level of independent functioning with minimal direction.
- A trainee is acceptable provided the individual meets the established work standards within [*n*] weeks of completion of the mandatory training program for this job.

Skills

- fluent in English, with special emphasis on alphabetization
- able to process work, error free, within prescribed deadlines and time frames
- able to process work, using both alphabetical and numerical filing systems

Physical and Mental Demands

- ability to withstand the pressure of continual deadlines and receipt of work with variable requirements
- ability to concentrate and maintain accuracy in spite of frequent interruptions
- ability to be courteous, tactful, and cooperative throughout the working day
- ability to use judgment in carrying out all phases of the work
- ability to maintain confidentiality with regard to all phases of the work
- visual acuity of 20/60 in at least one eye (with/without corrections)

- color perception
- hearing sensitivity bilaterally within normal limits (0–24, db HL) aided/nonaided or speech discrimination within functional limits for telephone and personal communication
- ability to communicate verbally
- manual dexterity
- moderate physical effort: lift/carry up to 30 pounds continuously during workday
- ability to lift supplies/equipment occasionally
- continual bending, stooping, kneeling, crouching, reaching
- ability to use standard office equipment including computers, photocopy and facsimile machines, and readers/printers

Special Requirements

This worker substitutes for messenger to deliver priority records for direct patient care and therefore needs to meet the same requirements as the messenger job requirements.

Working Conditions

- exposed to hazards from electrical/mechanical/power equipment
- subject to irregular hours occasionally
- uses computer equipment extensively
- travel outside the department is required because some files are located in a remote storage area on the organization's campus

Bloodborne Pathogen Risk

There is no direct patient care contact. Tasks involve no exposure to blood.

Checklist for Compliance with Occupational Safety and Health Administration Ergonomics Regulations—Storage and Retrieval Clerk

Indicator	Yes	No
Performance of same motion or motion pattern every few seconds for more than two to four hours at a time	✓	
Fixed or awkward postures for more than two to four hours	✓	
Use of vibrating or impact tools or equipment for more than three to four hours during a shift		✓
Forceful hand exertions for more than two to four hours at a time		✓
Unassisted frequent or heavy lifting for more than one or two hours	✓	
Job duties with potential for causing or aggravating musculoskeletal and nervous systems—for example:		
• lower back injuries	✓	
• tendon disorders		✓
• carpal tunnel syndrome		✓
• eye strain	✓	
• noise		✓
Ergonomically correct workstation, including		
• desk height	✓	
• chair height	✓	
• video display terminal and screen positioning	✓	

Equipment and Space Allocation and Layout Grid—Storage and Retrieval Clerk

Number of Employees

Day_________ Evening_________ Night_________

Key Activities

The following work volumes need consideration in planning space allocation, both for files and for sorting areas:

1.

	Daily Number of Medical Records			
	Pulled	**Held**	**Returned**	**Refiled**
Inpatient				
Outpatient				
Emergency services				
Internal department use				
Research studies				
Committee, administrative, and special review use				

2. number of continuous care and late receipt reports for sorting and filing
3. number of records pulled and held [designate time period held on site] for records designated for outsourced processing
4. filing and retrieving all health records and related reports: inpatient discharges; outpatient; emergency care

Contact with Clients and Patients

None; no additional space required.

Contact with Professional Staff

Frequent contact, but usually occurs by telephone/requesting system.

Intradepartmental Relationships

- frequent, continual interaction with incomplete health record processing and word processing
- regular but infrequent interaction with other department units

Extradepartmental Relationships

- frequent, continual interaction, but most requests are made by electronic transmissions or telephone
- holding areas for large numbers of health records pulled for research and special studies needed

Other Contacts

- microimaging company coordinators (or commercial storage)
- space needed to hold records pulled for outsourced processing (microimaging or commercial storage)

Privacy and Security Considerations

- All material processed is confidential patient care documentation.
- Night shift personnel work alone in this area of the facility.
- Computers and related equipment are attractive items for theft.
- Display screen of computer needs to be placed so that material cannot be read by others.
- There is limited access to work area.
- There are special security alarms for night shift personnel.
- There are equipment locks/antitheft devices on all equipment.

Noise Control

Acoustical ceiling.

Lighting and Electrical Needs

- close work; detailed clerical work processing throughout the working hours
- convenience lighting at workstation
- overhead ambient lighting: 100 foot candles
- direct lighting at workstation: 100 foot candles
- grounded outlets
- power surge protection
- sufficient outlets to eliminate the need for extension cords

Telephone and Other Communication Devices

Telephone:
- internal access lines
- external line
- equipment secured from unauthorized access

Temperature and Humidity

- standard specifications for worker comfort to enhance productivity: heating, air conditioning
- standard specifications for equipment care, with special regard for computer equipment requirements
- humidity control: 40–50 percent

Special Architectural Support or Weight-Bearing Considerations

- standard office equipment: 150 pounds per square foot
- additional weight-bearing support needed for filing shelves holding [*n*] records of an average weight per shelf unit of [*n*] pounds

Work Surface Requirements

- range of motion availability: work done while sitting at desk
- range of motion availability: work done while standing
- sorting space
- distribution of completed work
- table height: adjustable up, down, and tiltable; lock-in position for height adjustment feature
- no sharp edges

- allowance for adequate leg room
- allowance for easy movement from one task to another

Flooring

- resilient
- no carpeting (static reduction)

Equipment and Ergonomic Considerations

- chairs
  - height adjustable
  - high backrest
  - adequate lumbar support
  - lock-in position: backrest
  - backrest adjustable: forward tilt; up or down
  - stable (five-leg brace)
- video display terminal (VDT) space
  - VDT tiltable
  - VDT movable to desired distance for ease of viewing
  - VDT with glare-free features
  - keyboard: adjustable height to maintain straight wrists

Square Footage

- standard allowance in net allowable square feet (NASF)
  - per employee: minimum of 120 NASF
  - per supervisor: minimum of 150 NASF
- aisle space: five-foot minimum; provide extra allowance in active file area for ease of access by employee with file cart

Source: Joan Gratto Liebler, *Medical Records: Policies and Guidelines*, Aspen Publishers, Inc., © 1996.

THE HIRING PROCESS

INTERVIEWING: GUIDELINES FOR QUESTIONING

Although common courtesy should prevail in your interview behavior at all times, courtesy itself is not enough. You must be constantly aware of questions or comments that could be taken as discriminatory in some way although not intended as such. An applicant may *volunteer* information related to the following precautions, but you may not ask for this information.

Questions To Avoid

You may not ask any question that requires the applicant to reveal *age, date of birth, race, religion,* or *national origin.* The direct questions—"When were you born?"—should be easy to avoid. Watch out, however, for indirect questions through which a person can claim you were "fishing" for specific information. For instance, a question that is not allowed is one such as "I'd say we've both been around about the same length of time—both early baby boomers, perhaps?"

The matter of age has become a particularly sensitive area in recent years, calling for heightened awareness on the part of the supervisor. Although the Age Discrimination in Employment Act (ADEA) has been in place since 1967, it was given added scope and influence by the Age Discrimination in Employment Amendments Act of 1986, effective January 1, 1987. Although mostly the concern of the personnel or human resources department, this law nevertheless has implications for the supervisor.

The 1986 act prohibits mandatory retirement for most employees and removes the age 70 limit on ADEA protection. Therefore, stay away from all questions related to an applicant's long-term intentions, such as, "How long would you plan on working before thinking about retirement?" because of the age-related inferences that one might draw.

There is no safe question that the supervisor can ask about age, except perhaps to inquire whether an apparently young person is of legal age to enter full-time employment under the circumstances required of the job in question (in most instances, at least 18 years of age). Avoid all questions that either directly or indirectly call for age-related responses. Also, you need to assure yourself that all the qualifications you are seeking are truly related to the job. Evaluate individual applicants on their individual capabilities and qualifications, not on your general beliefs or personal preferences ("An older person just couldn't keep up," or "Someone her age would resist new technology," or "I want someone who's more likely to stay 10 or 20 years").

Similar to concerns about age, there are few if any safe questions the supervisor can ask about disability, whether a job candidate's disability is evident or not. The Americans with Disabilities Act (ADA) (1990) provides a national mandate barring bias against persons with disabilities. This act calls for supportive and accommodating behavior by employers in maintaining disabled persons in the work force. Concerning the employment selection interview and the disabled person, the supervisor should ask questions about the applicant's qualifications and experience that focus strictly on the essential functions of the job. The job's peripheral activities that have no bearing on its essential functions—for example, occasional filing or report delivery related to the position of a billing clerk—are subject to "reasonable accommodation" by the organization and have no bearing on the person's capabilities as a billing clerk.

You may not ask if the applicant has a recommendation from a present employer. This may be taken as discriminatory, as it may be difficult for the applicant to secure such a recommendation because of reasons other than job performance (e.g., race, religion, political affiliation).

You can no longer ask the identity of the person's nearest relative or next of kin, even for the simple purpose of having someone to contact in case of illness or accident. This can be taken as probing into the existence of spouse or family, which you cannot do. Even asking about "the person to be notified in case of illness or accident" is risky until the applicant is actually employed.

It is generally permissible to ask if an applicant is a U.S. citizen or is legally eligible for employment. However, this should not be an active concern of the supervisor if the personnel department is fulfilling its proper role in complying with the Immigration Reform and Control Act of 1986 (IRCA). This law requires employers to hire only U.S. citizens and lawfully authorized alien workers, and provides penalties and sanctions for employers who knowingly hire or continue to employ illegal aliens or who fail to verify legal eligibility for employment.

In compliance with IRCA, the personnel department must require an applicant to produce certain proofs of identity and employment eligibility within three working days after an offer of employment is made. For your part in helping the organization comply with IRCA, you should resist the temptation to prevail on the personnel department to allow a much-needed new employee to begin work before the necessary proofs are produced.

Immigration reform has provided the work organization with a set of risks and pitfalls of a kind never previously experienced, and these risks and pitfalls cannot be avoided by backing away from the problem. The supervisor who might seek to avoid IRCA problems by not considering an applicant because of foreign appearance or language can face discrimination charges as defined by other laws.

In asking about the applicant's military service, you may inquire only into the general training and experience involved. You may not ask the character of the person's discharge or separation. Whether the discharge was honorable, dishonorable, general, or otherwise remains privileged information that the applicant may reveal voluntarily but that you may not request.

You may not ask the marital status of the applicant at the time of the interview. Particular sensitivity has developed along these lines in recent years. Many women have been able to claim, with considerable success, that they were denied employment because of marital status. Employers often proceeded on the assumptions, sometimes statistically substantiated, that

- Young women recently engaged often quit shortly after they get married.
- Young, recently married women may leave after a year or two to begin families.
- Unmarried women with small children tend, on the average, to have poorer attendance records than other workers.

Even if an applicant, male or female, has willingly revealed marriage on a resume, you are not permitted to ask what the spouse does for a living. In the case of a married female applicant, you are also forbidden to ask her maiden name because this question can be interpreted as probing for clues to national origin.

You may not ask if the applicant owns a home or a car. This may be interpreted as seeking to test affluence, which may in turn be taken as discriminatory against certain minorities. You may, however, ask if the applicant has a driver's license if driving is a bona fide occupational qualification (BFOQ), that is, a requirement of the job. (Generally, you are on your soundest footing when all questions of a personal nature relate to BFOQs.)

You may not ask if the applicant's wages were ever attached or garnished. Credit information is privileged information; it may be volunteered by the applicant but not requested by the prospective employer.

You may not directly ask any applicant's height or weight. Neither of these factors should have a bearing on the applicant's suitability for the job unless there is a specific job-related requirement (BFOQ) that is uniformly applied to all applicants.

Beware of asking an applicant to take qualification tests. Preemployment tests have long been under fire as discriminatory in matters of age, race, and economic background. Preemployment testing is best left to professionals who design tests that are specifically related to the requirements of the job, statistically validated as nondiscriminatory, administered consistently and in good faith, and evaluated impartially.

There are also pitfalls to be encountered in asking an applicant's educational level, such as completion of high school or possession of a college degree. An employer may require specific educational levels when these are directly related to job performance (again, BFOQs). Otherwise, it may be possible to show a pattern of employment discrimination. You can require, for instance, a nurse to possess a diploma or degree and a state license because these are essential to the performance of the job as it is structured. However, you cannot require a housekeeping maid or kitchen helper to have a high school diploma because it is possible to demonstrate that people in these job categories may perform equally well with or without the diploma. Effective personnel department procedures should take most of the burden off the interviewer in this matter.

You can no longer ask if an applicant has ever been arrested. An arrest is simply a charge, not a conviction. It has even become risky to ask if a person has ever been convicted of a crime. Most courts have ruled that after a few years have passed following conviction and correction, the individual need not be called on to reveal this information. Unless the job is clearly related to safeguarding money or security (a BFOQ), it is best to refrain from this line of questioning.

You may not ask whether an applicant is or has been a member of a union or has been involved in organizing or other union activities.

You may not ask any obviously older applicants if they are receiving Social Security benefits. It has been demonstrated concerning older persons applying for part-time work that some employers have discriminated in favor of applicants receiving Social Security payments, as a person receiving a combined income may be more likely to remain on the job longer than one to whom the part-time job is the sole means of support.

Questions To Ask

The questions you are permitted to ask are broad and in many instances open-ended. This is as it should be; remember, you are interested in learning as much as you can about the applicant in a limited amount of time and the way to do this is to listen to the person talk. Try these in conversation with the applicant

- What are your career goals? What would you like to be doing 5 or 10 years from now? How would you like to spend the rest of your career?
- Who have been your prior employers, and why did you leave your previous positions?
- What did you like or dislike about the work in your previous positions?
- Who recommended you to our institution? How did you hear about this job opening?
- What is your educational background? What lines of study did you pursue? (Be careful, however, of attempting to delve into specifics as cautioned in the list of questions to avoid.)
- What do you believe are your strong points? What do you see as your weaknesses?
- Have you granted permission for us to check references with former employers (see following section)?

If the personnel department has not already done so, ask the applicant to explain any gaps of more than a few weeks' duration that appear in the resume or application. Some applicants will omit mention of unsuccessful job experiences or other involvements that they believe might reflect negatively on their chances of being hired. As the hiring supervisor you should be in a position to make a fully informed decision based on more than just selected pieces of a candidate's background. Also, you share a responsibility for ensuring that the organization is protected from possible negligent hiring charges should an employee who was hired without reasonable background verification cause harm.

Employment References

The whole topic of employment references represents a quagmire of potential legal traps for both the supervisor and the personnel department. Ideally, the personnel department should have secured the applicant's signed permission to check references as part of personnel's screening interview, calling for a specific signed release for each former employer. For good reasons, many applicants ask that their present employers not be approached for reference information, but they ordinarily grant permission to check with most—but not always with all—previous employers. No reference checks should be performed by anyone in the absence of an applicant's signed authorization to do so. Even if a signed release is presented, reference checking should be left to the personnel department.

References must be checked systematically in accordance with strict guidelines governing the kinds of information requested and the kinds of responses to expect. In these litigious times, many unsuccessful applicants are quick to charge that they were not hired because of defamatory information acquired from previous employers. It is therefore important for all references to be checked by persons who do so regularly enough to be sensitive to the legal pitfalls that can be encountered. For example, an applicant might claim to have been defamed in being labeled on a reference check as "uncooperative and unreliable"—and can succeed in pursuing such a claim if there is insufficient information in the individual's past employment record to "prove" such contentions. Reference information used in making a decision not to hire needs to be substantiated in the past employment record. For instance, to stand up as valid if challenged, a reference of "poor attendance" should be backed up (in the personnel file maintained by the employer supplying the reference) with attendance records or with records of disciplinary actions dealing with attendance.

Although you might be tempted to use personal contacts such as your counterparts at other institutions to check on potential new employees, in no way should you ever use information so obtained in making an employment decision.

Source: Charles R. McConnell, *The Effective Health Care Supervisor*, 3rd ed., Aspen Publishers, Inc., © 1993.

THE ACTUAL INTERVIEW

Assume you have reached the point where you are well aware of questions you should avoid and well advised of the kinds of questions you should ask. In addition, assume that you and an applicant are now face-to-face in private and that you are mindful of the edge you hold in this interchange and of the possibly uncomfortable position of the applicant. Having reached this stage, proceed according to these guidelines:

Put the Applicant at Ease

At the beginning of the conversation you need to put the individual at ease and instill a degree of confidence. You might want to try several different topics at the start of the interview—for instance, the weather, the ease with which the person may have found your office, or an invitation to enjoy a cup of coffee—to get the person talking and take you a step toward conversational rapport. Whatever opener you employ—and usually it need be only brief—it will get you off to a far better start than the shock of something like "Good morning. Why do you want to work here?"

During these first few critical minutes, try to avoid making judgments and freezing a picture of the applicant in your mind. First impressions are often difficult to shed, and when formed while the person is not yet at ease they can be unfair.

Avoid Short-Answer Questions

Avoid asking questions in such a way that they can be answered in one or two words, and especially avoid questions that can be answered simply "yes" or "no." For instance, a question such as "How long did you work for County General Hospital?" might simply be answered: "Three years." This gives you very little information. Rather, a request on the order of: "Please tell me about the work you did at County General Hospital," requires the person to use more than just a couple of words in response. Your purpose is to learn about the applicant, and you can do so only by getting the person to talk.

However, you should avoid permitting the applicant to wander off the subject for minutes at a time. When this occurs, interrupt (as politely as possible) with another question or a request for clarification intended to draw the conversation back to the focus of the interview.

Avoid Leading or Loaded Questions

Avoid questions that lead the applicant toward some predetermined response. For instance, if you ask "You left County General because the pay raises weren't coming along, is that right?" you are channeling the applicant toward a response that you may have already decided is correct. It is far better to ask, "Why did you leave County General?"

Leading questions can be a particular hazard when you are talking with someone who is shaping up favorably in your eyes. In the process of unconsciously deciding you like this person, you may begin to bend the rest of your questions in a fashion that calls for the answers you would like to hear. Most people are sensitive to leading questions and, depending on the nature of the questions, will feel either forced or encouraged to deliver the answers that seem to be wanted.

Ask One Question at a Time

Avoid hitting the applicant with something like "What kind of work did you do there and why did you leave?" This is in fact two questions, and although they may well be properly asked one after the other the person should be given the opportunity to deal with them individually. Combining or pyramiding questions tends to throw some people off balance; a person prepared to deal with a single question is suddenly confronted with two or three at once. It is always preferable to limit your questioning to one clear, concise question at a time.

Keep Your Writing to a Minimum

Try not to take voluminous notes while the prospective employee is talking. This can be disconcerting to the individual, creating the impression that everything that is said is being taken down in writing. Also, it is distracting to you. Writing and listening are both communication skills subject to their own particular ground rules and neither can be done with maximum effectiveness if you are trying to do the other at the same time. The more note-taking you attempt, the more it detracts from your listening capacity. Take down a few key words if you must, but focus most of your attention on listening to the applicant. If you need or desire a written report of the interview, generate this report immediately after the applicant leaves and the conversation is still fresh in your mind.

Use Appropriate Language

At all times deliver your questions and comments in language appropriate to the apparent level of education, knowledge, and understanding of the prospective employee. If you are a nursing supervisor interviewing an experienced registered nurse, you will likely talk on a level at which you would ordinarily expect to communicate with a registered nurse. However, if you happen to be interviewing for the position of ward clerk, talking with a person who has never worked in a hospital, you should alter your language accordingly. Always assume a reasonable degree of intelligence—avoid talking down to the person—but do not dazzle or confuse the applicant with unfamiliar terminology.

Do More Listening Than Talking

Throughout the interview be interested and attentive, never impatient or critical. Avoid talking too much about yourself or the institution. Remember, you are not selling yourself to the applicant—it is supposed to be the other way around. Also, you are not necessarily selling the institution to the applicant, although if the interview moves far enough in constructive directions you may wish to answer the applicant's questions about the institution. However, even on this score there are precautions to note: specifics of certain features of employment like insurance, retirement, and other benefits for which you may not have all the details should be left to the personnel department and broached only when you are ready to extend an offer of employment and the individual needs this information to aid in making the decision.

Indicate Some Type of Follow-Up

Conclude the interview with a reasonable statement of what the applicant may expect to happen next. It is true you generally cannot (and probably should not) make a definite statement at this time, but you should suggest what may be expected and when it might occur. For instance, you can always say something like "We'll let you know our decision after we've finished all scheduled interviews, say within a week or 10 days," or "You should be getting a letter from us next week," or perhaps simply "We'll call you by Friday." In any case, conclude the interview with some simple indication of impending follow-up.

Follow-Up

Follow-up is no problem when you decide to extend a job offer to an applicant—you will extend the offer and the person will either accept or decline the job. In either case, the interview process has been taken full circle.

However, even in instances when you do not wish to extend a job offer you should follow up and complete the interview cycle. Follow-up by the institution is a simple but deserved courtesy; although the applicant was looking for a job, you were also looking for an employee, and this particular individual traveled to meet you and gave you a certain amount of time.

Appropriate follow-up takes very little time. Once you have decided you do not wish to extend a job offer, a short, polite letter to that effect is appropriate. Also, you can use this same approach to let individuals know that although you cannot extend a job offer at the present time you would like to keep their applications on file for future consideration. Depending on your organization's employment system, these letters might originate with you or they might go out from the personnel department. In most organizations the personnel department will take care of applicant communication, but it is within the realm of reason for you to follow up with personnel to make sure this communication has occurred. In any case, and even for the most clearly unqualified of applicants, you should conclude the interview process with an answer. It is a courtesy due the applicant, and it serves to protect the image of the institution as an employer in the community.

The employee selection interview is a hazardous process filled with opportunities for miscalculation and misjudgment. It offers no guarantees that you will always locate the right person for the job. However, the interview is the best available way of gaining information about prospective new employees. As such it will continue to remain one of the most important kinds of personal contact for the supervisor.

Source: Charles R. McConnell, *The Effective Health Care Supervisor*, 3rd ed., Aspen Publishers, Inc., © 1993.

HISTORY AND MAJOR PARTS OF THE AMERICANS WITH DISABILITIES ACT (ADA)

The sponsors of the ADA found that discrimination against people with disabilities existed in such areas as employment, housing, public accommodations, education, transportation, communication, recreation, institutionalization, health services, voting, and access to public service. Discrimination encountered in these areas ranges from intentional exclusion to overprotective rules and policies to inadvertent exclusion caused by existing architectural, transportation, and communication barriers. They also found that people with disabilities had no legal recourse to help them fight the discrimination they encountered.

In reviewing other civil rights law, ADA sponsors determined that people with disabilities, as a group, had been overlooked. They also determined that this group deserved special protection against discrimination. To remedy this problem, they drafted the ADA to accomplish the following:

- provide a clear and comprehensive national mandate for the elimination of discrimination against people with disabilities
- provide clear, strong, consistent and enforceable standards addressing discrimination against people with disabilities
- ensure that the federal government plays a central role in enforcing the standards established in the ADA on behalf of people with disabilities
- invoke congressional authority, including the power to enforce the Fourteenth Amendment and to regulate commerce, to address the major areas of discrimination that people with disabilities face daily

It should also be noted that although the title of the ADA includes "Americans," its provisions protect everyone with disabilities, regardless of their citizenship status or nationality.

MAJOR PARTS OF THE LAW

The ADA is patterned after the Rehabilitation Act of 1973 and contains five major sections:

1. Title I—Employment
2. Title II—Public Services
3. Title 111—Public Accommodations and Services Operated by Private Entities
4. Title IV—Telecommunications
5. Title V—Miscellaneous Provisions

Compliance with Title I requirements is the primary focus of this information.

Title I: Employment

Title I deals with the hiring, treatment, and accommodation of applicants and employees with disabilities.

- *General purpose*: To provide protection against discrimination to people with disabilities in employment-related matters such as job application procedures, hiring, advancement, discharge, compensation, training, and other terms, conditions, and privileges of employment.
- *Effective date*: July 26, 1992, for organizations with 25 or more employees; July 26. 1994, for organizations with 15 or more employees.
- *Covered entities*: Private employers, employment agencies, labor organizations, joint labor-management committees, and state and local governments.
- *Protected individuals*: Qualified people with a physical or mental impairment that substantially limits one or more major life activities; those with a record of such an impairment; or those who are regarded as having such an impairment, who are able to perform the essential functions of a job with or without reasonable accommodation.
- *Enforcement and remedies:* The Equal Employment Opportunity Commission (EEOC) is the primary enforcing agency. Remedies available to people with disabilities who have been discriminated against include compensatory and punitive damages, back pay, front pay, restored benefits, attorneys' fees, reasonable accommodation, reinstatement, and job offers.

Source: McGladrey and Pullen, *The Americans with Disabilities Act: A Practical Guide to Cost-Effective Compliance*, Sheshunoff Information Services, © 1992.

WHEN A PERSON HAS A PHYSICAL OR MENTAL IMPAIRMENT THAT SUBSTANTIALLY LIMITS ONE OR MORE MAJOR LIFE ACTIVITIES

The following discussions clarify the concepts of "physical or mental impairment," "substantially limits," and "major life activities" as referred to in the ADA.

PHYSICAL AND MENTAL IMPAIRMENTS

A comprehensive list of all diseases and conditions that constitute a physical or mental impairment is impossible to provide, given the assortment of possible impairments. However, this section does provide information that will assist you in understanding the EEOC's interpretation of physical and mental impairments and who is considered to be disabled under the ADA.

A physical impairment is defined by the ADA as any physiological disorder, or condition, cosmetic disfigurement, or anatomical loss affecting one or more of the following body systems: neurological, musculoskeletal, special sense organs, respiratory (including speech organs), cardiovascular, reproductive, digestive, genitourinary, hemic and lymphatic, skin, and endocrine.

A mental impairment is defined by the ADA as any mental or psychological disorder, such as mental retardation, organic brain syndrome, emotional or mental illness, and specific learning disabilities.

Neither type of impairment takes into consideration any medication or assistive device that may be used to reduce the impairment. For example, if a person has an artificial limb, that person is considered impaired even though the prosthesis may reduce the impact of the impairment.

WHAT IS NOT A DISABILITY

Exceptions to the ADA definition of disabled are as follows:

- Conditions related to stress and depression may or may not be considered impairments, depending on whether the conditions have been documented as physiological or mental disorders.
- People with contagious diseases are considered impaired. However, if the disease poses a direct threat to the health and safety of others, you as an employer are not required to hire or retain the person with the disease unless the threat can be reduced or eliminated through reasonable accommodation.
- Physical characteristics, such as left-handedness, 'normal" height and weight, and hair or eye color are not considered impairments; they would not be categorized as physiological or mental disorders. Also, a physical condition like pregnancy or a personality trait like absentmindedness is not considered an impairment as it is not the result of a physiological or mental disorder.
- Environmental, cultural, or economic disadvantages, such as a lack of education or a prison record, are not considered impairments. Neither is homosexuality or bisexuality. The ADA specifically exempts the following sexual and behavioral disorders from being considered disabilities:
  - transvestism, transsexualism, pedophilia, exhibitionism, voyeurism, gender identity disorders not resulting from physical impairments, or other sexual behavior disorders
  - compulsive gambling, kleptomania or pyromania
  - psychoactive substance use disorders resulting from the current illegal use of drugs
- Current users of illegal drugs are not protected under the ADA.

Substantially Limits

The EEOC regulations define "substantially limits" as unable to perform a major life activity that the average person in the general population can perform; or significantly restricted as to the condition, manner, or duration under which an individual can perform a particular major life activity as compared to the condition, manner, or duration under which the average person in the general population can perform that same major life activity.

In determining whether an impairment substantially limits a major life activity, the EEOC regulations provide three factors to consider:

1. the nature and severity of the impairment
2. the duration or expected duration of the impairment
3. the permanent or long-term impact, or the expected permanent or long-term impact, of, or resulting from, the impairment

It is important to consider these factors because the ADA may cover an impairment or condition experienced by one person but not another. It is the *effect* of an impairment or condition on the major life activities of the person that determines coverage. The EEOC provides the following example: Although cerebral palsy frequently significantly restricts major life activities such as speaking, walking, and performing manual tasks, an individual with very mild cerebral palsy that only slightly interferes with his or her ability to speak and has no significant impact on other major life activities is not an individual with a disability under this part of the definition. If, however, the person is regarded as having an impairment and/or has a record of the impairment, the person would be covered under those portions of the definition of disabled.

If a person has more than one impairment, each impairment by itself may not limit a major life activity. However, if when combined they limit one or more major life activities, the person is considered disabled under the ADA.

Substantially Limited in Working

EEOC's regulations give specific attention to defining "substantially limited in working." Therefore, the following discus-

continues

When a Person Has a Physical or Mental Impairment that Substantially Limits continued

sion will help you determine whether this major life activity is limited.

Under this definition, a person is considered disabled if he or she is significantly restricted in the ability to perform either a class of jobs or a broad range of jobs in various classes as compared to the average person with comparable training, skills, and abilities. A person would not be considered disabled if that person were substantially limited in performing only one particular job.

The following factors should be considered when determining whether a person is substantially limited in working in your organization:

- geographical area in which the person may reasonably expect to find a job
- type of job from which the individual has been disqualified
- number and types of jobs using similar training, knowledge, skill, or ability from which the person is qualified within the geographical area
- number and types of other jobs in the area that do not involve similar training, knowledge, skill, or ability from which the person is also disqualified because of the impairment

Major Life Activities

The EEOC regulations define "major life activities" as functions such as caring for oneself, performing manual tasks, walking, seeing, hearing, speaking, breathing, learning, and working.

The definition above is not intended to be a comprehensive list of major life activities; it only provides examples. Activities that are basic in nature and that the average person in the general population can perform are generally considered major life activities.

Temporary Impairments

The ADA covers some temporary impairments. To determine whether a temporary impairment is covered, the extent, duration, and impact of the impairment must be considered. Temporary, nonchronic impairments that do not last for a long time and that have little or no long-term impact usually are not considered disabilities under the ADA. For example, colds, sprains, and broken limbs generally would not be considered disabilities. However, if an employee who held the position of encoder had a broken arm that took longer than normal to heal and during this time the employee did not have use of his or her hand, he or she would be considered disabled.

Source: McGladrey and Pullen. *The Americans with Disabilities Act: A Practical Guide to Cost-Effective Compliance*, Sheshunoff Information Services, © 1992.

WHEN A PERSON HAS A RECORD OF A SUBSTANTIALLY LIMITING IMPAIRMENT

The second part of the ADA definition of a person with a disability provides that someone with a record of having an impairment that substantially limits a major life activity will be protected against discrimination in employment at an organization. This definition applies regardless of whether the person is currently substantially limited in a major life activity. It also protects people who may have been misclassified or misdiagnosed as having a disability. Included under this umbrella of protection are people with a history of cancer, heart disease, mental illness, or other debilitating illness, whose illnesses are either cured, controlled, or in remission. The following examples were provided by the EEOC:

- A job applicant formerly was a patient at a state institution. When very young she was misdiagnosed as being psychopathic and this misdiagnosis was never removed from her records. If this person is otherwise qualified for a job and an employer does not hire her on the basis of this record, the employer has violated the ADA.
- A person who has a learning disability applies for a job as a secretary/receptionist. The employer reviews records from a previous employer indicating that the applicant was labeled as "mentally retarded." Even though the person's resume shows that he meets all the requirements for the job, the employer does not interview him because he doesn't want to hire a person who is mentally retarded. This employer has violated the ADA.

Source: McGladrey and Pullen. *The Americans with Disabilities Act: A Practical Guide to Cost-Effective Compliance*, Sheshunoff Information Services, © 1992.

WHEN A PERSON IS REGARDED AS HAVING A SUBSTANTIALLY LIMITING IMPAIRMENT

The third part of the Americans with Disabilities (ADA) definition of a person with a disability provides that anyone who is regarded by the employer as having a substantially limiting impairment is protected from discrimination. This means that a person need only be *perceived* as having a disability to be covered by the ADA. This part of the definition is provided to protect people who are perceived as having disabilities because of misconceptions, fears, and stereotypes about the disability.

A person would be covered under three circumstances:

1. The employer treats the person as if that person has a substantially limiting impairment even though the impairment in fact does not substantially limit a major life activity.
   Example: An employee who has controlled high blood pressure works in a stressful position. The high blood pressure does not limit her work activities, but the employer fears she may suffer a heart attack if she continues with her present job. Because of this fear, the employer reassigns her to a different position. In this situation, the employer has regarded her as disabled.
2. Because of the attitudes of others toward a person's condition, the person is considered to have a substantially limiting impairment.
   Example: An experienced bank teller who primarily worked in a drive-through was passed up for promotion to head teller because she had a prominent facial scar. A less experienced part-time teller was promoted instead, because the employer presumed customers would not want to look at the teller with the facial scar. Because the bank perceived and treated her as a person with a substantial limitation, it has discriminated against her on the basis of a disability.
3. The person is treated by the employer as having a substantially limiting impairment even though that person has no impairment at all.
   Example: An organization discharged a manager on the basis of a rumor that he had acquired immune deficiency syndrome. Although he in fact did not have any impairment, he was treated as having a substantially limiting impairment and therefore would be covered by the ADA.

QUALIFIED DISABLED INDIVIDUALS

To be protected under the ADA, a person must not only be disabled as defined earlier, but also must be qualified for the position he or she occupies or is applying for. A qualified person with a disability will satisfy the education, experience, skill, and other job-related requirements of the position he or she is seeking or currently holds, and will be able to perform the essential functions of the job, with or without reasonable accommodation.

Two steps should be used in determining whether someone is qualified:

1. Determine whether the person meets the necessary prerequisites for the position at your organization, such as education, work experience, specialized training, skills, licenses, and other job-related requirements. If the person meets all the prerequisites, he or she is "otherwise qualified" for the job, not considering the disability. If, however, the person meets all prerequisites except those that are affected by the disability, you should ensure that the prerequisite that screened out the person is job-related and consistent with business necessity.
2. If the person meets step one, the next step is to determine if the person is able to perform the essential functions of the job, with or without reasonable accommodation. To do this
   - Identify the essential functions of the job the person is applying for at your organization.
   - Determine whether the disabled person can perform these functions unassisted or with a reasonable accommodation.

Organizations must focus on the essential functions of a job when considering whether a disabled individual can qualify. Job functions that are only minor cannot be used as a basis for disqualifying someone with a disability.

Source: McGladrey and Pullen. *The Americans with Disabilities Act: A Practical Guide to Cost-Effective Compliance*, Sheshunoff Information Services, © 1992.

ORIENTATION

HEALTH RECORD/UTILIZATION REVIEW DEPARTMENT: GENERAL OVERVIEW OF FUNCTIONS

The staff of the department provides support for the health information/health record and utilization management needs to ensure quality patient care and to facilitate administrative, medical, staff, and other information requirements of the hospital, all with a commitment to ongoing performance improvement.

DEPARTMENT SCOPE AND SERVICES

Health record maintenance, retrieval, and analysis; transcription; release of information and claims processing; coding and abstracting; reimbursement support services; health science library services; clinical and statistical information gathering; utilization management; medical staff and administrative support.

DEPARTMENTAL CUSTOMERS

The HR/UR department facilitates the needs of many customers—first and foremost, the patient. Secondary customers include the medical staff, patient family members/friends, administration, managers, ancillary staff, governmental and accrediting agencies, physician offices, referral hospitals and medical centers, third-party payers, utilization review agencies, and all others with legitimate information needs.

PATIENT POPULATION

The hospital provides services to all patients presenting for care. HR/UR staff is trained in providing services to all members of the patient population regardless of age, socioeconomic status, ethnic/racial background, age and/or behavioral/developmental challenges. Policies are written to address the needs of children (minors) as well as those of patients who may have transferred the responsibility of their health care to others (durable power of attorney/health care decision responsibility). On an as-needed basis, the manager will seek assistance from administration, social services, or other areas to meet specialized patient needs.

HOURS

The HR/UR department is staffed Monday through Friday, 7:30 A.M. through 5:00 P.M. with Saturday A.M. coverage for transcription. Transcriptionists will respond to calls to transcribe dictation in emergency situations. After hours the department and component offices are kept locked; access can be obtained by contacting the nursing supervisor. Medical staff members are provided keys to the dictation room on request.

DEPARTMENTAL MEETINGS

Departmental meetings are held at 10:30 A.M. the fourth Wednesday of each month. A listing of meeting dates is posted in advance. Agenda items include administrative concerns and issues, departmental changes, new programs and policies, and individual concerns. Department members are encouraged to provide input into the agenda items or report informally at the departmental meeting. Minutes are maintained with copies provided to those staff members who are unable to attend. Regular attendance is strongly encouraged.

DEPARTMENTAL POLICIES AND PROCEDURES

An HR/UR departmental policy and procedure manual is maintained in the HR office to provide guidance and instruc-

DEPARTMENTAL ORGANIZATION

Board of Trustees			
Chief Executive Officer			
Manager, Health Record Department			
Clerical Section	Transcription Section	Coding Section	Utilization Review Section
1–1.0 HR Clerk 1–0.8 HR Clerk 2–0.5 HR Clerks	3–1.0 Transcriptionists 1–0.8 Transcriptionist 1–0.4 Transcriptionist	2–0.8 Coders 1–0.4 Coder	1–1.0 UR Coordinator
Volunteers and students also participate in departmental operations.			

continues

Health Record/Utilization Review Department continued

tion in carrying out key departmental functions. All policies and procedures are developed with the assistance of the staff impacted and presented as informational items at the monthly departmental meetings.

PROBLEM RESOLUTION MODEL

A problem resolution model has been developed and education provided to assist staff in constructively dealing with conflict. The steps are as follows:

- First step—Staff is strongly encouraged to resolve problems among them as a first course of action. The manager will encourage this whenever possible. If the problem cannot be resolved at this level, then. . .
- Second step—Problems that cannot be resolved on a one-to-one basis among staff members shall be referred to the manager for resolution. The manager will meet with the staff members involved in an attempt to resolve the issue. If the problem cannot be resolved at this level, then. . .
- Third step—Problems that cannot be resolved with a meeting of the staff and the manager may be referred to the personnel department. The personnel director and the manager will take steps to access additional expertise in resolving the issue. This may include input from division directors, administration, and other applicable resources.

ADMINISTRATIVE POLICIES AND PROCEDURES

Pertinent administrative policies and procedures are maintained in the HR department. All new or recently revised administrative policies are presented at departmental meetings as informational items.

JOB DESCRIPTIONS AND PERFORMANCE EVALUATIONS

Copies of job descriptions are maintained in the departmental policy and procedure manual. Job descriptions are developed with the assistance of the staff impacted and from standardized data sets available to management. Performance expectations are included in the job evaluations; job descriptions are approved by administration.

Corresponding with each job description is a performance evaluation tool. Performance evaluations are carried out annually on the anniversary of the employee's hire date. Copies of the evaluation tools are made available prior to the evaluation process with an opportunity for feedback from the staff member prior to the actual evaluation. Performance evaluations are scheduled by the manager; sufficient time is allowed to offer staff members opportunity for feedback. A copy of the completed performance evaluation is provided to the employee for personal records.

DEPARTMENTAL PARTICIPATION IN THE HOSPITAL SAFETY PROGRAM

In conjunction with the hospitalwide commitment to safety, the members of the HR/UR department hold responsibility for ensuring a safe environment for patients, staff, students, volunteers, and all others visiting the hospital. Departmental disaster plan and safety manuals are maintained in the outer office for easy reference. Department members participate in the safety program through the following four mechanisms:

1. Development and responsibility for departmental safety policy.
2. Participation in actual and drill emergency situations. (During an actual disaster, the HR/UR department will serve as the personnel pool for the hospital.)
3. Attendance at hospital inservices that provide training and education in safety-related areas.
4. Regular reporting of adverse occurrences that may affect safety in the hospital.

PARTICIPATION IN INFECTION CONTROL PROGRAM

While the members of the HR/UR department are not actively involved with hands-on patient care, indirectly there is participation in the hospitalwide infection control program. Specifically, the staff of the HR/UR department assists the infection control coordinator in the identification of infection control issues, the comparison of databases, and the analysis of health information related to infection control issues.

PERFORMANCE IMPROVEMENT ACTIVITIES

Performance improvement activities are considered part of an ongoing environmental process. Key statistical performance indicators are kept routinely. Opportunities for improvement are identified through various channels, especially through customer feedback. The HR/UR department is committed to ongoing enhancement of departmental services as well as participation in hospitalwide efforts to improve services. Members of the staff serve on various work teams and provide input on health information topics. Furthermore, the department supports activities outside the realm of health information functions by providing analysis of clinical and statistical data.

Courtesy of Door County Memorial Hospital, Sturgeon Bay, Wisconsin.

INTERDEPARTMENTAL RELATIONSHIPS OF THE HEALTH RECORDS DEPARTMENT

Accounting:	We work with this department on budgets, payment for materials and services received, petty cash, check requests, equipment inventory, and employee payroll.
Administration:	We receive direction from the administrative officers in the form of policies, memos, department head meetings, conferences, and department meetings. They are available to help us solve problems or to give advice.
Cardiology:	We provide this department with patient information. It provides us with reports of tests on patients.
Education Department:	This department is responsible for most of the education classes in the hospital, i.e., orientation, inservices, and continuing education. It provides calendars to keep us informed about what is available. It also has the responsibility to schedule the use of all classrooms and conference rooms.
EEG Department:	We provide this department with patient information. It sends us the results of tests on patients.
Emergency Department:	We provide this department with patient information; in addition, we store this department's records.
Employee Health:	This department provides our employment physicals and yearly follow-up tests. It also handles employees who become ill or injured on the job.
Financial Services (Billing Department):	We work very closely with this area to provide diagnosis and procedure codes on discharge for billing purposes.
Environmental Health Services (Housekeeping):	This department keeps our office clean so we have a pleasant place to work.
Human Resources: (Personnel):	Every employee works closely with this department all during employment at this hospital. This department provides us with explanations of personnel policies and employee benefits. This department maintains each employee's personnel file and keeps track of wages, promotions, changes in status, etc.
Information Desk:	This function is staffed by volunteers. They provide information on hospitalized patients to the public and families.
Information Systems:	We abstract directly onto the computer in order to receive our indexes for Joint Commission and state licensing requirements. Data processing provides us with lists, such as admission, discharge and transfer (ADT) lists, daily census reports, etc.
Laboratory:	The laboratory provides the lab work for the employee physicals. It provides us with the original reports of all outpatient and inpatient lab work. We provide it with necessary patient information.
Medical Library:	This resource is supervised by the director of medical records, and we maintain a very close working relationship. The facilities of the library are open to all employees to use either before or after their shift or at break times.
Medical Staff Office:	This office processes all of the applications for privileges, maintains information necessary for the committees of the medical staff, and maintains the listing of the medical staff. We work closely with the medical staff secretary on certain committee functions.
Nuclear Medicine:	This department provides certain diagnostic procedures. It provides us with reports of tests on patients. We provide it with necessary patient information.
Plant Services:	Includes three major areas: grounds, maintenance, and the power plant. It provides us with all the maintenance support, including heat and air conditioning.

continues

Interdepartmental Relationships continued

Public Relations:	We provide this department with news items about our area for the hospital newsletter and possible publication in outside papers. If we have VIP inpatients or a disaster, this department is the only one that will release information. We transfer relevant calls to this department.
Purchasing:	We work with this departmentto get the supplies and equipment we need to run our office.
Quality Improvement:	Most of the data obtained by the quality improvement coordinator for review of patient care is obtained through the health record and the monthly indexes. Thus, charts are retrieved for the quality improvement coordinator and various medical staff committees upon request. In addition, the health information management specialist and quality improvement data analyst play an active part in generating and reviewing patient care data and report results to the quality improvement coordinator.
Radiology:	This department provides us with the reports of outpatient and inpatient X-rays. We provide it with patient information.
Rehabilitation Services:	This department provides us with reports of patient treatments. We provide it with necessary patient information.
Respiratory Therapy:	We provide this department with patient information. It provides us with reports of outpatient and inpatient treatments.
Safety and Security:	This department provides us with systems, programs, and people to deal with emergency situations. We work with it to keep our area safe and secure. This department also handles lost-and-found items.
Social Work:	We provide this department with patient information and store its records with ours.
Telephone Central:	The operators are the main phone contact with the hospital. They help us with phone problems.
Volunteers:	Volunteers provide us with many services free of charge.
Utilization Management:	We provide this department with patient records that are necessary for it to review. In addition, DRGs are an integral part of the necessity for health records and utilization review to maintain an effective, communicative relationship.

Courtesy of Shady Grove Adventist Hospital, Rockville, Maryland

TELEPHONE GUIDELINES

Good telephone habits give people the feeling they are speaking with a friendly, helpful, and considerate employee. Please remember when you are on the telephone that you represent the hospital and that you are responsible for maintaining our reputation for quality health care. When answering calls, the following guidelines should be followed:

- Be courteous, polite, and pleasant.
- Communicate interest and concern.
- Speak slowly and clearly.
- Make requests rather than give orders.
- Listen and make sure you understand the reason for the call.
- Answer calls promptly (first, second, or third ring whenever possible).
- When answering the telephone, identify yourself and the department. Example: "Health records, Mary speaking, may I help you?" or "Good morning, health records, may I help you?"

PUTTING CALLERS ON HOLD

- If you need to put a caller on hold, say, "May I please put you on hold?" or "Could you please hold?
- When you come back on the line, say, "Thank you for holding," or "I appreciate your patience."

TAKING MESSAGES

Always have paper and pencil handy so you can write down messages, including the following information:

- caller's name
- organizational or departmental telephone number
- date and time call was received
- your name on the message
- what call was in reference to

Courtesy of Shady Grove Adventist Hospital, Rockville, Maryland.

COMPUTER TRAINING NEEDS ASSESSMENT

Today's Date: ______________________

Name: ______________________ Department: ______________ Title: ______________

Manager's Name: ______________________ Shift: ______________

Please answer the following questions:

(circle one)

1. Are you familiar with computer hardware? Yes No
2. Have you used a mouse? Yes No
3. Are you familiar with basic computer terms? Yes No
4. Rate your perception of the following:

	Never Used	Use a Little	Fairly Competent	Very Competent
DOS				
Windows				
AmiPro				
Maven				
CC:Mail				
Freelance Graphics				
Lotus Notes				
Approach				
EIS				
Code 3				
MIS				
CERNER				
DOLBY				
MEDIC				
Lotus 1-2-3				
NHS Occupational Medicine				
SmartSuites Organizer				

5. I need intermediate-level classes in: (List)

____

____

6. I need advanced-level classes in: (List)

____

____

____

Source: Rebecca Sykes, "Information Management Plan and the Role of the Health Information Management Professional," *Topics in Health Information Management*, Aspen Publishers, Inc., © February 1996.

ORIENTATION OVERVIEW CHECKLIST

ORIENTATION TO HEALTH RECORDS DEPARTMENT AND SHADY GROVE ADVENTIST HOSPITAL

_____ explanation of organizational/departmental chain of command

_____ location of work station and coat rack

_____ location of cafeteria, canteen, rest rooms, water fountains, stairways, elevators, and public phones

_____ explanation and discussion of the confidentiality of the health record

_____ explanation of chart flow and chart control

_____ explanation of microfiche and roll film

_____ location and instructions for PC

_____ location of health records department policies and procedures manuals

_____ safety management/risk management

_____ hospital and health records continuous quality improvement process

ORIENTATION TO INDIVIDUAL JOB

_____ description of job; requirements of position

_____ synopsis of position; work flow preceding and following completion of duties

EVALUATION AND FOLLOW-UP

_____ evaluation process (45-and 90-day evaluations for full-time employees and 120 days for part-time employees; annual evaluation)

_____________________ _____________

EMPLOYEE SIGNATURE **DATE**

Courtesy of Shady Grove Adventist Hospital, Rockville, Maryland.

ORIENTATION EVALUATION FORM

We are glad to have you as part of the Health Record Department team. Please take a few minutes to complete this brief questionnaire. Your input will be greatly appreciated.

EMPLOYEE: ______________________________

POSITION: ______________________________

SUPERVISOR: ______________________________

HIRE DATE: ______________________________

1. Did the orientation cover all the areas you wanted discussed?
   YES ____ NO ____

If not, what additions can you suggest? ______________________________

____

(Use back of form for extra space.)

2. Were you satisfied with your orientation?
   YES ____ NO ____

If not, why? ______________________________

____

(Use back of form for extra space.)

	(Circle one number in each scale.) Rating Scales				
	Low			High	
3. How well did you understand the locations in the hospital where charts are to be taken?	1	2	3	4	5
4. How well was the supervisory structure explained to you?	1	2	3	4	5
5. How much responsibility are you now willing to assume?	1	2	3	4	5
6. How clearly and understandably was your own work explained to you?	1	2	3	4	5

7. Did you feel that you wanted to go into more detail in
   (Circle one) no some most all areas?
8. How soon do you think you'd like to have the next orientation follow-up session?
   (Circle one) one day three days one week two weeks
9. What do you want help on right away? ______________________________

____

(Use other side of form for extra space.)

10. What suggestions would you like to make to improve the Orientation Program for the next employee? ____________

____

(Use other side of form for extra space.)

ACKNOWLEDGMENT STATEMENT

I have read the Orientation Packet that applies to my employment in the Health Records Department.

Each section of the packet has been discussed with my supervisor.

I understand the policies and procedures for which I am responsible and am aware that I am subject to disciplinary action if I am found to be in violation of the guidelines within this packet.

I agree to abide by the policies and procedures recorded in this packet and realize my responsibility in becoming aware of revisions or additions to them, for in so doing, I will enhance interdepartmental communication and operational effectiveness at this hospital.

______________________________ ______________________________

Signature of Employee Date

Courtesy of Shady Grove Adventist Hospital, Rockville, Maryland.

SEXUAL HARASSMENT

WHAT IS SEXUAL HARASSMENT?

Sexual harassment occurs if an employer or manager makes the granting of sexual favors a condition of continued employment or promotion in the company, or if a hostile or embarrassing atmosphere is created in the workplace as a result of lewd remarks and obscene language. Allowing employees to make unwelcome advances to coworkers also falls under the definition of sexual harassment.

Although at one lime only the exchange of sexual favors for preferential treatment on the job was considered sexual harassment subject to sanction under Title VII of the Civil Rights Act of 1964, the current definition is much broader. Today, courts consider any unwelcome sexually oriented behavior—which need not result in physical contact—that creates a term or condition of employment to be sexual harassment. Sexually suggestive comments alone may constitute sexual harassment under Title VII if they create a work environment that the employee reasonably feels is hostile, abusive, or offensive. Sexual harassment need not involve the conditioning of concrete employment benefits on sexual favors. Specifically, a successful claimant does not have to prove a loss of any economic benefit, but only that, given the "totality of the circumstances," the employment environment is hostile, abusive, or offensive as a result of sexually suggestive conduct.

Source: James O. Castagnera, *Employment Law Book*, 2nd ed., Panel Publishers, A Division of Aspen Publishers, Inc., © 1993.

THE SEXUAL HARASSMENT POLICY

SEXUAL HARASSMENT

Sexual harassment is a form of sex discrimination. Under the law, employers are liable for sexual harassment—whether or not they have knowledge of offending behavior on the part of their employees or even the public. Therefore, many companies choose to start with a strong policy against sexual harassment, coupled with a program of educating supervisors and employees generally.

The policy must be included in an employee handbook and otherwise communicated to employees. A sample memorandum communicating a change of policy and procedures appears below.

SAMPLE POLICY

This company believes that each employee has the right to be free from harassment because of age, color, creed, national origin, or sex. Sexual harassment is defined as any of the following:

- unwelcome physical contact
- sexually explicit language or gestures
- uninvited or unwanted sexual advances
- an offensive overall environment, including the use of vulgar language, the presence of sexually explicit photographs or other materials, and the telling of sexual stories

Sexual harassment can come from superiors, fellow employees, or customers. Men as well as women can be victims of sexual harassment. This company cannot stress enough that it *will not tolerate any form of sexual harassment.*

The manager at each location is responsible for dealing with harassment incidents, which includes dealing with complaints that employees bring to his or her attention and identifying harassing situations on his or her own. Similarly, the regional supervisor is responsible for his or her region, and the president of the company is responsible for the company as a whole.

Complaints against employees or customers are to be brought first to the manager, who will investigate the matter. If the allegation is sustained, the responsible employee will be disciplined. If harassment continues, the responsible individual will be terminated *immediately*. Responsible customers who do not change their behavior after a polite request from the manager will be denied entrance.

If the complaint is against a manager, it is to be brought to the regional supervisor or any regional supervisor if the supervisor for the region is not available. If the complaint is against the regional supervisor, the president is to be contacted. If, at any point in this process, the employee is dissatisfied with the investigation being conducted, the employee is to bring the matter to the attention of the president's office.

Source: William J. Quirk, *Company Policy Manual*, 3rd ed., Panel Publishers, A Division of Aspen Publishers, Inc., © 1992.

SAMPLE COMMUNICATION OF SEXUAL HARASSMENT POLICY TO EMPLOYEES

To: All Employees
From: ______________________________, CEO
Subject: Sexual Harassment
Date: ______________________

This company believes that each employee has the right to be free from harassment because of age, color, creed, national origin, or sex. Because of the current rise in sexual harassment charges across the country, we wish to clarify our procedure for dealing with this problem.

It cannot be stressed enough that this company *will not tolerate any form of sexual harassment.* Should you feel you are being harassed, please follow these guidelines to help remedy the problem.

Harassment by other employees or by customers at the individual units should be brought to the attention of the manager, who will then investigate the matter. If the allegation is sustained, the responsible employee will be disciplined. If harassment continues, the responsible individual will be terminated *immediately*. Responsible customers who do not change their behavior after a polite request from the manager will be denied entrance.

Should you feel the manager has not investigated the matter to your satisfaction, contact ______________ at __________ *immediately*.

Should the harassment originate from the management in a location, the regional supervisor for that unit is to be contacted. If, for any reason, that supervisor cannot be reached, any supervisor will respond to your complaint.

Should the harasser be the regional supervisor, please contact me directly.

Sexual harassment is defined as any of the following:

- unwelcome physical contact
- sexually explicit language or gestures
- uninvited or unwanted sexual advances
- an offensive overall environment, including the use of vulgar language, the presence of sexually explicit photographs or other materials, and the telling of sexual stories

It can come from superiors, fellow employees, or customers. Men as well as women can be victims of sexual harassment.

Please sign and date the attached, acknowledging that you have read this notice.

Source: William J. Quirk, *Company Policy Manual*, 3rd ed., Panel Publishers, A Division of Aspen Publishers, Inc., © 1992.

TRAINING DESIGN

ABOUT TRAINING DESIGN

A specific training program is developed for each job in the health record department to foster uniformity of practice in carrying out the work, to provide a safeguard against errors that put the patient and/or facility at risk, to comply with regulatory and accrediting agency requirements concerning training, and, finally, to ensure that the facility has an adequate and motivated work force.

The training program is based on two major management documents:

1. the job description for the position
2. the relevant policies and procedures, with their associated guidelines

The basic purpose of each segment of the training program is to acquaint the trainee with the underlying principles and knowledge base necessary for the work to be performed. Practice activities follow.

Learning Objectives

These are stated in stylized language. Usually the learning objective contains

- the statement of the main focus: what is to be demonstrated or stated
- the level of mastery *or* an acceptable performance level, such as "error free" or "with 100 percent accuracy" (When mastery-level performance is adopted, a realistic time limit to obtain mastery—for example, after [*n*] practice sessions—may be stated.)

- any conditions such as use of specific regulations or use of designated equipment
- time frame/performance standard, which may be presented in stages, with an initial phase of untimed performance followed by progressively increased performance levels until the work standard is met

These learning objective elements may be stated in whole or in part at the beginning of the training design for each unit and need not be repeated. For example, the various activities or processes that the trainee carries out must be in accordance with the specified policies and procedures. Having stated this condition initially, the training specialist need not repeat it for each learning objective.

Content

It is useful in on-the job training to present the material in the job context, followed by discrete job elements, presented in one of two orders:

1. strict job performance order, giving the trainee a cohesive sense of the overall work flow
2. technical knowledge-based content, followed by specific administrative and procedural processes, giving the trainee the underlying principles that may then be used to guide actual practice

These approaches may, of course, be mixed according to the nature of the material to be teamed.

Methods

The traditional lecture method is used to present factual material, such as the content of regulations or the format of a health record. This method is used in conjunction with the demonstration/presentation of samples and practice material in the flow of the lecture. For example, key points of an adequate authorization for release of information might be discussed, using a sample authorization as a basis for the lecture.

In the interest of fostering the immediate involvement of the trainee, practice activities based on actual materials or examples drawn from the work are used. As an example, a series of fictitious letters requesting information about patients, representing a mix of typical requests, might be used as the basis for teaching the procedural steps used to process these requests.

In jobs involving routine and problematic interaction with patients/clients and members of the public, simulated activities may be carried out. Routine activity may be presented in role playing, and problematic situations may be illustrated and practiced through critical incident interventions.

A comprehensive activity, the in-basket exercise, may be used initially as a method of providing an overview of typical work. It is then used as the final, comprehensive evaluation tool.

Evaluation

For material of a factual nature, where precise knowledge should be demonstrated, fact tests are used. More commonly, in the job setting, the trainee will be evaluated through performance tests. The trainee has activities to carry out; these activities are drawn from the usual work of the job. The final evaluation may be carried out in stages: practice activity, followed by real work activity under immediate supervision, followed by real work activity with diminishing levels of immediate supervision.

The evaluation brings the training process full circle. The trainee has been given specific training objectives to attain, appropriate didactic and practice materials have been explained, and practice activities with appropriate correction and feedback have been given. The evaluation, therefore, consists of determining the trainee's capacity to perform the work described in the job description and specified through the detailed policies and procedures of the department.

Source: Joan Gratto Liebler, *Medical Records: Policies and Guidelines*, Aspen Publishers, Inc., © 1991.

SAMPLE TRAINING DESIGN: RELEASE OF INFORMATION SPECIALIST

Assumptions

The learning objectives presented in this training design are based on these four assumptions:

1. Performance condition: the activity is carried out according to the prescribed policy and procedure.
2. Acceptable level of performance:
   - *alternative one*: 100 percent accuracy level is attained.
   - *alternative two*: mastery-level competence is attained (no stated accuracy level is given).
3. Time frame/performance standard:
   - *during training:* the activity is accomplished at [60 percent] of the established performance [time] standard.
   - *final, comprehensive evaluation:* the trainee meets fully the stated performance [time] standard.
4. These learning objectives relate to the release of information; therefore, this phrase is not repeated in each objective or evaluation statement.

Overall Learning Objective

At the conclusion of this training sequence, the trainee/employee will demonstrate the ability to process written and oral requests for the release of information

- according to the standard policies and procedures of this facility
- with 100 percent accuracy
- within the performance [time] standards established for this work

The training sequence that follows is intended to develop the trainee's capacity to meet this comprehensive objective.

General Orientation and Introduction

Purpose

To acquaint the trainee with the general content and scope of the release of information processes.

Content

- review of job description: release of information specialist
- overview of policy and procedure manual
- explanation of learning objectives:
  - performance conditions
  - accuracy level (or mastery level)
  - performance standards

Methods

- *In-basket activity*: The trainee is given a representative sample of the various types of requests in the usual form in which such requests are received.

  After the trainee has read and reviewed these requests, the correctly completed responses to each request are given.

  NOTE: All examples used at this stage of orientation and training are fictitious.
- *Discussion*: The trainee has a brief discussion with the trainer in order to answer immediate questions and concerns and to present the outline for the detailed training to follow.

Evaluation

None; at this stage of the orientation, the trainee will not carry out activities.

Privacy and Confidentiality Principles

Purpose

To acquaint the trainee with the underlying principles of ethics and with privacy and confidentiality directives as these apply to the release of information about patients of this facility.

Learning Objectives

- The trainee will identify the applicable codes of ethics and directives relating to the release of information about patients of this facility.
- The trainee will compare the privacy and confidentiality directives contained in
  - federal and state regulations
  - accrediting standards
  - professional association codes of ethics
  - institution's Patients' Bill of Rights
- The trainee will apply these concepts to practice examples of release of information requests processed by this department and by related departments.

Content

- general principles relating to patient privacy and confidentiality: ethical and legal aspects
- specific directives and codes of ethics:
  - federal and state regulations
  - accrediting standards
  - professional association codes:
    a. American Hospital Association
    b. American Medical Record Association
  - institution's Patients' Bill of Rights
- policy and procedures reflecting these principles
- practice examples

Methods

- lecture
- practice activity: comparison of directives
- practice activity: application to typical requests

Evaluation

The trainee will complete worksheets

- comparing the various directives
- applying these directives to practice situations

General Requirements for Authorization

Purpose

To acquaint the trainee with general principles relating to the need for patient authorization.

Learning Objectives

- Given [______] written requests containing various types of written requests, the trainee will determine the need for authorization for each request.
- Given the same set of written requests and a mix of authorizations, the trainee will determine the adequacy/validity of each authorization for those requests needing authorization.

Content

- general underlying principles used to determine need for authorization
- the patient's capacity to authorize
- designated representatives of a patient who may authorize on behalf of the patient
- circumstances in which no authorization is needed
- requirements for valid authorization
- formats of authorizations:
  - insurance claim form
  - patient's own wording
  - facility's recommended form

Methods

Lecture is followed by practice activity. The trainee is given a representative sample of written requests, including a variety of authorization formats and a mix of both adequate and inadequate authorization statements.

Evaluation

A performance test consisting of fictitious written requests and a mix of authorizations is used.

- The trainee will determine which requests require authorization.
- The trainee will determine which authorizations are adequate/valid when compared to the listing of the required content for an authorization.

Special Authorization Requirements

Purpose

To acquaint the trainee with requirements associated with special classes of requests and the need for special authorization.

Learning Objectives

- Given [_____] written requests containing a mix of requests requiring special authorizations, the trainee will determine the specific type of authorization needed for each.
- Given the same set of written requests and a mix of authorizations, the trainee will determine the adequacy/validity of each authorization.

Content

- general underlying principles relating to special situations and requirements associated with the selected release of information from restricted records
- specific laws and regulations relating to the following categories of requests:
  - psychiatric records
  - employee patients/clients
  - adoptees and adopting parents
  - records requiring extraordinary security
  - child abuse cases
  - older adults abuse cases
  - HIV/AIDS-related cases
  - mental handicap/mental retardation cases
  - psychiatric cases
  - drug and alcohol use cases
  - sexual assault cases
- patient's capacity to consent
- designated representatives of a patient who may authorize on behalf of the patient
- circumstances in which no authorization is needed
- requirements for valid authorization
- formats of authorizations:
  - insurance claim form
  - special emphasis on billing reports in HIV/AIDS-related cases
  - patient's own wording
  - facility's recommended form
- court order for release of record

Methods

Lecture is followed by practice activity. The trainee is given a representative sample of written requests including a variety of authorization formats and a mix of both adequate and inadequate authorization statements.

Evaluation

A performance test consisting of fictitious written requests and a mix of authorizations is used.

- The trainee will determine which requests require special authorization.
- The trainee will determine which authorizations are adequate/valid when compared to the listing of the required content for a special authorization.

Selecting Health Record Information for the Response

Purpose

To acquaint the trainee with

- the content and format of the health record
- the appropriate response for each type of request
- the abstract form and its content and use

Learning Objectives

- Given a listing of health record data/information questions and [_____] fictitious health records, the trainee will complete the worksheet by indicating the answer to the specific query and the health record form on which the data were contained.
- Given [_____] health record reports containing abbreviations, the trainee will write out the correct meaning of each abbreviation from memory.
- Given [_____] fictitious written requests, the trainee will determine the appropriate response:
  - use of abstract format
  - selection of specific documents
- Given the same requests as in the previous learning objective, the trainee will
  - complete the abstract form for each request in which such a form is indicated
  - select specific documents as indicated

Content

- the health record: detailed content, detailed format
- approved abbreviations and their meaning
- abstract form: content
- guidelines for determining the use of the abstract form
- guidelines for selecting specific documents

Methods

- *self-study packet:* guided questions for each form in the health record; sample health records
- *self-study packet:* standard abbreviation list; guided questions to drill on the meaning of abbreviations; guided questions to drill on the meaning of abbreviations in the context of health record reports

Evaluation

A performance test is used.

- The trainee will complete questions based on specific health records, indicating the source document containing the requested information.
- The trainee will write out from memory the correct meanings of abbreviations contained in the health record reports.
- The trainee will determine the need for
  - an abstract form

  or

  - selected documents
- The trainee will complete abstract forms as indicated by the nature of the requests.
- The trainee will select specific documents as indicated by the nature of the requests.

Administrative and Procedural Steps

Purpose

To acquaint the trainee with the detailed administrative and procedural steps for the release of information from patients' health records.

Learning Objectives

- Given [_____] written requests, the trainee will process each request in the eight-step sequence established in the procedure manual.
  1. performing preliminary sorting and processing
  2. making entries in the release of information log
  3. determining patient status
  4. requisitioning the patient's health record
  5. preparing the cover letter
  6. determining and calculating the fees
  7. photocopying and reassembling the health record
  8. processing outgoing mail

Content

- examples of types of written requests:
  - U.S. mail
  - interdepartmental mail
  - fax
- categories of requests:
  - direct patient care
  - third-party payers
  - government agencies
  - review agencies
  - attorneys

- initial processing:
  - sorting and date-stamping
  - handling confidential mail
  - routing mail for further processing
- priority matrix: purpose and use
- release of information log:
  - purpose and use
  - content
  - staged entries: initial logging through final entry
  - computer security safeguards
- determining patient status:
  - accessing the patient master index
  - interpreting information in the patient master index
  - recording information on the request/inquiry
- requisitioning the patient health record:
  - preparing the requisition form
  - coordinating with the Storage and Retrieval unit
- preparing the cover letter:
  - purpose
  - sample formats
  - appropriate response statements and cover letters
- processing fees:
  - fee schedule and guidelines
  - determining applicable fees
  - calculating the fees
  - handling money received
  - transmitting fees to Accounts Receivable
- photocopy process:
  - equipment use
  - safeguards to prevent misfiling during processing
- reassembling the chart:
  - chart order
  - problem and misfile identification: notification of Storage and Retrieval unit and correction of misfile or problem
  - inclusion of original request, authorization, and record of material released
  - return of record to Storage and Retrieval unit
- final preparation for mailing the completed response

Methods

- lecture and demonstration of each step
- immediate practice activity following the lecture and demonstration of each step

Evaluation

Stage 1: The trainee will be given one standard request to process through the complete procedural cycle.

Stage 2: The trainee will be given one nonstandard request to process through the complete procedural cycle.

Stage 3: The trainee will be given [_____] written requests reflecting a mix of materials typically received. The trainee will process these requests through the complete procedural cycle.

Telephone Inquiries and Requests

Purpose

To acquaint the trainee with the procedural steps used to process telephone inquiries and requests.

Learning Objectives

- Given written descriptions of telephone request scenarios, the trainee will
  - determine the nature of the request: emergency or routine
  - process each type of request according to the procedure for the type of request or inquiry
- Given simulated events, the trainee will participate in role playing the response to telephone inquiries and requests.

Content

- public relations and client service aspects
- guidelines to determine the nature of the request:
  - emergency
  - routine
- detailed procedural steps for processing each of the types of requests

Methods

Lecture is followed by

- written answers to practice situations
- role playing
- critical incident process

Evaluation

- The trainee will complete a worksheet indicating the proper handling of each type of request.
- The trainee will participate in role playing to respond to fictitious requests.
- The trainee will respond to simulated critical incidents relating to emergency and problem requests.
- The trainee will respond to actual telephone requests under the immediate direction of the trainer.

In-Person Inquiries and Requests

Purpose

To acquaint the trainee with the procedural steps used to handle in-person inquiries and requests.

Learning Objectives

- Given written descriptions of in-person request scenarios, the trainee will
  - determine the nature of the request: emergency inquiry, routine inquiry, or request for access to health record
  - process each request according to the prescribed procedure for each type of request
- Given simulated events, the trainee will participate in role playing the response to in-person requests.

Content

- public relations and client service aspects
- guidelines to determine the nature of the request:
  - emergency inquiry
  - routine inquiry
  - request for access to a record
- detailed procedural steps for processing each of the three types of requests

Methods

Lecture is followed by

- written answers to practice situations
- role playing
- critical incident process

Evaluation

- The trainee will complete a worksheet indicating the proper handling of each type of request.
- The trainee will participate in role playing to respond to fictitious requests.
- The trainee will respond to simulated critical incidents relating to emergency and problem requests.
- The trainee will respond to actual in-person requests under the immediate direction of the trainer.

Subpoenas and Court Orders

Purpose

To acquaint the trainee with the processes involved in accepting and responding to subpoenas and court orders.

Learning Objectives

- Given a fictitious subpoena (or court order), the trainee will carry out the procedural steps for processing the legal instrument, from receipt through final preparation of the health record for use in legal proceedings.
- Given fictitious scenarios, the trainee will role play giving testimony at
  - a deposition
  - a court hearing: general health record
  - a court hearing: psychiatric or other restricted-access records

Content

- court system and jurisdiction:
  - general concepts
  - court jurisdiction specific to this health care facility
- subpoena, court order, and deposition:
  - definitions
  - sample form and content
  - process by which a subpoena or court order is served
  - elements necessary for acceptable content of a subpoena or court order
- procedural steps for responding to a subpoena or court order
  - determining patient status
  - computing processing fees
  - notifying Risk Management
  - maintaining the release of information log
  - requisitioning the health record
- specific considerations:
  - "no record" status
  - record on microfilm
  - record unavailable due to loss, misfile, or routine destruction
- checking the record for completeness
- detailed preparation of the record:
  - numbering the pages; preparing a table of contents
  - photocopying
  - certifying a copy as a true copy
  - computing additional fees; preparing the bill
- delivering the record at the court proceeding:
  - following general courtroom behavior
  - entering the record as evidence
  - giving testimony
- handling a request to leave the original record or copy
- response to depositions:
  - general proceedings
  - answering factual questions

Methods

- Lecture followed by a practice activity for each procedural step.

- Role playing participation as a witness in a fictitious court proceeding.
- Role playing responses to questions at a fictitious deposition.

Evaluation

- Given a subpoena (or court order), the trainee will
  - determine its acceptability
  - carry out the procedural steps for responding to the subpoena (or court order)
- Given simulated events, the trainee will participate as a witness in a fictitious court proceeding.
- Given simulated events, the trainee will participate as a respondent at a deposition.

Final Evaluation

Stage 1

- The trainee will complete a comprehensive in-basket examination that includes a representative sample of all the requests typically processed by the release of information unit.
- The trainee will complete role-playing and critical incident activities reflecting telephone, in-person, and legal proceeding inquiries.

Stage 2

- The trainee will, under direct supervision, process [_____] written requests and [_____] telephone and in-person requests, as received in the work unit in the course of a working day.

Stage 3

- Over a period of five consecutive working days, the trainee will meet the work standard/performance standard at progressing levels of productivity:

Day 1	60%
Day 2	70%
Day 3	80%
Day 4	90%
Day 5	100%

Stage 4

- The trainee will, under direct supervision, process [_____] responses and participate in legal proceedings as required by subpoenas and court orders.

Source: Joan Gratto Liebler, *Medical Records: Policies and Guidelines*, Aspen Publishers, Inc., © 1991.

PERFORMANCE EVALUATION

GENERAL PERFORMANCE STANDARDS

The following performance standards have been developed with application to the nonexempt positions of the Health Information Management Department. Personnel shall be responsible for meeting the standards. These standards have been developed to provide uniformity and guidance in evaluation of employee performance. Performance will be monitored to ensure that standards are being met. Failure to meet the standards may result in progressive disciplinary action following these steps: oral consultation > written consultation > written disciplinary action > suspension > termination.

1. Personnel shall assist in the achievement of meeting the departmental mission of providing accurate and timely information.
2. Personnel shall provide an excellent quality of customer service to patients, public contacts, ancillary personnel, and departmental coworkers.
3. Personnel shall support the overall goals and objectives of the department and medical center administration.
4. Personnel shall report immediately to administration any occurrence that may disrupt departmental operations or project a negative and/or unprofessional image.
5. Personnel shall strive to work as a cooperative team, offering assistance when needed to patients, ancillary personnel, and coworkers.
6. Performance of duties shall be accomplished with minimal supervision along the guidelines set forth in individual and departmental policy and procedure manuals.
7. Personnel shall adhere to the 15-minute/30-minute break and lunch periods.
8. Personnel shall report to work at the set time. The standard of not more than one period of tardiness per month shall be adhered to.
9. Personnel shall not leave their work area prior to the set end time. It will not be acceptable to leave the work area before the end of the workday shift.
10. Personnel shall avoid excessive absenteeism (refer to the hospitalwide attendance policy).
11. Personnel shall perform duties in a courteous and professional manner.
12. Personnel shall not disrupt work activity or patient flow by unprofessional behavior.
13. Personnel shall use work time in an effective and appropriate manner:
    - Personal phone calls shall not exceed more than one per day.
    - Personnel shall not leave the work areas without informing a coworker while performing job duties.
    - Personnel shall not leave the work area for any other reason not relating to performance of job duties without notifying administrative personnel.
14. Personnel shall strive to provide a safe and comfortable work environment for fellow employees and staff with respect for their rights as individuals.
15. Personnel shall report free time to administrative staff for additional work assignment.
16. Personnel shall be responsible for the completion of their assigned duties in a timely manner, with variances reported to administrative staff.
17. Personnel shall limit schedule changes (not including vacation, illness) to not more than one per pay period.
18. Personal illness and vacation time shall be used in 30-minute increments.
19. Personnel shall notify administrative staff of the inability to report to work in a timely manner. It will not be considered appropriate to leave messages with other staff members unless administrative staff members cannot be contacted.
20. Personnel shall provide an appropriate notice of absenteeism:
    - first/day shift—within one hour of start time
    - second/evening shift—within four hours of start time.
    - third/night shift—within eight hours of start time
21. Personnel shall respect the equipment available and make every attempt to be fully knowledgeable in operational matters.

Courtest of Door County Memorial Hospital, Sturgeon Bay, Wisconsin.

ACCOUNTABILITY STANDARDS: HEALTH INFORMATION MANAGEMENT SPECIALIST

Financial Management: How well the financial resources of the organization work unit are managed.

1.0 15% FINANCIAL MANAGEMENT

1.1 5% Operating budget margin [approved expense budget (-) actual expense (=) approved expense budget] is between 3 and 6 percent.

1.2 5% Payroll expense per unit of service is between $10.25 and $10.75.

1.3 5% Total expense per unit of service is between $10.50 and $11.00.

Productivity: The measure of human resource utilization against work unit activity.

2.0 20% PRODUCTIVITY

2.1 5% STAT transcribed reports (histories and physicals, consultations, diagnostic imaging exams, and operative reports) are transcribed within 24 hours.

2.2 5% Retrieval of records for studies is done within three days of receipt of request 95 percent of the time.

2.3 5% Records requests for patient information (release of information) are processed within seven days 95 percent of the time.

2.4 5% Records on hold for diagnosis are processed within 10 days 90 percent of the time.

Quality of Service: How well the services of the work unit are provided.

3.0 25% QUALITY OF SERVICE

3.1 5% Number of patient complaints received is fewer than _____/year.

3.2 5% Joint Commission and other accrediting or licensing surveys note less than three deficiencies per survey.

3.3 5% Departmental quality improvement monitoring indicates compliance to thresholds 95 percent of the time.

3.4 5% Hospital admission reviews for designated patients are completed within 24 hours of admission or within the first working day 92 to 97 percent of the time.

3.6 5% Compliance with review agency requirements is within 90 to 97 percent for certification regarding reimbursement, with no payments being disallowed and denied. Admissions/charges by third-party payers and peer review organizations are successfully appealed for reversal of decisions 90 to 95 percent of the time.

Human Resource Management: Management of the work unit's employee relations program.

4.0 20% HUMAN RESOURCE MANAGEMENT

4.1 5% Employee perceptions of administration and manager will be between 90 and 100 percent of the norm as measured by the Employee Opinion Survey.

4.2 5% Employee participation in the Employee Opinion Survey is between 80 and 95 percent.

4.3 5% Performance appraisals are conducted on all employees within five days of their anniversary date with fewer than three instances of being late.

4.4 5% Departmental meetings are conducted on a regularly scheduled basis each month, with no more than one canceled each year.

Medical Staff Relations: The measure of success at developing or monitoring positive physician relations.

5.0 10% MEDICAL STAFF RELATIONS

5.1 2.5% Responses to information requested by the medical staff or medical staff committees are responded to within 10 days or as appropriate.

5.2 2.5% Monitoring of incomplete and delinquent medical records is performed on a regular basis with weekly reports provided to medical staff members at least 48 of the 52 weeks per year; monthly reports and trend sheets completed by the tenth of the following month.

5.3 2.5% Contacts with physicians regarding utilization review issues are initiated within 72 hours and resolved within five days 80 to 90 percent of the time.

5.4 2.5% Maintains positive physician relationships as observed from physician comments, informal observation of problem-solving with physicians and feedback from the Medical Director.

Situational Leadership: The manager's ability in such areas as working relations, situational leadership, and quality of staff work.

6.0 10% SITUATIONAL LEADERSHIP

6.1 2% Completes requested projects as assigned by CEO according to established guidelines and submits 90 to 95 percent on scheduled date.

continues

Accountability Standards continued

6.2	2%	In situational leadership, this manager demonstrates the ability to respond positively to changing circumstances so as to maximize the opportunity or minimize the problem. Always acts decisively and takes effective action.
6.3	2%	In working relations, this manager consistently demonstrates positive interpersonal relations with all constituencies. He or she cooperates harmoniously with others in the accomplishment of the hospital's goals and shares information appropriately and in a timely manner.
6.4	2%	This manager consistently completes staff assignments in a timely, thorough, and appropriately detailed manner.
6.5	2%	This manager consistently advises and provides inservice education on health information–related topics (confidentiality, release of information, informed consent, etc.).

Courtesy of Door County Memorial Hospital, Sturgeon Bay, Wisconsin.

DISCIPLINARY ACTION AND TERMINATION

DISCIPLINE

A bit of research into the origin of words will reveal that *discipline* comes from the same root as the word *disciple* and as such actually means "to teach so as to mold." Originally, teaching was the key to discipline—to shaping or molding the disciple. However, we have come to think of discipline, and thus disciplinary action, as punishment.

The true objective of discipline should not be punishment. It should be correction. Thus, one of the primary requirements of disciplinary action is that the employee be afforded the opportunity to correct the behavior that prompted the action.

Conduct versus Performance: Separate Progressive Paths

In all but the few legitimate instances in which immediate termination is appropriate, corrective action must be progressive. That is, it must follow through a number of steps in which subsequent similar infractions are addressed with increasing severity. At each step in the progressive process two pieces of information must be made clear to the employee: what must be done to correct the problem, and what may follow if the problem is not corrected. Throughout the process it is essential to view the sequence of occurrences exactly as it would be viewed—and often is viewed—by an empowered outsider such as an investigator for a civil rights or employee advocacy agency, by asking: Was the employee given every opportunity to correct the offending behavior?

In applying corrective action it is also necessary to make a distinction between problems of conduct and problems of performance. Although traditional progressive disciplinary processes may work well for problems of conduct, such processes are not appropriate for performance problems. The employee who has broken no work rules and violated no policies is not appropriately handled with a progressive disciplinary process for work performance that falls short of standard or expectation.

The supervisor always needs to ask: Is the employee not capable of performing as expected under present circumstances? If the employee cannot, for one reason or another, perform as expected, it is not a discipline problem, and to treat it as a discipline problem is to burden the process with a layer of negativity that serves only to impede correction.

Portions of this section excerpted from *The Health Care Supervisor*, Vol. 11, No. 3, pp. 70–80, Aspen Publishers, Inc., © March 1993.

Conduct Problems: Traditional Progressive Discipline, Plus

Counseling

The first step taken to address a specific kind of errant behavior should be counseling. One to one, supervisor to employee, the employee should be told what was done that was wrong, why it was wrong, what the organization's rules are concerning this behavior (with specific use of handbooks, policy manuals, and other written references), what the possible consequences of this kind of behavior are, and the period of time within which correction is expected. All of this needs to be accomplished without reference to any kind of warning; it is simply an important, job-related discussion between supervisor and employee.

Any such counseling session should be thoroughly documented by the supervisor in notes retained in departmental files.

Oral Warning

Repeated errant behavior following counseling should be addressed using the more formal early stages of the progressive disciplinary process, specifically the oral warning. It should be stressed that the oral warning stage, often regarded as a counseling session, should be utilized only *after* the employee has failed to respond to counseling.

The oral warning should be documented by the supervisor, preferably on a corporate form created for that purpose. If it is documented, is this not actually a written warning? It certainly may seem so, but the difference between a written and oral warning lies in what goes into the employee's personnel file. The record of an oral warning should be retained in department files; it should go into the official personnel files only as part of a subsequent warning for the same kind of behavior.

If it is truly to be an oral warning, why document it at all? Because the oral warning is a step in the progressive disciplinary process, and when an employment relationship breaks down and legal problems result, it can become necessary to provide evidence that each step in the process was followed.

Written Warning

The written warning follows in turn as necessary, with this documentation automatically included in the employee's personnel file.

An employee whose improper behavior has not been corrected following counseling, oral warning, and written warning is in a position in which failure to change will lead to loss of income via suspension and perhaps loss of employment.

By this stage the supervisor and employee have been together on the subject of the employee's behavior problem at least three and perhaps four, five, or six times. It is time for the supervisor to bring other organizational resources into the process.

Before Suspension

The supervisor should at this point, before proceeding to the suspension step, *refer the employee to one of two available sources of further assistance: the employee health service or the human resource department.*

If in any of their numerous contacts the employee has given the supervisor reason to believe he or she may be experiencing health problems of any kind, a referral to employee health is in order. If the problem appears to perhaps lie in employee attitude or in possible difficulties unrelated to health, the referral should be to human resources or perhaps to an employee relations specialist or employee ombudsman.

This referral puts the employee in contact with someone who can possibly point the way toward resolution of some underlying problem. Also, a knowledgeable person other than the supervisor is brought into the process, and this new participant may be able to get through to the employee where the supervisor could not. Finally, this step gives the employee one more distinct opportunity to correct the problem behavior.

Suspension and Discharge

If the referral step is unsuccessful, suspension without pay and eventual discharge may follow as necessary. However, a well-functioning referral program for employee behavior problems will significantly reduce the use of the clearly punitive steps of suspension and discharge.

Should you feel you have cause to discharge an employee, you should take your case to the personnel department for thorough review *before* taking action. Given the legal environment of the times, most organizations today require human resource or administrative review and concurrence in such cases. This review will attempt to determine whether all bases have been covered from a legal perspective and whether the record clearly demonstrates that the employee was given the opportunity to correct the inappropriate behavior. This review, because of the time required, serves another extremely important function: it ensures that no employee is ever fired on the spot or otherwise terminated in the anger of the moment.

Some severe infractions must of course be dealt with as they occur. However, an immediate firing is never the answer. The offending employee should instead be sent home and immediately placed on *indefinite suspension* pending investigation and resolution.

Not all kinds of infractions will require the application of all the foregoing steps. A mild infraction, such as tardiness (within a few minutes of starting time) may, if it becomes chronic, eventually require all of the steps described above. A more serious infraction, such as sleeping on duty, may call for a written warning or suspension on the first violation and discharge on the second violation. The organization's human resource department ordinarily provides guidance for determining the severity of disciplinary action for specific infractions.

Performance Problems: Warnings Not Applicable

It is inappropriate to apply a progressive disciplinary process to an employee who is exhibiting substandard work. The substandard performer has not broken the rules; to group this person with the supposed rule breakers is to lend a negative aspect to a process that must be as positively oriented as possible.

Substandard performance can be simply described as the production of unsatisfactory results that prevent an employee from attaining or maintaining the job standard. The job standard may be further defined as the acceptable level of output achieved by employees in the same or similar job classification, or the standard level of results, *defined in advance* by the supervisor and clearly identifying the quantity and quality of output expected.

For the Newly Identified Substandard Performer

The supervisor's primary objective should not be to get rid of the substandard performer, as is frequently the case, but rather to show the substandard performer how to perform acceptably. The supervisor should

- Review the job standard with the employee, ensuring that the standard is known and understood and, ideally, that the employee accepts this as a reasonable expectation.
- Counsel the employee, developing an action plan specifying what must be done to attain standard performance and a timetable for doing so, documenting this thoroughly, as any counseling session should be documented, with a copy of the complete plan supplied to the employee.
- Conscientiously monitor the employee's progress against the improvement plan, providing assistance as necessary.
- Remove apparent obstacles to the employee's success when possible and make reasonable accommodations to enhance employee performance.

If this process does not correct the problem within the agreed-upon time period, it should be repeated in essentially identical fashion in terms of the creation of a mutually acceptable plan of correction—with necessary modifications from the earlier plan, based on what was encountered in the process—and an agreed-upon target date.

Again to the Important Plus

The *second* time the employee is taken through the corrective counseling and instruction, the process should include referral to either the human resource department or the employee health office. The reasons for doing so are essentially the same as for making this referral for an employee exhibiting conduct problems, and the advantages of doing so are likewise the same: a new person who can possibly help is brought into the process, and the employee is given the chance to address a possible underlying problem that may be causing the apparent performance problem.

How Many Times?

Depending on how much, if any, improvement is noted from one time to the next, the foregoing process might be applied three or four times. When, finally, every reasonable opportunity to improve has been extended multiple times without lasting change occurring, a last-ditch deadline should be established. When this deadline arrives, employment should end unless all conditions of the plan of improvement have been met.

Dismissal, Not Discharge

When it is necessary to release an employee for reasons of substandard performance, the action should be identified as a dismissal for failure to meet job standards, and not as a discharge. The distinction is important; a discharge for cause is a firing, and a person so terminated has lost employment through inappropriate conduct and in most parts of the country is not eligible for unemployment compensation. However, an individual who is dismissed for inability to meet the standards of the job is not considered wholly responsible for the termination, so the action is regarded more as a layoff than a discharge and the person so terminated is usually eligible for unemployment compensation.

Source: Charles R. McConnell, *The Effective Health Care Supervisor*, 3rd ed., Aspen Publishers, Inc., © 1993.

WORKERS' COMPENSATION

WORKERS' COMPENSATION: THE BASICS

WHAT IS WORKERS' COMPENSATION?

Whether under federal or state jurisdiction, workers' compensation is a mandated, employer-funded benefits delivery system that ensures that persons who develop workers' compensation–related injuries or illnesses will receive appropriate benefits. While the nature and extent of the benefits varies between the federal program and state programs, which are different from state to state, they all include

- medical care
- temporary disability benefits
- permanent disability benefits
- death benefits

WHAT TYPES OF BENEFITS DOES WORKERS' COMPENSATION PROVIDE?

Under either state or federal regulations, workers' compensation guarantees that a person with a workers' compensation–related injury or illness will receive reasonable medical services necessary to evaluate and treat his or her injury or illness. In addition, workers' compensation programs provide wage replacement benefits for those workers with injuries that temporarily preclude their full compensation, permanent disability benefits for those with permanent impairment, and death benefits to the survivors of an employee who dies as the result of a workers' compensation–related injury. It should be noted, however, that the extent of wage replacement, permanent disability benefits, death benefits, as well as the provision of any other benefits (for example, vocational rehabilitation) will vary with the jurisdiction: federal or state and state to state.

HOW IS WORKERS' COMPENSATION INSURANCE MADE AVAILABLE?

In addition to state-subsidized workers' compensation insurance funds, workers' compensation insurance is sold by a wide variety of national and state insurance companies. In some states, all of these insurance options are available. In other states, the sole option is the state insurance fund. In those states with private and state-subsidized insurance vehicles, an employer with a poor workers' compensation record may find that its only option is the state program or an insurance pool for high-risk employers. While some insurers sell directly to employers, others use insurance brokers as intermediaries. The cost of insurance for a particular employer will vary with the nature of the work performed by that employer, its prior workers' compensation experience (if any), and the size of its payroll.

WHY IS WORKERS' COMPENSATION A GROWING CONCERN FOR EMPLOYERS?

For years, employers have viewed workers' compensation as either a fixed insurance expense or simply as a component of salaries, wages, and benefits. More recently, however, employers have been increasingly aware of both the direct costs of workers' compensation and the indirect costs associated with such tasks as reporting, program compliance and administration, and lost opportunity.

As the direct costs have escalated, increasing numbers of employers have come to focus on the fact that workers' compensation costs can have a considerable impact on the bottom line. In fact, workers' compensation costs can threaten a company's very viability. As such, many employers now realize that workers' compensation is a cost center and can be better managed—given the proper tools—to benefit the bottom line.

MAY WORKERS' COMPENSATION INSURANCE BENEFITS BE INTEGRATED WITH OTHER EMPLOYEE BENEFITS?

With regard to both the administration of benefits and the provision of health care services, so-called 24-hour care is the buzz phrase for the integration of group health and workers' compensation. While there is considerable interest in this approach, workers' compensation is a highly regulated benefits delivery system that goes well beyond the provision of medical care and related services. In addition, there are many regulatory and administrative differences between workers' compensation and group health. As a result, full integration of the rights of an employee (and employer) under workers' compensation with the employee's benefits pursuant to a group health plan will prove to be a complex undertaking. However, some states have begun experimenting with the concept, and many managed care organizations are anxious to add workers' compensation services to their programs.

HOW ARE WORKERS' COMPENSATION BENEFITS TAXED TO AN EMPLOYEE?

They are not. Workers' compensation is an employer-funded, no-fault system that guarantees that a worker with a workers' compensation–related injury or illness will receive certain benefits. In this regard, workers' compensation benefits can be considered a right of employment. In return for an employer-funded, no-fault benefits system, labor agreed that a worker with an alleged, workers' compensation–related illness or injury could not (with specified exceptions) file a civil tort action for related damages against his or her employer. In other words, while employers pay the full tab, workers' compensation is the

continues

Workers' Compensation: The Basics continued

sole remedy for an employee with an alleged workers' compensation–related injury or illness.

ARE THERE DIFFERENCES IN WORKERS' COMPENSATION LAWS BETWEEN ONE STATE AND ANOTHER?

Regardless of the state, the overriding principles of workers' compensation remain the same. There are, however, many state-to-state differences with regard to such factors as employer, employee, and physician injury-reporting requirements, the employer's ability to direct medical care, reimbursement for medical services, the acceptance of subjective complaints as a factor in permanent disability determination, wage replacement, permanent disability benefits, dispute resolution, and the provision of benefits (for vocational rehabilitation, for example).

Source: John C. Garner, *Health Insurance Answer Book*, 4th ed., Aspen Publishers, Inc., © 1996.

WORKERS' COMPENSATION COSTS

HOW EXPENSIVE IS WORKERS' COMPENSATION?

The direct cost of workers' compensation is primarily a function of medical care costs, temporary disability payments, and permanent disability awards. For a particular employer, workers' compensation costs will vary directly with the type of work performed, injury frequency, and injury severity. Over time, an employer's insurance costs may be modified either up or down, based on its work injury experience (i.e., frequency and, to an extent, severity). In recent years (especially in some states), system abuse (for example, increased utilization of medical services), fraud, and litigation have created a dramatic increase in the costs associated with workers' compensation.

Other factors that contribute to the costs associated with workers' compensation include administrative costs (such as responding to regulatory requirements) and the costs of state-specific benefits (for example, vocational rehabilitation). While the direct costs associated with workers' compensation are readily apparent, employers also have a number of indirect costs. In this regard, some analyses have demonstrated that issues such as reduced production, lost opportunity, and workers' compensation–related overhead expense can be larger than the direct costs noted above.

WHY ARE WORKERS' COMPENSATION COSTS RISING?

While the costs of most goods and services will rise with inflation, in most states workers' compensation costs have increased much more rapidly. The reasons for this fact may vary from state to state, but, in general, the pace of increase can be attributed to combinations of the following factors:

- excess utilization of medical services
- cost-shifting from capitated health care to fee-for-service workers' compensation care
- fraud
- litigation-related costs

WHAT ADDITIONAL FACTORS ACCOUNT FOR GROWING WORKERS' COMPENSATION COSTS?

Other factors that can contribute to increases in the cost of workers' compensation include:

- advances in medical technology
- compliance with increasing state and federal regulatory requirements
- the Americans with Disabilities Act (ADA)

HOW DOES THE ADA AFFECT WORKERS' COMPENSATION?

When an injured worker is permanently impaired in a manner that precludes him or her from returning to usual and customary employment, ADA regulations may require that the employer provide "reasonable accommodation" in an effort to bring the employee back to work. The definition of *reasonable accommodation* is case- and employer-specific.

ARE PSYCHOLOGICAL DISORDERS BECOMING MORE IMPORTANT IN WORKERS' COMPENSATION CLAIMS?

The frequency and severity of psychological disorder claims experience in workers' compensation varies widely among states. Primarily, this fact is a reflection of whether the state acknowledges workers' compensation–related stress as a bona fide workers' compensation–related injury and considers subjective complaints to be a factor in rating permanent impairment. Those states that do (for example, California) have experienced a dramatic increase in both psychological injury claims and fraudulent claims. Workers' compensation rates in California declined when the legislature changed the requirements for stress claims from only 10 percent work-related to 50 percent work-related.

HOW DOES STRESS TRANSLATE INTO A COMPENSABLE DISORDER?

In those states that acknowledge psychological stress claims, when it is accepted (by the payer) that the source of an employee's stress was work-related, the claim becomes compensable when the injury claim results in the claimant's receipt of medical care or time off from work. In some states, the contribution of work-related events to the claimant's level of psychological stress must exceed a defined threshold before the claim will be covered under workers' compensation.

HAS STRESS CONTRIBUTED TO RISING WORKERS' COMPENSATION COSTS?

Not surprisingly, yes. A psychological stress claim is typically based on subjective complaints. Because such complaints can be difficult to refute, disputing such a claim often results in a costly battle of expert opinions. While the battle is waged, the allegedly injured worker may be receiving temporary disability benefits. Not all states acknowledge workers' compensation–related stress as a bona fide source of a workers' compensation–related injury. Those that do have experienced a dramatic increase in stress claims and resultant costs related to medical care, temporary disability, permanent disability, and dispute resolution.

Source: John C. Garner, *Health Insurance Answer Book*, 4th ed., Aspen Publishers, Inc., © 1996.

Index

D

U

V

W

Lightning Source UK Ltd.
Milton Keynes UK
UKOW012007251111

182708UK00002B/26/A

9 780834 212312